3/8/10
From one
writer to
another
Sally Sorrow

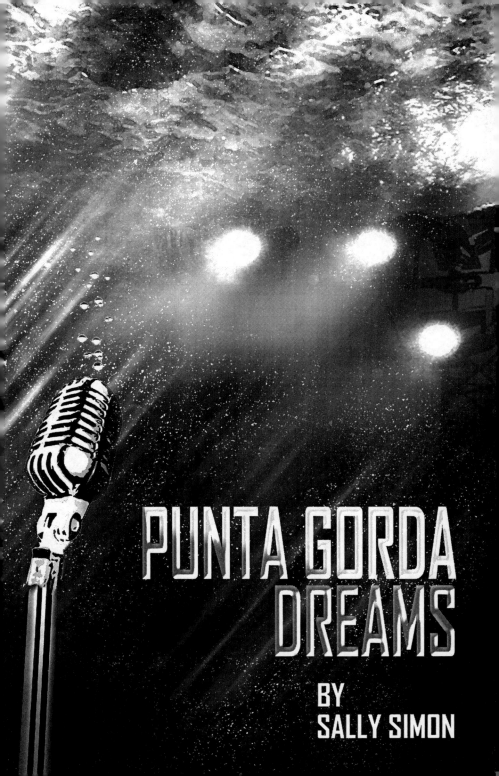

Sally Simon Books, Inc.
21495 Eldred Ave.
Port Charlotte, FL 33952
(941) 391-2331

Copyright 2005 by Sally Simon
All rights reserved

ISBN.0-9748356-1-9

This book or any part hereof may not be
reproduced without
the written consent of the author.

Printed in the USA

Acknowledgments

This is the place where the writer gets to gush like a Grammy Award winner.

Some of my helpers don't want to be mentioned here, so I'll respect that.

Shyness, worries about potential conflicts of interest, or dislike of the spotlight in general are all valid reasons why some of my helpers aren't mentioned here. Thank you for your help. You know who you are.

I won't go into each listed person's field of expertise. If you know these people, you'll be able to tell which areas they helped me with. I'm doing this alphabetically because I can't think of a more equitable way to do it.

James Abraham
Dena and Verne Hall
Linda Kern
Jane Wanroy
Steve Widmeyer

I would also like to thank the cast of real people and businesses who have agreed to be in this book by name.

And, as always, to the unsuspecting strangers I have met and spoken with, thank you for your help with minor characters and plot ideas.

Dedication

This book was completed prior to August 13. 2004, when Charlotte County, Florida, was hit by Hurricane Charley and effected subsequently by three other category four hurricanes, turning the area into something that resembled a war zone and leveling forever many well-known landmarks, some of which are in this book.

Publication of this book was storm-delayed.

Heroes emerged from the hurricanes–brave, resourceful citizens as well as the patient, caring rescuers who came to help us.

Some of you I know.

Some of you I don't know and maybe never will.

But you know who you are.

This book is dedicated to you.

# Punta Gorda Dreams

Trevor Daniels ended his signature song, "Guitar-Man," with a quiet flourish. The lights went down on the stage as the capacity crowd erupted in applause. The curtains swept closed and Trevor stalked from the darkened stage, his long dark hair moving across the strings of the guitar slung over his back, his light gray eyes intent.

He left the whistling, clapping crowd sounds and the thumping of feet pounding in the huge hall behind him. He stumbled between dangling wires backstage and over extension cords and around boxes and crates. He kicked one crate for good measure.

The vehemence of the kick reverberated all up the long, lean length of his body, even moving the loose white fabric of his signature Dani-shirt and causing the thin sparkle of a beaded necklace to shift against his collarbones.

The kick felt good, he thought.

"If I have to sing that song one more time, I'm tempted to cut my tongue off."

His brother Scott paced beside him, his walkie-talkie in his left hand.

"Got a little burn-out there, Guitar-man?"

"Yeah, I do."

"Fans kinda expect Trevor Daniels to sing that song. Ya got three curtain calls before ya had to sing it."

Trevor shot his brother a hot-eyed look.

"Fuck 'em."

Scott Daniels grinned back at him in the darkness, his teeth gleaming white.

"Hard to do, Trev. There's too many of 'em. Even for you."

Trevor chuckled, letting go of his anger and frustration.

"Thanks, Bro."

"Give that tune a rest, Trev. Recycle somethin' else. The fans'll live."

"I'm pretty much sick of singing anything Trevor Daniels ever wrote. And I wasn't even the one who wrote 'Guitar-Man'. Remember? That was Dad."

"Whoa. Got a lot of territory there, Trev. Do somebody else's stuff then. Cover some Dylan. Do some of what comes in the mail from young kids as demos."

"Maybe I'm getting sick of the whole business."

Scott's assistant, Jesse Tweak, held out his hands as the brothers passed him.

"I'll take Blondie."

Trevor handed over his Gibson acoustic guitar.

Scott flicked the button on his walkie-talkie.

"We're comin' out about now. Tighten it up out there."

Together the brothers hit the quick release bars on the backdoor of the auditorium and emerged into a screaming crowd of people waving shirts and photos and CDs and Sharpie markers. Scott's troops, in their distinctive yellow T-shirts with TREVOR DANIELS BAND SECURITY emblazoned in red front and back, held the line as Trevor's fans surged forward. Trevor slowed his pace, scribbling his signature—or what passed for it these days—on objects held out to him or waved around his face. He had what his brother thought of as his idiot-grin on his face.

It wasn't that Trevor didn't appreciate his fans, Scott thought. He did. And he would stay right there on the glistening asphalt signing away until the last fan was satisfied.

But he was tired. And sweaty. And chilling off rapidly in his sweat-soaked white gauze shirt and blue jeans.

The night air sent icy fingers around Scott's exposed neck and Scott watched Trevor move his shoulders restlessly as the same breeze dried the stream of sweat on his skin, and sucked the billowing white shirt to his body.

Scott turned his broad back towards the bulk of the crowd and straightened, giving Trevor a bubble of space directly in front of him so that at least he could breathe.

It took the better part of an hour until the last dewy-eyed matron was gripping her program to her chest and repeating her thank-yous breathlessly over and over again. Scott's troops gently herded her in the direction of the front parking lot, one of their numbers going with her to her car as a safety precaution. Scott knew Trevor was very proprietary about his fans, their welfare, the value they received, and their safety at his shows, before, during, and after.

As Trevor said, this wasn't a mosh pit, for God's sakes. It was music.

Scott eyed the thin, handsome face beside him in the dim parking lot light.

"Get into the tour bus and get out of them wet duds. Take a good long hot shower and wash all that smoke and sweat out of your hair. I'll handle this out here."

"I hate the smoke, Scott. I wish we could do something about that. Change the law or something. I don't know. It hurts my throat and it makes my eyes sting. It makes it hard to breathe."

"That's a fight for another day, Trev. Go take your shower and stretch out while you can. Travel tonight and open phone lines at a local radio station tomorrow morning. A gig tomorrow night."

"Story of my life."

Scott slapped him on the back, turned him toward the tour bus parked ten feet away, and gave his butt an affectionate parting whack.

"Move it, moron."

"Thanks, Bro."

The Daniels brothers' relationship had changed little over the years. Trevor wriggled. Scott pounced. Trevor flew high. Scott followed with a net. They shared women, sometimes literally. They shared dreams and liquor and life in general. Scott kept Trevor grounded. Trevor kept Scott alert. They had helped one another home, covered one another's asses, held one another's heads to puke and had lied one another out of hell.

The personnel in the Trevor Daniels Band had changed over the years. Trevor had once complained to their father that he couldn't seem to keep a drummer, to which Jarrett had replied that he needed to run an ad that read: *Wanted—workaholic, knowledge of percussion optional.* Jake Benson, one of his oldest if not closest friends, continued to play bass guitar. Danielle Moran, known as Dani, moved to costumes. Her friend Margaret White took on the job of caring for Trevor's hair. His brother Scott drove the tour bus or the bland white Hyundai they towed behind it and handled security. Jesse Tweak was Scott's back-up and Mitch Evans was Jesse's back-up for everything else.

Various cousins filled the ranks of the road crew.

Various wives had come and gone.

The road was a killer for relationships and Trevor was on the road at a minimum of three hundred days a year. Even his detractors called him the hardest working artist in country-western music. Trevor considered he was doing a job and shied away from labels. Few knew he also wrote for another record company under his old name, Trevor Lane. Fewer still understood the need that drove Trevor.

The need to let the music out.

Paradoxically, the road was killing the music in him.

It was literally killing him, too, Scott thought.

In the tour bus again, Scott surveyed his younger brother. Trevor was stretched out in a narrow coffin-like bed along the right side of the converted diesel bus. His eyes were closed. His long dark hair, freshly washed, was dripping into and soaking the pillow his head lay on. The bright blue afghan their now-deceased grandmother had crocheted for him was drawn up to his chin.

"Hey, moron."

"What?"

"Wrap a towel around that mop of yours. You'll be asleep in the wet spot of your own hair on your pillow."

"Too tired."

"Moron."

Scott tossed his walkie-talkie onto the tiny kitchenette table, and reached above him for the available supply of fresh towels behind a latched cupboard. He pulled one out and down, unfolded it and tossed it unceremoniously over his younger brother's face.

They all worked hard, Scott thought, but Trevor worked the hardest.

Trevor's voice came from beneath the towel.

"Thanks, Bro."

"I ain't gonna wrap it for you."

"Okay."

Trevor stayed motionless. Scott shook his head.

"Give me that darned towel. Am I gonna be liftin' your head, too?"

"Probably."

Scott snagged the towel from his brother's face. Under it, Trevor's eyes were open, and twinkled up at him, irrepressible fun shining past the grayness of fatigue. Scott snorted.

"Wiseguy."

"Yep."

"So, while you were in here with time on your hands, what did you cook us for dinner?"

"Nothin', honey."

"Take-out, huh?"

"That or drive-thru. I don't have the energy left to crawl into a Cracker Barrel. I might not have the energy left to chew."

"We'll see about that. I'll wave some food under your nose when we get it and see if you come alive some more then."

Scott frowningly considered his younger brother.

"Helluva concert, Trev."

Trevor had his eyes closed again.

"Bite me."

"I don't think so."

"Fuck you."

"In your dreams."

Trevor smiled at their familiar routine of insults and chuckled as Scott lifted his damp head to shove the towel under and flip the pillow to a dry side as well. Scott wrapped the towel around Trevor's wet head and Trevor opened his eyes briefly.

"Thanks, Scott. Really."

Scott squeezed Trevor's shoulder and picked up his walkie-talkie again, depressing the send button as Trevor closed his eyes once more.

"You know the drill, guys. What's for dinner? Trevor's bushed but that don't affect you all. So, did it used to fly, walk or swim? Fax me back the vote and we'll move this circus down the road once we're all locked down."

Scott clicked off his walkie-talkie and came to sit on the other bunk bed, directly opposite Trevor in the bus. His big hands dangled between his knees, tossing the walkie-talkie back and forth like a football. It had served as such many times before. Not a good thing for a walkie-talkie.

"Ten more calendar days till we're home, Trev."

"God bless calendar days."

"God bless patient wives."

Trevor shifted his shoulders on the narrow bed.

"You let me know when you want off this ride, so you can get a life, Scott. I know this constant touring was a factor in Tiffany leaving you and Scott Junior."

"Maybe. But it wasn't the whole problem. I'll let you know when I want off. You?"

"I guess not yet. Will somebody please let me know when?"

"You'll know."

"Scott, I can't even think straight anymore."

"Well, heck, Trev. You don't have to think about it right this red-hot minute. I'll shut up and let you get to sleep."

"No. I like hearing your voice. It keeps me connected. It keeps me from spiraling out into the darkness."

"You're in deep doodoo if my voice can do all that for you."

Trevor chuckled.

"Thanks."

"Darned Yankee-serious pills you been takin'."

"Yeah."

"I guess you're too tired to get laid."

Trevor opened one eye and focused it on his brother's perfectly serious face.

"Let me get back to you on that one."

Trevor closed the one eye again and Scott chuckled.

"Uh-huh. I thought so."

"Yep. Too tired to even sleep through a blow job."

"Darn."

"Exactly."

Scott's walkie-talkie crackled and he held it to his mouth, automatically depressing the answer button.

"Yeah?"

"The vote's for Arby's. We'll be faxing over our order."

"Gotcha."

Scott clicked off the walkie-talkie and set it in a specially-built holder near the door of the bus.

"You heard?"

"Yep. I'll have my usual. God, I love the romance of the road."

The fax machine, built into its own special holder, rang, squealed, and Scott turned to it. It delivered a sheet of paper that Scott picked up. Names of the band, the roadies and others Scott didn't even recognize crisscrossed the paper along with their orders. Scott scratched one eyebrow. Now they were feeding the floozies, he guessed. No matter. Trevor wouldn't care.

Trevor's voice sounded behind him.

"Scott?"

"Yeah?"

"Get one of those guys with too much energy and time on his hands to drive this behemoth. Get Jesse Tweak to drive. Take a break."

"And what? Trust this precious cargo to just any little piss-ant? I don't think so, mister."

"Bite me."

"Fuck you."

"In your dreams."

"As if."

Warmed again by the familiar routine, both brothers smiled, Trevor with his eyes closed still, and coasting off to sleep and Scott with his wide open as he climbed behind the big wheel of the diesel bus and fired her up.

They'd had some wild times out on the road on the way to the top, Scott reflected. Playing corn festivals and sheep festivals and festival festivals. Playing high school gyms and parking lots. Playing Walmart parking lots. Five or six acoustic pieces with Trevor signing autographs for the five to six hundred people who showed up in the course of the day.

Scott remembered he'd once announced over the intercom at a Walmart that whoever bought the most Trevor Daniels CDs that day would get an autographed pair of Trevor's jeans, right off his body. One lady bought twenty-six CDs, and he and Jesse had held a big dark-patterned sheet up around Trevor while he stripped off his old jeans, signed them with a Sharpie marker and then clawed his way into a fresh, stiff pair of Walmart specials.

Then it was on to their next stop, just a few minutes away by Lear jet, as things got better. And as things got better, Trevor did more. More meet-and-greets. More radio talk shows. More. Always more.

Trevor's first CD went gold and hung around seventeen with a bullet on the Billboard charts, going up to platinum. His second CD was released immediately and went quickly to gold. His agent had been more than happy to pay the RIAA its fee for verification of sales. For Trevor and the band, it was always on to the next Kroeger's or Piggly-Wiggly or radio station open phone lines that their cousin Stephanie could book for them to mesh with the tour schedule Trevor's agent, Barbara Kincaid, had arranged.

Politicians didn't meet and greet as many people as The Trevor Daniels Band did.

Trevor had slept around some, Scott reflected. He'd even slept with his agent. When Trevor was fifteen and Barbara Kincaid was twenty-one, she had seemed old to Trevor. But they hadn't met face to face until Trevor was twenty-one and she was twenty-seven. She hadn't seemed old to him then. And by the time he was twenty-three, Barbara Kincaid, at twenty-nine and divorced, had seemed perfectly fine to Trevor. It hadn't gone on to be more than good safe sex and a closer business relationship, but Trevor sometimes laughed at himself when he remembered the first time he'd heard her name brought up. He'd been afraid she wouldn't want to be working for a kid. But their grandmother Bernice Daniels had been right. Talent was ageless.

\*    \*    \*    \*    \*

*"I'm so tired. I'm just so tired."*

*"Tired of what? Fightin'? Runnin'? Bein' scared? Bein' alone? Never deny your needs, boy."*

Trevor awoke, sweating and disoriented, with his lungs painful to every breath. Worries from his desperate youth cycled over and over again in his head and mingled with his adopted father's steadying voice in his mind. He felt as if his life was a loop in some computer program or a repeat button on a CD player. He felt the swaying of the tour bus beneath him and wondered if the wheels turned at all and if he ever actually went anywhere. It all looked the same.

And he was so tired.

Trevor looked up pitifully into the ever-watchful eyes of his older brother seated on the opposite bunk bed.

"Jesse driving?"

"Yep."

"Scottie, make it go away."

Scott's big callused hand came down on Trevor's forehead, almost making him cry out in pain at the tenderness of the gesture.

"Trev, you need a doctor. Maybe even a hospital."

"No."

"Bull. You been out cold since before we pulled into Arby's last night. You ain't eaten in over twelve hours. You're burnin' up with a fever. I did your open phone lines thing with the radio station myself. They weren't happy about it, but they'll live. What am I gonna do tonight? Put sand in your sneakers, tie Blondie around your neck and stick a broom handle up your butt to keep you upright onstage?"

"Maybe."

"Heck, Trev, you didn't even bite on that broom stick line. You're so sick right now ya done broke your funny bone. Maybe we should have a doctor travel with us on tour."

Trevor's head buzzed. He felt Scott's weight shift onto the edge of his bed. Scott's hand moved to his shoulder, radiating warmth and comfort.

Scott's voice rumbled over the creaks and roars of the diesel bus.

"Okay. Too sick to strategize. I can pull rank on you, you know. I'm your health care surrogate. And I'm your older brother. I'm bigger than you are. I can take you."

Trevor didn't even feel his lips twitch at the mild joke. He found he was concentrating on every breath he took and that those breaths weren't going very deeply into his lungs. That wasn't right, he thought, and he tried to fight off a rising wave of panic. He didn't mind dying, but he hated hospitals. There might be a hospital in his near future.

Scott moved his hand to the side of Trevor's neck, rolling his thumb up into Trevor's hairline.

"Maybe there's a clinic or somethin' somewhere. Yeah, a walk-in clinic. Get a prescription for stuff. Get it filled. Keep on goin'. Be off schedule maybe two hours, tops. Phone ahead to the engagement. Whatcha think?"

Trevor nodded. Aches and sharp pains had invaded his body and he felt himself shivering as well.

Scott picked up his walkie-talkie, never breaking physical contact with Trevor, and began to reorganize the schedule.

"All ya'll, listen up. Trevor's sick. We're off at the next exit that looks like it has a town with a doctor anywhere in it. Got that? We're gonna be thinkin' on our feet here. Roadies, go on to the engagement. Band, do the same. Dani and Margaret, suit yourselves. I'm puttin' Dani in charge of explainin' the situation to tonight's gig to minimize any panic. Jake, you handle the rest. I'm keepin' Jesse with us to do the drivin' and I'll be stickin' to Trev. Everybody got that?"

Everybody did.

Dani and Margaret continued on with the group that was convoying up the interstate. Margaret was the one who always drove the van that she and Dani owned, and Trevor had had a full set of what he considered electronic necessities installed in it–cell phone, walkie-talkie, fax machine, laptop computer with full tour information including maps, addresses, phone numbers, and contact persons. Dani could handle her end while they rolled.

Scott clicked off his walkie-talkie. He felt the tour bus slow marginally and heave slightly to the right. He figured Jesse was taking an exit to some small town.

"Maybe a nurse to travel with us, Trev. Don't need no doc if you'd try to keep yourself in a little bit better shape than this. This is all gonna cost more than ten tickets to your show. God knows how you'll stand the economic strain what with a full house of some forty thousand folks at forty to sixty bucks a pop, depending on seat location. Some freebies with this doc might make the service a bit faster, too."

The bus paused as if for a stop sign. Jesse never quite came to a full stop unless he had to, Scott thought. They pulled away again, every matchstick the tires went over feeling like speed bumps to Scott as he watched Trevor flinch. He leaned over and moved a finger under the bottom of the blue afghan. He felt the cuff of a frayed pair of jeans and smiled.

"Well, thank God you thought to put on some jeans last night. I'd have had to charge double if I had to dress you, too. Gonna have to carry you in as it is."

There was no response from Trevor. Scott knew him well enough to know he wasn't sleeping, just conserving his energy. And hiding.

Scott lifted another edge of the afghan and smiled.

"Good deal, Trev. Got a decent flannel shirt on, too. You can keep your Grammy-afghan. We'll get you that doc and some drugs, Trev. You'll be fine."

Jesse in the driver's seat hadn't said anything. He spoke now.

"Got a gas station comin' up, boss. Exit sign says Tidewater, Virginia. Gas station'll know where docs are, too."

"Do it, Jess. Good work."

Jesse nodded and hauled on the big steering wheel, pulling to one side of the gas station parking lot, mindful of low clearances near the pumps and turning radiuses for leaving later. He put the bus in park and turned to Scott. Scott nodded and Jesse scrambled out the door. Scott closed it behind him to keep out drafts and diesel fumes.

*      *      *      *      *

Once inside the clinic, Trevor wouldn't let Scott pull rank.

"It's not fair to the guy ahead of me that I didn't plan ahead on this like he did. I'll wait my turn."

Scott growled low in his throat, surveying the miserable bundle of his younger brother propped up in a gray plastic chair against one wall of the clinic, his afghan around him. He felt a feather's edge of fear and could almost hear their father's voice in his head. *Are you tellin' me your brother died in the waitin' room of some clinic in some backwater town in Virginia because some guy with a splinter in his finger was ahead of him?*

Scott didn't want any parts of that in his future.

Years of being with Trevor on and off the road had taught him something of the way Trevor got things done. He himself preferred brute strength and intimidation, but that wasn't going to work here, he thought.

Scott assessed the staff behind the frosted glass check-in window.

Two women.

He rolled his shoulders, glanced at a slumping Trevor and tried to find some middle ground between his brother's sense of fairness and his own sense of dignity.

He stood up and walked slowly to the window to see what wriggling his worm could get him in the way of faster service for Trevor. He smiled his big lazy grin at the redheaded nurse-receptionist, sucking in his gut and giving her his best imitation of Trevor's big-eyed look.

He hoped he didn't scare her off.

He read her nametag.

"Carla? I'm Scott. I got me a real sick baby brother out here. Any way you can scoot him in front of a guy with a hangnail or a bullet wound or somethin'?"

Scott looked over his shoulder to Trevor wrapped in his afghan with his eyes closed, and dropped his act. Carla must have sensed his genuine concern and looked around him to Trevor.

"How long's he been sick?"

"Days, I'd guess. He's been hidin' it. We got engagements and he don't like to whine. I'm worried about him."

"He looks familiar, but both of you are strangers here. Maybe it's just the hair."

"My brother's tour bus is out in the parkin' lot. I'd guess half the town knows by now. That pitiful lump of humanity over there is Trevor Daniels."

Carla put her hand over her mouth and looked again.

"Oh, my God. Becky here is a huge fan. Bring him on into exam room three. Becky'll be thrilled."

"I thank you, ma'am."

"You're his brother? You don't look at all like him."

Scott grinned.

"Different mothers. Different fathers, too. Long story. I'll be right back with him."

Scott strode purposefully to Trevor's chair and nudged him partly awake.

"Your turn, Trev. Never mind standin' up. It's faster to carry you."

Trevor never even protested as Scott scooped him up, trailing Trevor's beloved afghan behind him. Carla was holding the door to the back open. She bent and picked up the end of the afghan and threw it over Scott's shoulder as he walked past her.

"I'll do his vitals. It'll be quicker. And I'll alert Dr. Brownie. Becky is going to be just so thrilled. You have no idea."

Scott stood with Trevor clasped in his arms at the entrance to the examination room. Trevor seemed asleep, but Scott knew he was hiding again. Hiding from his weakness. And hiding as much of himself as he could from a potential fan.

"She best not be bringin' in no camera for a photo or no stuff to autograph. Trevor don't need that right now."

"Lay him down over here. That's good. She wouldn't do that. She's a fan, but she's a nurse first. I'll get all the paperwork for you to fill out and bring it back here. Insurance?"

"Out the yin-yang, ma'am, but we ain't messin' around with no insurance. You take VISA?"

Carla popped an electronic thermometer into Trevor's mouth.

"Are you his health care surrogate? Yes, we do."

"I am. Got the papers in my pocket for you to copy."

"Very efficient."

The thermometer beeped and Carla pulled it out.

"Saints alive. A hundred and four. He is sick. Is he allergic to any antibiotics that you know of?"

Carla ejected the disposable cover from the thermometer into the trash and hung the thermometer back in its wall holder while Scott considered the question.

"No, ma'am. None that I know of. He's allergic to hospitals, though."

"Too bad. That's Dr. Brownie's call, not mine."

Scott watched Carla apply the blood pressure cuff and employ her stethoscope. She scribbled notes on a post-it and then felt Trevor's pulse, scribbling more notes.

Scott watched her with worried eyes.

"Is he gonna be all right, ma'am?"

Carla looked up to the big, concerned face.

"He's very sick, Scott. I'll bring the paperwork."

"Ma'am?"

"Carla."

"Carla, I'd like to send you somethin' for bein' nice enough to help me out with Trevor here. You got a boy friend or a husband might get jealous if I did?"

Carla smiled up at him through her lashes.

"No, I don't. But I'd do the same for a tree frog that looked as sick as your brother does. A gift will not be necessary."

"No, ma'am. I didn't mean to offend you. I'm just real grateful for the help."

"You're welcome. I'll go tell Dr. Brownie. And Becky. Don't be offended by Dr. Brownie. He can be rather gruff. Give me your paperwork. I'll xerox it and get it back to you. Your driver's license, too, please."

Scott gave her the requested items and Carla left, closing the door behind her.

Trevor stirred on the exam table.

"I can't believe you're wriggling your worm while I'm dying."

"I wriggled my worm to keep you from dyin', moron. Looks like I might have caught a fish anyway. Can't blame

15

me if I get two good things out of one wriggle. You shut up and rest and let me handle this for you."

"Okay."

A young girl with blonde curls peeked around the edge of the door as it opened. Scott could tell by her rounding eyes that she yearned to have a camera in her hands. As though Trevor was Shamu at Sea World or something, Scott thought.

The girl came quietly in with a clipboard full of forms, her eyes glued to Trevor's still form. Scott broke her concentration.

"Whatcha got there, missy?"

"Becky. I'm Becky. Forms. You're Mr. Daniels?"

"I am. Give me that there clipboard and a pen, Becky. I'll make short work of this stuff."

Scott took the clipboard with its attached pen from her slackened grip and flipped quickly through the forms. It worried him a bit that he didn't know the answers to a lot of the questions. They had never come up. Had Trevor ever had measles? Was he allergic to penicillin? Had he had any operations?

"Trev?"

"Hm?"

"I'm gonna be askin' you a lot of questions. I'm right sorry about that. Okay?"

"Yeah. Okay."

Scott listed all the questions and got his responses. Sometimes Trevor didn't even know the answers. He'd had quite a few broken bones in his earlier years before Jarrett, Scott thought, but Scott Junior was always falling out of trees and off ladders, so that was maybe no surprise.

Scott handed the completed and signed forms on the clipboard to Becky, nudging her slightly to break her trance as she gazed at what Scott considered to be a fairly rough-looking Trevor in his trailing afghan. Becky woke up, handed him his driver's license and left the room with her forms.

"Trev, you got one without even wrigglin'."

"Much good it'll do me."

"There is that."

"Don't let them put me in a hospital, Scott. Please?"

"Stay healthy then."

"Please?"

"We'll see. I can't make no promises 'til I know more. Carla says you're sick."

"I don't need Carla to tell me that."

"Shut up and get well then."

Scott found Trevor's hand under the afghan and gave it a squeeze. Trevor squeezed back.

The door opened again and an elderly man in a white lab coat entered. Scott drew protectively closer to Trevor on the exam table. The man pulled out a small flashlight.

"I'm Dr. Brownie. Sit him up."

Scott helped Trevor erect and held him there with an arm around his shoulders. The doctor leaned in.

"Say 'ah'."

Trevor did and the doctor peered in his throat with the flashlight. He peered in his eyes and then into his ears with an otoscope. He listened to Trevor's chest with a stethoscope and felt under his chin and around his neck with long fingers. Trevor sat and took it. The doctor straightened.

"You've got a heavy bronchial infection there, young man. Your lungs are all clogged up."

"Yes, sir."

"Your throat's red. Got some white pustules there. Carla says your temps a hundred and four. Vomiting? Diarrhea? Stomach pains?"

Trevor stirred.

"No, sir. Sore throat. Cough. No cough. Hard to breathe. Hurts to breathe. Chills. Fever. Sweats. Weak. Dizzy. Tired."

"Walking pneumonia and a strep throat for starters. You're a mess. Gonna get laryngitis pretty soon, too. Injection of antibiotics; guaifenesin syrup for the congestion. Plenty of liquids. Rest. No singing. No playing. No nothing."

The doctor turned to Scott.

"If he's not on the mend in three days, I want him back in here."

Scott nodded.

Dr. Brownie focused on Trevor again.

"What accent do I hear there?"

Trevor blinked.

"Uh, New York, I guess. And some Florida cracker."

"Can't be both. You sing for a living?"

"Yes, sir. Raised in New York City. Raised in Florida. I sing and play guitar."

"Well, you won't be doing much singing for now, young man. Thank God. My girls tell me you're a country-western star. I can't stand country-western music. Twangy sentimental poop."

"Hospital?"

"Not yet. It's healthier to stay out of hospitals if you can."

"Amen to that."

"Hillbilly. I saw that fancy bus of yours in my parking lot. I never heard of you."

Trevor's shoulders straightened.

"Okay. So you can't know if you're going to like my music or not."

Scott shifted his feet, sensing the doctor's growing animosity towards Trevor and hoping to draw his fire.

"We're on the road, sir. We'll have that tour bus out of your parking lot in just a little while now. We'll be on our way to Richmond."

"No, you won't. You'll be right here in Tidewater, Virginia, living in that fancy bus of yours. Or in a motel. Your boy here's sick. You got that?"

"Yes, sir."

The doctor turned to Trevor again.

"I don't like Johnny Cash. I don't like Hank Williams. Why should I like you? Button up your shirt."

Trevor's plaid flannel shirt was part of his usual undercover outfit. Having the tour bus in the parking lot with its sides reading The Trevor Daniels Band had made that

18

irrelevant but Trevor had been chilly and the flannel shirt had made him feel warmer. Trevor buttoned the shirt now, his fingers clumsy.

"'Cause I'm different, Dr. Brownie. What music do you like?"

"Lawrence Welk. Know who that is? And the classics. Chopin. Strauss."

Trevor smiled.

"Now you're talking. My aunt's Mary Buck and my birth father was Shawn Lane. Scott, do we still have any of my serious CDs on the bus? Or Mary's?"

"Got a few."

"Would you mind?"

Scott nodded and vacated the room. Trevor eyed the elderly doctor.

"Mister, I got concert obligations for the next nine calendar days. I gotta do them or folks get disappointed. If I give you backstage passes to the show in Richmond, have you got something in your closet that'll keep me on my feet 'til I can get back home at the end of this tour?"

The doctor frowned at him.

"You're rich. You can afford to buy what I'll be prescribing. I save my samples for patients who can't afford to get their prescriptions filled. I'm not a sports team doctor. I don't consider it part of my duty to keep you on your feet, just to keep you from dying. I don't want your CDs. Here's your prescriptions."

Dr. Brownie scribbled fiercely on his prescription pad and tore off the small sheet, handing it to Trevor.

"Money can't buy you everything, young man. Just you think about that."

Trevor blinked and folded the prescription, sliding it into the left breast pocket of his flannel shirt.

"Why are you angry at me? Is it the hair? I'd like to give you some backstage passes. I'd kind of like to know there'll be a doctor in the house in Richmond. And I'd like to give you my CD, signed. No strings attached. I'm glad this clinic was here and open when I needed it. That's all."

Scott came back into the room with two boxed CDs, one a pre-autographed one of Mary Buck's from a stack that Trevor kept simply for the pleasure of being able to hand them out to his aunt's fans. The other was his instrumental work under the same label that carried Mary Buck. Scott had thoughtfully brought a Sharpie marker as well, and, knowing Trevor, a stack of backstage passes to their next engagement.

Trevor smiled his thanks at Scott as he took his own CD, opened the box and scribbled his full name across the top in marker. Trevor Lane Daniels. He waited for the marker to dry and then closed the case. He smiled again and handed the case along with Mary's CD to the doctor.

"How many passes? Please? I'd be honored."

The doctor accepted the offering of the CDs and two backstage passes, nodding his begrudging thanks

"All right, Mr. Country-Western, stand up and bend over. Carla will be in with an injection."

Trevor slithered from the table and stood swaying on his feet.

"No hospital?"

"No hospital. Not yet. This is going around here. You must have caught it wherever you've been and brought it along with you. It wouldn't have hit you so hard if you weren't so run-down. Carla described it to a tee."

Carla came in carrying two hypodermic needles and Scott turned away, not because he didn't want to see Trevor's butt, or hadn't before, but because needles made him queasy and he knew he'd faint dead away like a girl if he saw one go into Trevor's flesh. He'd be embarrassing himself in front of potential nookie. Not sexy at all.

Trevor dropped his jeans down, bent over and Carla poked him in the butt with the two needles. He pulled his jeans back up.

Scott turned back once he heard the distinctive sound of a sharps container rattling. The doctor scowled at him as though it was all his fault.

"Get some meat back on his bones. Chicken soup. Lots of liquids. Lots of rest. Tylenol or a cool cloth if his temp goes up. Buy a thermometer if you don't have one."

"Yes, sir."

"Pair of kids out on your own with no damned sense."

"Yes, sir."

"You can cover him back up and get out of here."

"Yes, sir."

Scott watched as Trevor straightened his posture somewhat. Whatever had been in those injections seemed to be fast-acting, Scott thought. Trevor was looking better already.

They filled the prescriptions. Scott got the medications into Trevor and then rolled him into his bunk bed. They hit the road again, Scott phoning up the florist the family used back home in Punta Gorda, Florida, to arrange for flowers to be delivered to one Carla Simpson at the Tidewater Clinic, Tidewater, Virginia. When Trevor raised an eyebrow at him, Scott blushed.

"Business expense."

In Richmond, Trevor collapsed on stage.

Dr. Brownie wasn't there, but his nurses Carla and Becky were, courtesy of the backstage passes.

# Chapter Two

Scott had been standing with Carla and Becky back stage, chatting up Carla under his breath while he kept an eye on Trevor. He saw the moment Trevor began to go down amid shocked gasps and hysterical squeals from the crowd. He had his arms under Trevor before he hit the floor.

Scott's troops cordoned off the stage and Scott scooped Trevor up, carrying him quickly out from under the bright lights.

Capturing Blondie from around Trevor's shoulders, Jesse Tweak stepped to the open mike as the band members looked at one another wildly.

"Ladies and gentlemen. Mr. Daniels has been ill with a chest cold for a couple of days. We been real busy on the road. He's fine, but we'll have to cancel this show. I'm real sorry about that. You all will be gettin' a full refund. Your box office here will handle that for you. Again, I'm real sorry. Trevor's real sorry, too. You all go home now. And drive safe."

Jesse switched off the mike and bolted off stage. He grabbed Mitch Evans on his way past him, leaving the band, security and the roadies to do their jobs. His job was to secure Blondie and to be Scott's backup driver.

Jesse and Mitch followed hurriedly in the wake of Scott who was plowing through the backstage area with Trevor in his arms, preceded by security team members and accompanied by Carla and Becky.

The tour bus stood ready. There were no lingering fans out back this early in the show. The bus doors were open. They all flowed inside, Jesse and Mitch bringing up the rear. Scott growled to Jesse over his shoulder.

"Get this thing rollin'."

Jesse nodded to Mitch. They rolled.

Scott had pre-located the nearest hospital and already discussed the route with Jesse, not liking the look of Trevor since they'd left Tidewater, Virginia.

Scott laid Trevor on his bed, then stood back to let Carla in. She muttered under her breath to him.

"Dr. Brownie's going to be furious. He knew the moment you left the clinic that you weren't going to cancel the Richmond concert. I came prepared."

Carla pulled her purse open, whipped out two neatly wrapped and filled hypodermic needles and Scott collapsed heavily onto the floor. Carla looked down at him in disgust.

"Great."

She then rounded on Jesse.

"You with the guitar. Any alcohol in here? Not for drinking."

Jesse gaped at her.

"Uh, yes, ma'am. We got a first aid kit."

"Get it."

Jesse hurried to comply, stepping over Scott's inert body. Carla glanced at Becky.

"Men. Help me roll Trevor over, Becky. We need his butt. Make sure he doesn't smother in the pillow."

The two women rolled Trevor over. Jesse brought the first aid kit and Carla gave him her instructions.

"Get this bus to Richmond General Hospital right now."

Jesse dropped the first aid kit on Trevor's bed and sped to obey, propping Trevor's guitar hurriedly in its custom-built corner as he joined Mitch up front to superintend the trip.

Carla unzipped Trevor's jeans. Becky hauled them down. Carla wiped with an alcohol swab from the first aid kit and stuck one after the other of the two hypodermic needles into what passed for soft tissue on Trevor's lean, hard body. They pulled up his jeans, rolled him onto his back and covered him up.

Becky, awestruck, smoothed her hand over Trevor's pale forehead. Scott groaned and sat up. Carla whipped out her cell phone.

"Richmond General? Emergency room, please. I'll hold."

She looked down at a dazed Scott.

"You are so worthless."

"Yes, ma'am. Whatever you say."

"Has he been taking the medication at all?"

"Yes, ma'am. All of it. I seen to that. Lots of liquids. Lots of rest. Chicken soup. He seemed fine 'til this mornin'. Then I got worried. I done set up the plan with Jesse in case I was right. We're goin' to Richmond General right now."

"Dr. Brownie liked the CDs Trevor gave him. Both of them. He knew you'd run out of time, too. He sent me with the proper medication in case there was a problem. The third day. Remember?"

"He seemed like he was goin' on fine. I'm tellin' ya."

"And I'm telling you Dr. Brownie was furious."

"Not no more furious than our daddy's gonna be. No way to cover this up from him. He's got TV. He'll hear the eleven o'clock news. I thought Jesse did a right fine speech for bein' shook up. Didn't you? Is Trevor gonna be all right?"

Scott stayed on the floor but reached out hands to his brother.

"Come on, Trevor. Don't be stupid and die or anythin'. Come on. Daddy's gonna kick my butt and it's all your fault. You stay here and take your licks, too, you moron."

Trevor's eyelids fluttered and Scott squeezed his hand. Trevor opened his eyes a slit.

"Angels?"

"You moron. It's Carla and Becky. Quit tryin' to scare me so much, will ya?"

Mitch lurched the bus to a stop and Jesse opened the doors, sprinting into the emergency entrance of Richmond General Hospital. Carla could see him snag the first person in hospital attire he found and was gripping them firmly by the arm. She hung up her cell phone, fuming furiously to herself. She'd been on hold the whole time.

"Scott, get Trevor. Becky, get Jesse before he's arrested for assault."

24

Carla led the way into the emergency room waiting area and approached the admissions clerk.

"Trevor Daniels. Heavy respiratory infection. He collapsed on stage. I'm his private nurse. Get a cubicle and a doctor for him right now. It may take a while for his personal physician to get here."

The clerk scrambled into the back. Scott nodded, Trevor in his arms, Trevor's head resting on his shoulder.

"Daddy's gonna like you, Carla. You're not married, right?"

\* \* \* \* \*

Jarrett Daniels didn't dignify the occasion of his youngest son's hospitalization with a mad dash northward by truck or plane. He didn't acknowledge the event at all, which caused Scott's nerves to twitch and his skin to crawl. Not hearing from Daddy about this fiasco was infinitely worse than hearing from him about it, he thought.

From a hospital room smothered in bright flowers, it was Trevor who placed the phone call to their father.

"Hey, Dad. How's it goin'?"

"There goes one of your nine lives, boy. You just watch it."

"Yes, sir. Scott took me to a doctor. A fan of Aunt Mary's. Mine, too, now I guess. Anyway, he gave me prescriptions and advice and at least I took the prescriptions and some of the advice. I'm fine now."

Trevor quickly held the phone away from his ear, just in case his father decided to turn up the volume on his voice a little.

"Son?"

Trevor brought the phone back to his ear again.

"Yeah?"

"I'm not gonna tell you a thing you haven't already told yourself. And you can tell your brother he can breathe again, too. He did a fine job. My hat's off to him for gettin'

25

you to that doctor in the first place. He did everythin' he could."

"I messed up."

"You know exactly what you did."

"I'm sorry, Dad."

"Like I said, I'm not gonna tell you a thing you haven't already told yourself."

"I disappointed you."

"Some. What are your plans now?"

"Doc wants me resting. Scott's got something going with our nurse. Oh, we've got a new employee. A nurse. Her name's Carla. She'll be coming with us on the road. When we go back on the road. Whenever that is. I'll tell you later all she's done for us. I asked her to sign on. I asked her her price. She told me and I doubled it. Worth every penny, Dad."

"That's your call, son. Where are you plannin' on doin' your restin'?"

"Home. Can I come home?"

"You're gettin' too old to come home, son. Mary don't need this."

Trevor sniffed.

"Please? Then I'll go back up to The Ice Palace. Scottie and Carla'll be with me."

"My older son is importin' it from Virginia now?"

"Yes, sir. I believe he is."

"Then come on home to your old room here in Punta Gorda, monkey. Let your brother and his lady try out the benefits of that house of yours on Longboat Key. Scott Junior can stay with his maternal grandmother just as if the tour was still on. Give my older boy time to work some magic for himself. It's time he did. It was a pity Tiffany took off, but Scottie deserves to move on."

"I think he has, Dad. Carla's real nice. You'll like her. She'll fit right into the family just fine."

"Hang up the phone and go to sleep, Trevor. We'll have the bed all made up for you when you get here."

"Thanks, Dad."

"You're welcome, son."

Trevor hung up on dead air, but he felt at peace. Home. He was going home. He slid down in the white-sheeted hospital bed and closed his eyes. He let the medication take him away.

\*　　　\*　　　\*　　　\*　　　\*

*Sunlight and flowers. Bees humming. The air smelt like grass and dirt. And pine trees. The wind sighed through the pine trees. Grass was tickling the palms of his hands and he gripped a handful, pulled it out and put it in his mouth.*

*"No, no, baby. Don't eat the grass. Cows eat grass. You're not a cow. You're a little boy. My little boy. Little baby boy Trevor. Come give Aunt Mary a kiss."*

*He looked down at white shoes with jingle bells on them, then fell slowly over onto his side, laughing. A blonde curl dropped in front of his eyes and he tried to grab it, but poked himself in the eye with his finger instead and started to wail.*

*Mary scooped him up and nuzzled her face into his neck.*

*"Trevor, Trevor, Trevor. Hush, little baby. Aunt Mary'll give you a big kiss. Make it all better."*

*She smacked a wet kiss onto his cheek and he giggled again, forgetting his pain and frustration.*

\*　　　\*　　　\*　　　\*　　　\*

"Hey, moron. You make it all right with Daddy for us?"

"Hm?"

"Scott, let him sleep."

"No way. If he sleeps now, he'll be up all night."

"He's not a baby."

"Sure he is. And he gets cranky, too."

Trevor opened one eye to see his older brother grinning down at him, one arm around the waist of their nurse. His nurse.

"Hey, that's my nurse."

"Come and get her."

"I'll show you cranky."

"I can take you."

"You can right now. But you just wait."

"Darn, I'm glad you're back, Trev."

"Glad to be back, Bro."

"We goin' home?"

"We're going home. I'm going to Punta Gorda. The Ice Palace is totally available."

Scott turned to Carla and nuzzled his nose and then his lips into her neck, making her laugh.

"You're gonna like Sarasota, sugar. Big-assed house there. What about Scott Junior, Trev?"

"Dad says he stays with Martha, just like he would if the tour was still on."

"Yes! Not that I don't love my son. I do. And you will, too, sugar. Helluva kid. But, oh, my, yes. The Longboat Key house all to ourselves."

"There's Buddy."

"We'll do fine. I'll just toss him some KFC and we'll be cool."

Carla turned in Scott's arms to look up at him.

"Who's Buddy?"

"Trevor's cat. Big, fluffy gray-striped tom cat."

"Oh. Trevor, go back to sleep. This clown just had to see if you were all right."

"I'm fine. Dad says you did good, Scott. All my fault. Well, we knew that."

"Home. Goin' home. God, I love goin' home."


## TREVOR'S GOD


I woke up from a nightmare.
God sat beside my bed.

He held me in his arms
And this is what he said,
"Hush now, Trevor,
Don't you cry.
Jarrett's gonna sing you
A lullaby."

God drives a dented pick-up truck.
God pays the power bill.
God works to make an honest buck;
Keeps peaches on our windowsill.
God taught me how to love.
God taught me how to pray.
God taught me how to be
Everything I am today.
Some folks think God's in Heaven,
Looking down from up above.
I know God's right beside me,
With smiling eyes of love.

\*     \*     \*     \*     \*

Scott hung around Trevor's hospital room two days later while they waited for Dr. Brownie to finally release Trevor. Trevor had been writing music and lyrics again on one of the lined, spiral tablets he always kept with him. He was sitting up in bed in his patient gown. Scott, in jeans and a plaid shirt, was sitting on the same bed, fiddling with the call button.

"Nice idea, these things. Maybe we could hang one around your neck. Then maybe you'd let folks know when you need help. I'd sure feel safer."

"I don't need one. Since I met Dad, I've surrounded myself with safety."

Scott lay the call button down.

"Well, who wouldn't want safety? Especially since when I first met you, you was real puny. That long hair of yours made you a walkin' target. Kept me real busy in my early teens bustin' heads of folks for lookin' at you funny."

Trevor chuckled and smiled warmly at his brother.

"Me looking funny never kept the women away."

"There is that. But, heck, Trevor, everybody wants to feel safe. It's just a whole lot easier to feel safe when you know you've got backup. I got froggy with my mom after I knew Daddy would back my play if I wanted to live with him. And it's a helluva lot easier to run away from home when you're in the town you was born into. Got friends all over the place. Got forts out in the woods to live in. I was safe as a bug in a rug, and I knew it. And I am bigger than you are. I been strikin' accidental terror in people since I was seven. 'Course, that was with the six-year-olds, but still. I bet you never struck terror in anyone in your life. It ain't your style."

"I struck terror in Dad once. I remember being surprised about that. It was the second time I'd seen him. Up in the hospital back home. I had all these tubes going in me and wires taped to me. I was hurting and scared and feeling sorry for myself. He came up there to ask me questions, doing his cop-thing. I don't remember what he said to me, but it ticked me off and I started to try to sit up and get out of that bed. I got about as tangled up in wires and tubes as I did that day you found me with my hair stuck in the big live oak tree in the side yard. I kind of panicked. I guess I scared Dad then. He grabbed me real quick to stop me thrashing around and getting up. And he grabbed me too hard. He didn't mean to. I knew that right away, but it hurt and I yelped and he let loose of me a little. I saw in his face that he cared that he'd hurt me. I'd struck terror in him thinking he'd hurt me. I grabbed him and bawled. Best thing I ever did for myself. That changed my whole world. Looking back, I think that change Dad's whole world, too."

Trevor reached out to grab Scott's arm. Scott pulled it away, jokingly frowning at him.

"Get your fag hands off me."

Trevor grinned at their usual routine.

"You love it. You know you do. I taught you all kinds of stuff you never knew before we met. I'll bet I'm striking terror in you right now."

"You are that, you manipulative little weasel. I'm scared to death you'll blurt out something about those early days of ours together to Carla."

Trevor gave him the big-eyed look.

"I would never do that."

"And I learned when I was sixteen that I didn't want to see your hairy butt again."

"My butt wasn't hairy in those days. My body wasn't hairy."

"It ain't too darned hairy now, Trev. Except that mop on top."

"I wax. And I shave."

"Geez, Trev. I didn't need to know that."

"Just striking some terror."

"You are that. Quit."

Dr. Brownie walked into the room without a word to the two brothers and applied his stethoscope to Trevor's chest. He straightened and returned the stethoscope to his lab coat pocket.

"You've got asthma."

Trevor's mouth dropped open.

"What? Asthma??"

"That's what I hear in your lungs right now. It has a very distinctive sound to it. Apparently you got it later in life. These things happen."

Trevor snapped his jaw shut.

"Well, I'm screwed now."

Dr. Brownie frowned at him.

"Not necessarily. You have to keep on top of it. Prevention beats out treating symptoms once they start. It can be controlled these days with medication. You'll need to get a peak flow meter..."

Trevor scowled at the doctor.

"Medication? No. I hate medicine. What's a peak flow meter?"

31

"It measures how well you breathe out what you breathe in. Gas exchange, oxygen for carbon dioxide, is a very real problem with asthma. Why no medication?"

"Long story. Diet? Exercise?"

"Never hurts. The asthma may have a food trigger. You'll have to find out."

"Me? You're the doc."

"And they're your lungs. Your responsibility. Exercise? Not when you're having an attack. Maybe your asthma is exercise induced. When do you feel breathless?"

"When I'm in love."

Scott slammed Trevor between the shoulder blades so the doctor didn't have to.

"Trev, the guy's tryin' to do his job here. You ain't helpin'."

"I don't want to deal with this."

"Deal with it. If you've told me once, you've told me a dozen times that smoke in the concerts makes it hard for you to breathe. And I never seen anybody shun cold air like you do. When we was out skiin' in Colorado, I liked to never got you outside and onto the slopes."

"The cold air hurts when I breathe it. I wheeze."

"Well, there you are. It ain't goin' away, Trev. You just been ignorin' it. Daddy know about this?"

"No. Don't tell him, Scott. He worries."

"He's right to worry about you, moron."

Dr. Brownie interceded dryly.

"Boys? In spite of Mr. Hillbilly's marked lack of cooperation—and denial is a fairly common reaction to bad news—you've been finding the triggers and avoiding them all along."

Dr. Brownie fixed serious eyes on Trevor's face.

"If the person you loved the most in the world got this news, what would you do?"

Trevor raised stricken eyes to Scott.

"Dad."

He turned to the doctor.

"Full testing, if necessary. Medication. Lifestyle changes. Care. What?"

The doctor was laughing at him now.

"And you don't rate as high as your loved one?"

Trevor's eyes slid away.

"No. He's special."

Scott bumped shoulders with him.

"Moron. You're the meal ticket. I don't fancy drawin' no unemployment checks. Best get this under control."

Trevor narrowed his eyes at the elderly doctor.

"No news leaks. One hint of this in the media and I'll know where to look."

Scott saw the doctor begin to stiffen and drew his fire again.

"He's rude when he ain't feelin' good. Don't pay him no mind. Make the prescriptions out to Trevor Lane. Ain't no one gonna care if some longhair composer guy's got asthma, Trev."

Trevor Lane, the composer, began an exhaustive series of tests for allergy triggers while he was in Richmond, Virginia. Arriving in the white Hyundai wearing sunglasses and a baseball cap with Scott doing the driving and most of the talking, Trevor had scratch tests done.

"I'm not giving up Buddy. I'm holding firm for that."

"Probably ain't cat dander, Trev, or you'd have been gaspin' for breath every time you nuzzled your face into that varmint's fur. Could be cut grass."

"No more lawn mowing? Now you're talking."

"I been readin' up on this asthma thing, Trev. I figured one of us ought to know what we're doin'. Ain't nobody real sure what causes it or what sets it off or whether or not there's genetic predisposition..."

"That's the longest word I've ever heard you use."

"I been practicin'. And that's what the docs are doin'. Practicin'. It's the practice of medicine, Trev. Like you and your guitar."

"If I hit an A-chord, I hit an A-chord, goddammit."

"This ain't that easy. Go get scratched up and let's see what we got."

*    *    *    *    *

Trevor was on the phone to their father at least once a day from Richmond, Virginia.

"Coming home, Dad. Be there tomorrow."

At his end, Jarrett picked up one of Trevor's glossy new promotional photos.

"You know, you ain't never took a bad picture yet."

"It's all planes and angles of light, Dad."

"You got a great smile. Real warm eyes."

"That's the photographer. He tells me to let the light in and I think of you. Works every time. My warm eyes'd be getting some john hot right about now if it weren't for you. I'd be nothing but a guitar-playing street hustler if it weren't for you."

"Well, you'd have been a good one."

"Darned straight."

At his end, Trevor sobered.

"You know what I mean."

"I do. You're a guitar-playin' street hustler now. You just hustle a bigger, better crowd."

Trevor cracked up.

"And you'd be a grumpy old hermit living alone."

"Well, at least I'm not livin' alone. Mary says I'm grumpy? She's lyin'. And you ain't livin' alone."

"That pretty-boy face you're talking about in the photos isn't getting me what I want."

"It could get you all the casual sex you could handle."

"I've got that. That's not what I want."

"Bambi?"

"Bobbi."

"Whatever."

"I had a chat with Buddy back when about casual sex. I don't think he paid any attention to me. Now I'm the one who feels like a darned tomcat."

"Small wonder Buddy ignored you, what with Bambi in bed with the both of you. And don't tell me Buddy left the room because he's a gentleman."

Trevor laughed.

"He didn't. He doesn't. He sits up on that shelf over the headboard and scores my ladies like a judge at the Olympics. He hasn't signaled a ten yet."

"Cat's got his standards."

Trevor heaved a sigh.

"I'm lonely, Dad."

"Come home. Reconnect with some real people. Find your roots again. You're tired and sick and bummed out."

# Chapter Three

They got into Punta Gorda, late.

Scott had refused to let Trevor drive himself home in any of the vehicles he owned. Scott and Carla had dropped him off at the house that had been his home since he was fifteen years old before doubling back to the white marble, metal and glass house on Longboat Key that the Daniels brothers irreverently referred to as The Ice Palace.

Trevor entered the backdoor of the unlocked frame house on Olympia Avenue. He walked easily to his old room through the darkened house, turning on the old bedside lamp once he was there. Looking around the room, he saw no changes. The Dolly Parton poster from Jarrett's youth was still on the wall next to an embarrassingly large poster of himself that Mary had had created from a photo of him in green tights playing Peter Pan for a local children's theater in Sarasota.

The only thing he had taken with him when he had moved out was the poster of guitar chords that Jarrett Daniels had given him the day of his debut as a musician upstairs at Big Dog's on a Tuesday night many, many years ago.

It stayed on the tour bus with him, a reminder of home.

Trevor set his old camo green backpack on the floor next to the bureau, aware that his arms were tired and felt almost floaty after the minimal weight of the backpack left them. The only thing he unpacked and unfolded was the afghan his now-deceased grandmother had crocheted for him. He'd gotten that when he was fifteen years old, too, and had met her for the first time. It had stayed with him through troubles, a reminder to him of her love for him.

Trevor spread the afghan lovingly on the empty bed, toed off his sneakers, shut off the lights and flopped on the bed on his back in his clothes, folding the wings of his Grammy-afghan around him. He sighed and looked up to heaven to thank God for his blessings.

And looked up into a ceiling filled with luminous, glow-in-the-dark stars. It took his breath away. Awed, he felt he could look right straight up to heaven.

"Wow."

His Aunt Mary's voice floated through the silent house to him.

"You're welcome, Trevor."

Trevor smiled as he lay on his back and watched the stars overhead, relaxing and remembering his family life in Punta Gorda.

He remembered the beginning of this, what he considered to be his real life, when he had been learning to be a good ole boy and hanging out with his newly-acquired older brother Scott. The insistent music machine within him had been quiet then, taking a break, chilling out, refueling.

He'd jabbered and run and played.

He'd embarrassed Scott.

He'd intrigued him.

And he'd gotten him women.

In the groove and happy, he'd allowed his natural aptitude for persuasion to flourish. Jarrett Daniels had laughed at him and let himself be manipulated. His Aunt Mary had challenged him on it. Scott just shook his head and reaped the benefits. His adopted grandmother Bernice Daniels had warned him never to use his power for evil. He'd given her the big-eyed look and she had tapped his nose with one arthritic finger. He heard her voice in his head now.

*"I'm on to your ways, little bird. Grammy loves you. You don't have to be doin' all that Yankee snow job on Grammy. Or Jarrett or Mary, either. If you want somethin', you just ask for it politely and we all will consider the request. Might get a no. Might get a yes. You'll always get the reasons for the vote, baby. Save that talent you've got for the outside world."*

Looking back on those times, Trevor realized he had been learning to live.

His high school days had been a pleasant blur of easy A's and hot sex in the boonies with the old blue Chevy pickup truck Jarrett had given him. If Scott played football for the Desoto High School Bulldogs, the whole family went to Arcadia to watch, Grammy in her wheelchair included. If he himself played guitar in Arcadia, the whole family did the same. If he played Winter Haven, he stayed with his Uncle Richard's family. When he played LA later, he stayed with his Aunt Cass and her family.

After that first Christmas, when Grammy had gathered all available family down to Punta Gorda, blocking off one wing of the Best Western Water Front, he had never had a valid reason to feel alone again.

Peering out from behind Jarrett's broad back, his eyes wide and his heart nervous, he had been overwhelmed at first by the number of eyes turned towards him and been inclined to retreat behind Jarrett's comfortable bulk. But Mary had surreptitiously grasped his hand, her own sweating, and he had realized his aunt was meeting these same strangers for the first time, too. Mary had had a lot riding on it, he'd realized, having not yet been married to Jarrett.

Somehow that insight had helped and he had stepped forward, remembering what Jarrett laughingly called his perfect manners. He had relaxed himself, smiling tentatively and trying very hard to grasp and retain all the names and relationships tossed at him.

His cousin Stephanie had definitely stood out. With her pale blond hair and big blue eyes, she had clung to him dreamily. "Oh, I just love you so much!" It had unnerved him as a fifteen-year-old boy, but it had broken the ice.

Looking back, Trevor realized his life through his remaining school years had been both a never-never land and a good base of experience for his current occupation.

He and Jarrett and a tutor had traveled with Mary as she fulfilled her concert tour obligations and closed off her career as a concert violinist, heading towards her goal of retirement to Punta Gorda, Florida. Millie Crawford, the retired school teacher who had gone with them as his tutor, had laid a good foundation of geography and history for him to be able to appreciate, to some extent, the things he saw, or at least as much as it was possible to prepare a teenaged boy to appreciate, say, the Grand Canyon. Just another really big hole in the ground, but cool to spit into. He had spat off the Eiffel Tower, the Coliseum, and dozens of balconies throughout Europe.

By the time he was ready to attend Charlotte High School, Mary had succeeded in retiring. In spite of being on world-wide tours, Mary and he had never lost the newly-acquired Punta Gorda roots Jarrett Daniels had allowed them to put down. It hadn't been as difficult to start high school because he'd already known his peers there from the preceding summer of his sixteenth birthday.

Trevor realized that the span of time between meeting Jarrett Daniels and beginning the end of Mary's tour life had been, for him, magical. He had found a home. He had found a father. Two of them, in fact. He had discarded one mother and gained another in his aunt. He'd gotten a brother. And friends. And connections. A wonderful grandmother.

A family.

He had been safe and sound and loved and pampered and spoiled. He had never taken any of it for granted and he still didn't.

Scott and he had roamed wild between his rollerblades and a new bicycle for Scott, courtesy of Jarrett. Scott's wheels could take them further, with more stuff on board, including Trevor. Scott's legs were older and stronger than Trevor's had been. Bicycle trips to Murdock and the Port Charlotte Town Center Mall had been a piece of cake for Scott.

The two of them had explored the semi-abandoned streets of greater Port Charlotte as well. Scott had fished in canals while Trevor had jabbered and Scott had told him to shut up. He had introduced Scott to a bewildering universe of sexual techniques far in advance of both their years and their inept peer group. Technically, he knew quite a lot, between the bad experiences of one Christopher de Nunzio, the man he had gone to live with after being abandoned by his birth mother, and his subsequent adventures on the road before meeting Jarrett Daniels. There had also been the educational benefits of the VCR tape accidentally left in his first father's effects of some slim boys frolicking at a waterfall in Brazil, which in later life had become a bit of a running gag between the two brothers.

As Trevor fell asleep, words and music and flashes of images began to flit through his head.

### I'M FREE

C C  F  B  A    B B  C    F G
I lay on the banks of the Pontchartrain,

  E   F   G   G    A G F E
My backpack tucked under a tree

G F  A   A  A  G   A C  C   C
I lay down in wonder under the sky

A   Bb     C    C  Db  Eb Eb Eb
And watched the stars flow over me.

Gb  Gb  Eb
I'm free now.

 Eb
I'm free.

C Db  A  B    C     B G A G  A
I saw the bright lights of New Orleans.

A  C   C   D   D    A B   A

I saw the moon glow on my hands.

A C   C   D   D D   D A B   A
I felt the heat, and the grass and the breeze.

A C   C C   C A A
I felt myself understand.

G  A  A
I'm free now.

G  A
I'm free.

I've got one pair of shoes, but they're mine.
No bully can take them from me.
Got a razor, some socks, and a Swiss Army knife,
But it's something better for me.
I don't mind sleeping out in the rain
'Cause I can.
I've had fancier homes in my life
But I ran.
Wrap my long hair around me;
With myself I'll surround me.
It's everything I've wanted to be.
I'm free.
I'm free.

\*      \*      \*      \*      \*

"Jarrett, your son is insane."

Jarrett Daniels raised an eyebrow and looked at his beloved second wife Mary. It was breakfast for two on the outside deck at the house on Olympia Avenue, plus one today. Trevor was still in bed asleep, but his brother Scott was very much awake and present. Jarrett lifted his eyes to look up into the big live oak tree above them.

41

"My son, huh? You can't be talkin' about Scottie here. I'm guessin' your nephew Trevor is just fine."

"You know what I mean. Scottie, tell him."

Jarrett turned a bland look to his older son and Scott squirmed in his chair.

"He's weird, Daddy."

"By whose standards?"

"Well, he's gettin' weirder."

"Casual sex, his talk about gettin' a piercin' in his belly button and those hairdos Margaret's been turnin' out for him to wear onstage don't count?"

Both his listeners became uncomfortable and Jarrett frowned at them.

"Is he doin' anythin' that might be harmful to himself or to others?"

Scott dropped his eyes.

"No, sir."

Mary's chin came up.

"Certainly not."

"Then leave the boy alone, the both of you. Can't a man have some peace to explore a new hobby?"

But later, when Mary had gone out shopping at S.S. Rainbow in Fisherman's Village with her tennis buddy Linda Kern, and Scott had returned to Carla at his rented house east of Sarasota, Jarrett knocked on Trevor's old bedroom door. Trevor's smiling voice answered him.

"Come in."

Jarrett slowly opened the door, prepared for almost any sight. Over the years, he'd seen a few. He looked briefly for Trevor at eye level and again at the miniscule desk with its outdated computer. Not there. A movement caught his eye and he adjusted his bifocals to study it.

Trevor sat on the braided rug, cross-legged, wearing boxers and an old cast-off shirt of his. He'd been wearing them for years, Jarrett thought, and they still didn't quite fit him.

Trevor looked up with his brilliant smile, his hands full of Legos.

"These are really cool, Dad."

Jarrett carefully lowered himself to the floor. He tried sitting cross-legged, but his knees didn't much like the sensation. He squatted on his heels for a while, watching Trevor work with the bright, primary-colored plastic blocks, then gave it up and sat back up in the chair by the desk.

"Recapturin' your childhood, Trevor?"

"Yep. Only I never had these."

"There's a lot of stuff from your childhood you never had, Trevor. As I recall, I offered to buy you anythin' you wanted back then from Toys R Us."

"I know. But I wasn't ready then. I'd gotten so much already from you and never had the payback come. I didn't want to press my luck. Then I got too old for toys."

"And now you're not?"

Trevor grinned companionably up at him.

"Yep. Now I'm not. I'm trying to get into it, Dad. The colors and shapes and the whole potential of the thing. Cars and buildings and all kinds of make-believe."

"Recapturin' a sense of wonder?"

"Yeah. I've lost track. I hate my own songs. What I've been churning out lately is dark and edgy. It needs getting out, mind you. But I don't really like it once it's out. And God knows who'll ever play or sing it. Scott says the new band Jake's been working with maybe. Rock, ya know. Apparently I'm country."

"You are?"

"That's what I said."

"I hate labels. So, you're goin' back to the basics you never had?"

Trevor blinked, fingering the bright plastic building blocks. He tilted his head and became thoughtful. Jarrett felt the years fall away and almost could imagine a much younger Trevor sitting before him.

"I'm still missing the boat, aren't I?"

"I don't know, son. It's your boat."

Trevor sagged. Jarrett nudged his bare foot with the toe of his sneaker.

"Hey, boy. Lighten up."

"I'm not that kind of crazy. I know Mary and Scott think I'm crazy."

"Of course, you're crazy. You've always been crazy. Who cares? The point is, are you crazy that you're hurtin' yourself or others?"

"No. Well, maybe myself."

"That would be my guess."

Jarrett nudged Trevor's foot again with his sneaker.

"Offer still holds for that shrink. That offer never expired."

"I'm not that kind of crazy. I've been over the Spath boys raping me for years."

"I know it. But I'm not sure you're over a lot of other things. What the talk shows these days call 'unresolved issues' ain't like a head cold, over when it's done. They're more like the chicken pox. The chicken pox can come back any time later in life as the shingles. Real painful, the shingles. Not nearly the same kind of fun as the chicken pox. Chicken pox is aggravatin' and drives you crazy. Shingles just makes you crazy. You might still have some of them unresolved issues left over from that time you was livin' with your birth mom."

"Maybe. I don't know. I hate spilling my guts. It's different talking with you. Recently Scott's been getting the overflow. And that may be why I'm finally becoming receptive to this shrink idea. There shouldn't be any overflow."

Trevor waved a handful of Legos.

"Dammit, I'm a grown man. And I'm sitting on the floor in my old room playing with Legos, for God's sake!"

"Hey. Don't throw them things around. They hurt when you step on one later in your bare feet. I ought to know. Done stepped on enough of them myself. Got my old red carryin' case full of them up in the attic."

"You've got Legos?"

"I got a lot of stuff from my childhood I been savin', hopin' to use again when I had children of my own to share it with. The timin' wasn't right for Scottie or for you. I got hopes for grandbabies. Scott Junior's comin' right along. I'm bidin' my time."

"You don't play with your toys on the floor of your bedroom."

"I would if I could. It'd be the livin' room floor, though. There's more space. Havin' kids gives a man a good excuse to revert back to bein' a child himself. Get you some kids to hang out with and front for you, Trev. Go be a Big Brother or somethin' once you're all healed up again. Great things, kids. Gotta getcha some. Later. Not right now. How about you bring them Legos out to the kitchen table? It'll be easier for me to work on them there. The floor ain't my friend right now."

Instant concern washed across Trevor's face.

"Are you okay?"

"Of course, I'm okay. All that darned football in my youth done caught up with my knees and my back some days, is all. Today's just one of those days. Enjoy your body while you got it, boy."

Trevor grinned.

"I do."

"Other parts of your body, Trevor. Not just your close personal friend."

"I do."

"You know what I mean, boy."

Trevor got up from the floor, gathering his Legos together.

"Yeah. I do. So, who's your pick of the shrinks?"

"It's up to you. I hear good things about Rosamma Panjikaran."

"That's my gal, then. If she'll have me."

Trevor and Jarrett took their Lego pieces out to the kitchen table and sat down in their usual chairs. Jarrett started building a house.

While they continued to build Lego dreams in companionable silence, Jarrett studied his youngest son's profile.

Vulnerable, he thought. That was the look that made Trevor so appealing. Even behind a seemingly carefree grin there was vulnerability. Did Trevor know it? Maybe. Did he use it? Probably. Was it real? Absolutely.

Small and nearly defenseless when younger, Trevor had had to use the talent available to him to survive. Silence. Grit. Fast legs for running. And charm. The whole package was innately Trevor now. The charm he could put on and take off like a coat. But the vulnerability stayed. He was tougher than he looked. And more fragile than he cared to admit. Trevor's huge volume of musical talent fed from his life experiences, which meant some wounds were kept open purposely to bleed.

Trevor felt everything in a sharp, unfiltered way. Great joy, great pain, great fear, great regret. There were no modifiers, no parameters. From his eyes and ears to his skin and fingers, it was all sensation and input to Trevor. All feeding the thirst of the music machine within him.

Trevor needed the music.

But the music needed Trevor.

Jarrett was still hoping to figure out a way to help Trevor install some roll bars on himself, because it seemed at times as if he was on a crash course with life itself.

Trevor tired quickly, his Lego projects on the kitchen table in various stages of completion, and not a single one finished. Even with these tiny toys, Jarrett thought, Trevor was manic and obsessive. He had to do more. He had to finish.

Jarrett laid a hand on Trevor's arm.

"Trevor. They're toys. They'll be here later for you to play with. Like I said, I got more in the attic. Slow down, son. Enjoy what you've got. Right now, get back to bed. You're tired. I can see it in your eyes."

Trevor nodded and stood waveringly up from the kitchen table. He didn't try to put away his toys, another sure sign he was under par, Jarrett thought.

Jarrett steered him to his bedroom and into his bed, where Trevor lay face down on his pillow. Jarrett brought the jar of Vick's Vapor Rub he'd bought when he'd learned of Trevor's congested lungs down from the top shelf in the closet. He shoved Trevor's shirt up his narrow back, opened the jar and, scooping out a handful, smoothed it onto Trevor's back, feeling every bone and sinew and muscle under the pale skin. He felt the tension slowly melt out of Trevor and a totally new sensation move in.

"We're not like those boys in that VCR tape from Brazil, Trevor. We're like regular buddies. Got the love. Got the affection. Just not gonna have the sex."

"This feels so great."

"It's a massage, Trevor. I figure there's about three ways to get a good massage. One is to pay down good cash money at a spa or a massage parlor or a doctor's office. Another is to get tangled up in the sheets with a good-lovin' woman. And there's a voluntary act of lovin' kindness from a close, personal friend. In this case, your dad. Gotta get you a willin' woman, boy."

"I do. I've got plenty."

"Wiseguy."

"They've got little hands."

"Little hands is good."

"Yeah, it is. But for this, big hands feels better." Jarrett frowned.

"I can almost put my hands clean around you in places, bird-man."

"Maybe that's why this feels so good."

"Could be. Could need a little domination there."

"Keep dominating, big boy."

"Watch the sex talk."

"Yes, sir."

Trevor had his eyes shut and a relaxed smile on his face.

47

"Mary do this for you?"

"Nunna."

"Nunna?"

"As in, it ain't nunna your business."

"Oh. Sorry. Just making conversation."

"Shut up and relax. Quit with the charm and the schedules and all that stuff. Just float some."

And Trevor floated. Jarrett could tell when he floated to sleep and covered him in his Grammy-afghan.

Satisfied that his youngest son was on the mend, the next day Jarrett threw him out of the house again, sending him back to his own residence in The Ice Palace on Longboat Key in Sarasota.

## Chapter Four

In the stark glass whiteness of the Longboat Key house, Trevor pulled on boxers and another old shirt of Jarrett's. His hair looked like he hadn't brushed it in days, and he couldn't have cared less. He pulled on socks against the cold of the glossy white marble floors and felt he now looked like the antithesis of anyone's romantic vision of him.

He wished he didn't have all this darned hair on his head, too. Even his scalp ached. He didn't feel like doing much of anything, least of all the music. It still hurt to breathe and he was conscious of every breath he took.

The music machine within him was quiet again, having shut down. That was a rarity and right now, a blessing. He couldn't work up any enthusiasm for either picking up his discarded clothes on the floor of his bedroom or having a snack. He wasn't hungry. He wasn't thirsty. He wasn't anything. He considered the possibility that he was going into an emotional down cycle and discarded it. He was simply as bland as white bread.

He nuked himself a big mug of hot water and added the medication for the congestion in his lungs. He shoved his big cream leather recliner closer to the fireplace so he could stare at the gigantic family photo over the fireplace as he sat. He found even that slight exercise tired him and winded him. He wrapped his Grammy-afghan around himself, slumped into the recliner and hugged the warmth of the mug to his chest, sipping from the rim.

All around him the vast whiteness of The Ice Palace was silent, though sunny. He relaxed his shoulders into the softness of the afghan and the recliner, staring mutely at the huge, vivid photographic portrait of his family over the fireplace. Just seeing the grinning faces warmed and relaxed him from within while the hot liquid and the medications did their magic.

He finished the mug of liquid and set it on the floor beside him. His cat Buddy padded down the carpeted stairs and jumped up into the recliner with him, purring and rubbing his face up into Trevor's face for attention. Trevor fondled the kitty ears, relaxing into a familiar routine with his old friend.

"You sure are handsome, you devil you. Let me check your ears. Wow. Those are some clean ears, dude. You got you some honey cleaning your ears for you? Huh? Bet that feels real nice. A warm wet tongue up in your ear. I better just quit that sex talk, huh? I ain't found the right lady to do my ears for me yet. Though I've had my ears done. Where'd you find a willing pussy around here? Got you a high-tone woman, boy? Bring her on home here. We got plenty of room."

Buddy circled like a dog on Trevor's lap and finally curled up, twenty some pounds of added warmth to fight the inner chills of Trevor's bones. Trevor continued to absently fondle Buddy's fur and let his mind drift. He pulled the wings of his afghan closer around him and closed his eyes.

*     *     *     *     *

He dreamed of babies.

One baby, actually.

In a sunny room full of toys and pastel colors.

It was a little boy, old enough to stand well enough, with blonde curls and light-colored eyes. He couldn't quite see the color of the boy's eyes because of all the reflected light shining around the baby and making the pupils of his eyes almost mirrors of light. The little boy's blue pajamas were fuzzy, had feet to them, and a pink rabbit on the left breast. The little boy couldn't leave the room, but he didn't seem to mind. He didn't speak, but he seemed content and safe. Trevor watched the little boy and studied him. The little boy knew Trevor was watching and studying him and didn't seem to mind that, either, shyly smiling at him once in a while.

Trevor woke lazily around sundown, Buddy still in his lap, with the conviction that another piece of a puzzle had fallen into place. He didn't even know what the puzzle was. He made a mental note to ask Mary if she had any pictures of

50

him from what he thought of as the before-time. He had always been so intent on delving into his deceased father's life, that he had never explored that period between his own birth and his parents' divorce.

Perhaps it was time for him to explore that period, Trevor thought.

He smiled to himself, absently massaging his fingers into Buddy's deep fur and setting off the cat's purr-motor.

He reached for the pencil and pad of paper on the table next to him and began to write.

\* \* \* \* \*

Down in Punta Gorda, his family continued to worry about him.

Mary Buck Daniels paced back and forth in front of Jarrett.

"He shouldn't be living alone."

"He's a grown man, Mary."

"That horrible big house of Shawn's. He hates it. Shawn hated it. It was for entertaining and for an investment. Not for living in."

"He could move if he chose to."

"He'd move right back here if he had the choice."

"And I won't have it, Mary. Birds leave the nest."

"We bring him here every time he crashes anyway."

"That's different. I'll always do that."

"Scottie says you spoil him."

"God knows I try."

"Scottie says he's a spoiled brat."

"Well, he is spoiled. And he is a brat. So I suppose that equals out to bein' a spoiled brat. Scott was probably havin' to fork out more money for speedin' tickets. Trevor sure does have a weakness for speedin', and the cops sure do know that old truck of his, and that hair. Easy pickin's."

Jarrett reached out hands to his wife and slowed her pacing down, finally stopping her.

"There ain't an ounce of harm in Trevor, Mary. He's never floated on the family money, not from either side. He ain't no trust fund baby, tramplin' on folk's feelin's and scoffin' at the law. Well, except for them speedin' tickets, maybe. He don't never use his power for evil or for gain. Sex don't count."

"Spoken like a man."

"I am a man, honey. You're a worse mother hen than I ever was about that boy. Darn it, he's old. He's not a baby. He's a man. He ain't done a thing wrong in I don't know how long. Stupid, yes. Dumb, yes. Risky, yes. Bad, no. He's hard workin' and responsible and honest and loyal."

Mary grabbed the collar of Jarrett's shirt and shook him, her bottom lip caught between her teeth.

"Why am I so worried?"

Jarrett chuckled.

"Because it's Trevor. Because his own brother calls him a moron. Because he's got no more sense than a baby bird. Because no matter what he's doin', he's an accident waitin' to happen. Because Trevor's never borin'. Trevor's an adventure."

"He's lonely, Jarrett."

"Can't be. He's got us."

"We're family, Jarrett. It's not the same."

"Nookie? He can get all that he wants, too."

"Jarrett, you ape, he doesn't have a special someone."

"He's got Bambi runnin' in and out of The Ice Palace up there now. Or Thumper. Whatever."

"Her name is Bobbi, Jarrett. And I'd categorize their relationship as business, not personal."

"Well, I'll be darned if I can figure out how to help him with this."

Mary ran her hands up into her short, blonde curls.

"You can't, sweetheart. He has so few opportunities. He never slows down long enough. He never drops out of that rat race he's in. I know how it is. Thank God I had you and Trevor with me on those last few tours. Thank God I met you at all!"

52

Jarrett kissed his lady and gave her a big hug, rocking her tiny body from side to side.

"Maybe the boy'll get lucky, too."

"How?"

"Gonna have to be God's plan, Mary. Nothin' we can do to slow him down. If gettin' sick on this last tour didn't slow him down, nothin' will."

Mary shook her head.

"Well, perhaps we can talk him into a few days out on Sanibel, incognito. Or just picking up on some of his old friendships here."

"All his ladies from high school went off to college, married, and moved away. Ain't nothin' left in town for Trevor or in the county, either, Mary. Charlotte County's curse. Bright young people growin' up and movin' out 'cause there ain't no money to be made here unless you're a doctor or a lawyer. None of Trevor's old crowd of ladies went either of those ways. He's out of luck here at home."

"Oh, Jarrett."

Jarrett kissed her on the forehead.

"He'll be fine, Mary. God's plan. Gotta have faith."

"I suppose. What choice do we have?"

*     *     *     *     *

Scott had dropped by The Ice Palace and Trevor had asked him to stay over. Scott had declined, but said he'd pop in from time to time to check up on his brother. He preferred his own small house and double garage with Carla now in charge of it. Trevor was wrapped in his afghan in his recliner and Scott had dragged another chair in from the living room to park next to it. He flopped down into the chair now and Trevor showed him some of his recent efforts at lyrics.

I PLEDGE ALLEGIANCE TO MY DAD

I pledge allegiance to the man
Who guards me while I sleep–

53

A smiling man with gentle hands,
The kind you'd like to meet.
And in the republic of my heart,
To which he holds the key,
I'd gladly die a thousand deaths
To keep him worry-free.

Dispensing, through my teenage years,
Justice when I fell,
And helping me to liberty
From my tiny bedroom cell.
Through the rocket's red glare of my teenage years,
He kept his faith in me.
By the dawn's early light of illegal beers,
He firmly grounded me.

The Statue of Liberty lifts her lamp
Beside the golden door,
But I was the homeless, tempest-tossed
Drifting to his shore.
Oh, beautiful for loving me,
He sees beyond the years,
And hopes to make my future bright,
Untouched by any tears.

Oh, God above,
 I do so love
The man he lets me be.
He guides me with good parenthood.
He means the world to me.

Scott quietly handed the single sheet of paper back to
his brother, uneasy with the song's sentimentality.

"Trev, I don't think this one is gonna sell. It's kinda
sacrilegious to the USA."

"I don't care. I had to get it out. The music machine
isn't a cash register. It just does its own thing. Good or bad.
Hard or soft. Fast or slow. Economically feasible or a bomb.

Politically correct or a fiasco. It just doesn't pay any attention to anything but itself."

"Chill. Will you chill? I'm just sayin'.."

"Sorry. I know."

Scott eased back in his chair.

"Tell ya what. Send it off to Barbara Kincaid. Could be a Broadway show in it somewhere."

"Will you quit? You care less about the money than I do."

"Is that even possible? How about this idea? You ready?"

Trevor rolled his eyes.

"What now?"

"Just do it up for Daddy. A one-shot deal. All this real personal, gotta-get-it-out stuff. That's who you're singin' and writin' this all to anyway, ain't it?"

Trevor thought about that. A slight smile twitched his lips and his eyes crinkled at the corners.

"Yeah. You're right. They are. Just me and Blondie and Buddy sitting on the bed, messing and thinking."

"Just get into one of those low-budget demo shops and do it up for Daddy. I think there's one in North Port. Maybe even in Port Charlotte."

"Thanks, Bro. He'd like that. Here. Tell me what you think of this one."

Trevor handed another handwritten sheet of paper to his brother.

DADDY LET ME

I'd been working tip jars
And hanging out in bars
When Daddy met me.
I was out on my own
And looking for a home
When Daddy met me.

I was dying of fright
And looking for the light;
I was looking for love
And I thank God above
That Daddy met me.

He took me in his arms.
I knew I'd never come to harm
When Daddy met me.
He wiped away my tears
And calmed down all my fears.
He came to get me.
He said, "I need a son."
I said, "Let me be the one."
I said, "I see the sky."
He said, "It ain't too high."
He said, "You'll be a star."
I said, "It's way too far."
He said, "We are a team.
Everybody needs a dream."
And Daddy let me.

Scott handed the paper back to Trevor, a slight smile
on his face.

"Now you're talkin'."

"Don't make the cash register sound, Scott. This is
personal."

"The Daddy CD?"

"Yeah."

"I like this one. Some of them others you write is too
edgy for me. I like comfort myself. This makes me feel all
warm and squishy."

"That'd be the stuff rising up over your ankles, Bro.
Yuck."

Scott gave him the chuckle that reminded Trevor so
much of their father and looked at him with Jarrett's eyes.

"Just messin' with you, Yankee."

"Wiseguy."

"Yeah. I am. Go put this on the Daddy CD, Trev. I'm serious. I really do like this one."

"Thanks. I've got to have a chat with Mary one of these days, too. I've been getting flashes of something from the before-time."

"Before-time? What the heck is that?"

Trevor laughed.

"Sorry. I forgot. It's what I think of as the time before I met Jarrett. In this case, I guess I mean maybe the time before my parents divorced and I went to live solely with my birth mother."

"Call Mary up."

"Good idea. I keep forgetting about these modern conveniences."

"You'd starve at a picnic. Can't even put batteries in a microcassette recorder unless they got pictures of which way they go. I swear."

Trevor pulled his cell phone out from the folds of the afghan he still wore. It was the same cell phone Jarrett Daniels had given him when he was fifteen. Scott looked at the cell phone now and shook his head.

"Trev, you best put that thing up on the wall between an 8-track tape and a Rubik's cube. You got you an antique there. There's just so much duct tape can handle."

Trevor brought up the cell phone's directory, found Mary's cell number and pressed the call button, smiling at his brother.

"Still works. Mary? It's me. Yeah. Fine. Got a question. No, got a request, I guess. What color was my hair when I was a baby? No kidding. Can you dig out any photos of me from way back then? Cool. I'm thinking about age two, maybe. How many volumes?"

Trevor looked over at Scott and lifted his eyebrows comically.

"That many? Geez. No, no. That's fine. I think that self-storage unit in Port Charlotte is a great place to keep them. Listen, don't worry about it now, but I've been getting interested in the time when I guess it was you who were the one taking care of me, not Lisa. I'll check the pictures out when I'm down there next. No, nothing's wrong. Say 'Hi' to Jarrett. Scottie says 'Hi'. Love you. Bye."

Trevor clicked off the cell phone and sat staring at the Jarrett-antique in his hand, then looked up at Scott.

"As a baby, I had blonde hair."

"So?"

"I've been dreaming about a little blonde baby boy."

"You ain't never seen baby pictures of yourself?"

"Nope."

"Geez."

Trevor leaned back in his chair.

"I've been poking around the bottom of the music machine, messing with some of the stuff that spilled out before I met Dad. Got a lot of old, nasty stuff in there I haven't had the nerve to clean up. I've started cleaning up now."

Scott shook his head.

"I'm glad I ain't got no talent. You're hintin' at some nasty stuff with this one you got right here."

Scott poked his finger at another sheet of paper he had picked up. Trevor hadn't given him this one to read.

## IN MY HEAD

I'm remembering things best forgotten.
Parts of my past that were rotten.
I wake up in a sweat,
Seeing visions I've let
Myself bury.
I'm not in a hurry
To go there again.

It's all in my head.
Those people are dead
Or out of my life.
They can't give me strife
Unless I let them.

Why do I let them?
They're nothing to me.
Dead leaves on the tree
Of my life.

Let me grow.

The dead branches tangle me up.
Stuck in my tree,
I need to fly free.
I have weapons.
My brother is always beside me.
And his son.
I've found fun
Can chase off the shadows for me.
And my father.
Just saying his name has such power.
The nightmares scurry away.
Brand new day.
I can grow.

Scott passed the sheet of paper to him and Trevor saw what he had read.

Trevor shook his head ruefully.

"There's days I'd rather not have this talent, either, Bro. Days I'd rather be able to fix cars or put batteries in the right way. Thank God Dad taught me how to work construction, or I'd be totally worthless."

"You're totally worthless anyway, moron."

"Thanks, Bro."

Scott considered the family photograph over Trevor's fireplace.

"You know, I think the family had high hopes you and Stephie would pair off."

"Yuck. That'd be like dating my sister. Gross. She's my first cousin."

"You ain't related by blood."

"We're family, for God's sakes."

59

"She was in love with you the moment she saw you that first Christmas."

"She was nine years old. She got a crush on me, was all."

"Carried it well into her late teens."

"She's been over it for a while. Thank God."

"I think Aunt Myrline wanted to keep the money in the family. And the two of you would have made pretty babies."

"Well, I really hate to disoblige Aunt Myrline, but Steph and I don't really click. She's nice. I like her. I love her. She's my cousin. But love and marriage? No. I much prefer her in the front office working publicity and making pretty babies with Ed Foster from accounting. She wupped my ass at tennis. She can put batteries in her own phone. She can program her own VCR, DVD, TV, whatever. She has a master's degree in marketing and she scares me to death."

"She's a tiny, little blonde girl in a business suit, Trev. I'm tellin' you, you could take her."

"Not when she starts with all those facts and figures. I can feel my eyes rolling into the back of my head. I don't understand every third word she says. She points and I sign."

"Good plan."

\*      \*      \*      \*      \*

Later in the day, Jarrett in Punta Gorda phoned Scott in Sarasota.

"How's Trevor doin', son?"

"Feisty. He's crankin' out about three full songs with lyrics a day right now. Not stoppin' for full orchestration. Just chordin' and movin' on. Says he don't need no stinkin' nursemaid."

"You watch him. It's about now he needs one the most. You tell him I said to shut up and park it. Or I'll tell him myself if you want. Might work out better that way."

"I'd appreciate that, Daddy. There's only so much guff that Trev'll take from me, older brother or not. I got no hold on him when he gets wound up and goes Yankee on me."

"Sit on him. Literally. You outweigh him."

Scott raked a hand through his short hair.

"Daddy. He's a man. That don't work out so good after a while. And if he's ticked off, he'd think nothin' of havin' me arrested for assault, the weasel. Oh, he'd be sorry later, and all. But when he's ticked off? Well."

"Fine. I understand. He ain't gonna never get that ticked off at me. Be a cold day in hell."

"I'm sayin'."

"You think he might be up for a surprise visit?"

Scott considered this.

"I think he's been half expectin' one before now. He might be gettin' worried he ain't had one."

"That'd be just like him Well, pencil us in for tomorrow about 10:00 a.m. Hide all the keys to the vehicles. Hide his cell phone, too. Unplug the cordless phone from the wall and clip off the plug end."

"Geez, Daddy. It shouldn't come to all that."

"He's a witch when he's thwarted, son. You have no idea. Just try not to get caught, or he'll melt you like you was an ice cube in the sun. Boy's got a darned nasty temper and he's cranky when he's healin' and startin' to feel froggy."

$$*\qquad*\qquad*\qquad*\qquad*$$

Scott, sitting easily on one of the white stools pulled up to the white counter in the kitchen of The Ice Palace, watched Trevor bounce from table to counter to drawers in a frantic search.

"Scott?"

"Yeah?"

"Where's my keys?"

Scott mentally got down into a defensive crouch and waited for the handoff.

"What keys?"

61

"The keys to the MG, or the truck. Whichever."

"Goin' somewhere?"

"Out. What's it to you?"

"Nothin'."

"So, where's the keys?"

Scott glanced at the wall clock. A quarter to ten. Gonna be a rough fifteen minutes or so, he thought.

"I dunno. You hungry? I'll go poke around in the fridge. Bound to be somethin' in there to eat."

"I'm not hungry. I want out."

"Go for a walk. I'll come, too."

"I don't want to walk. I want to drive. My own vehicle. By myself. Alone. Geez. Where's the keys?"

Scott sniffed.

"Game of poker?"

"No."

"Game of chess?"

"Not on your life. You'd wup me. You always did at chess. Where's my keys?"

"Lay in the sun by the pool?"

"I'm all laid out. And you're about to be. Never mind. Forget the keys. I'll call a cab."

Full of edgy nerves, Trevor turned to the cordless phone and tried to get a dial tone, looking puzzled when he got nothing but dead air.

Scott glanced at the clock again. Still a quarter to ten? How? He hadn't unplugged the clock.

Trevor squinted at the phone, his vision still a little bleary from a low-grade fever and the medication. Then he squinted at the base.

Maybe he couldn't put batteries in the right way, Scott thought, but even Trevor knew phones plugged into phone lines. This one didn't. Not anymore.

Trevor picked up the end of the phone line with its connection neatly snipped off by dykes. He frowned at it, then frowned at Scott. Realization was slow to come.

Still under par, Scott thought, glancing at the clock. Had time stood still?

Trevor flung down the phone with its snipped line.

"You frigging asshole. Where are my keys? Where's my cell phone? Not in my room. I checked there. Not anywhere in my house. I've looked. Never mind. I'll hot wire the truck."

"You don't know how to hot wire the truck. I never taught you."

"I'll figure it out. Then I'll drive my bumper up your ass."

Trevor slammed out of the door that connected the kitchen to the garage through a mudroom. Scott could hear him in the garage, flinging tool chests open and closed, looking for God only knew what. Maybe a spare set of keys, Scott thought.

Scott shifted in his chair.

Even if Trevor did have a spare set of keys, or two, he thought, and got one or the other of the vehicles in the garage started, he'd never get out of the garage. The garage door openers now had no batteries in them and the chain was off the drive sprocket, just in case.

Trevor stomped in through the door from the garage and then out the huge sliding glass doors that lead to the pool deck and the long dock on the Gulf beyond, shouting at Scott as he went past.

"I'll take the boat."

Not with the battery to that disconnected and locked in the back of my van, Scott thought. He glanced at the clock again and muttered to himself.

"All right. If he pops the hood of the pickup truck, disconnects that battery, hauls it down to the boat, and installs it, I'll let him have the keys to the boat. If he's not too winded to take them. Fair is fair."

Trevor slammed the sliding glass door back so hard it rebounded, the huge plate glass wall of it shivering with the impact.

"You fucking son-of-a-bitch."

Trevor's eyes were molten hatred, but he was panting and pale. Scott slid eyes to the clock and then turned a bland face towards his brother.

"Problem?"

"You know there is. I don't like this, Scott."

Trevor paused and licked his lips, lowering his eyelids.

"I'm a prisoner in my own home. I've done prisoner in a house before. I don't like it."

"You ain't no prisoner, you two-bit actor, you. Walk out the front door. Go on. Open the door and walk out."

"I don't want to walk. I want to drive."

And there it was, Scott thought. They were about to go down to the line.

"What's your hurry?"

"My time. My freedom. My keys. My car. My truck. Now, Scott. Right now."

Scott delayed his reply as long as he could, edging up from his seat at the broad kitchen counter.

"How about I teach you how to restring a guitar?"

Just before Trevor went postal on him, Scott heard the front door chimes. He grabbed Trevor around the shoulders in a bone-crushing hug and steered him to the door.

"Lookee there, Trev. Doorbell. Company comin'."

Scott glanced at the clock and prayed.

"Let's go see who that is."

"Get your arm off me."

"Come on. Let's go peek at least."

He bodily dragged a furious and squirming Trevor with him, aware that Trevor's struggles weren't as vigorous as they should have been, nor as lasting.

He really was tired, Scott thought.

Scott flung open the door, his scowling brother clamped to his side and an idiot-grin on his face. He needn't have bothered with the grin.

Jarrett and Mary stood on the threshold, several Neiman-Marcus shopping bags at their feet.

Trevor melted like wax out from under his brother's arm and threw himself on his father's chest.

"Dad."

Jarrett patted Trevor's back and shook his head.

"Good work, Scott. Darned fine work. He's hard to handle when he's like this. Could you get some of these shoppin' bags for Mary?"

"Yes, sir."

\*　　　\*　　　\*　　　\*　　　\*

The three of them, Mary, Jarrett and Trevor sat outside on the pool deck at The Ice Palace in white Adirondack chairs with plump green and white striped cushions. It was Trevor's favorite part of the house with its view of the water. Relieved of nursemaid duty, Scott had bolted for his van and driven off with the boat battery still in the back.

Trevor ran his finger down the side of the can of soda he held while Jarrett and Mary enjoyed theirs.

"Mary, how did you survive on the tour circuit? It's killing me. I know Jarrett and I were with you for the last few years, but I don't remember much of it. Not really."

"I'm a very focused and disciplined person, Trevor. I was even more so back then, before I loosened up and learned how to live. I have skill. I never had your creative temperament."

"Then how about my dad? How did Shawn cope?"

"Your father had his life partner Doug. That's a big difference. And I had Jarrett and you. It's important to know that, when you come off that stage, there are people who love you waiting in the wings. A tour bus or a hotel room is not the same thing at all."

Trevor turned his can of soda slowly in circles, focusing on it and blushing slightly.

"Shawn didn't always have Doug."

Mary laid a hand on Trevor's arm.

"And Shawn didn't always handle the tour life well, Trevor. Wild women. Wild men. Drugs. Over-indulgence in anything and everything. Trying to keep himself alive and killing himself in the process. It was from a one-night stand of unprotected sex that he contracted AIDS. It only takes one time, Trevor."

Jarrett leaned forward.

"You've stopped growin', boy. You've settled. You've gotten lazy. You're recyclin' old tunes and old words. I tell ya, you done stopped growin'.""

Trevor looked up, his temper flaring.

"I'm at the top of my game! I've got more money than God. I make more money than an oil sheik. I got good grades in high school and college. I've never done a bit of harm to anyone. What the hell do you want from me!?"

Jarrett ignored the tirade, waiting for Trevor's brain to catch up with his emotions.

It did.

"Oh, my God, Dad. I just heard myself. Geez. I take it all back. Drifting? I've been drifting? I'm not having that."

"It's my fault, Trevor. I wanted my little boy so much I never let you grow up. I was always there for you to catch you when you fell. My fault. I'm sorry for that."

"No."

"Oh, yes. I'm gonna be backin' away from that. I should have been backin' off about the time you was sixteen, but you were still so needy, and genuinely so."

Jarrett flashed him a grin.

"And you can be real charmin' and precocious. I can be real lazy, too. And I liked doin' for you. I still do."

Jarrett shook his head.

"But I didn't do you no favors by makin' things so easy for you. I'd like to say I wouldn't do it again, but that's a lie. Now you're stuck tryin' to fix my mess."

Distress sharpened Trevor's voice.

"No! I'll admit in some ways I was more a man at fifteen than I am now. You taught me how to trust, so I did. Before that, I closed off everything and took care of myself."

"Grow, Trevor. Figure out how to grow. Your music is sufferin'. You're sufferin'. I hate to see you sufferin'."

"I'll try. You know I'll do anything for you."

"And that's another problem I caused. You got to do the growin' for yourself, not me. I'm sorry, son."

Jarrett shifted in his chair.

"Listen, your aunt done dragged a mess of photo albums up here with us. Had me drag 'em, I should say. Said you'd been askin' about them. You wanna take our sodas back inside and spread out across that hunk of glass in the livin' room you call a coffee table and see what she's got?"

Trevor smiled, relaxing.

"I'm so glad you don't mind me being moody. I hate that in myself."

"You're sick, boy. You're cranky now. It'll pass. You got the sweetest disposition of anyone I ever met usually. Apology accepted."

Trevor turned to Mary.

"I'd love to see what you've brought. I've been having dreams. Or flashbacks. I don't know which."

Jarrett stood up and patted Trevor's back.

"Well, come on inside, boy. You got any real food in this house or are we gonna have to lower the property values around here by draggin' in a pizza delivery?"

Trevor grinned.

"Pizza. Definitely."

After splitting a large pepperoni pizza two ways, less Mary's one slice, they turned to the bags of photo albums that Mary had brought.

Mary started with pictures from when Trevor was a newborn in the hospital. She fingered one now lovingly.

"You weighed 6 lb 5 oz. You were nineteen inches long. It was 10:40 a.m. on a Monday. Your father and I were both there."

Jarrett leaned over to look. Trevor wrinkled his nose.

"Yuck. What an ugly kid. And trust a woman to know all those weird stats on a baby."

Jarrett sniffed.

"Darn, Trevor. You was a bald frog. All red splotches and snot all over you."

Mary jabbed him in the ribs.

"He was a beautiful baby. He still is."

Jarrett grinned at Trevor.

"Trust me, boy. You'll remember your own baby's stats when the time comes. Scottie was 9 lb 3 oz. About 6:00 a.m. I don't remember the day of the week."

Trevor laughed.

"You needed a forklift to move him even in those days."

Trevor turned his attention back to the photo albums.

"Yuck. How many pictures do you have of that ugly screaming thing?"

Mary laughed.

"As many as I could take. Between us, your father and I took two rolls of Instamatic film before the nurses threw us out."

"Wow. Lisa and baby. Shawn and baby. Mary and baby. Shawn and Mary and baby."

Trevor's long finger pointed ahead in the album.

"Who's that?"

Mary smiled.

"Your maternal grandmother, my mother. Lisa's mother. Mary Elizabeth Conwell Buck. And that's your grandfather, Harold Buck, there. Those two in the waiting room with cigars are both your grandfathers, the tall thin one your paternal grandfather, Shawn's father, Jason Lane."

"How'd I wind up with Trevor for a name? I never asked."

"Your grandfather Lane's grandfather. You came into this world with a crowd of people pantingly eager to spoil you and protect you. That woman holding you there is your paternal grandmother, Shawn's mother, Jason's wife, Matilda Crossan Lane. You were their only child's first child. Their only son's first son. The sun rose and set in you."

Trevor glanced at her with his old eyes.

"Sun went down hard, Mary."

"That was no one's fault, Trevor. Hard on you, but a result of forces and tradition in the law that sealed your fate in your early years. By the time Lisa divorced Shawn and gained sole custody of you, all the grandparents were dead, or out of the picture. I was a maiden aunt with an unstable home environment–I traveled to make my living. You already know the law's position back then regarding even visitation with a homosexual father. Lisa was in charge. Then Lisa left with you. And then Lisa disappeared. You were MIA–missing in action."

Mary looked fondly up at her husband.

"And then you turned up living with some man in Punta Gorda, Florida. Jarrett Daniels. Remembering that letter Jarrett sent still makes my blood boil. Luckily for him, it's not possible to purchase a handgun in Delaware or to fly with one to Florida. I was furious enough to do murder."

Trevor nudged Mary to get her back on track.

"Where's the good stuff?"

"It's all good stuff to me, Trevor. Great stuff. These first pictures represent great joy and hope."

"How about some where I've at least got hair?"

Mary reverently turned stiffened pages jammed with photos as Trevor scanned them quickly and dismissed them as near duplicates of others.

"Wait. Who's that?"

It was a black woman holding him now.

"That was our housekeeper. Formerly Lisa's and my nanny. God rest her soul, she's been dead for years, too. Shawn performed. I performed. Lisa ignored you. I suppose Mary Alfreds was the person who raised you the most consistently."

"I'm black? Lisa hated blacks."

"Lisa hated. No, you're not black, you idiot. And you weren't raised black, either. Mary and her family weren't slaves, nor the children of slaves. They never picked cotton in the south. They weren't inner-city, ghetto-born welfare recipients, either."

"No. That was Lisa. I didn't mean black, really. I guess I meant, well, in spite of all this white hope and joy, it was black love for me for my early years or months. Right?"

"Months. And not all day, all night. Shawn hovered. He canceled his remote engagements and limited himself to Washington, Philadelphia, Baltimore, Boston and New York. I did the same. He and I changed diapers and walked the hallways with you. It was Shawn who discovered that if he took you for a ride in his car, you went to sleep. You loved riding in that car."

Mary's face took on a dreamy quality.

"Shawn had a black Jaguar XKE. If that wasn't a sight! Shawn in the driver's seat and you in the passenger seat, tooling around sleepy Newark, Delaware, with that distinctive Jaguar purr lulling you to sleep. He always had a classics station on the radio. You'd sleep in Shawn's arms, too, afterward. It was nothing to come into your nursery room and find you asleep in Shawn's arms and Shawn asleep, still in his tuxedo, in the ladder-backed rocking chair we kept there, Bach or Strauss playing in the background."

"And my sainted mother?"

"Asleep in her own suite of rooms."

Mary sighed.

"She never bonded with you. She didn't have it in her, I suppose. And I think she'd begun to suspect there was someone else in Shawn's life. I think she thought it was me. I'd moved in to help take care of you. She wouldn't, and Mary Alfreds deserved her sleep, too. Shawn hadn't met Doug yet, but there were others. Your mother wasn't happy."

"And you? You never did get Shawn."

Mary gave him a quick grin.

"I got you, babe. I had my career. I was closer to Shawn than anyone was. Certainly your mother. I took the shift 7:00 a.m. to 3:00 p.m. because of my evening obligations along the East Coast, the same areas your father had. That included breakfast, lunch and active playtime. Mary took 3:00 p.m. to 11:00 p.m. That included dinnertime and putting you to bed. Mary Alfreds sang you lullabies, too."

"My music has ethnic roots. Wow. Not just Darryl's grandfather Ben."

"Shawn took 11:00 p.m. to 7:00 a.m. He abandoned the cocktail circuit and any hope for his outside interests to be with his 'Pride and Joy'. You were a very well loved and cared-for baby. Your grandparents, when they were alive, came over to visit with you. But they were very, very old people, mentally and physically. They could watch you with joy, but hadn't the energy to participate. Your paternal grandfather, Jason, died of a heart attack when you were ten-months-old. Matilda died within a month of him, from not caring to be alive any longer."

Mary smiled ruefully at him.

"Sudden-death syndrome. Well-documented in couples who have been together and been close for decades."

Mary slid her hand into Jarrett's.

"Your maternal grandfather, Harold, simply went senile and had to be placed in a nursing home. He faded away and was dead by the time you would have maybe been four. My mother moved in with me to my house on Orchard Road, the one you remember from coming up to see me in Newark the year we truly met and you were fifteen. I moved from that house to come be with you and Jarrett. My mother kept house for me and was my base and security through all the upheaval of the divorce and losing you and then Shawn's death. She died quietly in her sleep about a year before you and I re-met one another."

Trevor looked up from studying the pictures and trying to piece together his backtrail. He looked at the stacks of photo albums around them, and then at the woman beside him, her eyes misty with tears and love.

"Aunt Mary, I've under-rated you for years. I'm sorry for that. I apologize. You were one tough lady. You hung in there. I'm sorry I never really met the rest. I did, but I was too young to remember. This is great, hearing about them from you. You're making them all come alive for me again. Thanks."

Mary put her arms around Trevor, hugging him and burying her face in his neck to kiss him there. She sniffed.

"I just love you so much, Trevor. I never stopped loving you all those years you were missing."

Jarrett straightened in his chair.

"Will you two quit that? You're chokin' me up now. Boy, did you find what it is you been lookin' for?"

Mary sat back away from Trevor, wiping her eyes. Trevor kissed her on the cheek.

"Yeah. I think so. At least I seem to be on the right track. Mary, do you have any pictures of me from about age two to four?"

"Certainly."

Mary closed the album they had been going through and opened the fronts of others until she found what she was looking for.

"Here we are. Trevor from roughly age one to maybe two. Too early?"

"I dunno. Let's see."

Trevor flipped quickly through the pages, worrying Mary with his apparent disregard for the stiff, old pages.

"What's with the hat? Did this kid ever not wear a hat?"

"Hats keep warmth in, Trevor. We humans lose most of our body heat through our heads."

"Ah. Here we go. Hair at last."

"Oh, yes. Easter. Aren't you darling in that bunny suit with ears and a tail?"

Jarrett peered over.

"Priceless."

Trevor wrinkled his nose.

"Geez. Women. I look like such a dork. No son of mine, I'll promise you, will ever be wearing one of those things. But blonde curls. Somehow I knew it was going to be blonde curls."

Trevor looked over to a puzzled Mary.

72

"I've been dreaming about a baby, Mary. A quiet kid with blonde curls. Did I have blue fuzzy pajamas with feet and a pink rabbit on them?"

Mary opened her eyes wide.

"Yes. You did. You remember?"

"Not exactly. I see him in my head. When I'm asleep. My room? What colors were in my room?"

"Pinks and blues and yellows. Nothing too bright. We didn't want to over-stimulate you."

"I may have met myself. Weird."

"You liked your room. You'd sit for hours on the rug and make faces at your reflection in the cheval glass mirror there.

"Mirror?"

"You loved it."

"Describe. Please?"

"Let me think. Mahogany. Oval frame. It's been a long time, Trevor. We angled it so you could see yourself when you sat on the rug."

"That's what I've been seeing. I'll be darned. Not me as an adult looking in some kid's room. Me as a kid looking at myself in a mirror. Smiling, mugging, laughing. Sometimes just playing and ignoring myself. Watching myself out the corners of my eyes. I'll be darned. Cute kid."

"You're cute now."

"Yuck. Well, you're my aunt. I guess you gotta say stuff like that."

Trevor laughed at her.

"Thanks for the photos. Lots of good stuff here. Overwhelming."

"You should see what I have now that you're famous."

Jarrett leaned forward.

"No, he shouldn't. It'd swell his head. No wonder you kept a hat on that kid's head, Mary. Only way to keep it from swellin'. Wear more hats, son."

"Wiseguy."

"Definitely so."

73

"I love you both so much. That sounds so corny and trite when I say it out loud."

Jarrett gripped Trevor's arm and gave it a slight shake.

"The basics are always corny, boy. Love you, too. Quit givin' your nonsense to Scott. He's only tryin' to look out for you. And he's only doin' it because you won't look out for yourself."

Jarrett shifted back in his chair.

"Well, then. As long as I've got you here in one place, I want to go over some business with you."

Mary began packing albums into the Neiman-Marcus bags.

"Oh, Jarrett, no."

"Oh, Jarrett, yes. I'll go light."

"See that you do."

Mary finished packing up her photo albums and wandered out of the room, leaving her men to discuss business.

Jarrett leaned forward in his chair again.

"Little Stephanie's been trackin' your approval ratin'. Ain't that cute? She approved of you herself right off. Anyway, it seems you're still right up there, but folks are gettin' bored. Same songs. Same sets. You mix up the line-up but same same. You do well in the South, the Southwest, and the Mid-west. Not so good on either coast. Your longhair label does good there. I know Mary sawed away on the violin at the same tunes for years, them dead dudes, but I can't see how the heck she did it night after night. I'd purely hate that. And I sure don't understand them audiences of hers. I never seen the likes of people could sit on their hands so. Your core fans are beginnin' to show a statistical tendency to sit on their hands, Trevor. That ain't good in your game."

"They're bored and I'm bored. The band's bored."

"Take a break. Or let Jake take the band around. He can slip in some of his. You know he's been itchin' to.

74

Freshen yourself up. Get back to your roots. Get back to what you wanted to do in the first place."

"I guess I'm scared of change."

"Well, who isn't?"

Trevor leaned forward and blew out a breath.

"I'm scared I'll look out over the footlights and there won't be anyone out there at all. Just a vacant house like it is for rehearsals. It's hard to get the fire up in rehearsals. You need a good crowd."

Jarrett slapped a reassuring hand onto Trevor's shoulder.

"Ain't gonna happen, boy. They'll come for the name now as much as the music. That empty house didn't never happen on your way up. You're good. If you dropped off the face of the earth–and I would be seriously ticked off if you did that–and started at the bottom callin' yourself Zeke Calzone, you'd draw a crowd. Music draws people, Trevor. It always has and it always will. Your music, and your playin', and just plain you, draw people. So don't you never think you'll play to an empty house. It ain't gonna happen."

Jarrett released Trevor's shoulder and reached into one of the Neiman-Marcus bags to pull out a VCR tape.

"You don't never pay attention to interviews and stuff, but I thought you might like to see Scott in this one off a local cable channel. Patty Harrison of The Gilded Grape– and The Gilded Grape Too–sponsored it. Well, she's Patty Pitts now. Did you know her daddy built the building where the Port Charlotte post office is now and ran it as a bar, Floridian Recreation, till it got bought out and turned into The Sandtrap, another bar? We sure had some good bars back when. Before your time by several decades. But I digress. You mind if I just slip this tape into your machine here? Got the remote handy? Okay. Hit it."

Trevor picked up the complicated remote control that Scott had idiot-coded for him with numbers to push. His wall-sized TV came alive and his VCR/DVD player moved smoothly forward internally.

A local cable station's talk show set appeared. The interviewer's back was to the camera. Scott, in his usual jeans and long-sleeved plaid shirt, the sleeves rolled up his massive forearms to the elbow, lounged in a tan armchair.

The interviewer spoke.

"Are you jealous of him?"

"Trevor? Jealous of Trevor? Nah. I maybe used to be. For about a week, tops. That's when I first met my dad. I was jealous of what Trevor and my dad shared. I seen some weird stuff go on between them. About spooked me. Trevor knew my dad before I did. Turned out he only knew him about a month longer, but I didn't know that then. They was real close. Still are. They got this voodoo communication thing goin' on. The both of them can just tell right off by lookin' or even over the phone if somethin' ain't right with the other one. At least for Trevor, my dad can tell he's in trouble before Trevor can sometimes. I swear to God, I don't know how it works. But, yeah, I was jealous of that back then. But now? Heck, no. You couldn't pay me cash money to be my brother and deal with what he's dealin' with. That music he's got in him is a witch on his back sometimes. And I'll tell you to your head, that fame and fortune stuff ain't all it's cracked up to be. Me, I sleep at night. Trevor don't always. If I'm sick, one of the cousins takes over my job. If Trevor's sick, he still goes on. If I get tired of doin' this job for a livin', I can just quit it. No big deal. Trevor can't. If he walked out, he'd put the equivalent of a small town out of work, between us family on the payroll and all the associated parts of the record and entertainment industry, right down to some little off-shore company makin' them white gauze Dani-shirts to sell to wannabes. He's huge. And he feels it, too, right down to his toes. Got a real fine sense of responsibility, my brother does. I don't envy him that, or his music or none of it. It's all a darned curse, if you ask me. And I guess you did."

"Your brother is rumored to be brilliant."

"People are always sayin' Trevor's a genius. I guess he is. My daddy says he has no sense of his own physical limitations. I say he ain't got no sense at all. So, I treat him like he's a moron and it works fine for the both of us."

"There are also rumors that he's ruthless."

"Ruthless? Listen, Trevor works hard. He expects his employees to work hard. He don't expect any of us to do what he wouldn't or hasn't done himself. But he darned well expects good value for the good wages he pays. If you're a slacker, you're off the team. He'll fire family, too."

Trevor watched as Scott shifted his weight in the interview chair.

"There's a herd and a half of people lined up to work for The Trevor Daniels Band in one capacity or another. Tons of musicians. We got us an interview panel of Trevor's core people set up now. Life on the road's rough. It don't hardly matter sometimes whether a musician is brilliant or not. It's just diggin' ditches most times. But they gotta be willin' to work hard and love it, like I said. And they gotta be compatible with the existin' staff, so to speak. Gettin' along is real important, 'cause we all can get edgy and up in one another's faces once in a while. Gotta flow like a team and not let any of that interfere with the job. We done been through a load of musicians. Trevor had to fire another guy not so very long ago. The guy was a sneak and a backstabber. That can tear up a band and the whole darned house of cards can tumble. So that guy had to go. His true personality slipped underneath our radar 'til it was darned near too late. He got a decent severance package. He ain't starvin'. He could have had it good. Trevor says the seeds of his own destruction were planted at birth. I say he was a moron that didn't know when he was well off and messed up. Comes down to the same thing."

Jarrett took the remote control from Trevor's slackened grasp and pressed stop, hit rewind and sat quietly while the tape rewound. Mary had wandered into the dining room and was seemingly intent on a collection of cut-glass lead crystal vases displayed there on glass shelves behind glass doors.

Jarrett got up to extract the tape. Trevor hadn't spoken. Jarrett came back and dropped the tape into the top of one of the shopping bags, sitting back down on the sofa beside Trevor.

"Been takin' your brother for granted? I know I have. I'll be tryin' to make that up to Scott. I thought you'd like to see how he represents you. How he presents you to the world."

"He's always there for me. Maybe I do take him for granted. I swear I never meant to."

"We none of us ever mean to take any of our loved ones for granted, boy. Another one of our blessin's it's hard to remember. Try to be mindful of your blessin's. I'm tryin' hard to be mindful of mine. I enjoy, but I forget to be mindful. Easy to do."

"I'd be nothing without you. And Mary. And Scott."

"Not so. You was always somethin'."

"What can I do to make amends?"

"I don't know that you've got anythin' to make amends for, son, but I do. We're different. I wanted to show you a side of your brother you might not have noticed. He ain't the big dumb ox his momma let him think he was."

"I never thought that. He knows how to do a whole lot more things than I do. Practical things. We're a team and I love him. He's brighter than he thinks he is."

"Just you remember the concept and the meanin' behind them perfect manners you was brought up with. Thank you is short for maybe I-am-thankful-to-you-for-what-you've-done-and-who-you-are."

Trevor struggled to sit more upright on the sofa, still easily tired out. He looked Jarrett directly in the eye.

"Thank you."

"You're welcome, son. Now give me a hug."

Trevor did, slumping tiredly against Jarrett for a moment. Jarrett hugged him tighter for a moment before releasing him.

"Meat and grease, boy. Flesh up them bones. You need a strong constitution for the work you do. Ditch diggin' is easier. Mary? You ready? Let's roll."

When the door closed behind them, Jarrett paused momentarily to gaze upward into the high, arching entrance that covered the front of the huge house before looking worriedly down at his wife beside him.

"Have I sacrificed one boy for the sake of another, Mary? I swear I never meant to do that."

Mary tucked her arm through her husband's.

"Oh, please. Both of them have had wonderful opportunities. They're a team. Either one of them could back away from it if they chose to. I've no doubt they will eventually. And go right back to being what they've always been. Close personal friends and brothers. An auto mechanic and a composer. The ultimate odd couple."

"I just hope both my babies are all right."

## Chapter Five

In The Ice Palace, Trevor sat hunched morosely in his recliner, turned now to face out the sliding glass door wall and across the pool to the water beyond. He had his Grammy-afghan over his head, only his eyeballs peeking out.

It was icy in The Ice Palace this morning, he thought.

Which only made sense. On many levels. Sometimes he felt as though he were living in Superman's father's house. All glass and white marble and angles and planes. Great light. Great place to live.

If you were a penguin.

Trevor pictured a penguin waddling across the glossy white marble floor, and he realized he had no trouble at all seeing a herd of them there. Silly, flightless birds in tuxedos, squawking and walking.

There was a herd of them here every other weekend when he was off tour, he thought. And he was one of them. Stephanie had arranged it. Good publicity. Blend into your community. Improve your image.

"Huh."

The sound echoed faintly in the cavernous house.

He guessed this had been Superman's father's house. It had belonged to his birth father. There was little of Shawn Lane here. Mary or Doug had it all in safekeeping. The plantings outside were appealing. Especially the trees. God had made that, Trevor thought. Not man.

"Shawn, how could you stand it?"

And, of course, he knew the answer. Shawn's letters to him as a boy had made that clear. Doug. Doug had kept him sane. Doug had kept him grounded. Doug had kept him safe. Doug was older and not in the business. Doug was first his lover and finally his life partner. Doug was family now.

"I've got Scottie. I've got Jarrett and Mary."

He knew it wasn't the same.

80

"God, how the heck am I going to even meet anybody? I'm not settling for any of those easy bimbos or any of those Ms. Penguins, either."

Trevor shifted in his recliner.

He hadn't felt this trapped-in-a-house since he was a cast-off preteen boy. At that time, he'd had little to no choice in the matter. Even his adult imagination quaked at what one Christopher de Nunzio might have done if he'd tried to leave that house. His memory did quake at some of the things that had happened to him after he had left it.

Well, he wasn't a solitary, homeless boy now, he thought. He had choices. And he'd better start making better ones. That short span of time with Dr. Brownie in Tidewater, Virginia, had been a wake-up call.

"Why do I have to be darned near dead to listen to good advice?"

Stubborn, he thought. And, when healthy, moving too fast. Heedless. Like Scottie said, a moron.

"Health. Money can't buy health. I miss health. Running. I miss running."

When he was a preteen boy and living with Christopher de Nunzio, he hadn't been able to run. Had that been yet another factor in the psychological horror of that period in his life? Probably, he thought. He needed to run.

"Trev, get a grip. You're sick. Balance. You gotta learn balance, dammit."

Trevor blew on his fingers under the afghan, shivering in his boxers and T-shirt, and watched a red-gold glow of sunlight toast the sides of some palm fronds as it moved off the eastern sky over the water and lit the vegetation he was staring at. It blew a rocket blast of color through the glass wall in front of him and started bouncing and reflecting off the marble and glass and mirrors of the house around him.

"Yeah. Much better. God's fireplace fire."

Trevor shifted his legs.

"Gotta write that down."

He slid his stockinged feet to the glossy marble floor and stood up in his afghan. He padded over to the kitchen counter where a lined tablet and pen lay, one of a dozen such idea stations positioned around the house. In his bedroom. In his bathroom. Definitely in all his vehicles. He picked up the pen and scribbled down the fireplace line for possible future use as a lyric. Finished, he lay the pen back down and walked carefully to the refrigerator on the sheet-ice marble floor. He opened the door to the refrigerator, releasing a blast of artic air, searching for inspiration.

Nada. Niente. Zip. Zilch.

He closed the refrigerator door again. Leftover party food. Which meant it was pretty well non-food. Almond-stuffed olives. A bag of curly endive. It looked like pizza delivery was in his future.

He brightened at the thought.

It was a wonder he didn't weigh three hundred pounds, he thought. Years of lean living and semi-starvation had left him with a deep and abiding love for what he considered to be real food.

He slipped a little on the marble floor as he padded to the thermostat.

"Sixty-eight degrees. Bull. I'll bet it's warmer outside."

Trevor slipped again and caught his balance. And smiled.

Fun.

That's what he needed.

Trevor pulled the afghan off his head and up from the floor. He took a few quick steps, locked his legs, and slid a short distance on the icy floor. And chuckled. He did it again. And again. Longer lunges. Longer slides.

He was warming up.

He took off the afghan and tossed it into the recliner. He did a powerful fast break, locked his legs and slid, howling with laughter, into the dining room. He clipped his hip on the edge of the dining room's heavy glass-topped table and laughed through a different howl as he spun and landed on his butt.

He got up, still laughing.

"That's it. Table's gotta go."

Trevor put his hands to the edge of the huge table and shoved. His stockinged feet slithered backward. He peeled off his socks and tried again, getting more purchase with his bare feet. The table resisted, but he finally clunked and bucked one end of it nearer the back wall. He did the same with the other end. He found he was winded, but not badly so. There was no wheeze. While he hadn't been noticing, the medications had been working.

He breathed in deeply. No pain. Good. He hated pain.

Limber and warmed up, Trevor took his socks back with him into the kitchen, put them on, and sighted his path. He took off running, locked his legs and slid, whooping, into the dining room, past the table by the wall and veered left through the archway and on into the living room.

"Cool! Not a bad ride at all."

He ice-skated around the big room, his hands linked behind his back, humming 'The Skater's Waltz' under his breath and proving to himself simultaneously that he was crazy and that his housekeeper was excellent. Neither grit nor dust bunnies attached to his socks. Cat hair didn't count. Buddy kept an endless supply of that available. He pirouetted, pretending he was Brian Boitano or that Elvis guy. Not Elvis Costello, the musician. That Nancy Kerrigan guy. He shied away from imagining himself as Nancy Kerrigan. Yuck.

A deep voice echoed out at him across the mirror-finished marble floor.

"What the heck are you doin'?"

Trevor skidded to a halt, caught in his boxers and socks, hair wild, chest heaving. He grinned at his brother lazing against the archway between the dining room and the living room.

"Having fun. Check this out."

Trevor ran and slid.

"Cool, huh?"

"You are such an embarrassment."

"What? I'm in my own house. Nobody's going to see this. Kick off your shoes. This is fun."

"I done did this when I was a kid. In school on them terrazzo tile hallways. You get a real long slide with no interruptions."

Scott took off his sneakers and did some test slides.

"Darn, Trevor. You had the Zamboni in here already today? This stuff's smooth as glass."

"I'm telling you. Just watch it. The pond's real slick this morning, too."

"The pond?"

"Yeah. Here in the living room. The bobsledding is between the kitchen and here, mostly through the dining room. I had to move the dining room table. I did move the dining room table. Heavy sucker."

Trevor reached out hands to his brother and Scott batted them away.

"Get your fag hands off me. I ain't skatin' doubles with you. Will you shut up with that 'Skater's Waltz' you're hummin'?"

"Bro, I feel great. My lungs are clear. I can leave the house. Please, please, please, please let me leave the house."

"You seem fine. Crazy, but fine. Watcha wanna do?"

"I want to run. Not today. Not now. Not right this red-hot minute at least. I'm starving to death in here. I'd like to go down to Pizza Hut and inhale a Meatlovers. Then I'd like to go jogging. You can watch. Jogging on the beach. Going nowhere. Just back and forth. What do you think?"

"I think if you eat pizza and jog, you'll puke. That's up to you. But I'm agreeable. You'd best shower off and put on some real clothes. And don't get your head wet. Pull all that hair out of the way. We ain't got all day to let it dry and you're all fussy about not usin' a hair dryer on it. Heat damage. Gettin' split ends. I declare. You are such a girl."

"Bite me."

"In your dreams."

"Good idea about the hair. Maybe I'll braid it into a coronet around my head."

"Maybe you'll wake up some mornin' with it beside you in bed and me loomin' over you with a pair of scissors in my hand."

Scott was pulling on his shoes while Trevor peeled his socks off again.

"These last few weeks while I've been sick, the idea of having short hair has been appealing to me. I couldn't take care of this mess. There were times I thought the weight of it would pull my head off my shoulders backwards. It's getting to be a nuisance."

"Cut it. I'm willin'. I'm tired of havin' a sister."

"Bull. You love it."

Trevor waved girly-hands at his brother, grinning, and Scott grinned back at him, giving Trevor back their old shared joke.

"Get your fag hands off me."

Scott followed Trevor up the stairs to his bedroom and flopped across the California king-sized bed with its white satin coverlet to fondle Buddy's ears.

"Why the heck you keep usin' this dust-catcher of a bedspread?"

Trevor shrugged.

"It came with the house. It's not my job to keep it clean. Buddy likes it."

"Buddy don't care about it, either."

Trevor quickly braided his hair and wound the braid up on top of his head, sticking in two thin lacquered chopsticks he'd gotten in New York City over a dozen years before. He casually stripped off his T-shirt and boxers and began to move the controls on the shower as he brushed his teeth with his other hand.

Scott eyed him.

"I'm tryin' to figure out what you'd look like without all that hair. You look right goofy with it pulled up on your head like some geisha. Or you should. Anyone else would."

85

Trevor turned his head, laughing, the early morning grunge of a beard offsetting the geisha look.

"Maybe it's time to find out."

"Don't go rushin' things. You're always one to go rushin' things."

Trevor laughed and finished brushing his teeth, rinsed the toothbrush, spat in the sink, gargled with mouthwash, spat that out, and rinsed down the sink. Scott watched him.

"You're a neatnik, too."

"Early training. I've been considering something else, too."

Trevor opened the frosted glass shower door with its etched details of an egret in flight over marsh grass and stepped into the intersection of several jets of water at various levels.

Scott rolled over on the bed.

"What now, rat boy?"

"Ferrets. You know I had that ferret thing all figured out. Lab rats in college were cool. Real friendly. Mice were cute. Ferrets were like mice-rat things. How could I know they'd be more like squirrels with an attitude? Or raccoons in disguise? How did I know they'd open every cabinet in the house and then every box in every cabinet? How did I know they liked to swing from chandeliers? Who knew they could pick locks? It was a nightmare. Thank God they escaped to breed in the wild after I gave them to that elementary education major."

"I'm just sayin', Trevor. Some of your ideas. You don't plan too far in advance on some things."

"A gym. I've been thinking about joining a gym."

"What? And use the membership when? Nice charitable donation there, Trev. You'll never be in town to go there."

"A franchise place where we can find a branch in any city we're in. Reciprocal agreement places. You know."

"You fixin' to get laid?"

Trevor stuck his head out the shower doors, the ends of his hair dangling wetly on his shoulders.

"Why? Maybe not right now. Not this red-hot minute."

"It's been my experience that if a guy gets interested in goin' to a gym, he's interested in gettin' buff. If he's interested in gettin' buff, he's interested in gettin' laid."

"Oh."

Trevor went back to showering.

"No, actually I was thinking more along the lines of good health and some fun. Apparently my body was, too. I need to run. Running isn't that safe in strange towns or in cities. It probably never was, but I had no choice. I've got choices now. Since I need to run, it might as well be on a treadmill of my own choosing."

"Buy a treadmill and put it on the tour bus. Run while you ride."

Trevor shut off the shower. Scott rolled off the bed, opened the linen closet door, took out a huge white monogrammed bath towel and had it ready to hand to Trevor when he stepped out. Trevor grinned when he saw Scott in front of him and took the towel.

"Thanks, Bro. I forgot to get one out."

"I know it. Can't never plan ahead well. Nice tattoo. That hurt when you was gettin' it?"

Trevor scrubbed his face with the towel.

"Hurt some. Killed my sex life for about two weeks. I had to put this AD ointment on it for a couple of days and then put lotion on it 'til it all healed. Who knew? A local gal down in Port Charlotte did it. Came highly recommended in a three-county area. Lisa Schmoldt at Level 5 Tattoo."

Trevor continued to rub himself dry while Scott watched.

"I planned ahead on that one. Sketched what I wanted and where I wanted it for months. Scheduled the appointment myself for when we had a tour break. Good darned thing. I was up here wearing a pair of old baggy swim

87

trunks most of the time or going naked to keep that mess from sticking to my jeans and peeling all the design off."

"Ya see there? Planned ahead but didn't research the product well enough. Ladies like it?"

Trevor grinned.

"Oh, yeah. Real good investment. Sort of a decorative framework to my masterpiece."

Scott snorted.

"You are so full of it. Dry off your masterpiece, stick it into some jeans and let's go kill some pizza. And get them chopsticks out of your hair. I swear."

Trevor finished drying off, flung the towel over the shower door and picked up a pair of faded and ratty jeans from the back of a Louis XV chair. He pulled them on and zipped them, searching for his Walmart sneakers. Scott opened a drawer in the antique bureau and pulled out a Fighting Tarpons T-shirt with Trevor's high school mascot of a fish in boxing gloves on it.

"Why do you even bother to fold this shirt? I've seen the homeless wearing better clothes."

"They do. Force of habit. If I'm holding it, I'm folding it. Thank you very much, former-mom Lisa."

"You'll make some woman a wonderful wife."

"Give me my T-shirt. Geez. Are we ready yet?"

"Chopsticks out. Baseball cap and shades on."

"Oh. Yeah. Forgot."

Trevor complied, pulling his braided hair out the opening in the back of an old Texas Rangers baseball cap

"Now? Can we eat now?"

"We can eat now."

The brothers clumped down the stairs together, Trevor eyeing the wrought iron banister for sliding possibilities.

"Why don't you ever wear a cap and shades?"

"I ain't as pretty as you are. Ain't no one lookin' for my autograph."

"Oh. Well, they should."

"Whatever for? I ain't got no talent. I ain't famous."

"You've got a real talent for covering my ass."

"Been doin' it for years. Been doin' it since I met you, about. That's what big brothers do. They look out for younger brothers."

Trevor smiled and bumped his shoulder into Scott, which didn't budge Scott but sent Trevor himself ricocheting off a wall. Scott shook his head.

"Watch it, moron. You're gonna hurt yourself."

"I'm really glad I've got you, Scott. An older brother. I always wanted one, you know. This is perfect."

"I ain't your valet, though. You best learn how to take a shower and get out the towel first."

Trevor shifted his shoulders uncomfortably.

"What would you do if we didn't do what we're doing now? Living on the road, I mean."

"Get married and raise babies. I did that once. I really liked that. I'd like to do that again."

"No. I mean for a living. What would you do for a living? What's your serious dream of what you want to do for a living when you grow up?"

"Get married and raise babies. Heck, Trevor, you pay me more darned money to do nothin' than any six people I've ever met. I live cheap. I done invested most of my paychecks in land and stuff. Been rentin' out the land. Got a nice little nest egg. Don't know if there is a word for what I want to do. Just live clean with a good woman and raise babies. Tinker with cars. Got a real weakness for cars. Maybe open up a small mechanic's shop. I guess that's what I'd be doin' if this pipe dream of yours hadn't taken off. I'd be a grease monkey. And a happy one."

"You're a good one. I've been so self-absorbed I never questioned what you really wanted to do. I just dragged you into this life with me."

"Can't drag me where I don't want to go. I could always be a mechanic. Comin' with you, I seen places and done things I never would have seen and done. You done broadened my horizons with all your silliness. I had fun, mind you. I ain't complainin'."

89

"I guess I'm not the only one getting stale, huh? About that gym."

"Here we go again."

Outside, Scott slid behind the wheel of his 1976 Ford van and Trevor slid in the passenger seat, closing the pale blue door and holding on to the door frame with his arm out the open passenger window just in case the latch let loose.

Scott turned his head to his brother.

"Buckle up, moron."

"Oh. Yeah. Forgot."

Trevor did so and Scott turned the key in the ignition, shaking his head.

"Tell me about the gym, Trevor."

"I'm serious."

"You always are."

At Pizza Hut, they ordered the pizza to go and then sat in the restaurant to eat it, enjoying one another's company. Scott chewed steadily as Trevor bit down on a slice of his pizza and then almost swallowed it whole. Scott squinted at Trevor's pizza.

"No anchovies?"

"I'm trying to eat healthy."

Scott snorted. Trevor removed another slice of pizza from the box.

"Bro, that doc in Virginia kinda scared me. And he's right. I've been letting myself slide, so to speak. I've got to eat better. I've got to exercise. I love to eat. I love to run. I love exercise. The basketball and a portable hoop are definitely coming on the next tour with us. I've got to take charge of myself. Dammit, I've let first Dad and then you take care of me. Dad got a life. You need to get one, too. Heck, I need to get one. Exercise is good for me and I know it. Dad knew it, too. It keeps me sane. Saner. Well, nearly sane, anyway. I've got this asthma thing under control."

Trevor paused for breath and a mouthful of pizza, hiding behind his sunglasses and beneath his basketball cap. He was supremely unaware of the notice his gestures and his enthusiastic voice were attracting in the small restaurant.

Scott wasn't, and kept his usual weather eye out for trouble. One hint of fan recognition, he thought, and he'd have Trevor whisked out of there before he could gulp down his soda. He had seen the results of a fan feeding-frenzy. Not pretty.

Trevor gestured with his pizza slice.

"Anyway. It couldn't hurt. Well, maybe for a while it would. But, Scott, my first dad died of AIDS. I'm not him and I don't do what he did, but maybe I'm prone to problems with my immune system. Who knows? Safe sex is one thing, but I was seriously run down before that last tour and certainly on it. I gotta watch it. I went down on that stage like a ton of bricks. It scared me."

"Scared you for a while. Now you're back at it, rat boy."

"They were ferrets. This is a gym. What harm could there be?"

"I shudder to think."

"Come with me to the gym, Bro. It'll be great."

"Yeah. That's just what I need. Joinin' your craziness."

"Sure it is. What the heck? If it sucks, we'll quit."

"I ain't never known you to quit nothin'. Not even stuff you don't like. And hardly ever stuff that ain't good for you. What's different about this, I'd like to know?"

Scott watched a college-aged girl with long straight dark hair frown and tilt her head to one side, puzzled.

Uh-oh, Scott thought. Fan alert.

Trevor rattled on.

"A change of lifestyle. I gotta be on the bus anyway. But we can factor in an hour or so once in a while. Spread the schedule out. Say a half-hour of B-ball when the mood strikes us. Like I said, take a portable hoop in the tour bus with us. God knows we've got enough guys for a team. Gals, too, if they can handle it. As to the gym, factor in maybe an hour every other day or so. Maybe an hour and a half, allowing for travel time in there. Use the Hyundai to get there. No problem."

The college girl reached into her purse and drew out a small notebook and pen, making eye contact with Scott.

"Trev."

"Yeah?"

"Grab the pizza and your drink. Gotta go."

"Huh?"

"Gotta go, moron. Fan at twelve o'clock."

"Where?"

Trevor swiveled in his chair to follow Scott's gaze. Scott groaned. The college girl's eyes went round. Trevor grinned. Scott stood up and grabbed the pizza.

"Get your drink, rat boy."

"There's only one of her."

"Now there is. You just wait and see what follows. Grab your drink."

But Trevor flowed out of his chair and went to stand looking down at the stunned college girl.

"Hi. I'm Trevor. Are you a fan?"

"Yes," she breathed.

"Cool. Autograph?"

"Yes, please."

Trevor took the pen and notebook from her frozen fingers, scribbling his name.

"What's your name?"

"Claire Miller."

"Nice to meet you, Claire."

Trevor scribbled the same thing on her notebook and handed her back her pen and notebook. Scott loomed over him from behind. Trevor grinned.

"I gotta go, Claire. See ya."

The girl never replied.

Scott nudged Trevor and he moved himself to the door. Scott followed with the pizza, glancing right and left for incoming fans. He breathed easier once they were out in the sunny parking lot.

"You got a real weakness for what Aunt Mary calls 'reckless enthusiasm'. I ain't never seen the likes of you. I'll bet she sleeps with that notebook under her pillow tonight."

"She was just a kid."

"And you're so old. She'd have followed you to Texas."

"As if. Want me to hold the pizza or drive?"

"Hold the pizza. I'll drive. It'll be cheaper that way. Less speedin' tickets to pay out."

"About that gym."

"Listen up, rat boy."

"Ferrets. They were ferrets."

"Ferret-boy. Whatever. You done ice-skated your livin' room today. Had a nice ride in the big blue van. Got to dangle your feet under a restaurant table. How about you quit while you're ahead? Mull over this gym idea. Sleep on it. See how you feel in the mornin'. Heck, Trev, it's your first day out of the house in two weeks. The gyms of this world will be there in the mornin'."

"Sleep on it? 'I gotta know right now.'"

"Meatloaf. 'Paradise by the Dashboard Lights'. Darned hippie geezer rock singer. And you can stuff it about that gym. Take the pizza and get in the van."

Trevor slid into the van and sat holding the pizza box Scott had shoved at him on his lap. He remembered to put on his seat belt. Scott got in, glanced from force of habit to make sure Trevor did indeed have his seat belt on, and nodded.

"Good short-term memory, moron. Could you try, along with the other lifestyle changes you're contemplatin', to internalize some of the good advice you've heard over the years? From me. From Daddy. From Aunt Mary. From Dr. Brownie. From anyone?"

Trevor gave him the big-eyed look.

"I'll try."

Scott turned the key in the ignition and backed out of the parking slot, watching in all directions in his mirrors.

"I'm serious. Don't you never think twice?"

Scott frowned at him and Trevor dropped the act.

"I'll try."

"Good enough."

"Scott?"

"Yeah?"

"Maybe I just need to get out and meet some real people again. Ya know?"

Scott glanced over at Trevor's unguarded face.

"You won't have incognito at the gym, Trev. You just look like you."

Trevor shrugged. Scott frowned through the windshield.

"Move out of that darned Ice Palace, Trev. Keep it for Stephie's parties. Get yourself a snug little place up here in town somewhere. An apartment near the college. Get out them old rollerblades and blend in with the rest of the long-hairs."

"Maybe."

"Ya see? Right now you're startin' to crash and burn. You ain't got a lick of sense."

"I love you."

"We'll check out a gym in a few days. See if you get any funny looks. One darned fan comes up for your autograph, we're outta there. You need a break from this life, Trev. You need a place to go meet real people where they don't fall all over you for who you are. That's gonna be tough to find, maybe. We'll check it out."

"Thanks, Bro."

"You're welcome, moron."

Trevor held the pizza box on his knees and rubbed his thumbs absently on the edges of it, looking straight ahead as Scott drove them back to Longboat Key and The Ice Palace. Scott glanced at Trevor's profile once, knowing he was up to something. Hearing some song, or words, or working at some idea in his head. Nothing bad. Nothing scary. But he was up to something. Always thinking, his little brother. He might kid him about towels and ferrets, but no one had a better grasp of the big picture than Trevor did when he was well rested. But Trevor needed to stay well rested, and well fed, and well cared for. By himself or someone. He was brilliant but he was absent-minded.

94

Scott knew he'd follow him into Hell.

Back in The Ice Palace, Trevor snuggled up in the recliner with his Grammy-afghan again, limp as a noodle, and dropped off to sleep. Scott slid the remaining pizza into a Tupperware container and snapped the lid shut, knowing full well Trevor would nuke it later for a snack. He opened the door of the huge white refrigerator and shook his head. The inside was as cleanly white and vacant as the rest of the house.

Scott set the pizza in its container on a shelf at eye level where it would be easy for his brother to find later. He pulled out a bag of shaggy green vegetation and threw it in the trash. He pulled out the jar of almond-stuffed olives, polished it off, and tossed the empty jar into the trash as well. That left the pizza and an open box of Arm and Hammer baking soda, a trick both of them had learned from their father, who had learned it from his mother. It was a cheap way to keep down odors in a refrigerator. Odors against what in this refrigerator, Scott couldn't have said. There wasn't even any beer in there, let alone food. Just some cans of Dr. Pepper.

Scott closed the big door and opened the side with the freezer in it.

A box of frozen fried chicken and an ice-encrusted pack of grouper with freezer burn. Pitiful, Scott thought. For a man who could buy Miami, it was pitiful. Heck, it would have been pitiful for a man who couldn't afford shaving cream and toilet paper at the same time.

Scott closed the freezer door.

\*     \*     \*     \*     \*

Trevor rested.

Trevor ate.

When he felt he was ready to resume his usual work schedule, Trevor shoved himself back up onto the stage again. Onto the tour bus. On to the remaining tour obligations.

At a concert in Jacksonville, he broke off singing in the middle of a phrase and stopped playing. The band, confused, stumbled to a halt, looking at one another.

Trevor pointed out into the audience.

"Hey! You out there in the third tier. About middle, maybe ten seats in. What the heck you think you're doin'? I said this was a smoke-free concert and I meant it. I'm workin' here. Do I come out on the job site and mess with you when you're workin'? No. I don't. I couldn't care less how many of them coffin nails you chain-smoke on your own time. But you ain't gonna be doin' that here. Somebody grab them cigs away from that guy."

Trevor waited while there was the slight sound of a tussle from the third tier and a tall man triumphantly waved a pack of cigarettes at him, gave a whoop, and grinned.

Trevor nodded at the man.

"Thank you, sir. Mr. Smoker, you're gonna be enjoyin' this concert from the parkin' lot if I see that happen again. That goes for any and all of you. I'm workin' here. This is my job site. My lungs are my livelihood. Ain't none of you gonna be messin' up my lungs. We got that straight?"

There were scattered murmurs from the crowd and a shouted yeah or two of support in the uneasy silence.

"Ladies and gentlemen, I'm right sorry to come down on you all like that. I feel like the preacher hollerin' to the choir because nobody came to church. You all been doin' just fine, puttin' up with my craziness about smokin'. You all been suckin' it up for darned near two hours now. I appreciate that. That ain't easy to do. The band and me'll pick it back up now at the first of the last stanza. I'll throw in a brand new tune–one you all ain't heard yet–for good measure."

Trevor nodded to Jake, who rallied his musicians and off they went, Trevor jumping in on cue.

The publicity he got from the incident was hugely in his favor. A few detractors sneered at him, but Trevor's reply to his critics was that the audience had a choice. Stay and lay off the smokes, or leave the concert.

## MY LUNGS ARE MY LIVING

My lungs are my living.
How would you like it
If someone messed up your work hand?
I've done my playing
In smoky, old barrooms.
But this time I'm taking a stand.

Smoke in my concerts
And you'll love the seating.
Asphalt and curbs and your car.
I'll have your money.
You'll lose your ticket.
Best not to press me too far.

The stage is my jobsite
For two to three hours.
I know this job doesn't look tough,
But the smoke clogs my lungs up.
I can't breathe real easy.
My singing can sound kind of rough.

So, if you want value,
Don't mess up my product.
Let me do my finest work.
You paid out good money
To come see and hear me.
Don't lose it by being a jerk.

\*     \*     \*     \*     \*

After a concert in Joplin, Missouri, and on their way to one in St. Louis, Scott sat heavily down on the seat in the tour bus's kitchenette while Jesse drove. Trevor was already slouched in the opposite seat, staring out the windows at nothing.

"Trevor, I messed up, and you can fire me over it if you want. You got a right."

Trevor shifted in his seat, pulling his mind back from nowhere and focusing on his brother.

"What the heck are you talking about?"

"A reporter. I done been flappin' my gums to a darned reporter. I didn't know that, but the damage is done."

"What damage? What reporter?"

"Vicky Lynn. The newest backup singer. Turns out she's a reporter. Who knew? I sure as heck didn't. I just thought she was a groupie. But I didn't need to go flappin' my gums about your business to anyone. Fire me."

"Get real. I've had reporters claiming they interviewed me in Dallas when I was in Detroit. I've had stuff quoted I never in a million years said. Let her write it, whatever it was. Let her print it. Fuck it. Fuck her. Or did you?"

"Nope. She offered. That's when it came out she was a reporter. I turned her down. I'm hopin' to be a happily married man. I love Carla and I'll take my vows seriously. God knows what that reporter'll say, though. I messed up, Trev. Fire me."

Trevor just shook his head.

"Maybe you're guilty of a minor security breach. Maybe you get a warning along the lines of, 'Don't do it again.' It's not a firing offense for you or anyone. I mess up. Am I going to fire myself?"

"You can't. You're the deal."

"I'm darned sure giving myself a warning. I'm an effing moron."

"You are that. So am I. Fire me."

"I'm not firing you, Scottie. You can forget about that. You're not stepping off this bus. It may be headed off a mountain road and plunging to the bottom of a ravine but, by God, you're going down with it same as I am."

Scott leaned closer, scanning his brother's face.

"Are you all right, Trev?"

Trevor shook his head.

"I'm tired, Scott. Really, really tired."

Scott considered him.

"You talked to Daddy recently?"

"No."

"I'll be darned if I'm not gettin' to be like Daddy. I don't like the look of you, Trev. What's wrong?"

"Everything. Nothing."

Scott pulled his cell phone off his belt, and, keeping eye contact with Trevor, punched buttons from memory. He listened as it rang, but never broke eye contact with Trevor.

"Jarrett here."

"Daddy? It's me, Scottie. I got Trevor here. I'm puttin' him on the phone."

Scott stuck the phone out to Trevor, who didn't move to take it. Scott narrowed his eyes at his brother and brought the phone back.

"Daddy? He won't take the phone. Holler at him, will ya?"

He held the phone quickly away from his ear.

"Trevor!"

Scott handed the phone to Trevor again, finally picking up one of Trevor's hands, clamping it around the phone and holding it near the side of Trevor's head.

"Trevor!"

Trevor winced.

"Yes, Dad?"

"Talk. Right now."

"Okay."

And Trevor stopped talking. Scott nudged him in the shoulder and Trevor blurted out the first thing that came to his mind.

"I'm all messed up and I don't give a damn and I don't care if the whole mother-fucking thing crashes and I don't walk away from it."

"Jesus, Mary and Joseph, boy. Get your ass back here on a plane right now."

99

"I can't. I've got engagements. I've got engagements for the next five years. I have to make an appointment with myself to take a piss. I want out and I can't get out."

"Tell Scottie to make it happen. Send the band to the minor engagements with a sorry-he's-sick memo. Have him contact the big ones and ask what they want, a cancel-and-reschedule or the band alone. I'll expect to hear back from Scottie within the next two hours, tops, as to when I can expect to see you comin' out that deplanin' tunnel at Southwest Florida International Airport in Fort Myers. You got that, boy?"

"Yes, sir."

"And don't think I won't be callin' Scottie to tell him the self-same thing if he couldn't hear me himself."

Scott moved Trevor's hand with the phone in it to himself.

"I heard, Daddy. He's real listless. And I had to 'fess up to somethin' stupid I did. That probably didn't help matters much."

"What have I got out there? A pair of morons? Scottie, you can't be responsible for how Trevor handles the pressure. You do good work. We all mess up once in a while. Anybody die because you messed up?"

"No, sir."

"Anybody hurt?"

"Maybe Trevor, later."

"Personal?"

"No, sir. Just the band and the career and such."

"No big deal. I'm sorry to drop all this on you, Scott. But you should know I'm proud to say I know you can handle it. I wish you were comin' off that plane, too. I miss both my babies. But I really can't see Dani and Margaret and Jake holdin' the whole thing together. Trevor'd worry about that, too. He may say he don't give a damn, but that's just the depression talkin'. We both of us know he'd worry about the band if you weren't there. I love you, Scottie."

"I love you, too, Daddy. I'll get him home to you. He'll be fine. We'll be fine here. I'll call you when he's gonna arrive."

Scott clicked off his cell phone and peeled Trevor's fingers from around it. He tucked Trevor's hand into his own hand and used the thumb of his left hand to punch buttons on his cell phone.

"Sheri? Scott Daniels here. Get me a one-way ticket to Fort Myers, Florida, ASAP, in Trevor's name. We're in St. Louis. We'll pick it up at the airport, but call me back on my cell with departure information. Bless you."

He clicked off and punched more buttons. Trevor's hand lay lax in his grasp, but Trevor's eyes remained on his face.

"Dani? Scott here. Tell Margaret to get out the playbook. Trevor's goin' home for a bit. He's fine. Not to worry. Have her fax out band-and-regrets to the B-team. Direct call with options to the A-team. For how long?"

Scott eyed Trevor and moved his thumb over Trevor's knuckles.

"I'd say two weeks safely. They can always get a pleasant surprise if it's less. Try not to panic the band. Jake's seen all this before. He can help break it to the band. Just say he's tired, okay? He is tired. I got Sheri gettin' him a ticket home. Try to keep folks off us back here, will ya? I'll drive him to the airport myself in the Hyundai. Have Gus get it ready, will ya? Trevor'll be travelin' light. Daddy's got a handle on it from his end. Trevor and I got it covered here. Daddy gave us two hours to make it happen. I'd like to see results in less than that. Have our boy up in the friendly skies and headin' home in less than forty-five minutes."

Scott clicked off his cell phone, secure in the knowledge that the network of organization he had in place would follow through on their orders quickly and efficiently because they loved Trevor.

Silence engulfed them. Trevor hadn't spoken since his last words to their father. Scott considered his brother.

"You takin' Blondie?"

Trevor shook his head.

"Geez, Trevor. I used to think you took that guitar of yours to bed with you."

Trevor blinked. Scott scowled at him.

"You been writin' any music?"

Trevor shook his head.

"Darn, son. You are a moron."

Trevor stirred.

"Call Dani back. Have Margaret cancel it all. If I'm slacking off, let the band slack off, too."

"Those were not my orders from Daddy."

Trevor rolled his eyes. Scott shook his hand sideways.

"I know, I know. It's your band, not Daddy's. Maybe the band doesn't want to slack off. Maybe they'd rather play and get a paycheck. Huh?"

"Give them the choice."

"What? And wind up with a fiddle player and one back-up singer? Sweet. This isn't a democracy here. It's a band, Trevor. And you're the boss. You tell. You don't ask."

"Dad tells."

"Only 'cause you can't seem to think straight about now for yourself. I'll bet he'd also say not to make a decision you couldn't undo later. Right?"

"I guess."

Scott's cell phone rang.

"Scott here. Good. Thanks, Sheri. See ya."

Scott clicked off the phone again and silence surrounded them once more. He stared into Trevor's bleak eyes.

"You can fly out in the clothes you're wearin'. I'll get your sunglasses and a baseball cap for camouflage. I'll walk you to the security area. I'd rather be gettin' on the plane with you. It's real temptin'."

"I'm not a little boy."

"What you are right now is a pile of nothin'. If you don't get on that plane, I will come lookin' for you and I will take you home myself and then come on back out."

102

"I'll get on the plane."

More silence. Scott stared at Trevor and Trevor stared back. Scott ran his thumb over the buttons of his cell phone.

"You been eatin' right? You always was scrawny."

Trevor shook his head and Scott sighed.

"Darn. You are like takin' care of a baby. I outta know. Scott Junior's got more sense."

Trevor's lips turned up at the corners in a slight smile at the mention of his nephew and his eyes softened. Scott grabbed the advantage.

"Scott Junior likes to hear his Unka Trev play guitar."

More light came into Trevor's face.

"Scott Junior likes to hear about the lizards on Marion Avenue surfin' behind the cars after a rainstorm. He likes to hear about them climbin' up the Clock Tower to see the Peace River."

"I like that song."

"Ya done a good thing when you wrote that, Trev."

"I like babies."

"I know it. You want to take Scott Junior's picture on the plane with you? You can borrow my wallet-sized one for the trip. I can get it back from you later."

"No. But thanks."

"You want babies, Trev?"

Trevor nodded. Scott smiled at him.

"Any number of women'd be more than happy to oblige you, Trev."

Trevor's lips lifted, but his eyes darkened. Scott hurried into another sentence.

"Maybe we should just put in a request with Santa Snake? See what pops out of the snake egg shell on Christmas mornin'?"

The light came back into Trevor's eyes again and Scott continued.

"You don't want to be goin' off without Blondie, Trev. You fly off light. I'll ship her on down to you. You all shouldn't be separated. It ain't right."

Trevor snuffled and gulped.

"Don't you dare sing that ridiculous song about mockingbirds and diamond rings or I'll really lose it."

"Not gonna. That's Daddy's job."

Scott's cell phone rang again and he answered it.

"Scott here. Good for you, Dani. Good for Margaret. Fast work. Well done. Gus finished yet? Good. I heard from Sheri. Me and Trevor's outta here. I'll call Daddy when Trev's up in the air. I'll be back when I can."

He clicked off and squeezed Trevor's shoulder.

"Time to go."

Trevor nodded and stood up.

## Chapter Six

In the white glow of the master bedroom of The Ice Palace, Trevor stretched sinuously under the white satin covers and rolled onto his back. His shoulders met a rounded warmth behind him. He sighed, shifting his shoulders against that warmth, snuggling his butt back, and smiling to himself as a hand went around his waist.

Little had changed about him physically in the years since he'd found a loving home and happiness in the sleepy town of Punta Gorda in Southwest Florida.

He'd gotten taller.

He'd gotten bigger.

He still wore his dark hair long, a trademark now. His cat, Buddy, had changed more, growing from a feisty kitten to a rounded tomcat with a sleepy attitude. His Gibson J-45 acoustic guitar would only get better. A modern day classic, she was still his main lady.

Blondie didn't have an agenda.

Which wasn't true of the lady currently sharing his bed.

Bobbi would have to go soon, Trevor thought. But not right now.

Trevor eased Bobbi's hand from around his waist and persuaded it downwards.

As the physical contact woke Bobbi and nudged them both towards arousal, they began a familiar pattern of smoothing and pressing, nipping and teasing. Through it all, Trevor stayed oddly detached.

This was a good enough deal, he thought. He got good sex and he got great eye-candy for the crowds. Bobbi got great sex. Trevor grinned to himself. Yes, he thought smugly, Bobbi got really great sex. And the boost her modeling career needed. Which was why Bobbi was in the deal at all. He had no illusions about that. Well, maybe a few. But that was kid stuff.

He was back off tour for a while again. Resting up. Writing. Keeping in touch with his beloved family less than an hour south on the interstate. He was lodging again in the Longboat Key house of his deceased birth father.

Life was good.

His career was good.

Sex was good. Oh, yeah…

But that part of his brain which always seemed to operate on a level of its own, whispered to him that what Jarrett said was true. He was drifting. Making do. Settling for less. It told him that the passion he brought to his music and gained from his music wasn't spilling over into what passed for his personal life. Life on tour left little time for a real life. Little time for sleep, let alone reflection.

But it left enough.

Trevor finished. Bobbi was happy and already drifting off to sleep. Buddy peered down at them from a shelf on the headboard and looked bored. Trevor chuckled and raised a long finger to scratch behind the tomcat's ears. He cuddled Bobbi to him because he knew that was what she liked and he could appreciate how good it made you feel to get what you liked.

He dozed for a while in the pleasant afterglow of sex, then awoke hungry for food and rolled out of bed. He stood looking down at Bobbi. Being a model, she even slept pretty, Trevor thought. She looked great day or night.

Trevor rubbed his face and headed for the shower to scrub off the sweat from sex.

Long years of practice had his morning routine down pat. He had his coffee maker set on a timer, so dependable was his routine. He showered and shaved, pulled on a pair of old Charlotte High School gym shorts and headed for the kitchen downstairs, his wet hair dripping down his back.

He staved off hunger with a Pop Tart while he heated a frying pan with butter and then cracked eggs into it, moving them around with a gold-plated fork to scramble them. He got out orange juice, did toast, poured himself a cup of coffee, shoved it all onto a big Haviland dinner plate and added the same fork he had cooked the eggs with. He grabbed the cordless phone from the kitchen wall, tucked it under his chin and juggled his way out the sliding glass doors and onto the deck facing the water. He spread his breakfast around the table there and sat down, propping his long legs on the chair opposite and dialed up Jarrett Daniels while he ate his eggs.

"Trevor. What's up?"

Trevor ginned. Caller ID. What a great invention.

"Nothing much. How's Mary?"

"Fine. That's eyewash, Trevor. What's the matter?"

Trevor smiled to himself, picturing this big man he loved so much, probably standing in his own small kitchen back home, scrambling eggs with a fork, too.

"You out on the deck?"

"Near about. Mary's sleepin' in, so I'm in charge of myself. You sound tired."

"It was a long tour. Once I got back to it. I'll bounce back. I go into rehearsals next month for the next round."

Trevor forked egg into his mouth, enjoying this connection with his father, even if it was only silence on both ends.

"Trevor?"

"Hm."

"You gonna talk about the weather next?"

"Why? I guess I've got about the same weather here in Sarasota as you do in Punta Gorda."

"Well, I've never known you to say so much drivel when you're talkin'. I thought you might start talkin' about the weather next. What's wrong, son?"

"Nothing. I don't know. Would you mind me coming down there? Maybe about now? I miss you, Dad. Can I come home?"

He hadn't meant to say that, Trevor thought. Jarrett's chuckle sounded in his ear.

"You never need an invitation to come home for a visit, Trevor. Just come on."

"I'd like that. I don't know what's got into me."

"We'll see you when we see you. Drive safe."

"I will. Thanks, Dad."

They both hung up and Trevor set the cordless phone down on the table, feeling more connected than he had in a while.

He finished his eggs staring out over the mangroves and brackish water to the fast, expensive boat that bobbed at the dock. A Donzi, it had been built right there in Sarasota. He knew he'd have traded it in a Yankee heartbeat for a sixteen-foot Glaspar with an ancient Johnson outboard on it. He realized he was homesick, which was stupid when you were a grown man and ludicrous when you lived less than an hour away from home anyway.

But home wasn't distance and it wasn't years, he thought. It was a state of mind. He was glad his subconscious, craftily devil that it was, had blurted out the truth. Glad he'd given himself this gift of a trip back home.

These were the people who gave him focus and grounded him. To them, he was very special and nothing special. The life he'd chosen for himself often seemed to run him. It seemed to have a life of its own. Because of what he did for a living, he was responsible for the continued employment of thousands of people, probably half of whom he had never seen or even spoken to on the phone. He loved the music and he loved the performing. But the time not spent creating or performing was becoming less and less appealing. Less and less fun.

If he threw in the towel and came off the road, he himself would not be greatly impacted economically. He had investments and a cash-and-carry mentality left over from his younger years. His personal tastes were embarrassingly simple. Okay, the boat that bobbed, neglected, at the end of his dock. And the tiny green roller-skate of an MG kept in the garage to avoid sun damage. He had no taste for jewelry, though some of his ladies had had a taste for it. Ditto exotic food, or pricey liquor. Clothes for the stage were just part of the job. The image.

But he couldn't throw in the towel. He had the twin responsibilities of his dependents and of his public.

It was just that sometimes the responsibilities seemed so huge, he thought.

And it was lonely at the top.

Bobbi was one of the better ones. She liked him well enough. They got along. Had they both been other than who they were in the public eye, they might even have been friends. But Bobbi had her eye on her career and was at least straightforward enough to not pretend a depth of feeling for him she didn't have. They were okay acquaintances and casual lovers, but that's as far as it went. In the drug-riddled stress-factories of their chosen careers, theirs was probably one of the healthiest relationships and one of the most honest.

It was hard to relax, hard to meet new people without agendas, hard to have a genuine life when you either worked or worked at work 24/7. The carnage was appalling, the hypocrisy rampant, the pace warp speed.

Home.

Trevor watched a snowy egret lift from a mangrove and flap slowly away as he sipped his orange juice and let the early morning sun warm him.

He was going home.

He closed his eyes and smiled.

He heard his own front door open and close, then the sound of Bobbi's Porsche starting up and pulling away. She came and went as she pleased, keeping in touch with him by cell phone, never showing up unannounced or unplanned in order to save him possible embarrassment. He appreciated her thoughtfulness, a nice asset in a friend, even a casual friend.

He didn't feel there was anyone in his life right now he could have depended on in a pinch–or trusted a half an inch out of his sight–except three people, two of whom he'd be seeing later today. His dad and his aunt. His brother Scott was the third. He could expand that number to Dani. Past that was tricky. Bobbi and the others didn't count. Not even his fellow musicians or the members of his band. But he had the people he completely trusted and that was doing darned good, he thought.

Trevor stared for a moment at the wisps of white clouds overhead, feeling relaxed, feeling a sense of pleasant anticipation. Going home. Yeah. That sounded good.

He got up and brought his dirty dishes inside, sucking on his coffee.

When he wrote, he sometimes forgot to eat or sleep, so he'd decided long ago that a good breakfast just made sense. It was about the only meal he could count on having with any regularity. He washed his dishes and coffee cup in the sink and put them to dry in a dish drainer on the counter. He set up his next morning's coffee in the coffee maker, made sure Buddy's food and water bowls were full, and went back upstairs to dress for the trip south.

Bobbi had made the bed.

Good girl, Trevor thought.

Buddy was sacked out now on the white satin coverlet. Trevor stuck his face down in the warm fur and nuzzled it, waking Buddy who tangled his claws in Trevor's hair playfully. Trevor laughed, untangled his hair from Buddy's claws and rumpled his fur.

He pulled on an old pair of socks and an even older pair of sneakers, a faded pair of jeans and a torn T-shirt. He pulled his long hair back into a ponytail, pulled on a gimme baseball cap, backwards, and added a pair of cheap sunglasses. He grinned at his reflection in the ornate mirror above the dresser.

Who needed Porsches and Armani suits anyway, he thought? He was going home, dammit. Not to the French Riviera.

From the top of the Louis XV dresser, he picked up the keys to the old blue Chevy pick-up truck that had been his first vehicle when he'd gotten his driver's license. The tailgate was missing and there was a dent in the passenger side door. Pilot error when he'd been eighteen hadn't helped the left rear quarter panel any, he thought. Another miscalculation had removed the second half of a SKI

COLORADO bumper sticker that had been a souvenir of a family vacation to Glenwood Springs, Colorado.

Trevor shoved his wallet into his hip pocket and clipped his cell phone to his belt. He figured he looked exactly like what he'd often been before when he'd helped Jarrett on some project around the house or around their hometown. A day laborer.

On his way out the door, Trevor glanced at the huge photographic portrait that hung over the white marble fireplace. It was of the five most important people in his world. His father Jarrett, his Aunt Mary, his brother Scott, his cat Buddy, and himself. They were layered like a totem pole, he thought, the clever photographer unconsciously capturing the family dynamics.

There he was at fifteen, he thought. In the middle. He was holding Buddy on his lap. Buddy already had that give-a-damn expression on his face. Mary's arms were around him from above and behind, smiling into the camera. And Jarrett's arms were around both of them from above and behind. His brother Scott lay on the floor with his head propped up. Good old Scottie, he thought. My right-hand man.

His grandmother had declined an offer to be in the picture, but had agreed to a separate one with Trevor and her alone together. It graced the white marble mantle in a plain silver frame. He was seated on the floor, cross-legged with his back towards her wheelchair, his head tilted back and his hair spread out across her lap. His Grammy's fingers were in his hair as she gazed down at him with love and he looked back up to her .Just looking at the photo made his scalp tingle with the memory of love flowing from her fingertips and into him.

He had never felt close to the pristine grandeur of this house of his birth father. Portraits of love helped warm for him what he and Scott had always referred to irreverently as The Ice Palace. He knew Shawn had rarely stayed here, but it was in the family. Stupid to buy or rent somewhere else when there was decent lodging available for free.

But cuddle up to this place? As if. He knew where his real home was.

*    *    *    *    *

In Punta Gorda, he spent the day just hanging out with Jarrett and Mary. They did nothing special. He helped Mary fold clothes before Mary went off to turn her newest batch of wine at The Gilded Grape Winery. He and Jarrett washed Jarrett's newest truck out on the driveway.

Trevor scrubbed vigorously at one tire.

"I don't know why I resisted therapy for so long."

"Because you're stubborn."

Trevor laughed.

"Yeah. That would be it."

Jarrett played the hose down one side of the truck, then flopped it onto the concrete driveway where Trevor could reach it.

"You best stay with that therapy for a while."

"I will. It's not as scary as I thought it would be. It's nothing like the books and movies show it. Dr. Panjikaran really doesn't do anything. I just babble and she nods. She sticks her oar in once in a while. Nothing special. Nothing spooky, but it is weird."

"You're healin' yourself. It always comes down to you and what's in your head. Same for all of us. Doc points out the steppin' stones. You do the walkin'."

"I don't think I was ready for this at fifteen."

"Everythin' in it's own time."

"You know I'd still be living here with you and Mary if you hadn't thrown me out."

"A man can't get good nookie when he's livin' with his folks. It ain't all that sexy."

"I get good nookie."

"If the half of what I read is true, you get stellar nookie."

Trevor laughed.

"I do well enough for myself."

Trevor picked up the hose to rinse off the tire he'd been working at and sighed.

"Aw, Dad."

"Don't you let that terrible emptiness inside you get to you, boy."

"I'm trying."

"Get out of it, Trevor. Get out of this business. You don't need this. Take your energy in another direction. You'll still be writin'. You'll still be makin' your music."

"I don't know what the heck I want."

"Fulfillment. We all do. You ain't gettin' fulfillment."

"Got a store nearby? Maybe I can go buy a pound or two."

"You know darned well you can't buy it. You've already tried that."

"I have."

"Try to figure out what Trevor wants and what Trevor needs, then figure out how to get it."

Trevor moved to another tire and began scrubbing it.

"Buddy brought in a whole mockingbird last week. Feathers all over the house. Left the carcass in the bottom of my shower."

"Darned cat always was a right fine hunter. Very thoughtful about puttin' the body in the shower."

"I nearly stepped on it."

"You ought to know enough by now to watch where you put your feet."

"Well, it did make it easier to clean up than if he'd left it under the bed."

"I'm sayin'."

Trevor slumped against the fender of the truck.

"Aw, Dad."

"Hush. You just hush and let the warmth between us flow."

Trevor straightened and chuckled.

"Mary's been taking you to those meditation classes of hers hasn't she?"

113

"She could take me to Hell and I wouldn't care. You and Mary and Scottie fulfilled me."

Jarrett turned to look down at Trevor's profile.

"You just gotta figure out what you want, what you need, and how to get it."

"Swell."

"Open yourself to the light."

"Get stuffed."

Jarrett chuckled and went back to scrubbing his side of the truck.

"Well, Yankee. You're in high cotton now. Got half the world wearin' them shirts Dani made for you. Mr. Daniels' wardrobe by Ms. Danielle Moran. Hair by Margaret White. The family's gonna be floatin' for years on the proceeds from the sale of the promotional items alone. There's even a plush toy Buddy-cat."

"It's not the money, Jarrett. Past the necessities, what the heck good does it do? But I've made a difference."

"Yep. Got half the world lookin' like Star Wars meets Bob Marley."

"That's not what I meant and you know it."

"I know what you meant."

"I count for something. I've made a difference."

"With your music? Yes, you have. By the way you live your life? Yes, again. You always counted for somethin', Trevor."

Trevor sagged against the fender again.

"I'm just a guitar-playing street hustler."

"You're tired. I can tell. Get off the treadmill, Trevor. The road's suckin' the life out of you. Take a break."

"I've got commitments. I've got responsibilities."

"Send the band out. Cancel and re-schedule."

"My fans."

"Will live. You written anythin' lately?"

"No."

"You've lost track of your dream, Trevor. You're all caught up in the day to day routine of the business. Tell me again why you wanted to do this."

Trevor flopped the hose he was holding back and forth, watching the light strike rainbows in the spray.

"I wanted really famous people to play my music."

"You done got that, boy."

"I wanted to see my name on labels. Written by Trevor Lane. Trevor Daniels. Sorry, Dad."

"That's all right. That was a dream you had before we met."

Silence.

Trevor shifted on his heels.

"I've got everything I ever wanted. Why am I not happy?"

Jarrett chuckled. He stood and brought his big hand down on Trevor's shoulder, giving it a squeeze before removing it.

"Why ain't you happy? 'Cause you only got the first part of what you wanted. 'Cause you ain't got the part you really wanted."

"That's ridiculous. What could I possibly be missing?"

"That's for you to figure out. But I'll give you a hint."

"What?"

"It ain't up there on that stage. You done covered that. And it ain't in them hotel rooms or on that tour bus of yours."

"You're making me blush now."

"Rightly so. It ain't up in that mausoleum of a house on Longboat Key."

"Buddy likes it there."

"Buddy'd like any house he shared with you."

"True. That's it for the hints, huh?"

"You gotta figure out the rest for yourself, Trevor. What a boy wants for his dream at fifteen ain't always what he wants for his dream later in life."

"Man. I'm a man."

"Huh. I done heard that one before."

"You know, if you were a woman and we weren't related, I'd marry you in a New York minute."

"I appreciate that, Trevor. Go tell that to Margaret. Or Dani."

"Margaret would eat me alive. Dani'd laugh at me."

"Go try that line on Mary."

"I will not. She'd probably wash my mouth out with soap."

"Rightly so."

"You know what I mean."

"I do. I'm not sure you do, though. Go crawl into bed before you collapse. Or stretch out on the old plaid couch in the living room. We'll work around you."

"What are you up to in there anyway?"

"Skylights."

"Geez."

"It oughta look right pretty when we're done. Let some light in there. 'Bout time."

"There you go, giving me ideas for lyrics again. God, I love you, Dad."

"I love you, too, son. Now get in that house and go to sleep."

Jarrett woke Trevor for dinner and the three of them ate baked chicken followed by cherry pie at the old kitchen table.

Jarrett shoved a large wedge of the pie over to Trevor.

"I wonder what your fans would think if they knew your best love songs so far have actually been written with your daddy in mind?"

Trevor slid warm eyes to his father.

"They're about to find out. I've finally got the right words and melody together to express how I feel about you. When I put that one out, the whole world's going to know it's okay to say you love your dad."

Jarrett crinkled his eyes in a smile at the intense boy-man he loved more than life.

"It took a darned long time for those words to come tumblin' off your tongue so easy, Yankee."

"Yeah, it did. It took too long, Dad. I've always had the music for it. Now the words and the music are getting together."

"You gonna stand up and give me a hug or are you just gonna sit there twitchin'?"

Trevor threw back his head in laughter and stood up to fling his arms around Jarrett.

"You make me so complete, Dad."

"You ain't complete yet, Yankee. You're a work-in-progress. You'll be complete soon, though. I can see it comin'."

Mary stayed silent as Trevor sat back down again, an easy smile on his face. He glanced at her now but addressed Jarrett.

"I think I crossed that line in the sand again, Dad."

Jarrett shook his head.

"You just ain't got enough selfishness in you to amount to a hill of beans. Always thinkin' to please other people. Me. Your fans. And you're tired. You been lettin' the tail wag the dog. You got into this business to get your music out there. I'm guessin' you ain't hardly had time to write at all. Been pullin' out old stuff from back when. Maybe even subbin' it out. Jake been writin' some of it? Straighten up, boy. Because if that's what you mean by crossin' that line in the sand, you are correct."

Jarrett leaned in closer to Trevor and dropped his voice.

"If you've been doin' any of that, son, you been whorin' again."

Trevor sat up straighter and Jarrett nodded.

"Been writin' marketable product, have ya? Trevor, this business don't want creativity. It wants saleable, marketable product. If song A is a hit, you're expected to write song B as soon as you can and make it as close to song A in style and content as possible. If Hank, Jr. is the hot property, you're expected, on your way up, to sound like

Hank, Jr. That all runs totally counter to who you are. You broke the mold once. Break it again."

After dinner, Mary opted to wash the dishes, allowing Jarrett more time alone with Trevor. It was obvious to her that there were still things Trevor needed to get out, but not with her around. That hurt a bit, but she consoled herself with the knowledge that Trevor would benefit more from Jarrett's help than hers at this point.

Jarrett and Trevor ambled into the living room and Trevor sat down on the couch there. Jarrett frowned at him.

"What's with you today? Somethin' botherin' you that you ain't said yet?"

Trevor slumped on the couch.

"I lost my girlfriend."

"Oh? Where did you have her last?"

"Very funny."

"Slide over, lover boy."

Trevor made room for Jarrett on the couch and Jarrett sat down, shaking his head.

"Your love life is a train wreck, boy. Who's missin' now?"

"Dani. I lost her to an older woman."

Jarrett cracked up. Trevor eyed his father with a certain degree of exasperation.

"It's not funny, Dad."

"The heck it's not. Especially the way you just blurted it out there. Margaret?"

"Yeah. What with me being off the road, she and Dani had time on their hands. They got married last week. A real quick civil union in Massachusetts."

"I'd guess it would have to be real quick with everybody's schedule. Well, who couldn't have seen that comin'?"

"Me."

"Always the last to know, huh? You ain't lost Dani. I'm guessin' you never had her. Not that way. You ever?"

"No. Well, we tried."

"There you go."

118

"I'm losing a friend here. Margaret hates me."

"She won't hate you now you're not the competition."

"Swell."

"Aw, give it up, Trevor. You and Dani been friends for years. I never saw a spark of anythin' special between you two ever. Am I missin' somethin' here?"

"No."

"Well, then? You ain't found your special lady. Look how long it took me."

"I don't have forever."

"It only seemed like it took forever, Trevor. It was worth the wait."

"Dani was the only female who never wanted anything out of me. Well, except for Grammy and Mary and Miss Millie. They don't count. You know what I mean."

"I know. You're talkin' eligible peer female here, Trevor, with the potential for a permanent relationship. You set high standards for yourself in the permanent relationship department. And I like that. You got just about all your bases covered when it comes to givin' and gettin' love. Grammy, Mary, Miss Millie, me. Buddy. Even Doug, in a way. And Dani. You're open and free with these people. Once you got over your fear, you opened up to the love and gave it and got it back. You're just not ready for the risk involved in openin' up to that special lady out there somewhere, so she ain't even showin' on the radar yet."

"I loved Dani."

"I know it. And you still do, just not the way a love-sick man loves his lady. You two never tangled sheets."

"We tried."

"And?"

Trevor chuckled and shook his head.

"We got to laughing too much and gave it up. It was all about as sexy as cutting up frogs in biology. I'd already seen the territory, so to speak, but Dani was curious, so we took a handful of condoms and a six-pack out into the boonies with a blanket and gave it a try. Finally we just lay

119

out in the back of the truck, sucking down beer, watching the stars, and listening to the racecars go around at the Charlotte County Speedway. She got a pretty good education on male anatomy and I got a darned fine blowjob, but we agreed it wasn't going to be our thing. I'm steak and Dani prefers the fish platter."

Jarrett nudged shoulders with him.

"So, I guess we finally know the awful truth."

"What? That Dani's a lesbian?"

"No. I kinda figured that out."

"What then?"

"That you're so ugly you'll turn a woman off men."

Trevor cracked up. Jarrett bumped shoulders with him again.

"There you go, Yankee. Lighten up."

Trevor blew out a breath, still chuckling ruefully.

"Self-service is playing a huge role in my life on the road."

Jarrett shook his head.

"I'll bet that'd be a blow to your image with your fans."

"My current love life off the road would be, too."

"You get. Don't tell me you don't."

"I get. But sex isn't love. I'm actually getting to prefer myself to anyone else, and that's kinda scary. I live with a tomcat, and I like his company better than even Bobbi's."

"You're a tomcat yourself."

"Yeah."

"Alex Villarreal's got a new animal clinic over on Collingswood in Port Charlotte now. You want me to take you over there and get you fixed, or what?"

"No."

Jarrett stared hard at the dark wood coffee table in front of them.

"Mary says we men don't need love to have good sex. I ain't so sure that's true."

"Well, Buddy sure doesn't need it. I've been settling for mutual lust and a certain degree of friendliness."

"There's your trouble, Trev. You've been settlin'. Never settle, boy."

Jarrett looked up and quirked a grin.

"You know, your darned cat got a better college education than you did."

"Hey. I got good grades."

"Bet he studied more."

Trevor gave his father the big-eyed look.

"What? It was all an education. And it was at college."

Later that night when he left for the house on Longboat Key, Trevor drove back more slowly than usual, cheating the ever-vigilant Charlotte County Sheriff's Department of the privilege of issuing him another well-deserved speeding ticket. It amazed him somehow the continuity his life had taken on once he became a Daniels. In a rough business, continuity was rare. Now, at a very good place in his life and his career, he couldn't be sure what that faint longing was that he felt at the edges of his world.

He slept better that night in The Ice Palace than he had since the pneumonia.

Maybe the shrink thing is working out, he thought.

### SECRET FUN

When the meeting of two souls occurs
It's beautiful to see.
I've seen it in some others
But never yet for me.
Souls as one.
Searching done.
Whole from half.
I watch them laugh.
Secret fun.
Secret fun.

Hands to hearts,
Eye to eye,
No pretense,
No more lies.
Naked souls
Clearly see
All the love
There for free.
Secret fun.
Secret fun.

Mary, Jarrett,
Scott and Carla.
Dani, Margaret,
Shawn and Doug.
Male or female doesn't matter
When you're having
Secret fun.
Secret fun.

## Chapter Seven

Trevor did a Christmas Special from New York City.

His rendition of "The Little Drummer Boy" was simple and straightforward. He sang it sitting in a single spotlight on a stool in a plain white T-shirt and jeans. Not even Blondie was with him.

He had a sprig of holly between his long fingers. Dani had directed Margaret to braid a dull gold metallic ribbon into his hair and it gave him a certain exotic look as the braid looped across the top of his head in a coronet. As he sang "The Little Drummer Boy," he easily became the poor boy with no gift but his music to give to the Christ Child. When he finished, he stuck the sprig of holly in his hair and grinned at his audience. The lights went up on his band and the fun began.

"Happy Birthday, Jesus" was the hit of the show.

It was a rollicking tune with warmth to it, as child-like as The Muppets meet Winnie-the-Pooh. The chorus was set to a polka beat. It was Ring-around-the-Rosy, Trevor-style.

His grandmother-by-adoption had tried to make a Christian of him, but Trevor continued to color outside the lines. His inner circle quietly enjoyed the sly references to his aunt and his adopted father. People in the audience were actually out in the aisles, dancing, by the time Trevor and the band finished and "Happy Birthday, Jesus" balloons dropped from the ceiling amidst pyrotechnics and streamers.

The CD was released the next day and quickly went platinum. Trevor quietly redirected the proceeds to a local Charlotte County food bank. Wearing sunglasses and a Santa Claus hat with his long hair stuffed up underneath, he took several shifts as a bell ringer for the Salvation Army once he was back in Charlotte County.

## HAPPY BIRTHDAY, JESUS

Happy birthday, little boy.
We're gonna celebrate.
Lots of people like you
And they sure do think you're great.

If one life can make a difference
It seems yours really can.
You brought us all some Peace on Earth
And, yes, Good Will to Man

Is the red for your blood?
They took a lot from you.
Is the green for your life?
God gave it back to you.

And what about the Wise Men?
Some silly birthday gifts.
A flock of angels in the sky?
I'd stick to Mary's kiss.

And Joseph as your step-dad.
He had a job to do.
The manger was a low place.
Herod's troops were coming, too.

Never mind the Father, Son and Ghost.
For me on Christmas Day,
It's, 'Pass the mashed potatoes,
Jesus Christ is here to stay.'

After the holidays, Jarrett, ever vigilant, dropped in on Trevor at The Ice Palace. When Trevor opened the massive front door, Jarrett eyed his son from the doorstep.

"I swear to God, boy, you could put on a fuzzy pink sweater and look good in it."

"I'm not Ed Wood, thank you very much. And pink isn't one of my better colors."

"What the heck's Dani been up to? Let alone Margaret. She hate you that much she'd mess up your hair?"

Trevor laughed. Jarrett shook his head at the complicated arrangement of twisted braids and metallic, colored mousse that added several inches to Trevor's lean length of six feet plus.

"You got Kiss meets Star Trek goin' on there, boy. And the clothes are Rod Stewart meets Vain. You got any tattoos? Any piercin's?"

"Got some tribal art down below."

"Well, at least it don't show in public. No tongue piercin'?"

"It would interfere with the singing. I think. No, nothing on the tongue. Small loop in the navel."

"Jesus Christ, boy. Well, have your fun."

"It's considered to be body art."

"I'm happy if you're happy."

Jarrett fixed a worried eye on the handsome face before him.

"Are you happy, son?"

Trevor chewed on his bottom lip as Jarrett stepped over the threshold.

"I'm antsy, Dad. I can't settle. I'm wired. I'm busy."

"Are you writin'?"

"No."

"You need to change that."

"I don't have anything in me."

"Lost it?"

"No, not exactly. It's there. But it's like the lawn mower when you cut the yard in the spring. The mower's going, but there's no grass coming out."

"Because there's no grass comin' in?"

"Yeah. The machine is chugging away. Empty."

"Take a break. Wash your hair. Get out your jeans and T-shirts. Get back to the basics."

"After the next tour."

"Bull. Tomorrow may never come, Trevor. This is worryin' you."

"I'm not unhappy."

"Well, that's a heck of a statement from a man who's already achieved his personal goals."

"Maybe that's part of the problem."

"Maybe it is, son. Your goals when you were fifteen were kinda shallow. Get your name known. Have famous people play your music. Those are darned fine goals for a fifteen-year-old. Maybe you need to establish new goals. Better ones, maybe. It's not always good for a man to achieve his goals. It leaves him edgy and incomplete."

Trevor nodded.

"That would be it. But what else is there, Dad? What the heck else is there?"

"Get out them jeans and T-shirts, Trev. Focus back on inside yourself. You're losin' track of yourself, maybe. Every man's goals are different. And they change. Might be your time to reassess. You're darned lucky you have the luxury of bein' able to reassess. Take it."

"After the next tour."

"That's a mistake, Trevor. I'm tellin' you."

*       *       *       *       *

And it was.

Jarrett picked a Saturday night to drop in unexpectedly for a visit to The Ice Palace, half-knowing and half-fearing what he'd find.

The music throbbed. The frenzied crowd moved like corks on choppy water. There was a sweaty feeling in the air. Trevor, wearing skin-tight black leather pants and a black leather vest, had opened the door, and now stood frozen at the sight of Jarrett on his doorstep.

Jarrett scowled at him.

"Drugs. You been doin' drugs."

Trevor's eyes drifted away and he didn't move to let his father in.

"Darn you, boy. Look at me. I thought we had an agreement. Nothin' illegal."

"I've had drugs for pain before."

"That's a quibble. Dammit, I can almost hear your arguments in my own head. 'Everybody does it.' 'It's out there.' 'I can control it.' Have I missed anythin'?"

"I can afford it."

"You can afford rat poison, too. Do you have to buy it and use it? Remember who you are, boy."

Not liking Trevor's lack of response, Jarrett grabbed Trevor's chin in strong fingers and brought it up so their eyes met. Trevor's eyes were simmering with dark rage and Jarrett narrowed his own.

"I said remember who you are, boy. Not what you were. You're better than this. You're smarter than this. What's gone wrong? If it's that dog-and-pony-show, get outta the circus. You don't need the cash. You don't need the fame. What the heck are you doin'?"

For Trevor, suddenly the years dropped away.

The undulating crowd vanished, the noise silenced and he was just a scared teenage boy on a quiet Punta Gorda street standing in the arching shadows of a tall banyan tree with the yellow glare of street light shining behind a big, kind man.

*"Are you all right, son? Not what you tell the docs, but what you tell me. Are you all right?"*

Trevor blinked and started to shiver.

"It hurts, Dad. Way up inside. I feel dirty."

Ignoring the noise and the crowd around them, Jarrett pulled a shaking Trevor slowly into his arms and folded him in close.

"Rehab, Trevor. Right now, boy. You don't want this. Get out of this life, son. It's killin' you."

"I ran into a ditch, Dad."

"I know, son. It'll be fine."

"The tour. The concerts. What'll I do?"

"We'll cancel and refund. You have healin' to do. Come on home with me right now."

"Will they send me to Ferndale?"

"We'll have to see about that."

Jarrett called the Sarasota County Sheriff's Department from his cell phone once he had Trevor safely in the passenger seat of his truck. He reported a loud party with the possibility of drugs and had the satisfaction of seeing flashing red and blue lights pass them, going the opposite direction, as he drove off Longboat Key. There'd be a scandal, he thought, but nothing like there'd have been if Trevor were there. This way, he could clean all the rats out at once and be done with it. He'd follow up tomorrow to make sure Buddy was okay.

*    *    *    *    *

The band took an extended break.

Two months later, Trevor's approval rating, according to Stephanie, was unharmed. Due to clever manipulation, his drug problem–or more specifically his fight to overcome the problem–was causing him to have an even broader-based recognition.

Ironically, he was becoming a hero.

Trevor had completely, ruthlessly and without a second thought severed his connections to anyone and anything from that part of his life. He had stubbornly held out for the most painful cold turkey allowable, hoping to internalize the horror against possible future temptations. His country following stayed loyal. His classical following stayed ignorant. His younger crossover audience voted him cool rather than dorky for his struggle. He did anti-drug promotionals for TV.

Trevor, in spite of himself, was still on an upward climb.

## TUNING MY GUITAR

My guitar is my life.
My life is my guitar.
Sometimes I need some tuning.
My strings get stretched too far.

Pluck softly.
Hear my tonals.
Strum wildly.
Hear my force.
But keep my strings adjusted.
Clean them up so they're not rusted.
Well kept-up, I can be trusted
To give beauty, truth and justice
To the melodies of life within my heart.

I broke a string.
I have no back up.
Some notes now
I cannot play.
I must be careful.
I must be patient.
Must make adjustments
So I can play.

Will you be kind?
Seem not to notice
When some music
Of mine you hear.
"That sounded different.

What is he doing?"
I'm only tuning
Myself by ear.

## Chapter Eight

But some things hadn't changed.

Trevor and Buddy were still living in The Ice Palace.

On a bright Sunday morning, Jarrett drove up to the house on Longboat Key, unannounced again. He knocked on the huge front door, ignoring the pretentious chimes of the doorbell. Since he didn't consider this to be his son's true home, Jarrett had never simply knocked on the door and opened it to walk in, even though he knew Trevor would have been fine with that.

Trevor opened the door to Jarrett wearing jeans and a T-shirt, barefoot, and flung his arms around Jarrett.

"Dad! Come on out to the deck. Dr. Pepper?"

"Sure. Where's Buddy?"

"Up in the bedroom, sacked out. He'll come if I press the can opener."

"Pavlov."

"Yeah. But it's a real convenient way to call him if he has a vet appointment. He hates going to the vet."

"Don't we all?"

Trevor snagged two cans of Dr. Pepper in his right hand from the pristine white refrigerator in the pristine white kitchen with its high domed ceiling. He shoved the refrigerator door closed with his hip and opened the sliding glass door onto the teak deck with his left hand, letting Jarrett go out first. He angled his chin towards the round teak table and chairs set up to face down the long length of the dock as it speared its way through the mangroves to the water beyond.

"Sit. Isn't this beautiful? I love this out here."

Jarrett eased back into one of the Adirondack chairs with its boldly striped cushions and Trevor flung himself into the other, grinning and handing one of the cans of soda to Jarrett. He popped his own can of soda and sat back in his chair, seemingly relaxed and buoyant.

"What's up?"

131

Jarrett popped the top on his own soda and took a drink, looking over his shoulder to the house looming behind them.

"Nice house."

"The Ice Palace? I guess. Buddy likes it."

"Buddy'd like wherever you were."

Trevor laughed and sipped his soda, contentedly gazing into the distance.

Handsome. Striking. Beautiful. Dynamic. Jarrett thought of all the adjectives over all the years that had been used to describe this young man and felt that none of them did justice to him.

Radiant. Forceful. Driven. Pulsating. It still didn't reach the core. Happy? Contented? At peace? No. Ageless, classic humanity? He'd have to check with Mary. Sensitive? Oh, my, yes.

Jarrett set his soda down on the deck beside him and reached out a finger to just barely touch Trevor's wrist as it lay on the arm of his chair. Trevor looked over, pulling his mind back from wherever it had gone wandering off to. He focused on Jarrett's finger on his wrist, and then looked up to Jarrett's face.

"What? What's wrong?"

Bright boy, Jarrett thought. Bright, sensitive boy.

Trevor sat up in his chair.

"Tell me quickly. Is it you? Is it Mary? What?"

"It's Dani, Trevor. She has cancer."

"No!"

Trevor surged up from his chair, fifteen years old again and his carefully constructed world in shambles.

"No!"

"She's takin' chemotherapy, Trevor. They think they got it under control. She's real bummed out, Trev. She looks awful. She's losin' her hair and the chemo makes her queasy."

"Money?"

"We got it covered. She needs her friend."

Trevor sucked it up.

132

"Of course. No question about it. I'll come. Right now. Buddy and my housekeeper are on real good terms. I'll leave her a note. She's got all the addresses and phone numbers already."

He turned to Jarrett, his face agonized.

"Jesus Christ, Dad. Dani's young."

"Cancer don't seem to care, Trev. This is breast cancer. They've taken one breast. They're hopeful. But she'll be off the road for a while. So will Margaret."

Trevor gulped. It would be his first real exposure to this disease–his first brush with the possible mortality of one of his closest friends. He breathed in through his nose to steady himself.

"What can I do to help?"

"Let her know you love her. Let her know she still looks like a sexy woman to you. And try not to fight with Margaret."

The last made Trevor laugh, as it was meant to, and the sharp edges of his horror smoothed over somewhat.

"Okay. I can do that."

"We'll take my truck. I'll drive."

"Don't trust me with your spiffy new truck, huh?"

"Darned straight I don't, Mr. Richard Petty. Pack what you need. We'll buy the rest back home."

Trevor staggered into the house, Jarrett bringing up the rear with their two opened cans of soda, sipping his while Trevor scribbled a hasty note to his housekeeper and propped it up by the phone. He handed Trevor his soda. Trevor shook his head, but Jarrett persisted.

"Business as usual, Trevor. Dani already has enough people pussy-footin' around her with long faces. Time to send in the clowns."

Trevor's face softened and he took the can of soda from Jarrett. Jarrett sized him up and figured he'd do.

"Don't forget your shades and your baseball cap, Fabio."

"Okay."

$*$     $*$     $*$     $*$     $*$

He was fifteen years old and she was fourteen. Trevor grabbed her and rolled her up and over his shoulders much as he would have Blondie. Dani, letting out a shriek, was laughing wildly as Trevor set her back on her feet.

"Wow! You're stronger than you look!"

Trevor's laughing eyes met hers.

"I hear that a lot. Come on, Dani. This place is great. Let's go explore."

He grabbed both her hands and grinned into her face, seeing the answering grin of fun from Dani. He could be silly with this girl. Serious by nature, it was a profound relief to him to simply be and enjoy for a short space of time. In Dani, he had met a kindred spirit. Haunted by her own demons, Dani, too, needed the release.

Laughing too loud, they raced the quiet near-dawn corridors of the Best Western in Punta Gorda, their sneaker-clad feet sending muted vibrations and echoes into the carpeted concrete. They raced towards as much as they raced from their fates. But they raced with, never against, one another.

They burst with a clatter out through the doors at the end of one corridor, finding sunlight and open air and the pool. Dani stopped, but Trevor scooped her up from behind and cannonballed into the pool with her in his arms, making her shriek again. They both came up laughing and splashing.

"You idiot! I've got stuff in my pockets. Important stuff. And shoes on."

Trevor laughed and shoved her head under. She came up spluttering and he laughed harder.

"Me, too. Shoes. Stuff. It'll all dry out. Don't be such a girl."

"I am a girl. Don't be such a boy."

"I'm a man."

"You are not. Stop!"

And Trevor shoved her under again. She came up even wetter than water could make anyone.

"Stop! I've got something for you. In my pocket. I don't know if I'll give it to you now."

Arrested, Trevor's eyes focused on her intently.

"A gift? For me? Cool."

His hands snaked out and grabbed her narrow waist, whipping her out of the water and onto the edge of the pool.

"Gift? You mentioned a gift? I distinctly remember hearing the word gift associated with my name."

Trevor hauled himself up onto the coping and sat dripping beside her. Dani hunched a shoulder.

"That was before you went all macho on me."

"Girl. You're such a girl."

"You want your gift or not?"

"Oh, yeah. I love gifts. What is it?"

Dani dug in her front jeans pocket and brought out a simple strand of tiny iridescent beads.

"I had to guess at the size of your neck."

"Eighteen."

"Bull."

"I'll grow into it."

She handed the necklace to Trevor who flopped onto his back and held it up to let the sharp morning sun glint off the irregular shapes and varied colors of the transparent beads. Dani leaned in.

"It took me forever to get it right. About ten percent of the beads wouldn't even string."

"It's beautiful."

Trevor turned glowing eyes to her, and Dani knew she would never find another person who so fully understood the choosing of each individual bead, the importance of this particular bead after this particular bead and ahead of this other particular bead.

Trevor looked deeply into her eyes.

"I'll wear it forever. I'll never take it off."

And Dani knew he meant what he said. She reached out her hand for the necklace.

"I'll put it on for you. The clasp is new and kinda stiff."

Trevor sat up, handed Dani the necklace and hauled his wet hair out of the way so she could have access to his neck. She fastened the clasp and then paused.

"You've got some real short hair at your neckline."

Trevor pulled out from under her hands and let his hair fall back into place.

"I never had a girl give me anything. Except for Dad and Grammy and Mary, I don't remember anyone giving me anything ever."

He frowned, remembering Christopher de Nunzio.

"Well, nothing good anyway."

Then he brightened.

"Thanks for the gift."

"It's the first one I ever finished. I'm not very good."

Trevor picked up her cool hands and held them for emphasis as he looked directly into her eyes.

"It's the most beautiful necklace I've ever seen in my whole life. When people ask me where I got it, I'll tell them it came from a lady admirer. Jewelry by Ms. Danielle Moran."

And he grinned at her.

\*     \*     \*     \*     \*

Dani was sitting by the water, looking out over the broad expanse of the Peace River. The ends of the red, black and white silk scarf she wore shifted in the slight breeze. Trevor came up behind her quietly on the soft grass and folded himself down into his favored position, cross-legged next to Dani's right side. She didn't even bother to glance over at him as she spoke.

"Hey. I heard you were in town."

"Hey, yourself. What's up?"

"Don't be a smart-aleck. You know what's up."

"Oh. Yeah. That. But I meant what's new and exciting or interesting?"

Dani glanced over at him now, her eyes hot. Then she caught him looking over at her with just the barest edges of his lips twitching into a smile. She chuckled and shook her head, nudging him with her shoulder.

"Wiseguy."

He nodded.

"Yeah. Pretty much. I liked your hair down free. Does it feel funny not having any hair after all these years?"

"Kinda. The scarf gives me something to hide my ears with. I'm getting used to it. I don't like the wigs. They prickle. And they're hot. They tell me the hair'll grow back."

"Is Margaret gonna be ticked off if I snuggle up to you?"

Dani shifted over and Trevor put his left arm around her shoulders. Dani seemed to sag into him for a moment, then just relaxed.

"Probably. She never did understand us."

"Yeah, well, I'm not sure I ever did understand us, either. I used to have some fantasies. That was way back. Then I quit that, 'cause who wants to have fantasies about his sister anyway? You're the closest thing to a sister I've got."

"I gave up the fantasies, too. For other reasons as well. Margaret doesn't get that. You're the closest thing to a brother I'll ever get."

Trevor leaned over, pulled Dani's top up from her waist and blew a wet raspberry of a kiss into her belly button, shoving her over backward as she burst out laughing and hammered his back with her fists. Her scarf fell off and she didn't bother to scramble to put it back on.

Her fingers were mock-choking a grinning Trevor, but she stopped, arrested by odd lumps she felt under her fingertips as they rested on the back of Trevor's neck.

"Trevor, what in the world have you got back there?"

Dani persuaded Trevor into bending forward. She parted the hair at the back of his skull with her fingers, squinting in the bright sunlight. Trevor's warm body moved under her cool fingers.

137

"My scars. I've never let you or Margaret mess with my hair back there, have I? I'm always the one to do the back of my neck."

Dani was parting the hair at the back of Trevor's neck and trying to peer at the roots of it.

"Wow, Trevor. I just thought it was part of your craziness."

"It is."

"No, I mean your serious craziness."

"It is."

Trevor sat back up and captured Dani's hands in his, running his thumb over her knuckles. He lifted his eyes to her face.

"I got those scars the first night I was in Charlotte County."

His eyes sobered.

"Past that, I won't be telling you any details. It was before you and I met. I'm still here, Dani. I survived and I truly believe there's nothing you can't survive with God's help, faith in yourself and the love of good people around you."

Trevor looked down at their joined hands.

"Yeah, it's chemicals you're taking to cure you of the cancer. But it's mostly you, Dani. Your willpower."

"I always wondered about your past, Trevor. You were so serious."

"I'm not as serious now as I used to be. I got older and smarter. Silly is good."

Dani chuckled at that and Trevor's eyes warmed. Dani touched his face.

"You were the only boy who could ever make me have fantasies."

Trevor grinned at her.

"Darned shame Margaret had fantasies, too."

"You were so wild and free! Nothing like the other boys here."

"We've all got our demons, Dani. I'm here for you. What do you want? What do you need? Need a hug? Need a kiss? Need a good tickle?

Dani's face crumpled.

"I guess right now I need a good cry."

Trevor pulled her into his arms.

"I've still got your necklace, Dani. See? You know I wear it all the time. I never take it off. It meant the world to me when you gave me that, skinny little weird kid that I was."

Dani snuffled into his shirt, gripping him tightly.

"Yeah, you were. You still are."

Trevor rocked her, absorbing her sobs for a while as Dani calmed herself somewhat.

"Trevor?"

"Yeah."

"I'm just so scared."

"What? Of dying?"

"No. I guess not. Maybe."

"Of being ugly and bald?"

"Wiseguy."

Trevor chuckled and then nuzzled Dani's neck, making her giggle again before she sighed.

"I'm scared of people looking at me funny, Trevor. Like cancer is catching or something. Like you can get it by being near me."

"People are nuts. Forget them."

"Easy for you to say."

"Yeah, it is. I never did give a darn about what people thought, I guess."

Dani sat up out of Trevor's arms and felt around behind her for her scarf. She found it, but she didn't put it on. She rubbed at her eyes with it to dry them.

"Why is that, Trevor? Why didn't you ever care what people thought?"

Trevor shrugged, smiled, and ran a finger under Dani's lashes to wipe at the last of the tears.

"Because they had no power over me, I guess. I wouldn't let them have that power. I care about what the people I love think of me. I care about the image I give. But not about how I look or act. Does that make any sense?"

Dani nodded.

"You are who you are and what you are, not what you look like?"

"Yep. That's it. Jarrett's always been better with the words. And you. All that poetry. Not me. I'm the music."

"And the hair."

"Yeah, well, we'll see. If some of the fans don't like it, well…"

"Forget them?"

"Yep. Forget them. You want me to shave my head? I will if you will."

Dani punched him in the shoulder.

"Wiseguy. You'll look cute and I'll look bald."

"My scars'll be showing, Dani. Big time."

"You'd do it, wouldn't you?"

"Sure I would. Doesn't change who I am or what I do. It's still me."

"And it's still me."

Dani shoved the scarf in her jeans pocket.

"You gonna be in town for a while?"

"Maybe. Why?"

"Margaret could use a break from driving me to chemo. Her nerves are shot. Mine, too. We could use a good laugh."

"You got it, sis."

Trevor kissed her cheek and Dani quirked a smile at him.

"Thanks, Bro."

$$* \quad * \quad * \quad * \quad *$$

The next day, Trevor lay diagonally across Dani's bed in the house she shared with Margaret on Wood Street in Punta Gorda. He was a gorgeous male animal, naked and

140

fully aroused. There was the familiar warm smile on his lips, but also the familiar clouds in his eyes.

Dani put her hands on her hips.

"Aw, Trev. What a sweet gesture. I can't believe I'm turning down what thousands of women would give their souls for, but this has never been what we're about."

"I thought I'd give it a try."

"You're trying to make me feel pretty. Thanks. Get up and put some clothes on, Trev. Just hang out with me, okay?"

Trevor rolled fluidly from the bed and unselfconsciously wandered to the chair where he'd carefully laid his jeans and T-shirt. Dani shook her head as she watched him, then frowned.

"Trev?"

"Yeah?"

"I don't remember a scar from your right butt cheek down the back of your leg."

Trevor paused in the act of pulling on his jeans, seeming to tense. His back was to her.

"Oh. That."

"You gonna share?"

"It's been there, Dani. You've just never noticed it before."

Trevor finished pulling on his jeans, zipped and fastened them, turning back to her.

"Is your knowing about my past going to help you fight the cancer, Dani?"

Dani sat down on the edge of her bed, considering this odd boy who had grown into such an odd man. Loveable, yes. But odd and unpredictable. His face was unreadable at the moment. Never a good sign.

"I guess you didn't get it saving a busload of children from sudden death in the Rockies? Or from a jealous husband late one night?"

Trevor shifted his weight.

"I'd have told you about the bus. And you know me better than to think it would be the other."

141

"Not gonna jolly you out of it, am I?"

"No. But I'll tell you if you want to know."

Dani looked down at her hands and spread her fingers on her jeans.

"Margaret's been surfing the net. She's no darned good at it, you know? Winds up in places she never wanted to be. Then just gets curious."

Trevor toed out a chair from Dani's computer table and sat down. He propped his elbows on his knees, the long fingers of his hands dangling loose.

"Writers. Worse than cats with that curiosity thing. What did she find?"

"Porn."

"She's a big girl, Dani. No pun intended."

"She showed the pictures to me and I told her she was nuts. I told her to shut up about them, too."

"Fierce Dani. Where's all this going, sis?"

"The little boy had long dark hair, Trevor. Those sites have a disclaimer that the models are eighteen or older, but I could tell that was a lie. How old were you, Trevor?"

Trevor ducked his head to let the dark fall of his hair cover his face.

"I was twelve. Maybe less."

"Trevor, that's horrible! That little boy was frightened to death."

"I never saw the pictures myself. By now, I thought they'd disappeared. Dad knows. No one else. Now you."

Trevor drew in a breath through his nose and looked up. He couldn't quite muster a cocky grin.

"Now Margaret. Swell. Guess I'll be finding out if I care what people think when they look at me after all. Thanks, Dani."

Dani surged up from the bed and dropped at his feet, grabbing his hands.

"No! I'm not going to exploit you. Neither is Margaret."

"Poor pun, Dani."

"Will you stop this? I told you because I thought you should know. I thought Margaret was wrong. The magazines are always looking for a scandal. That's all I thought, Trevor."

Trevor's face was closed.

"Well, what do you think now?"

"I think it was horrible! I think you were forced. What else would I think?"

"Do you think it's catching? Like people think your cancer is? Do you want to not be around me? Do I make you nervous? You got a million questions I won't like? Will it change things between us?"

"Trevor!"

"It was like your cancer, Dani. It was dirty and alien and I thought it would kill me. I hoped it would at times. Three months, Dani. I lived with the sewer-sucking sadistic slime that set up those pictures for three months. Because he was better than my witch of a mother who carved up the back of my leg with a steak knife. I left the dirt behind me when I met Jarrett Daniels. Or so I thought."

"Did that man rape you?"

"Fine line, Dani. Real close. Maybe he did. But I got my rape and my head scars at old Exit 31. Before you. Before Dad. But not by much."

"You never said."

Real temper flared up in Trevor now.

"Jesus Christ, Dani! How the hell could I? I was barely dealing with it myself. Like I said, Dad knows. Grammy knew, too. Mary doesn't. Not really. Now you do. And Margaret. Great. Just great."

"This hurts you, Trevor. What can I do?"

"Hug? Kiss? Tickle?"

"Don't be mean. You were never mean."

Trevor flashed fierce eyes at her.

"Will knowing all this help you fight the cancer?"

"I don't know!"

Trevor chewed his bottom lip, weighing the gains for Dani against the pain for himself.

143

"Okay. Grab us a couple of cans of Dr. Pepper, will ya? I'm putting on my shirt for this."

*     *     *     *     *

The next day, Trevor was back in the house on Wood Street, naked in Dani's bed again. She put her hands on her hips again and shook her head.

"Put your clothes on. You were always an easy lay."

Trevor grinned at her.

"Finest beef in a three-county area. I can't seem to even give it away to my nearest and dearest these days."

"Quit. Get up out of there before Margaret comes in and kicks your butt."

Trevor rolled out of the bed and began stuffing his legs into his jeans.

"As if."

"Want to wait and find out?"

"No. Come on down to the river with me, Dani. I've got a proposition for you."

*     *     *     *     *

Later that day, Trevor and Jarrett were alone in the house on Olympia Avenue. While Mary was out shopping again at S.S. Rainbow in Fisherman's Village, father and son were sitting on the old plaid couch. Jarrett took a sip of the Dr. Pepper he held.

"You're beatin' yourself up over somethin', boy. I can always tell."

"Margaret found the porn pictures Chris de Nunzio took of me on the Internet."

"And this effects you how?"

Trevor looked up and shook his head, chuckling.

"How do you do that? Nothing ever seems to surprise you. Nothing ever seems to shock you. You always make my disasters sound so ordinary or so trivial."

144

"Don't nothin' bother me much. I'm bothered that you're bothered. I thought you and I had this out when you was fifteen."

"We did. But I guess when the pictures didn't show up right away I began to think they never would. Just fooling myself, I guess."

"It's no more your fault now than it was then, Trevor."

"I guess I've got more to lose now."

"How you figure that? You ain't gonna lose the money."

"As if I cared."

"I thought not. You ain't gonna lose my love, or your aunt's love. You worried about Dani? What's Margaret got to say?"

"I don't know about Margaret. Dani told me she's okay with it, and she's got Margaret under control."

"Good for her."

Jarrett reached over and ran a hand up the back of Trevor's neck.

"If you follow through with this plan of yours you cooked up for Dani's benefit and volunteer your hair for Locks of Love, you're gonna be showin' a lot of scars, boy. Is that part of what's troublin' you now?"

Trevor leaned back into Jarrett's hand, enjoying as always the sensation of total love and acceptance. He felt his cares being eased away by this marvelous man who had become his father.

"They don't cut as much off as I'm planning on giving."

"That's my boy. Always goin' to extremes."

"Dad, when I'm telling it to you like this, it makes no sense. You always did have a way of making all my nightmares disappear. But I am worried. I'm just not sure why."

"Been takin' them Yankee-serious pills again?"

Jarrett dropped into the old joke between them and Trevor leaned into him. Jarrett leaned back.

145

"I'm not tryin' to belittle your fears, Trevor. God knows it could get ugly. The drug scandal should have taught you somethin'. Your friends will be your friends anyway. Your enemies will still be your enemies. I guess I can figure who you'd worry about the most, past me and your aunt and Dani."

Trevor looked up at his father.

"Yeah. My fans. You know how I feel about responsibility."

"I know it ticks you off that football players get away with drugs and violence and still get to be role models. I'm sure it ticks you off that you're still considered a decent role model. But you weren't at the age of consent when those pictures were taken and you can not take responsibility for what happened."

"Sure, I can. No one put a gun to my head. You think I want any of my fans, let alone the young ones, seeing those pictures?"

Jarrett shook his head.

"Trevor, you and I are gonna be wrestlin' over this guilt thing of yours for a while longer, I guess. We ain't seen eye to eye on the definition of choices yet. Dani tell you where to find these pictures?"

"Yeah. I got the address."

"You looked them up yet?"

"No."

"Well, then, let's go see what we're talkin' about."

Jarrett moved to get up and Trevor stopped him.

"I don't want you looking at those pictures. I don't want Mary seeing them."

"Trevor, I've got to know what we're dealin' with here. And so do you. I want to see if my Yankee is makin' a mountain out of a mole hill."

Jarrett finished standing up and ambled his way back into the master bedroom where Mary had long ago set up Command Central for Jarrett's, hers, and Trevor's various business interests. He started booting up the computer and could hear when Trevor's footsteps ceased at the open door.

146

"Come on in and sit on the bed, Trevor. You got that address handy?"

Trevor came into the room, reaching into his front jeans pocket. He brought out the slip of notebook paper Dani had given him.

"Yeah. I do. Here you go."

"Club Cock Tail?"

"Perfect, huh?"

"We'll see what we've got first. Hm. Gotta pay to get in there, Trevor. What the heck's Margaret been up to in there?"

"I couldn't tell you."

"Well, no way I'm payin' to see your butt, boy. Best give Dani a call."

Jarrett shut down the computer again and handed Trevor the cordless phone.

"Just have her print the darned things off, Trev."

"I don't want Dani seeing them."

"Hell, Trevor, Margaret's seen them. Right? Can you think of anythin' worse than that?"

With Jarrett's deadpan eyes on him, Trevor cracked up, glad to release some of the tension he felt. He was still laughing weakly when he got Dani on the phone to make his request and wiping his eyes when he hung up.

"Dani says she'll do it and walk them over to us. I can't believe you can get me to laugh about this."

Trevor was still chuckling and relaxing when Jarrett played his trump card.

"Why'd you do them pictures, Trevor? You say no one put a gun to your head, but I say they did. I have never known you not to regret them pictures. So what made you do it?"

Trevor sobered, the misery seeping back into his eyes.

"I wanted him to want me."

Trevor passed a hand over his face.

147

"No. That's not quite right. I wanted him to love me. I thought if I did what he wanted, he'd love me. I got into more than I bargained for."

"And less", Jarrett added. "Well, then, there's your story. There's your song. You did it so someone would love you. You got cheated because you didn't get the love. It wasn't a fair deal. Your fans can relate to unrequited love. They can relate to regret. You're too darned hard on yourself with that twenty-twenty hindsight, Trevor. Can't none of us have twenty-twenty hindsight."

Dani brought over the pictures, walking briskly through the balmy night air of the quiet streets to climb the steps of the Daniels house on Olympia Avenue. She had wandered freely in and out of there with both the Daniels boys all through their teens and early twenties and still felt she could simply knock and walk in. She did so now.

Trevor, who had been on the lookout for her, met her at the open back door. Dani solemnly handed him the brown clasp envelope of pictures printed on glossy photo paper from the Club Cock Tail site. She kissed his cheek and smiled slightly at him.

"You were a cute little boy."

Trevor winced.

"Thanks, Dani. Good thoughts. Catch ya later."

"'Night, Bro."

Trevor watched her stride off, the ends of her scarf lifting like hair in the darkening night. He closed the screen door and came back in to Jarrett with the envelope.

There were sixteen pictures.

Trevor frowned as he spread the photos out on the low coffee table in front of the couch and he and Jarrett sat down.

"I swear I remember more being taken."

"Probably a lot of duplicates. Or the photographer messed some up. Whatever."

"Yeah. These are enough, all right."

"Just like you described back when, son. Sit. Stand. Lay down. Show your butt. Darn, you were little."

"If it weren't for the hair."

"I know. I'm tryin' to hold it in, son. But I guess you know what I'd like to do to these men if they stood before me today."

"Yeah. Thanks. They're not all here, Dad. There were more pictures."

"Doesn't matter. It's enough. My poor, little, tiny defenseless baby bird."

"Aw, Dad. Don't."

"Look at them little fingers, Trev. Look at them thin arms and that narrow chest. This is a crime past horrible."

"It was a long time ago, Dad. Help me with damage control."

"For scars on your soul? Love. My love. You've always had my love. For yourself? The shrink. Tell the shrink."

"No. I mean for the fans."

"I done told you. That's the plan I'd stick to. Not your fault. Forced or coerced. Did it for love and got cheated. Pick one. No one is ever gonna lay the blame for these pictures on that tiny little boy, Trevor. It wasn't his fault. You're too close to this emotionally. Johnny Blackburn. You remember him?"

Trevor looked up from the glossy photos spread obscenely across the coffee table and tried to shift gears.

"J.J. Blackburn? High school track? Yeah. What about him?"

"He's got a little boy."

"Yeah. Jimmy. Cute kid. What about it?"

"Jimmy's twelve years old now."

"Wôw. When did that happen?"

"If these pictures were of Jimmy Blackburn, would you lay the blame on little Jimmy?"

"No! Of course not. He'd have to have been abducted or ran off or something. J.J. would never permit this or have a hand in it. Nor Melanie, either. My God. No."

"There you go. Not the fault of any little boy in pictures like this. Am I gettin' through to you yet, son?"

149

"Yeah. You are. Too close? I guess. Looking at all this, it takes me back to that cold, drafty warehouse. See that picture?"

"Yeah. 'Birth of Venus.'"

"What?"

"It looks like Botticelli's paintin' of Venus standin' on a shell, hair all flowin' around her. I remember seein' that one at the Uffizi Gallery in Florence–Italy, not South Carolina–when we was over there with Mary. I always liked that picture."

"Whatever. That's the one where I was so cold I was using my hair around me to keep warm. I've never been so cold in my life. Not even sleeping outside in the snow. This was much, much worse."

"Shock. Fear. Shame. And a darned big cold drafty building, just like you described to me back when. I sure hope that Chris fella and the photographer at least got a head cold out of the deal."

Trevor chuckled.

"No such luck. At least not for Chris. He was fine. The photographer? Who knows?"

Trevor bit his lip and looked up to Jarrett from scanning the photos.

"Mary can't see these, Dad. I don't want Mary to see any of this."

"That's a mistake, boy. A lie is always a mistake."

"I know it's a knee-jerk reaction. I guess I want to protect her from this."

Jarrett laid a hand on Trevor's shoulder.

"It's glossy pictures of the past, Trevor. She's already got two tons of the good ones. You're the flesh and blood, right here."

"Just go along with it, okay?"

"It's your secret, boy. Not mine. I'm just sayin'."

"Let's cover all this up. Get it all back in the envelope. Mary'll be back soon from S.S. Rainbow. You got anything stronger than Dr. Pepper in the house? Brandy would be good."

"I got Rock and Rye for colds."

"That'll do fine."

Trevor began sliding the photos together as Jarrett got out a Slurpee cup and poured two inches of Rock and Rye into it for Trevor. Trevor took the cup, smiling at the design. It had Michael Jordan on it. He looked at Jarrett over the rim of the cup as he took his first sip of the potent liquor.

"Why hasn't Chris de Nunzio been blackmailing me?"

"Too stupid? Sold those pictures about the time they were taken to turn a quick buck? Got nothing to sell? Don't follow country music? Don't know it's you, even if he does follow it. You don't look like that little boy no more."

"I've still got the hair. And my name's still Trevor."

"Can't figure out how to reach you?"

"Through the label."

"He might be dead. He'd have been dead if I'd have found him."

Trevor smiled.

"That's a wonderfully warm and cheerful thought. Thank you for that thought, Dad."

"I can't think of any humanitarian reason he hasn't tried to cash in."

Trevor took another sip of the Rock and Rye.

"It's like waiting for the other shoe to fall."

"Only if you let it be. Go on with your life, Trevor. You did before."

"I was young and dumb."

"You still are young and dumb."

Trevor grinned.

"Thanks, Dad."

"You're welcome, son. What would Grammy tell you to do?"

Trevor's eyes softened.

"She'd tell me to lighten up. And to be thankful to God for the beautiful day right here and right now."

"There you go."

Later that night, Mary snuggled into Jarrett in their big, shared bed. Soft moonlight and breezes flowed in the open windows along with the muted hush of traffic from Olympia Avenue.

"Jarrett, what are we going to do about this?"

"'Bout what?"

"Don't be an ignorant ape. Trevor's pictures, of course. He left the brown clasp envelope of them where he knew I'd find it."

"Mary, honey, what I'd like to do and what it's maybe smart to do are very, very different things. What I'd like to do is go back a couple of decades and murder your sister. And then I'd like very much to painfully harm both this Chris fella and the photographer. I'd like to wipe out the past for Trevor so's he'd never have to have suffered it, and never have to suffer the consequences now or ever again. But I can't do that."

Jarrett cuddled Mary closer to him.

"What I'm gonna do, and so are you, is be there for Trevor. Like we would be anyway. I'm thinkin' this will all blow over. Them pictures don't look a whole lot like Trevor now."

"He was so young. It was horrible."

"It was. Trevor knows they're there. And Dani and Margaret. Now you and me. But there ain't a lot of pictures of Trevor from when he was young. You've got the lot, I'd guess. Your sister never took any. My family's got some from later, but they ain't givin' them up. High school year book, maybe. But the scared and skinny kid in them pictures looks a whole lot different from the well-built smiling young man in them yearbook pictures. I'm bettin' on no trouble."

"I'd sue their asses off!"

"Whose? This Chris fella's? The photographer's?"

"That web-site."

"They just bought product, Mary. From a provider with all the proper releases and proofs of age, I'd guess."

"It stated he was eighteen. He looked eight."

152

"Doesn't matter. All that legal stuff would do is stir the pot and draw more attention, Mary. No help for Trevor that way. We're tryin' for less publicity on this one, honey, not more."

"How could they do such a thing? He was so little. And frightened. You could see he was frightened."

"God will get those men, Mary. I just know it."

"I'd like to help God out a little."

"Well, yes, so would I. It'd be a real temptation to me if they ever crossed my path. But that won't help the situation here."

Jarrett gave Mary an extra hug.

"Trevor'll be right mortified to have you know about them pictures. He's that ashamed."

"The taking of those pictures was not his fault. As I say, he left them where he knew I'd find them. Maybe subconsciously. I couldn't help but peek."

"He and I have done been over that guilt thing, Mary. I just can't seem to get through to him. He just keeps blamin' himself."

"What an idiot."

"I done told him that, too."

Mary made a movement as if to get up.

"I'll go talk to him."

"Not tonight, you won't. Remember, you ain't even supposed to have seen them pictures. Leave the boy be. Good enough for me he's stayin' in the house with us tonight and Dani was the one to break the news to him. That's two blessin's right there. I don't want him runnin' off to Sarasota sayin' he's fine till I know he's had at least one good night's sleep in his own bed in his own home surrounded by love. I done seen him tryin' to shoulder too much too young all by himself before."

"Will he stay? He came down initially to help Dani with her chemo."

"I don't know. He's a man now and street-legal to make his own choices. When he was a little boy, he had no one to turn to in trouble, so he never got in the habit of it.

153

I'm hopin' I've taught him he can turn to me. To us. But that's his choice for real now."

"I could just choke Lisa."

"Yeah. Me, too. Gimme a kiss, honey. Then shut up and let's get some sleep."

\*        \*        \*        \*        \*

Jarrett had gotten Scott down to Punta Gorda from Sarasota. If you struck at one Daniels, you struck at them all. Mary was out shopping at John's Pennywise Books. Trevor was off with Dani to a chemotherapy treatment. Jarrett knew they'd have the house to themselves. He faced his older son, hands on hips.

"You don't know a darned thing about your brother's past, do you?"

"No, sir."

"You ever ask him?"

"No, sir."

"Why not?"

"It didn't matter once I figured out he wasn't no threat to me. I just took him where I found him."

Jarrett ran a hand through his short hair.

"You weren't even curious?"

"Not after about the first two times we met. Trevor's Trevor. That's all I needed to know."

"Amazin'."

Scott's posture relaxed. This wasn't going to be the dressing-down for nebulous errors he had feared when he had gotten his father's call.

"What is he? An axe murderer? He'd cut his own foot off."

"His pictures are on a porn site on the Internet."

Scott burst out laughing.

"That little rascal!"

"He was twelve years old."

The light went out of Scott's face.

"Daddy."

154

"Yeah. Before I met him. Now we got trouble comin', maybe, and no fault of Trevor's. He was just a little boy. He had no choice."

Jarrett had begun pacing in agitated circles. Scott reached out a hand to stop his father and Jarrett looked up to his eldest son.

"There's your answer, Daddy. He was just a little boy with no choice in the matter. Simple. End of problem."

Jarrett smiled slowly.

"That's just what I told Trevor, but part of me thought it was a Yankee snow-job. You're brilliant, Scott. Brilliant. Thank you, son."

"You're welcome, Daddy. Somebody back then did this to my baby brother?"

"Yep. A long time ago, Scott. Trevor's been livin' with the knowledge of them pictures out there somewhere for years. He couldn't do a thing about them. Nor could I. Nor can we now. It's just there."

"Where can I see these things?"

"I can give you the web-site, but I've got printed copies of the pictures on photo paper. I've got them in the armoire in the bedroom now. It about makes me bleed inside to see them."

"I gotta see 'em, Daddy."

Jarrett nodded. Scott followed his father back towards Jarrett and Mary's bedroom, but waited in the doorway while Jarrett got out the brown clasp envelope from the huge armoire. He had never felt comfortable stepping through the doorway of this room and into the purple-flowered space where his father and second wife spent their intimate times.

Jarrett handed him the envelope silently and Scott opened it. He could easily recognize his younger brother, hair and all, his big eyes looking into the camera like a deer caught in the headlights.

Scott quietly and slowly studied each and every picture, noting details. In none of them did he see the spark that so characterized his brother. None of the vitality or drive or energy or hope or spirits. He ran through the photos twice slowly and came back to one. He ran his thumb over the glossy surface of the photo near the face of the little boy and quirked a smile.

Trevor was standing and facing forward, his long, dark hair almost to his knees, his feet bare, his face solemn. His right hand was across his breast, shielding his thin pale chest. His left was covering his genitals. His hair was pulled around his shoulders and body as though it had been a dark cloak against the cold.

Scott slid the other photos back into the envelope and closed it. He held this one up.

"I'd put this one on the cover of the new CD he's been workin' on. The one with all the lullabies."

Jarrett looked over Scott's shoulder. He remembered Trevor telling him years ago the details of this exact shot— about how cold the warehouse had been and how he'd used his hair to warm himself. Of all the photos, this one had no nudity.

But it had power.

"Perfect. We'll do it."

## Chapter Nine

Back on tour again–this time headed for Biloxi, Mississippi–Trevor was noodling on his guitar absently, one leg propped up on the kitchenette seat in the tour bus, leaning back into the angle formed by the back cushions and the armrest. Scenery raced by unnoticed in the rumbling vacuum of the bus as Jesse drove.

Scott sat down at the table opposite Trevor and began to play absently with the pencil he found there. Ignoring Trevor's notes on lyrics and the melody he had been working on, Scott began to doodle on Trevor's lined tablet in the shape of a Mustang GT.

"I done seen your pictures from off the Internet."

Trevor's hands stilled. The guitar went silent. Trevor closed his eyes and blew out a breath.

"Well. It doesn't get much better than this."

"Why didn't you ever tell me anythin' about your past?"

Trevor shrugged.

"Why didn't you ask?"

"I didn't hardly know you."

"I didn't know you."

Scott detailed a fender.

"After that, it didn't hardly matter."

"There you go, Bro."

"It don't hardly matter now, either, moron."

Trevor's lips twitched.

"I should know better than to play chess with you."

"You should."

Trevor opened his eyes and laid Blondie down on the seat beside him.

"What do you want to know?"

Scott concentrated on drawing a door.

"I don't want to know nothin'."

"Why'd you bring it up?"

"Daddy's worried."

"Swell."

"Not about the porn. We got that covered."

Trevor lifted an eyebrow.

"You do? How?"

Scott sniffed.

"Chess. Your 'Birth of Venus' photo'll be on the cover of your lullaby CD."

Trevor's eyes warmed.

"Sweet."

"I thought so. It looked like that baby could have used a good lullaby about then."

"Yeah."

Trevor thought back to those years on his own and bit down on his lip hard.

"What about Dad?"

Scott used the side of the pencil he held to shade in the body of the car he was drawing.

"He's worried that the leader is lost. Likened you to Moses in the desert, wanderin'. He figures you've lost sight of the mission somehow."

"What mission?"

"Hard to tell, Trev. It's your mission. What is your mission? Have you lost track?"

Trevor sat back in the seat.

"I don't know. I wanted my music to be played by really famous people. I wanted it to make a difference in peoples' lives. Blues for when you're blue. Hope for when you're down. Comfort. Joy. All the good stuff."

Scott sketched in some trees behind the Mustang.

"That new CD is gonna be beautiful, Trev. Them lullabies. Babies all over the world is gonna benefit. But there ain't a darned cut on that CD that's original. Not one."

"I always wanted to put out a CD with the old lullabies on it. That was a separate mission."

"All right. I didn't know that."

"Sorry."

"It's okay. I don't need to know stuff like that. And I guess you got what you wanted. The Trevor Daniels Band is famous, and God knows it plays your music."

Trevor rubbed his forehead.

"Mary said once that playing for her was like digging ditches."

"I know it."

"I guess she meant monotonous as well as hard work. Are we in a rut, Bro?"

"I don't know. Are we? It's your mission."

"I think we are then. I'm bored. Hell, you're bored and you don't even sing the darned stuff."

Scott flowed some road under the Mustang's wheels.

"Hard for the band to work up any enthusiasm when the leader can't."

Trevor sighed.

"You got any ideas, Bro?"

"Quit."

"Can't."

"Can't or won't?"

"A little of both. When I've got the music coming up in me, I can't quit. It just takes me over and rides me hard."

Scott rubbed the shading of the car with his thumb to blend it.

"You hit a dry spell?"

"Yep."

"How about the 'won't'?"

Trevor shifted restlessly.

"I'm not free here. I'm tied in. I've got responsibilities. Lots of them."

"When did this happen?"

"It was there all along, Scott. I guess it just never bothered me when I was younger."

Scott chuckled.

"Younger? I'm almost two years older than you are. I lust after cars that are older than the two of us put together."

It was Trevor's turn to chuckle.

"Yeah. Isn't that something?"

"What would you do to change it, Trev? What would make it fun again? What would make it fresh?"

Trevor slumped in the seat.

"Inspiration."

Scott finished his doodle of the Mustang GT and began filling in around it with more trees and bushes and added a fence line.

"I remember when I couldn't wait to leave Arcadia. Now I can't wait to get off this darned tour bus. If I see one more Cracker Barrel Restaurant, I may have to kill somethin'."

Trevor nodded.

"What's Dad's suggestion?"

"I don't know that he's got one. I guess that would depend on whether or not you've lost track of the mission."

Trevor sighed.

"Well, I think we can assume the mission is at least out of control. I've got the fame. I've got the music out there. I sound bored even to myself when I say that."

"Where do you want the mission to go?"

"Oh, I don't know. About now, straight to hell sounds good to me."

Scott gave the deep chuckle Trevor loved to hear. It reminded him so much of their father and that father's love. Trevor smiled to himself.

"Back to the basics, I guess. Back home. I always like to go back home."

"What's the story with that little boy in them porn shots, Trevor?"

Trevor rubbed his forehead again.

"Dad didn't tell you?"

"No, sir."

"I've got an ex-mother out there somewhere, Scott. A certified witch who's still breathing the same air I do, as far as I know. Those photos are the result of a young boy raising himself on the streets of New York City. I don't think I want to go that far back for my basics."

Scott added some flames to the side of the Mustang GT he'd drawn.

"I can tell that talkin' about your mom and all that back then don't make you bored."

"It makes me edgy and hostile, Scott. I don't want to go there."

"I don't remember any of your music bein' quite strong enough for edgy and hostile, Trev."

"I wrote that kind of music before I met Dad. Even some of it as I got to know him. It's ugly, mean stuff, Bro."

"Got any with you?"

"Sure. It's kinda like American Express. I don't leave home without it."

Trevor picked up Blondie and swung through a driving series of chords, dark and powerful.

"Rusty barbed wire
Tearin' up my brain.
I don't know how to stop it.
It's drivin' me insane."

Trevor stopped. He silenced Blondie and laid her back down on the seat beside him. Scott raised his eyebrows.

"Trev, that ain't country. That's rock."

"I know it."

"Ain't nothin' wrong with it, Trev. It just ain't country."

Trevor frowned.

"How did I get to be country anyway?"

Scott shrugged.

"Labels. Markets. Positionin'."

"I'm a Yankee."

"Not no more, you're not."

"When did this happen?"

Scott looked up, grinning.

"Darn, Trevor. We done assimulated you while you weren't even lookin'."

"I guess."

"Daddy's country. I'm country. Your whole darned band is country, ya moron. 'Cause you done recruited it in Punta Gorda, Florida, to start with."

"Aunt Mary is not country. Jake is not country. Darn it, I'm not country."

"You are now."

Scott looked up at Trevor again, still grinning.

"Where do you want to be? Who do you want to be?"

Trevor spread a smile at his brother.

"You are a sneaky, chess-playing, hide-my-brains weasel."

"Yep."

"All right then. I want to be Trevor Daniels, musical innovator and risk-taker. I want it to be virtually impossible to put a label on my product. I want women to weep when they hear my songs and men to nod their heads in agreement. I want power and flash and I want to be remembered long after I'm dead and in my grave."

"Yes."

"Write that down. Here. Give me that pencil, dammit. I gotta write that down. Real quick before I forget it."

Trevor was scribbling madly on the back of the paper Scott had been using for his doodling.

"You know what it is, Trevor?"

"No. What?"

"Ya done got to be a fat cat. I'm mellow. Daddy's mellow. Buddy done been mellow for years. You done got mellow, boy. Can't write good stuff if you're all mellow."

"Mellow's good," Trevor replied, still scribbling down his mission statement.

Scott shook his head.

"Nope. Grateful is good. Happy is good. Mellow is just sit on your butt and do nothin'."

Trevor finished his scribbling and tossed down the pencil, energy flowing through him.

"Yes. Good. I got it."

Scott laid a hand on Trevor's arm and looked him in the eye.

"Trevor?"

"Yeah?"

"Write about the little boy in those pictures. I want to know about the little boy in those pictures. I gotta know. You can help me feel the right way about that little boy. He was cold and scared. I want better for that little boy. I want to

162

know how he got there. I want to know what happened to him next. Tell me the story about the little boy, Guitar-Man."

Trevor blinked, his eyes big. He nodded.

Scott got up from the table.

"You want a Dr. Pepper?"

Trevor shook his head, his thoughts turning inward. Scott looked down at him.

"Can I tell Daddy you're kinda all right?"

Trevor nodded. He closed his eyes and leaned his head back against the cushions, letting his mind tumble back down the years to what he thought of as the before-time.

Before Jarrett Daniels.

\*    \*    \*    \*    \*

"Get him off me! Get him off me!"

Trevor, sweating and flailing around, fought the arms that held him.

"Trev. It's me. Scott. Take it easy."

Trevor's eyes flew open and he looked up into the concerned eyes of his brother. Scott gave him a little shake.

"Who do you want me to get off you?"

Trevor saw compassion there, and blurted out his answer before his mind could think twice about it.

"Chris."

"Who the heck's Chris?"

Trevor came more fully awake. He sat slowly up as Scott released him and glanced beyond them to be sure the door to the driver's area of the tour bus was closed. He didn't need Jesse Tweak hearing any of this, he thought.

Trevor shook himself.

"Oh. The guy behind the porn shots. The guy I lived with."

"Darn, Trevor. I sure would like to have him here. It'd be a pleasure to pull him off you and administer a little do-unto-you justice to him. Preferably with somethin' big with a lot of spikes on it pointin' the wrong way when it came out."

163

Trevor smiled and relaxed back against his pillows.

"That's what I like to hear. Really creative violence. Thanks, Bro."

"Daddy know about this?"

"He's known about Chris. That's where I got Blondie."

Trevor licked dry lips, watching his brother's face as he released each piece of information.

"Dad knows I traded sex with Chris for Blondie. He knows I stayed with Chris for three months and that Chris arranged the porn shots. He knows Chris participated in some of them."

Scott hadn't responded to any of the short, blunt statements. Sensing no disapproval from his brother, Trevor shifted his weight and divulged another piece of information.

"Scott, there's a video out there somewhere of Chris and me. Maybe a lot of them from different camera angles that same day. Even I don't know what's on them. They haven't turned up yet. Dad knows that much."

"What is it that Daddy doesn't know?"

Trevor gave his brother the last packet of information.

"He doesn't know Chris raped me."

Scott gave Trevor an exasperated look.

"Hell, Trevor, anyone lookin' at that little boy in them still photos could tell he was victimized. He don't look happy in any of those pictures."

"I told Dad I didn't like it, what Chris was doing to me. What he was making, no, having me do. I never told Dad it went from having to making."

"I'm bettin' he guessed, Trev."

"I told Dad I stayed to get Blondie. That was the deal, for true. Stay three months and I'd have Blondie. I told Dad I stayed to get Blondie. But the truth is I'd have been out of there the minute Chris finished with me the very first time..."

Scott leaned forward.

"Except that?"

Trevor gave Scott a rueful grin.

"Darn. You are so much like Dad."

Then Trevor sobered.

"I told Dad I stayed to get Blondie, but the truth is I stayed because I was too chicken to leave. I was too chicken to be on my own. With Chris, I had food and a bed. He never shared me with his friends. He could have. He could have done anything he wanted. He did sexually. What I just now woke up screaming? I used to scream that in my head. *'Get him off me, get him off me'*."

Trevor hugged himself.

"I was praying, I guess. Praying to God, or to my real dad in my head, or anyone I thought would listen."

Trevor looked up at Scott.

"I never did screamed it out loud, Bro. I only screamed it in my head, so it didn't count. When the three months were up, Chris gave me Blondie, twenty bucks, my red Swiss Army knife, and a handful of condoms. He gave me my camo backpack and he gave me my freedom."

Trevor sighed.

"Scott, part of me didn't want that freedom. I didn't want the sex with Chris. But I was scared to be on my own. I still am."

Scott shifted his weight on the bed.

"So, the truth at last. An abused little boy is scared to be on his own. Daddy told me all this happened before you was fifteen years old."

"I wasn't quite twelve. I made myself older in the story to Dad. I was always making myself older than I was. Heck, I told Dad I was eighteen when we met."

"No way he was believin' that. The bars still card you."

"I was chicken. When Chris gave me Blondie, I suddenly had no choice. Not really. I could hardly beg him to not throw me out. Part of me sincerely wanted out of there and away from him. I was scared. I was scared to stay. I was scared to go. I like being safe. I like feeling safe. I really, really like safe. Suddenly I was back out on the streets. With a very expensive, desirable guitar that might get me mugged

165

to death in the next three blocks. And twenty dollars in my pocket that felt like it was two million in gold bullion. I could feel it in my pocket, throbbing. I figured everybody could see that I had it and that'd get me mugged to death in two blocks. I was scared shitless."

Trevor shook himself.

"I had my backpack Chris had given me for doing the porn shots and all that. God only knows what I did in the video to earn that backpack as a bonus. He and the photographer had drugged me, so I don't know to this day what went on there. But I was stiff and sore for two days after I woke up."

Scott shook his head.

"Darn, weasel."

"Yeah. Suddenly, I was out of a home and out of a job. Blondie was almost as big as I was. Looking back as an adult now, I realize Chris probably thought I'd beg him to stay. Or maybe come back to him. Maybe he even had someone set up to rob me and get Blondie back. I don't know. I did my best defense back then. I ran. I was always good at running. Real fast on those short legs. I was what Dad calls all fed-up good. I was strong and healthy and tough. Blondie doesn't weigh much."

Trevor shifted again, looking reluctantly back into the past.

"After Chris closed the door behind me, I stood rooted on the front steps about three heartbeats, my backpack on my shoulders and Blondie gripped tight in my right hand. Then I lit out running, full speed, flying down the middle of the street to avoid anyone lurking behind parked cars or around the corners of buildings. I just ran and ran and ran. I didn't get tired–I was too wired–and if my legs cramped up, I never noticed. I was running for my life from everything I could imagine in my head, and my imagination's always been pretty good."

Trevor laughed suddenly and glanced at Scott.

"Did you know a human being can run an average of twelve to fifteen miles per hour? I think I did better than twenty-three miles per hour on day one of my freedom."

Scott sniffed.

"We should have got you to go out for track. I never thought of that."

"Swim team was out."

"Yeah, you still look goofy when you swim. Like some drowned rat scramblin' to find a piece of wood to crawl up on."

Trevor chuckled.

"I think the smartest thing I did that first day–after I quit running–was to buy a map of the city. That also broke up the twenty dollar bill into smaller bills. I put a five in the bottom of each of my socks, inside my sneakers. I put a five in my right pocket. I put the ones in my left. I put the change in my hip pocket. I didn't have a wallet. I figured I might have to ditch the backpack if I got in trouble so none of the money went in there. I folded open the map and figured out where I was. And then I figured out where I wanted to be. I just started walking to get there."

"Where'd you pick to be?"

"Out. Out of the city. I had this dream of being out in the country surrounded by trees and grass and stuff. I was gonna walk till I got to the country."

"Darn, Trev. You really was one dumb little kid, wasn't ya?"

"Yep. Scott, hand me back my tablet and pencil, will you? I've got work-product ready to spill out of me now."

While Trevor began scribbling on the tablet, Scott got up and made himself a cup of coffee with the on-board coffee-maker and then sat quietly down to watch his brother's efforts. When Trevor threw down the pencil, Scott took that for tacit permission to pick up Trevor's most recent work-product and read it.

# SCREAM IN PAIN

Ask the nice man please to feed you.
Hope to God he doesn't beat you.
Breathe a tiny bit more freely with the dawn.

Do you like that, little boy?
Slam me, slam me.
You're my tiny little toy.
Slam me, slam me.

Candy man has come to call.
Oh, yeah. Oh, yeah.
When you're short, the world is tall.
Oh, yeah. Oh, yeah.
I can hold you by one arm.
I can make you come to harm.
I don't have to be discreet.
I'll just knock you off your feet.
And if you want to run,
I'll just laugh and have my fun.
You'll be staying here for more.
You have no choice.

I can shove you in the dirt.
Oh, yeah. Oh, yeah.
I can make your body hurt.
Oh, yeah. Oh, yeah.
I can make your belly bleed.
I can make you eat my seed.
They'll never hear you cry.
You'll never see the sky.
Gagging in your throat,
You'll never have much hope
Of living out the next year of your life.

Scott looked up, stunned.

"Jesus Christ, Trev."

"It was an ugly time, Bro."

"I guess. Daddy knows about this?"

"Yeah."

"Jesus Christ."

"I couldn't tell you about this, Scott. Mary doesn't know about this. Not really."

"Understood. Are you okay?"

"Scott, it's been years. It's over."

"No, it's not, Trev. It's right here, right now. I can feel it in my own body. I can see it in my head. Wow."

"Yeah."

"I think you got it back, Trev. I ain't bored."

Scott shuddered and stood up again.

"'Scream in Pain', huh? Geez. It gave me the willies just readin' it. I gotta go shake it off some. Get yourself a Dr. Pepper and take a break, Trev. You've earned it."

Scott took a break, sipping his coffee and pacing in the narrow confines of the bus, but Trevor didn't. He picked up his pencil and tablet again. Scott watched him over the rim of his coffee cup. Trevor finished his second effort and silently handed it to Scott, who took it to read.


<u>LULLABY</u>

Lullaby and sleep tight.
Strangers feel you in the night.
Guardian angels 'round your bed
Have dark faces. Cover up your head.
Doors won't open.
Closets are dark.
Nylon cording
Leaves no mark.
If I should die before I wake,
I hope I have a soul to take.

Scott blew out a breath, trying to distance himself from the horror.

"I don't know about how marketable that one is, Trev."

"Doesn't matter."

Scott laid the tablet on the table between them as he sat down again.

"I think this could work with some of Jake's rock music behind it."

"Whatever."

"You got some scary stuff inside you, Trev. You got some Stephen King stuff in there."

"It's not make-believe, Scottie."

"I know. Didn't you have normal nothin' ever?"

Trevor glimmered a smile.

"After meeting Dad, I did."

"You got any more secrets, little brother?"

Trevor rubbed a hand over his forehead.

"Scott, I've got secrets I don't even remember I've got. Lousy stuff from that time on the road. Lousy stuff from Chris. I've kept it so long, it just leaks out once in a while in the music. Or when I'm asleep. I'm remembering stuff now I truly had forgotten about."

"Just as well, I'd guess. Daddy ever ask you where to find this Chris fella?"

Trevor looked up, puzzled.

"No. It was done with over a year or more before I met Dad. He had other stuff to worry about. Me, for starters. Why?"

"Well, ya know, I got me a low-grade urge to go up to New York City and get that slime-ball."

Trevor brightened.

"We could start from my former-mom's last-known address. I might be able to figure it out from there. Or from Darryl's grandfather's place."

Trevor looked up at his brother, his sudden burst of energy dipping.

170

"If I could remember where Darryl's grandfather's place was."

Trevor's face clouded over.

"Scott, I don't know where it was. I never knew the address. Chris picked me up from Ben's place and drove me to his place. I didn't pay any attention. I got out of the car and we went inside. Three months later, I came out. And ran."

"You was inside that place for three months? No comin' out to go nowhere? No comin' out to play? Nothin'?"

"Nothing. I stayed inside. That was the deal. No one was to know I was in there. When Chris was out, I just sat on the floor. No looking out windows. No going outside. No having anyone in. Nothing."

"Geez, Trevor."

"I'd forgotten that, Scott. I really had. No wonder I got depressed. Heck, I was just a kid. I've always needed to run around. I needed to play. I missed my friends. Darryl. I missed Ben."

"No school? No food shoppin'? Nothin'?"

"Nothing, Scott. Walls, food, and one bed. I sure as heck never slept safe in it."

"He was cruel to that little boy, Trevor. Past havin' his sex on you, he was cruel."

"I knew that about the sex, even then. Until just this red-hot moment, it never occurred to me how cruel he was to just seal off a young boy from the entire outside world."

Scott warmed to his project.

"We could go up there to New York City, find his sorry carcass, bring him on down here in my old Ford van, just you and me with him tied up in the back with a blindfold on. Take him out Bermont Road. Way out towards Palmdale. Stake him out naked on top of a big old pile of fire ants. Let him just scream and twist and suffer. Leave him out there with the blindfold off. Let him get toasted up in the sun. Let him get all thirsty. Let him watch the buzzards flappin' around him and pacin' up and down, waitin' for him to die. Go on out there with a case of cold beer and watch him, and

171

smile, and drink. Drink deep. Get shit-faced. Piss on him. Let him lick up your piss for liquid if he's thirsty enough."

Trevor leaned into Scott, smiling. Scott was already smiling. Both brothers had a warm, faraway look on their faces. Trevor sighed.

"That's just so beautiful, Scott."

"I'm tellin' ya. It could happen. It'd be my pleasure. The next time a bad memory from this Chris sneaks up on you, just bop it on the nose with that pretty little vision of revenge. I'm tellin' ya. This is doable. Got ways and means, opportunity and motive. Plant that sumbitch out the back of Uncle Richard's orange groves and nobody'd ever be the wiser. This dude can't have too many people care if he goes missin', I'd guess."

"Maybe Dad did that. Not the ant pile. But I know he hired detectives to go up there to the old neighborhood, looking for my former-mom. Maybe he asked them to ask around about Chris. As an adult now, I remember Chris' place was real stripped down. Maybe it wasn't even his real home, where he lived. Maybe he just kept me there. Maybe Chris wasn't even his real name. I wonder about all that now. I never thought of that before, either. Maybe Chris is already in the back of Uncle Richard's orange groves. That's a nice thought."

"Either way, Trev. Then or now is good."

*    *    *    *    *

## BLESSINGS

Most people count
The blessings you'd think of.
I do that most of the time.
But now and again
I sit down to count
The blessings of what might have been.

Thank you, dear Lord,
For that time down in Houston.
A cowboy made fun of my hair.
I lost my temper and stomped on his instep.
He laughed like he didn't care.
He picked me up by the scruff of my neck,
All his friends were standing around.
He shook me real good like a dog shakes a rabbit,
Said, "Listen up, boy, don't you get in the habit
Of messin' with folks too big for you to take down."
He laughed in my face, set me down on the floor.
His buddies and him slowly walked out the door.
I said, "Thank you, Lord,
For the lesson of humility."

Thank you, dear Lord,
For that time in Atlanta
I got two bucks and got robbed.
Crouched on the sidewalk, feeling rotten,
I nursed my head and I sobbed.
But I picked up my guitar and started to play,
And pretty soon grief and pain faded away.
Thank you, dear Lord,
For the gift and the comfort of song.

Thank you, dear Lord,
For the times I've been hungry.
I'm feeling full now today.
If not for the beatings and fear in the night
I'd never have learned how to pray.
The hard things in life
Are the things that can form us.
They make us or break us in time.
For the blessing of hardship, I lift my head.
I thank God above I'm alive.


Thank you, dear Lord, for the blessing of sadness.

I really know how to smile.
Thank you, dear Lord, for the blessing of drought.
I'll run in the rain by the mile.
Sickness and madness, depression and anger
All have their part in the play.
Thank you, dear Lord,
For the curses you send us.
It's getting better each day.

Most people count
The blessings you'd think of.
I do that most of the time.
But now and again
I sit down to count
The blessings of what might have been.
The hard things in life
Are the things that can form us.
They make or break us in time.
For the blessing of hardship, I lift my head.
I thank God above I'm alive.

\*     \*     \*     \*     \*

The bus, the band, and the brothers were back off
tour again. Jarrett drove up to Longboat Key, checking up on
his youngest son in person. Trevor opened the door at his
knock. He had on a white T-shirt, chopped off inexpertly by
scissors to stop just short of his abdomen. It had Magically
Delicious emblazoned across the chest in bright green. His
faded and frayed jeans were out at the knees and slung low
over his narrow hips. A gold loop pierced the skin of his
navel, lying against his smooth skin. Jarrett frowned at him.
"Jesus Christ, boy. What next?"
"What?"
"You're a darned belly dancer now."
"Oh. That."
 Trevor grinned.
"Chicks love it."

"Will they love it when it gets caught in their hair?"

"Apparently so. Come on in."

"It looks good on you, boy. 'Magically Delicious'?"

"Truth in advertising."

"You sure are somethin'."

"I swear this is the best I've felt since the summer you and Grammy fed me up on meat and grease. The shrink helps, too. Eating good. Eating right. Running. I'd slacked off on that. Big mistake. I dusted off the rollerblades. If it's good enough for Punta Gorda, it's good enough for Longboat Key."

"You got to have outgrown them things by now."

"True. Bigfoot's got nothing on me. Lucky I'm rich. Size thirteen is a bear to find and costs the earth when you do. I've been trying to get some use out of the pool, but I still swim like a drowned rat."

"Can't have it all, boy. Music?"

"Flowing and in the groove. Words. Music. Energy. It just ticks me off about myself that I lose the center so easily. And so often."

"You never had a center. Got it late in life, so to speak. You're still practicin'. You about got it now, I think. I hope."

"Me, too."

Trevor led his father out onto the back deck.

"Carla's up in Virginia, packing up stuff to move down here permanently. That was one whirlwind courtship my brother had. I can't believe he's married."

"Two weeks this Saturday."

"He comes over here and hangs out like a dying puppy. Scott Junior's up in Virginia with Carla, meeting cousins and stuff, I guess. A married man. Wow. He and Carla just clicked. Awesome."

"When it's right, it's right."

"Not for Shawn Lane. Not for you the first time. Heck, not for Scott the first time. What's with that?"

175

"Hormones. Stupidity. You name it. Some folks get it right the first time. Grammy and my Daddy. Richard. Fred. Myrline. Cass."

"Forgot. It just seemed so all of a sudden to me. Well, speaking of happily married people, and we were, Steph's on my case to mingle socially up here again. Of course, her idea of social is black tie in The Ice Palace, not a flannel shirt down at the Dew Drop Inn. For all her marketing, you'd think she'd know this isn't my core crowd."

"She does. She's wooin' butterflies for Trevor Lane Daniels, composer, Trev. You clean up good. Got them perfect manners from Mary's side of the family. No sense wooin' the bass in your live well. Fish for the snook out in the water."

"Got it. Makes sense. Well, she's got one on deck for tonight. I hope I don't die of boredom. Or from second-hand cigarette smoke."

* * * * *

Trevor looked out over the crowd of frantically undulating, intensely chic people dancing to the vanilla-disco music being played by a disc jockey of his cousin Stephanie's choosing. They reminded him suddenly of one of his Trevor Daniels concert audiences–faceless, moving humanity. Except he could orchestrate the behavior of a Trevor Daniels audience. It was focused on him as master of his production. He couldn't orchestrate these people who had come to meet Trevor Lane Daniels, composer. He found he didn't care to. They were laughing carefully and flirting with one another. Suggesting and dealing. They were seeming to have fun.

Were they having fun? Trevor wondered. Did they know what fun was?

Trevor slipped quietly out through the sliding glass doors.

It was quieter on the deck and darker, but there were still people here, sitting around the pool, drinking or passing joints. And other drugs. Men were glassy-eyed. Women, heavily made-up, were waxen beneath their make-up. He felt lonely, and dirty, and an outsider to something he no longer wished to be a part of.

He moved unnoticed past the group on the deck and down the dark steps to the sand.

Here, finally, the air was clean and the noise of music and voices was a distant buzz. He sat on the bottom step and took off his dress shoes and black socks. He stuffed the socks into his shoes, tied the laces of the shoes together. He pulled off his black bow tie, stuffed it in a pocket of his tux pants and unbuttoned the black studs of his tux shirt. It was easier to wear his tux jacket than to carry it, so he kept it on for now. He dug his toes into the sand, enjoying the sensation of warmth on the top and coolness underneath. This was closer to living than he'd been in the last few hours, he thought.

Trevor pulled his hair back out of his way, braiding it over his shoulder and wrapping the covered rubber band he always wore on his wrist around the end. The darned hair was getting to be a nuisance these days, he thought, requiring constant maintenance and care. It was hot. It was heavy. Some mornings he woke up with it wound around his neck like a noose. He was tired of it. He'd worn it pretty much the same way for darned near his whole life, he thought.

He remembered some of the first words Jarrett Daniels had said to him. *"Hey, boy. You need a haircut."* Trevor's lips twitched in a smile now as they had then.

He thought about all the hair he'd seen tonight. Women in curls and twists, moussed and lacquered into piles and ringlets. He tried to see them in his mind's eye as bald mannequins. He found he had no problem at all with that image. Half the men were bald anyway. No stretch there.

He thought of Jarrett's short hair. And he thought of Dani with her pathetic wisps falling out by the handfuls. Dani was facing her future without two of the items that

177

traditionally announced a female of the human species–her breasts and her hair. She'd still be a woman. She'd still be Dani. But she seemed to him now to be so defenseless. He thought of his birth mother, wearing her hair in a French twist to give her added height and elegance. He thought of Mary's mop of short, loose curls.

He wondered now why he kept his hair long. And why he had kept it long for such a length of time. Why had he ever had long hair to begin with? He tried to think back to the before-time. When had his hair begun to grow long? When had Lisa either permitted its growth or encouraged it? Why had she permitted it or encouraged it? Clearly, long hair had made him look more like his birth father. Why would Lisa have wanted that? What sick image had she been trying to superimpose on her baby? She hated his father. Long hair had made him look more like that father.

He remembered his Grammy's hands in his hair, combing the strands with her arthritic fingers. His lips twitched in another smile at the pleasant memory and his scalp remembered the sensation of love that had flowed from her hands as well. He remembered Jarrett washing the dirt and debris of his homeless existence from his hair in the hospital when he was fifteen and he felt his shoulders relaxing from a coiled tension he hadn't realized was there. Jarrett dampening and combing and cleaning his hair had been the most comforting sensation he had ever felt in his whole life.

It still was.

Having the hands of those he loved and who loved him in his hair had brought deep comfort to him. The memory, a sensory memory, still did.

He remembered pulling his hair around him for warmth and comfort in the vast cold warehouse while he waited for the endless instructions on how to position his naked young body for the photographer.

Over the years, his hair had brought him comfort. And a measure of protection. It had been his shield at times. Jarrett had claimed its thickness had saved his life the night the Spath boys had struck the back of his head with a short length of rusted rebar.

Comfort and protection.

He stood up from the steps with his shoes and began to wander slowly down to the water, admiring the reflected lights on the water, lifting his head to view the stars, several nebulous plans revolving slowly in his brain.

He wondered if Mary's hair stylist, Yvonne of Ya Ya Hair Hut in Port Charlotte, would know how to contact Locks of Love. If not his organization could find out. He wondered if Millie Crawford, now living in a retirement center in Port Charlotte, had any interest in selling her old house on Gill Street in Punta Gorda. A philanthropic organization hiding under the Daniels family umbrella had been maintaining her cats there for years. He figured Buddy might not mind a move into the house of his origins, and surely some dumb Yankee moving too slow would be thrilled to rent or purchase The Ice Palace, home of Trevor Lane Daniels and former home of Shawn Lane.

He figured he and Scott could bring up a U-Haul for the recliner and the wall photo, hitch the MG to the back of Scott's van and do the move to Punta Gorda in one day.

*  *  *  *  *

Trevor turned up on Jarrett's doorstep the next morning, still in his tux. Jarrett opened the screen door to let him in, seemingly unsurprised to have a son who lived in Sarasota climbing his steps in Punta Gorda.

"Mary's pickin' up some goodies at John's Pennywise Books. What's up?"

"I'm getting a haircut.

"What?"

"Yep. On National TV. Locks of Love. Big blowout for Dani. Free haircut for me. And I'm moving back to Punta Gorda."

"What? Not into this house, you're not."

"Nope. Into Millie Crawford's old place. Cats and all. Buddy'll love that. A whole harem of fine-looking feline females. Good sex has always been very important to Buddy. I've been busy on my cell phone."

Jarrett grabbed him into a bear hug, beaming.

"Welcome home, son."

Trevor hugged his father back, wriggling like a puppy, laughing and light-hearted.

"It's good to be coming home, Dad."

"Why the sudden decision to cut your hair?"

"Well, not so sudden. The timing just seemed so perfect, you know. Dani needed it. I wanted rid of it. Perfectly happy ending. I finally found a good reason to cut my hair. And I'm tired of looking like a girl."

"You ain't looked like a girl since you was sixteen."

"Well, then I'm tired of looking like a girlie-boy."

\* \* \* \* \*

Mary was flipping through the pages of a specialty catalog of rare and hard-to-find musical instruments she had downloaded from the Internet.

"I thought you said Trevor never asked for anything? This dulcimer he has me shopping for seems pricey enough."

Jarrett took her hand and ran his thumb over her knuckles.

"You think that's for him? Nah, that's for the music. He'll ask for the music. We got a real good drill goin' with that, 'cause he knows I'll never deny the music in him anythin'. He's proud of the music in him and he'll feed it anythin' it wants day or night. That's part of how those darned porn pictures came into bein'. He did it to get Blondie. And he'll ask for Buddy. Or for Blondie. Or for Dani. He'll ask for just about anybody or anythin' except himself. He will not ask for himself. You gotta guess. You ask him right now if there's anythin' he wants he'll look at you with a bland face and tell you he's fine."

"Well, maybe he is."

180

"He's a grown man, Mary. And he's movin' back home by choice. He's lonely and he's scared. He needs his family and he needs them closer than fifty miles up the interstate. That's a powerful lot of need in a grown man, Mary. The drugs and the liquor have never claimed him though he's had his chances. I dread the day we're not here for him."

"We'll always be here for him!"

"Not when we're dead, sugar. He no way reacted enough when Grammy died. He tucked it away. He ain't dealt with it. Not even in the music. He just won't risk the double whammy of needin' help for himself and havin' a cry for help rejected. He knows he can come to me. I'm always there when he lets it go too far. He just can't bring himself to ask before it does go too far."

Jarrett looked at their joined hands.

"He knows he's blessed by the love we three have for one another. But he's hollow inside, Mary. I can't figure a way to help him fill himself up. He needs to love himself."

## Chapter Ten

Trevor stood in the high hallway of Millie Crawford's old home on Gill Street, now his.

The light was fabulous in this house, he thought. He'd never noticed that before when he'd been in the big dark library with Millie Crawford and had his papers and projects spread across the huge library table there. Thick brocade curtains with fringed edges and braided and tasseled cords had held back the light.

The first thing Trevor had done when the sale was final was to rip down every curtain in the house, letting an explosion of light inside. The second thing had been to have the windows washed and then fully tinted with solar film out of deference to the feelings of the resident felines. His next step had shattered the nerves of the cats again. Millie having expressed no desire for the contents of her house, Trevor had had those items in which he had no interest appraised, shipped to auction and the proceeds put in trust for Millie. The house now devoid of furniture to hide behind and under, the cats temporarily moved into the lush tropical vegetation of the big yard, eating their meals after dark, when the workmen Trevor had hired had gone home.

He had gotten an army of various building contractors in, most of whom he'd gone to high school with, to upgrade plumbing and air conditioning, to repair and replace trim both inside and out, to re-roof with the newest in durable metal roofing, and to paint the big clapboard edifice a sunny yellow with white and blue trim. A salute to both his high school colors and those of his college alma mater as well, it was also a burst of joy from his heart. He loved to see the color yellow.

It found its way inside in various shades, warming the big, high-ceiling rooms. Crisp white trim sprang out in classic detail, and Trevor had the hardwood floors stripped, sanded, stained and resealed. He slung a hammer alongside men he hadn't seen since high school and loved every minute of it, from spackle in his hair to paint on his skin, to skinned knuckles, a black and blue finger from a misjudged blow with the hammer, to a red and peeling back from too much sun up on his own roof, working, guzzling beer and having the breeze off the Peace River fill his lungs and clear his senses.

Using Jane Wanroy of Careywood Design Group's landscape architectural renderings, Mary and Carla and some of the members of the Punta Gorda Garden Club had restored and replanted his wildly neglected yard. Under the umbrella of his general contractor's license, his brother Scott helped him with dry wall inside, yelling at him to stay out from underfoot. Jarrett helped him, working with him on paper concerning sight lines for rooms he wanted to combine and other areas he wanted to partition off. They built models of their plans with Legos.

He learned everything he never wanted to know about home ownership and periodic maintenance. He found his housekeeper from Sarasota had no desire whatsoever to work in Punta Gorda, let alone move there, at any price. He went Shopping Charlotte First as the Chamber of Commerce exhorted, and wound up with Jake Benson's mother as his new housekeeper, which worked out fine for both of them. He didn't have to have strangers in his house and Angie Benson didn't have to deal with a snooty employer who treated her like the hired help she was.

Trevor still drew the line at mowing his own grass and kept a succession of middle-school boys and girls in spending money until hard work killed off their initial greed. Mr. Daniels was fun, so the rumor went, but he was no pushover. If you wanted to make money, you worked for it. Smoke, drink, dope or have a bad attitude and you were off the payroll.

Trevor continued to live in The Ice Palace while the work on his home on Gill Street went forward. Buddy continued to be the main resident there as Trevor was still going out on tour. The touring became marginally better for him because he could dream about coming home to his new home and its projects and his renewed life, rather than just a sleep-over at The Ice Palace and the continuation of the soulless business of business in the limelight. His core people knew about his Punta Gorda project–Scott, Dani, Jake–but no one else and certainly not the media. This was to be his nest, his private pride and joy. When he was off-tour and working on his nest, he stayed with Mary and Jarrett in his old room in the house on Olympia Avenue, but it was clear to all of them that his heart had moved at last to another location.

### EVERYTHING AROUND ME IS MY HOME

Out my bedroom window I can see
All God's glory shining in on me.
Golden sunlight warms my face.
This is such a blessed place.
Everything around me is my home.

When we met I never realized
Just how much I hoped to see the sky.
In your smiling face I see
Everything I'll ever need.
Everything around me is my home.

When it's dark we sit together close.
That's the time I feel I need you most.
You put your arms around me.
You're my everything.
Everything around me is my home.

\*     \*     \*     \*     \*

Trevor, never one to let a good idea die, pestered Scott about the gym idea again. They settled on Gold's Gym for their needs and went to check out the one in Schoolhouse Square in Charlotte Harbor.

Gold's Gym, when they got there, was everything Trevor had hoped for. Self-absorbed young men and women were working out wordlessly to rock music or having minimal conversations with their workout partners. Sweat, metal, treadmills and anonymity. No one had even glanced at the door as they had entered in jeans and T-shirts, carrying Walmart gym bags. Trevor turned glowing eyes to Scott, who frowned him down.

"Okay. So far, so good. But try not to attract too much attention. Ya got a real problem with that."

Trevor nodded and began to step to the counter. Scott casually blocked his way and addressed the girl behind the cash register/computer.

"Two memberships. One month. Scott Turner and TD Buck. I'm Scott. That's TD. We're payin' cash."

"I still have to take your photographs, and you'll still need to sign paperwork."

"Of course we will. Can't get nothin' done no more without paperwork. Point the way to the paperwork, girl."

Somewhat bewildered by Scott's hostile attitude, she handed over two clipboards full of forms and two pens.

"I'm Melissa. Your trainer will be Rick."

"Oh, no, he won't. Here, TD, you start on that form."

"Rick has to show you how to use the machines. It's policy. There are safety issues."

"Okay. I'll buy that. But he ain't gonna be doin' no trainin'."

"Very well. But you have to take the tour and the instruction on whichever machines you're going to use."

"Done. You finished, TD? Good. Let's see this stuff."

Scott leafed through and scanned the several sheets, hastily checking off items and signing at X's. He took Trevor's clipboard from him and handed the girl the two clipboards and two pens, pulling his wallet out of his hip pocket.

"How much?"

Melissa told him and Scott forked it over.

"Bring on your Rick. Let's get this show on the road."

"You can change in the dressing rooms and come back out. They're right over there. I'll see if Rick's available."

"Swell."

Scott pointed his chin towards the changing rooms and Trevor headed that way. Scott followed, studying the crowd for recognition or interest of any kind. So far, so good, he thought.

In the changing rooms, Trevor found an open locker, and began simultaneously stripping off his clothes and shoes and adding and subtracting items from his gym bag, meanwhile sticking it into the locker. He beamed at Scott.

"Bro, you're brilliant. Fake names."

"Hope they don't ask for no ID with cash. Still gonna have our pictures took. And I should have thought to bring locks. Darn."

"No sweat. Buy them here. They've got them. I saw. This is going to be sweet."

"We'll see."

"You know, with you going all macho and doing all the talking, they're going to think we're a pair of fags working out together."

"Let 'em think it. Beats out the truth. And it'll keep both sexes off the both of us so you can have your leisure time."

"I sure won't meet many real people here."

"Can't have it all, TD. Can't have it both ways. Get yourself buffed up and ripped here. Go find somewhere else to meet real people. The beauty of this so far for me is no one hardly wants to meet no one here at all."

They both took the tour, bought locks for their lockers and had their photos taken. Scott looked like an axe murderer. Trevor, his hair severely scrapped back into a ponytail, looked like a con artist.

"Sweet."

"Hit the treadmill, rat boy."

186

"Ferrets. They were ferrets."

"Whatever. I'll take the one to your right. Hey. TV. Cool."

Trevor hit the treadmill with enthusiasm, punching buttons and changing speeds and incline levels on the machine. He set it to a fast jog and pounded along happily, glad to not be getting winded from lung congestion. Scott eased his more substantial bulk up from a walk to a slow jog. Trevor's ponytail was flying behind him and he was grinning. Scott reached out and punched him in the upper arm.

"What?"

"Put a lid on it, TD. Try for a lower profile."

"Oh. Okay. Forgot. Sorry."

"Huh."

"This is cool. I like this. I could do this for hours."

"We'll see."

Trevor certainly did his recommended half-hour warm-up on the treadmill with no problems, Scott thought. He was still going strong, a light sheen of sweat on his narrow body, as he hopped off the treadmill, still full of energy.

"Cool. What's next?"

"You tell me. You got the same tour I did, courtesy of Rick. You got your choices now, in any order you want them."

"God, Scott. You are so much like Dad. You have no idea."

"Watch your mouth, TD."

"Oh. Sorry. Forgot."

"As if."

"Bite me."

"Later."

Trevor considered the original question.

"I've got good arms. I've got good enough legs, I guess. Waist is good."

"Oh, please."

"You should talk. But I guess my chest is a little puny."

"It always was, TD."

"Well, we're looking for improvement here. That's the only flaw I can see in the overall perfection."

"You worry me sometimes."

"I worry you all the time."

"There is that. Bench press? This oughta be priceless. I'll bet Stephie could spot for you."

"I might surprise you. Yeah. That sounds good."

Trevor was a weenie, Scott thought, as they worked their way around the gym. But he was a determined and wiry one. He was tenacious.

Over the weeks that followed, both in Sarasota, and then Tampa, Lakeland, Winter Haven, Gainesville, Jacksonville, and on up and around the state on what the brothers thought of as the little tour, Trevor kept up with his plan for locating a Gold's Gym and setting aside an hour and a half to get there, get back to the bus, and still have a concentrated hour of physicality. He kept up with his plan for basketball as well, scheduling time-outs at pre-located rest areas where the whole entourage turned out to either play or cheer.

The band loosened up and intermingled more with the roadies. Carla, Dani and Margaret sat outside and sunned themselves on webbed folding chairs, drinking glasses of iced tea and listening to rock music on a portable radio. Dani was taking a break from chemotherapy. It was like a relaxed day at the beach—on asphalt.

The brothers did manage to meet what Trevor called real people. At the Gold's Gym in Miami, between a two day show booking, Trevor was sailing away on an already increased second set of bench presses and Scott was routinely spotting him, thinking that it was time to seriously bump up the weight on Trevor if he was sailing through a second set so easily. As always, his peripheral vision was aware of movement and he tensed.

The guy stood perfectly still, not interrupting the workout. Trevor finished, parked the weight back and sat up, grinning. Scott gave him a warning look and Trevor quickly put a lid on it. The man behind Scott shifted.

"You need a spotter? You gonna lift?"

Scott turned. The man stood with arms crossed and a weight belt on. Scott straightened, instinctively shielding any possible prying eyes from a closer look at Trevor.

"I wouldn't mind. And, yeah, I'd appreciate a spot."

"You can't get a decent spot from your buddy there. I'd like to lift some heavy weight myself, but I can't do it without a decent spotter, either."

"You got a deal. TD? Go play on the lat machine."

"Okay."

*    *    *    *    *

Trevor hopped around the changing room afterwards, hugely tickled.

"Scottie's got a boyfriend."

"Shut up."

"It's sweet."

"We're liftin' buddies."

"Does he want you?"

"To lift, yes."

Trevor made a crude gesture.

"Oooh, lift this, big boy."

"I'll be liftin' you in a minute."

"Is this guy straight?"

"I dunno. I suppose. It ain't come up in conversation, Trev."

"Well, I'm glad some things haven't come up, so to speak. Do you think he wants it nicely fluffed?"

"Quit."

"Seriously. No hitting on you?"

"No. Or I done missed it. Same thing."

"Not necessarily. But if you're cool, I'm cool."

"I'm cool, Trev. The guy's right. To lift really heavy weights, he and I both need spotters. It's common courtesy to ask or offer. No big deal. I wasn't offerin' or askin' 'cause I was with you. In the beginnin', I felt you needed a spotter. Now you don't. If you get to where you're liftin' more weight, you'll need a spotter again. Just pick any guy who looks like he wouldn't mind. Let me rephrase that."

"I got it."

"I miss the lure of the iron, Trev. I never realized how much I missed it. I lost track. I'm glad you had this wild-haired scheme about the gym. I'm havin' fun. This guy's okay. It's strictly business. Heck, I don't even know his name. It never came up. Don't start with the jokes."

"Wouldn't think of it. So, I guess if you don't know his name, you couldn't possibly know what he does for a living or if he's employed at all. Right?"

"Right. What of it?"

"Well, you can only lift heavy weights in Miami as it stands at the moment."

"And?"

"If he's unemployed, offer him a job if you think he'll fit in."

"Oh. Okay. We'll see."

"Think fast, big guy. We're outta the Miami-Dade area in two more days and on to Lauderdale."

"That's close enough to commute."

"Oooh. This relationship is serious."

"Quit. I'll see what I can see. We can always use more muscle on the security team. You ain't been hit in the head with a room key or a beer bottle yet but it could happen any day."

*     *     *     *     *

And, of course, it did.

In Fort Lauderdale.

A tiny box with a pink ribbon around it was lobbed from the heaving crowd of fans standing on the floor of the hall, hitting Trevor harmlessly on the chest, but making him briefly skip a beat before it slid down over Blondie and dropped to the floor at his feet. Manny, Scott's newly hired lifting-buddy, dove for it and covered it with his body, his military training crossing wires with his passion for old movies with bad plots.

Bomb, he thought, and lept to the rescue.

Trevor and the band played on. The rest of the security team scrambled, but couldn't identify the perp. Manny got up off the floor, carrying the pink-beribboned box in the palm of his hand, and exited, stage left, to take it to Scott for inspection. Scott rattled it, shook his head and slid it into his shirt pocket, forgotten as harmless.

But Scott knew it could have been worse.

There was virtually no way to protect Trevor on stage. For a wonder, he'd never had death threats or any riots at or before his concerts. He wasn't all that controversial a figure. But Scott began to think now in terms of security scans at entrances.

Manny had turned out to be an ex-Army, ex-police, ex-auto mechanic, ex-weight trainer, unemployed all-around good guy. Not married, not involved, and not gay, his worst vice, because of his intense concern for his body and its health, was a weakness for pizza. He was also an ex-cook, and filled in another gap in Trevor's plans for a healthier lifestyle.

Now it was the three of them huddled over the small box tied with pink ribbon as it sat on the kitchenette table of the tour bus and Jesse drove them on to Immokalee, where Trevor had a gig at the Seminole Gaming Palace. Manny handed around plates with rubber bottoms he had acquired from a marine supply store. They didn't slide on the table the way paper, plastic or china did. And they contained freshly cooked edible food that was also healthy. Baked fish, steamed carrots and rice pilaf. Even Scott wasn't sneering.

Trevor began to wolf his meal down while he held the plate, his pesky hair tied back in a rawhide cord that had belonged to his first father.

"What is it? It didn't hurt me when it hit. Just surprised the heck out of me. I lost a beat or two there."

Scott leaned over him.

"I don't think the fans noticed, Trev."

"I'll bet they noticed Manny diving for it. Thanks for the effort, Manny. It was great."

Manny blushed.

"I got carried away."

"Well, at least I didn't get carried off. Scott?"

"More security, darn it. Wands at all the entrances, I guess. Well, if you ever do run for public office, Trev, we'll know how to handle it. Geez."

Trevor picked up the box, abandoning for the moment his dinner fork.

"Too light for a room key, and why wrap it?"

Scott leered at him.

"Engagement ring? It's the right sort of box."

"How romantic."

Scott snorted.

"You are so sick. Open it up, Trev. If it's any good, we'll hock it."

Trevor set down his dinner plate. Scott whipped out his penknife and slit the pink ribbon, poking at the box with the knife because for some reason the pink ribbon irritated him. Trevor waved the knife away.

"Quit. Or open it yourself."

"It was meant for you, sweetheart."

"Please."

Trevor took the box in his long fingers and pulled the two halves of it apart. A folded note fell out. Trevor shrugged.

"Too small for a check. Wrong color. Checks aren't solid white."

Trevor picked up the note and unfolded it quietly, smoothing the barely two by three slip of paper.

"'Call me or you will suffer'. Whoa. Some fan. Phone number's from Florida, isn't it? 786 is one of our area codes. Right?"

192

Scott frowned.

"Semi-local to south of Miami, Trev. Lot of territory there. Lot of people. Creepy. Stupid, too. Easy enough to get the name and address for this number. I take that message as a threat, don't you, Manny?"

"I sure do. Library or Internet?"

"Your idea. You run with it."

"Me? Why me? I just got here."

Scott threw an arm around Manny's shoulders.

"Manny, old buddy, old friend, it don't take long to float to the top in the Trevor Daniels organization. We believe in lettin' people's creativity flow."

Trevor grinned at the big man's astonished face.

"Yeah, Manny. Never volunteer for anything in this family. It's easy to get hosed."

Manny got up from the table, his dinner forgotten. He got out a Ziploc bag and a pair of kitchen tongs he'd brought with him in the box of his belongings. He picked the box, the ribbon and the note up successively with the tongs, dropping them into the Ziploc bag while the brothers watched, and then he blushed.

"I watch too much TV, I guess."

Trevor hastened to reassure him.

"No. Good idea. I'm sure Dad would say something about preservation of evidence."

Scott glanced at his brother.

"Much good it does now you've pawed it with your fingers, Trev."

"Whatever. Dad?"

"Yeah. We better. Ten to one Manny's on the eleven o'clock news with that dive across stage."

"I give it an eight."

"I give it a ten. Don't do it again, Manny. Next time let the little weasel blow up. He's the target, not you."

"Well, thanks, Bro."

"You're welcome, weasel."

"I. R. Baboon."

"You are that."

It was Jarrett and Scott seated at the kitchen table in the house on Olympia Avenue back in Punta Gorda on yet another brilliant, sunny day. The Seminole Gaming Palace in Immokalee had been the last stop on the little tour and Jesse had driven them all back the night before, leaving the tour bus out at the Charlotte County Airport with the Lear jet. Trevor was in his old bedroom, catching up on his sleep. Mary was out in Englewood at a newly discovered bookstore on Placida Road called McBooks.

Jarrett leaned back in his chair, eyeing his oldest son.

"New ballerina on tour with you, son?"

"Liked that, did ya, Daddy?"

"And the occasion?"

"Nebulous threat to Trevor. We've got it handled. Got a phone number. Got a name. Got an address."

"Don't do anythin' stupid."

"Not gonna, Daddy. Not without you anyway."

"That's my boys. I try to keep both of you safe, Scottie. I want two sons. You understand?"

"Yes, sir. I do. Love you, Daddy."

"Love you, too, Scottie. Christopher de Nunzio, 213 SW Monroe St, Big Pine Key, FL. Tsk, tsk, tsk. Who'd have thunk it?"

"Is that who I think it is, Daddy?"

"Well, if it's not, the man was surely born under an unlucky star. Named Chris De Nunzio. And livin' in the Keys. And an idiot. Whether or not it is, he's in deep doodoo. Trevor ain't the President of the United States, but there's certainly laws against threatenin' people. Trevor knows what you've found out?"

"No, sir. I thought I'd run it past you first. Force of habit, really. Trevor's a grown man. This is his business."

"It's family business. You strike at one Daniels, you get us all up in your face."

"Have you seen Trev since we got back off the little tour? No? You're gonna like what you see, Daddy. I think your little boy done finally growed up."

It was true.

As with any project he committed to, Trevor had followed through to the extremes between Gold's Gym and Manny's healthy cooking. He was more rounded now than angular. More muscle than bone and sinew. He had filled out his baggy large tops and moved on to extra large ones. His neck had gone from size sixteen to size seventeen. Even his jeans had gotten shorter again somehow, though that may have been thigh muscle taking up the available space and raising the hems.

Since his teens, Trevor hadn't actually been scrawny. But now he was certainly very healthy and he looked it, acted it and moved it. A latent gentleness to his features now had hard muscle beneath it as well. He benched two hundred fifty pounds adequately, if not joyfully. It would never be his life-long love, as it was Scott's. But he could suffer the process to get the desired results.

After waking up, Trevor joined the conference at the kitchen table. Jarrett eyed the glowing face across the old kitchen table from him as he slid Trevor a glass of orange juice.

"Christopher de Nunzio. Ring any bells?"

"No. Should it? Wait till Mary meets Manny. I think they'll click."

"Florida Keys?"

"In my pocket. Old bad joke. What about them?"

"Threats to your career? Or to yourself?"

"Oh. That. Well, it wasn't really much of anything. Didn't mention career."

"Suffer. That was the word, wasn't it, Trevor? Suffer?"

"Yeah. So?"

"Are you bein' intentionally dense or is all this really not sinkin' in?"

"What?"

"Trevor. Listen to me. Chris. Key West. Suffer. Anythin' clickin' in there yet?"

Trevor set his juice down.

"All right. So?"

"We have to get to the bottom of this, son."

Trevor dropped the charm.

"Is he going to expose me? Who cares? How? With what? He's the one who committed the crimes. Not me. Blackmail? Yeah, probably. He ain't gettin' squat. Threaten my life? Whatever. Threaten my family? I'll kill him with my bare hands and piss on his grave."

Jarrett fixed his eyes on first one and then the other of his sons.

"When you call that phone number you found, this Chris fella talks and you listen. You don't talk much. If this is who we think it is, I don't want any backwash from this slime findin' either of you. I want check valves in place against this man's evil ever reachin' any of our loved ones. Do it all close to his home. Not here. Nothin' face to face until the very end. Set it all up in a room with no windows. You boys got that?"

Trevor nodded..

"Got it."

"You and Scott. Leave everybody else out of it. Especially Manny. He's new."

Trevor protested.

"Manny's cool. Manny got us the address and name."

"Manny stays out of it. This is family business. Got it?"

"Yes, sir."

"Good. Welcome home, son. You look good, by the way."

"Thanks, Dad. I feel good. This guy's nothing. He's a bogeyman to a kid. I'm not a kid anymore."

"That video tape is still out there, Trevor."

Trevor now dropped the act of careless unconcern he had hoped would fool his father.

"I want to nail this son-of-a-bitch low-life. The full force of the law."

"That would be messy, Trevor. A lot of your past would come out. What doesn't come out, any halfway talented attorney he hires will insinuate or even make up.

196

How you managed to stay alive for the year or more before we met will come out. There are consequences, son."

"I want him to pay. Fucking pedophile. Fucking sadist."

Jarrett studied the unaccustomed fierceness on Trevor's face.

"Been a lot of years. No witnesses left to that, I'm guessin'."

Trevor looked up, arrested.

"Witnesses? No. I guess old Ben is dead, God rest his soul. Darryl? Who knows? And he wouldn't be any help. He was just a kid himself. He was never a witness to anything Chris did. Nor was Ben."

"Your word against his, Trevor."

Trevor slammed his hands onto the table. Even Scott jumped.

"I'm the witness. God help me, I can describe that man's naked body down to each mole and birthmark. I knew his body for three months at a distance of not more than a half an inch, tops. All of his body. I want revenge."

Jarrett looked up into the stormy eyes of his youngest son. He had rarely seen this particular emotion in him. Anguish, yes. Pain and grief, yes. Fear? Years of fear he'd seen in those luminous gray eyes. But not this cold, bitter, harsh determination.

"Do you want revenge or do you want justice?"

"I want payback. I want suffering. And fear. A lot of fear. I want separation. I want sensory deprivation. Isolation. Dependency and horror. I want what he gave me."

"We need to know more about him, Trevor. We have a way to contact him. He can't be very bright."

"Greed makes you stupid."

"There is that. Do you remember anythin' about what he did for a livin'? If you can't remember or never knew, it's all right."

Trevor frowned, his mind searching the past.

"I thought Ben told me he was a musician, but I can't be sure. I may have equated a man having a guitar to sell with being a musician. Guitar was all he played with me. Looking back, I don't think he played it well enough to make a living at it. Of course, he may have been holding back. No reason to wow a twelve-year-old."

"Twelve? I thought you was fourteen."

"Uh. No. I was twelve. Maybe."

"Good God, boy. Bad enough when I thought you was fourteen. Much worse knowin' that all went on when you was so much younger."

"Sorry. I got used to bumping up my age. Old habit."

"Trevor, do you remember the Spath boys?"

"That's not a funny joke, Dad."

"It wasn't meant to be. Do you want revenge or do you want justice?"

"Do I want a trial for sexual molestation for this man? Or one for murder for myself? I'm older now, Dad. I'm far more aware of the consequences. A trial with this weasel won't hurt me the way the same thing coming out would have hurt me at fifteen. And he doesn't live in Punta Gorda. Punta Gorda people would be behind me all the way."

"Back when, this man sent you to the Keys. He lives in the Keys. You and me and Mary and Scott ain't never gone scuba divin' in the Keys, have we?"

"Dad, what you're hinting at is risky business. I don't want my revenge or my justice enough to risk my family for either one."

"Well, then, son, let's just lure him out and see what he thinks he's got. Maybe all you need to do is to look him in the eye after all these years. Go face to face with him. Maybe he's just a little boy's monster in a box with a loose lid. Needs to be dealt with, and the lid nailed down. You know my preferences."

Trevor leaned away from the table, rocking back in his chair, the heat fading from his eyes to be replaced by simple warmth.

"Scott seems to have a similar preference, Dad. He and I discussed ways and means before Chris ever showed up on the radar screens."

Jarrett smiled at both his sons.

"And left your dear old Daddy out of your plans. Selfish little boys. You all didn't want to share."

Trevor brought his chair back onto all fours.

"I agree with you, Dad. Let's see what he's got. I can't believe how stupid this guy is. But I sure have seen how hungry can make you stupid."

Trevor shook his head.

"The way this year's been going, I half expect to hear Scott's mom is suing you for bigamy or Lisa has come back to claim me as her own. Geez."

"He could have that video, son."

"Doesn't matter, Dad. I've moved on."

"Even if all we get is one copy of that video, we'll have to watch it, son. At the very least you'll have to watch it. Ignorance is not bliss. Ignorance is dangerous."

"I know. I also know it's not going be three boys frolicking in a waterfall in Brazil. I wish. It's going be ugly, hard and cruel. Even if we get one copy, we'll never find them all. All the knock-offs. God knows how many over the years. I'll be twelve years old forever in some pervert's video collection. But they won't have Trevor Daniels, Dad. They'll have that poor little boy, Trevor Lane. If anyone even remembers him. When I cut off this hair–and the day is fast approaching–it'll be very difficult to link the then with the now. I wish I could save that little boy. I have, to a certain extent, with your help and the shrink's. Now I'd like to be sure that there won't have to be any other little boys out there in the future."

Jarrett locked his eyes with Trevor's.

"There are always little boys, Trevor. And men, no, monsters like Chris."

"But maybe one less monster, Dad."

"Be very, very careful, son. I want two baby boys safe and sound. Not just one."

It was pathetically easy in the long run to lure the monster out of his box, the brothers found.

As the sun streaked red going down, they borrowed a used car scheduled for demolition from their Uncle Fred's car dealership in Arcadia and drove to the Miami-Dade area. They rented, for one night, a hotel room in a decidedly non-tourist area of town, then sat together on the one sagging bed, yellowed curtains closing off the darkness outside.

Trevor dialed the phone number provided in the note using the sticky, old black phone that squatted on the cigarette-scarred nightstand.

When the call went through, Trevor announced himself.

"Trevor here."

"Suffer? You want to suffer? I'll put that dog collar around your neck again. You'll pant. You'll beg. You'll lick my boots."

Easily able to hear the voice on the other end himself, Scott watched while uncertainty and fear crept over his brother's face. He watched Trevor's posture begin to slump.

Silently he took the phone from Trevor's grasp and laid it at a distance from both of them on the bed

When it seemed the sick monologue was at an end, Scott picked up the phone, listened to some heavy breathing for a moment, and then hung up. There was a pause while both brothers looked at one another and Trevor licked his lips nervously.

"I didn't handle that well, Scott. This is harder to do than I thought it would be. I should call back. I need to resolve this."

"I'm bettin' he'll call back, Trev. All he's got to do is *69. He's the one contacted you. He wants this."

The phone rang again and Scott watched Trevor flinch. Scott calmly picked up the receiver and put it to his own ear.

"Don't hang up on me, you dirty little sack of shit. You'll suffer if you do. I'll choke you with your own hair. Do you want that video? I've got it. Come and get it. Three million dollars, rich bitch. You can afford it. You owe me. I took you in"

This time Scott hung up and watched Trevor's expressive face.

The phone rang again and Scott picked it up to hear a now testy voice in his ear.

"Stop doing that. You'll never get what you want. Three million. End of Duval Street. Ten o'clock tomorrow night."

"No," Scott whispered forcefully into the receiver.

"What? Of course you'll be there, you silly little twink! I'll ruin you!"

Scott whispered again, trying hard to mimic Trevor's lighter voice tones.

"The tiki hut bar. Best Western. Big Pine Key. Same date and time."

"Oh, whatever. Come alone. Cash money!"

And Chris hung up.

Scott did, too, and then blew out a long breath, shaking his head.

"Jesus Christ, Trevor. What a moron. A slimy moron, but still. Three million dollars? He'd need a forklift for that in cash. Has he any idea at all? Maybe he figures you won't be able to raise that much. Maybe he hopes you'll beg for forgiveness and crawl back into your dog collar. What was all that about? Never mind. I don't care to know. Well, let's go down to the nearest Dollar Store and buy us some cash money. About fifteen pounds of it ought to do the job. Maybe two bags of fifteen pounds each. If anybody gets curious, we'll say it's for a practical joke. It is. Yeah, two bags of fifteen pounds each. You don't want to appear to be cheap. God knows what he's expectin'. What a total and complete moron."

The brothers vacated the hotel room and drove to Key West. They spent some downtime drinking in Key West that night. The next day, they bought the play money, did some more drinking, then slept off both the liquor and their nerves before the sun went down again.

By ten o'clock that night, both brothers were lurking in the shadows of the dark parking lot of the Best Western, Big Pine Key.

A man with a bald patch and a lank ponytail turned up at their rendezvous carrying a VCR tape in one hand. He entered the fenced area around the open-air tiki hut bar and peered around at the few other patrons in the sparsely populated bar. He wore thick glasses and a Hawaii print shirt. He wore sandals and shorts that showed his bony, hairy legs.

He looked like exactly what he was, Scott thought. A shifty-eyed weasel.

Trevor nudged Scott and pointed at the man, wondering as he did so about the tricks a child's mind can play on itself. And what the benefits of time, distance and love can bring. If this was the bogeyman of his childhood, the bogeyman had shrunk and become pathetic.

Trevor stood away from Scott and crossed the parking lot to the Christmas-light-decorated waist-high chain link fence that surrounded the tiki hut bar. He made certain his long dark hair, unrestrained by either braid or ponytail, was flowing free. No baseball cap, but he had his shades on, making it even harder for him to see in the ten o'clock darkness in spite of neon beer signs and strings of party lights. There was an adequate guitar player hooked up to an adequate amp, Trevor noted irrelevantly. He was currently wasting away in Margaritaville, as was the thin crowd at the bar.

The man with the ponytail finally tuned in to Trevor leaning on the chain link fence with his dark hair down and came over. He leaned into the fence from the other side and Trevor found he had no problem at all standing his ground. He wasn't twelve years old. He wasn't defenseless. And he wasn't alone. He was warmly aware of Scott lurking in the darkness somewhere behind him.

Chris' eyes, coyly sick, studied his face.

"The money?"

"The tape."

"Money first."

"Nope."

Trevor came away from the fence slowly and began to turn away. Chris' hand shot out to grab his arm.

"The money."

Trevor looked down at the hand. Sandy hair on freckled knuckles. He remembered that image, and that same hand vice-like around his upper arm as a child. The fingers could barely get a grip on his arm now. God bless bench presses, he thought irrelevantly.

He lifted cold eyes to Chris' face.

"Tape. Over there."

Trevor shook his arm loose easily from Chris' grip and strolled by prearrangement with Scott toward the end of the building that housed the motel. There was a convenient dock on a canal back there.

He heard the rattle and slam of the chain link fence gate and knew that Chris followed him. He slowed his pace, trolling his bait. Fishing had never been as appealing to him as it was now.

Chris' sandals scuffed the darkened parking lot and Trevor heard him muttering under his breath.

"You slut. You bitch. Run away from me, will you? I'll teach you. I'll make you pay. I'll tie you down."

Trevor turned the ugly flow off mentally and never paused till he was behind the end of the building where the sounds from the tiki hut bar were muted. A single bare light bulb mounted over the dock was still sufficient for the business at hand.

Once there, Chris stood close enough for Trevor to feel his body heat.

"The money, bitch. Give me the money. And don't think you're going to be so smart, Mr. Big Shot. I've left letters. If I'm not back by midnight, those letters go straight to the newspapers. It'll all come out for your fucking fans. Prancing up there on stage. Flaunting what's rightfully mine. I own you, twink. I always did."

"Tape."

"Right here, dog. Heel. Sit. Lick me."

"Tape."

"Where's the money? Give me my money."

Scott stepped out of the shadows three feet away, holding two lumpy floral pillowcases and Chris jumped. Scott merely set the pillowcases on the ground, opened one and pulled out a handful of play money. With darkness and distance, it looked real enough to Trevor. Apparently it looked real enough to Chris, too. He started towards it, greed overcoming his natural wariness of Scott.

Scott straightened.

"Tape."

"Take the fucking tape. Give me my money."

"Take your fucking money, creep-a-zoid. Come and get it. You can hand the tape to Trevor."

Chris turned back towards Trevor, his face avid.

"It is you, isn't it? I couldn't be sure. So many years. That picture on a CD cover of lullabies. You've grown. You're beautiful. Desirable more now than ever."

Scott shifted his weight.

"Quit the sex talk, ass-wipe. Trev, grab that tape and let's get on with this."

Christopher de Nunzio stood mesmerized.

"My willing boy-toy. My dog. My slut."

Scott simply reached out a long arm, snagged the tape from Chris' slackened grip as though it had been a football and stepped away from the pillowcases.

"Trev? I've got the tape. Finish it."

Eyes glowing in the dim light, Chris put out hands to touch Trevor's face and Trevor gritted his teeth. The hands veered southward and Chris' fingertips touched his stomach muscles through the fabric of his shirt.

Rage flashed up into Trevor, igniting decades of repression. His hands shot out and clamped around Chris' throat, his thumbs digging into the jugular vein. He watched in fascination as sweat beaded up on Chris' forehead and his eyes popped in fear.

He kept tightening his grip and shook with his own efforts to either kill or maim or terrify this creature from his past.

His brother's voice sounded behind him.

"Trev? Time's a wasting'."

Trevor was shuddering all down his body. Chris was dangling now by his neck, too stunned to even claw at the fingers closing the air supply off to his lungs as well as the blood to his brain, but now his facial expression was turning into something akin to bliss.

Shit, Trevor thought. A pedophile. A sadist. But also a masochist. He was giving this worm pleasure.

He loosened his grip without letting go and watched as disappointment filled Chris' eyes.

"I can't, Scott. I can't do it."

"Aw, hell. Hold the tape. Give me that thing. I'll do it. Turn your head."

Trevor did. There was a crunching sound and then a thud.

"You can look back now."

Trevor did. Then he looked down. There was Chris, at his feet like a dead rat. He was a dead rat.

Trevor looked up at Scott. A memory of Scott baiting his hook for him as a boy when they had gone fishing together flashed into his head. *"Give me that thing. I'll do it. Turn your head. You wriggle. I pounce. That's the deal. Remember?"*

Beautiful.

Trevor smiled at his brother in the dim yellow light.

"Thanks, Bro. You shouldn't have to be doing my dirty work for me."

"I'm not gonna. It's your job to piss on him."

"What about urine samples?"

"You ain't on no drugs. What do you care?"

"Oh. Yeah. Sorry. Forgot."

Trevor handed Scott back the tape, then unzipped his jeans, whipped out his dick and gleefully pissed all over

205

Christopher de Nunzio's hair, face, body, hands, legs, torso and feet. He shook off, put his dick away, and zipped up.

"Ah. That felt great."

"When ya gotta go, ya gotta go. Speakin' of which, we gotta go."

Scott casually shoved Christopher de Nunzio's body off the edge of the dock and into the water. The sound of the muted splash was deeply satisfying to Trevor.

"Got the tape?"

"Got it."

"Let's vamoose then."

"I'm takin' the three million with us."

"Okay. Why? It's play money."

"Waste of good play money to leave it. Junior and Robbie can toss it around and roll in it. Less evidence. And the dead don't need play money, either."

Scott looked at Trevor as they came under a streetlight, heading for their borrowed derelict of a car parked in the shadows.

"One less scumbag on the planet, Trev. Maybe one more little baby boy not sufferin' tonight."

Trevor nodded and drew in a careful breath, watching his own feet as they crossed the glistening darkness of the parking lot.

"We'll watch the papers. See if he makes his mark in history."

"Trev, the only mark that slime ever made in this life was the one on his shorts."

Scott drove them serenely out of the Keys, aware of his brother's silence.

"Trev, we're gonna have to watch that tape."

"I know. I don't want to watch it at home. I don't want it inside my own machine. How crazy does that sound?"

"Sounds sane to me. Let's buy a six-pack or something, get a room with a VCR at some decent little motel up the road here and watch this puppy. Just you and me. Unless you'd like to watch it all by yourself first."

"No."

"I got to watch it, Trevor. I just got to."

"It's okay. I understand. I gotta watch it, too. Dad, yes. Mary, no."

"Carla, no."

"Margaret, never."

"Amen to that. Dani?"

"Of course not. And no one else in the known universe, including Buddy. I don't even know what's on it and that's my vote."

"How good could it be, Trev? It's of a little boy not havin' any fun."

"It's of a little boy high on big-assed drugs. He might be having the time of his life. Who knows?"

"It was a little boy with no choices, Trev. That's what makes the difference to me. And I'd do what I did again."

*　　*　　*　　*　　*

Trevor sat on the sofa in the darkened motel room they had rented, staring intently at the images on the TV screen. Scott sat beside him, watching the same screen, but glancing once in a while at Trevor. Trevor was breathing slowly through his nose. Once in a while he shifted his weight. Once he rubbed his nose and swallowed. He blinked often.

Scott thought it was the longest tape he'd ever watched in his life.

The high, thin voice of a barely discernable male child repeated the same chilling words tonelessly over and over again.

"Oh, yeah. Oh, yeah. Slam me. Slam me."

The camerawork was blurry; the film grainy. The close-ups faded in and out, mostly concerned with what Scott considered to be extremely gross anatomy. There was the back of a younger Christopher de Nunzio's blonde head, a bald spot already in evidence. There was a glimpse of long, dark hair, some baby-sized fingers, one with a skinned knuckle. The little boy had a skinned knee, too. And narrow shoulders. And almost knife-like shoulder blades. His skin was as smooth and pale as a girl's. The long, dark hair hid his face throughout much of the tape.

He did very little in the scheme of things.

But he was sodomized.

Scott almost hit the stop button on the remote control a dozen times, but he didn't. He knew he'd never get up the nerve to watch this tape ever again. He had to do it now.

He didn't expect to enjoy this video one bit.

He didn't.

His beer sat on the end table, warming and going flat, forgotten. His stomach couldn't have tolerated water.

A long, long time later–or so it seemed to Scott– the tape ended with a kick in the ribs for the little boy from the man and his final orders.

"Get up, dog. Time to go."

The tape ended and a jolt of noisy static filled the room.

Scott closed his eyes.

"You didn't remember any of that stuff happenin'?"

"They jumped me and gave me drugs. So I'd enjoy it, they said. Doesn't look like it worked."

Scott sat up slowly.

"Explains a lot about you to me, little brother."

"It does?"

"Just part of who you are, Trevor. Nothin' big that'd stick right out. You can't stand people bein' mean to one another or to animals and especially to children. Explains you not likin' wrestlin' with me much when we were boys. I pinned you once and you got real hysterical. I never did that no more. It kinda scared me. You struck terror in me that time."

"I remember that. I didn't know you well yet. I guess I'd get flashbacks to this, or other stuff Chris did I was awake for. I do hate controls on me."

"Are you all right?"

"Yeah. Sure. I'm fine."

208

"If I'd have known, Trevor, I'd have taken my time killin' him."

"You didn't know. I didn't know."

"I'm sorry about all the jokes I've made over the years. That was no darned jokin' matter at all."

"Turn the TV off, will you? That sound's getting on my nerves."

"Mine, too."

Scott picked up the remote control and hit rewind on the tape, muting the volume. Now all there was in the room was the flickering light from the TV and the mechanical sound of the VCR rewinding the tape.

It clicked off soon enough and Scott hit eject, waited for the tape to come out the slot, and then turned the TV off.

Silence and darkness filled the room. Scott lay the remote next to his neglected can of beer and Trevor finally moved to rub his hands over his face.

"Choices. He took away my choices, Scott. So did my ex-mom. So did Dad when I was younger. Yeah. Surprise. Dad, too. But there's a difference. Lisa and Chris can go into the same sentence together. Dad never did a thing to hurt me intentionally in our whole life together ever. He lied. He took away my choices. But he never hurt me on purpose. Big difference. Huge difference."

"No wonder you can't bait a hook, let alone break some guy's neck."

"Yeah, I'm a wuss girl."

"No, you're not. You just understand really, really well exactly what it's like to feel pain."

The brothers stayed over that night at the motel. Scott sat up with all the lights on, unable to sleep.

Trevor slept briefly, then woke, wailing with nightmares

"Get him off me! Get him off me!"

Scott bolted to his brother's side.

"We got him, Trevor. We got him. He ain't comin' back. He can't hurt you no more, little brother. He can't hurt no one no more."

Trevor's eyes flew open.

"Scott, I can't tell what's real. I can't tell. Are you real? Did I make you up in my head to protect me? Where am I? Who am I?"

"I'm real. You're alive. Chris is dead. We're in a motel outside Miami."

"I couldn't tell. I couldn't tell if I made you up. I couldn't tell if I wished you up in my head."

"Why would you make up a brother who called you a moron?"

Trevor gulped down his panic and reason began to flow into his brain.

"I wanted it so bad I thought I made it up."

"I'm darned glad I ain't got your imagination. I'm real, moron."

"I feel like I'm twelve years old again. I feel trapped and scared and crazy."

"Well, maybe you're crazy. The jury's still out on that one. But you ain't trapped. And there's nothin' to be scared of. I'm here."

Trevor gripped Scott's arm.

"It was like every nightmare I've ever had in my whole life all rolled up into one. Fear. Paralyzing fear. Trapped. Desperate."

"I remember nightmares like this from when I was a kid. Thank God I outgrew them. I'd turn on all the lights and keep my hands and feet way inside the bed so the monsters under the bed couldn't grab me and pull me under the bed."

Trevor sat up in the bed now.

"There's no monsters under beds."

"Tell that to a kid with a nightmare. Them monsters was real to me. I can feel that fear crawlin' on my skin and dryin' up my spit right now."

"Yeah. What did you do?"

Scott chuckled.

"I was a lucky little boy. I had a TV and a VCR in my room. I'd pop in an old 'Dukes of Hazzard' tape with maybe six episodes I'd gotten off the TV cramped onto it and hit the play button. I could reach all that 'cause I'd planned ahead for what I'd do when I got a nightmare. I'd sit up there in bed and watch the good guys triumph over evil till my eyes closed and I'd drift back off to sleep to the sound of The General Lee's horn and fast cars jumpin' stuff."

"I played Blondie. After I had her. Before that? I just sucked it up."

Scott sighed.

"I guess neither of our momma's was any good for that kinda stuff, huh? Tiffany wasn't, either. Not for Junior. I'd be the one to get up when Junior had a nightmare."

"Dad'd get up for me."

"There you go. Carla's good with Junior."

"I'm glad."

"Yeah. Me, too. How are you doin' there, little brother?"

Trevor sniffed.

"I'm fine. Now. Well, getting fine. I'll do."

"We ain't got no 'Dukes of Hazzard' tape here, but I'll bet we could find some Three Stooges on this TV right now. Monsters don't like laughter, Trev."

Trevor chuckled weakly.

"No, they don't. God, I'm glad I've got you, Scott."

"It ain't no sin to be scared, Trev. I wasn't doin' any sleepin' after watchin' that tape of yours, either. Them two guys–Chris and the cameraman–was real monsters. I don't know how authors like Stephen King do it. I'd be awake all night watchin' The General Lee and Denver Pyle if I had an imagination like theirs. You didn't even need your imagination, Trev. It was the truth for you. You're always so darned hard on yourself."

"Stooges would be good."

"I done checked under the bed already. Ain't no monsters under there now."

"Thanks, Scott."

211

"You owe me, little brother. You get to be godfather
to Carla's and my baby."

"You're pregnant?"

"Not yet. But I got plans."

\*     \*     \*     \*     \*

### SAFE HOUSE

I like inside my safe house.
I like out in the open.
I like freewheelin' lovin'.
I never have been broken.

I been tore up
In my heart and in my soul.
Down on my luck,
But inside me
The spark
Still glows
And I know
I'll survive.
I'm alive.

So bring on your troubles.
I love a good challenge.
Got good love around me.
You can't take me down.

\*     \*     \*     \*     \*

Back in Punta Gorda in the house on Olympia
Avenue, Jarrett looked at his elder son's wooden face and
grim eyes.

"I take it that tape's pretty rough?"

"Yes, sir. It is."

"Got it with you?"

"I do. Got it right here."

212

Scott held up the VCR tape but didn't hand it to his father. Jarrett watched his older son's face.

"Are you gonna hand that tape over to me or do I have to pull it out of your fingers?"

"I ain't sure."

"Son, if you and Trevor done seen it and you're both still alive, how bad can it be?"

"Bad. It's bad. I don't want you to see it, Daddy."

"Choices, son. I have choices. Ignorance is not a choice that works out well in the long run. I'll have that tape, Scott."

Scott handed the tape to his father.

"Trevor doesn't want Aunt Mary to see it."

"Neither do I."

"Does Aunt Mary get a choice?"

"No, son, she does not. She gets a lie. For her own good. She'd be eaten up with guilt about what may be on this tape. For years she agonized over other things she couldn't have prevented. It will serve no benefit to anyone for Mary to see this tape."

"And yourself, sir?"

"Pretty cocky, aren't you, boy?"

"Yes, sir. I've seen the tape."

"Why'd you watch it?"

"I had to. I couldn't not watch it. I felt I owed it to Trevor. I owed it to myself. It's done with now."

"Well, there you go. Those are my sentiments exactly. Closure for all of us Daniels men. This may be one of those things that women really can't ever understand. Viewin' this tape would open up pain for Mary, and Carla, and Dani and even Margaret. But it brings closure to we three Daniels men."

"What the heck do we do with it afterwards?"

"That's up to Trevor. It's his tape."

A voice came from behind them. Trevor was lounging against the old Harvest gold refrigerator.

"Parts of it will go to Jake for incorporation as he sees fit into the video he's making for his cover of 'Scream in Pain'."

Scott stared at his brother.

"Trev! It'll be seen everywhere."

"My point exactly."

Trevor leaned away from the refrigerator

"Having a psychiatrist help me crawl around inside my head was a sound investment, Dad. It was also an affirmation that the advice I've gotten for free from you over the years was valid. It turned out you were right about a lot of things. You weren't actually wrong about any of it, but I can be self-delusional. I wanted to be sure. Now I am. My opinion of a really competent psychiatrist? Nearly as good as having a loving, caring parent."

Trevor frowned as he gathered his thoughts.

"Watching that video was actually a help to me, in a way. I could see for myself, as an adult, what was done to me as a child. The physical abuse wasn't nearly as corroding as the psychological abuse. Though it gave me nightmares, I'm glad I watched it."

Trevor lifted his chin.

"It's lost its power over me. Now it can forever lose its power over anyone in this family. Ignorance is not bliss and I did nothing wrong. I'm not hiding the thing. It's going to be out in the open and it's going to be doing some good, putting visuals to my music and lyrics. I'm moving on."

## Chapter Eleven

It was the final move of his final day at The Ice Palace.

Trevor was speeding down I-75 in his dented blue pick-up truck, radio blaring, the wind in his hair and around his face. His Texas Rangers baseball cap was on backwards. He had his shades on.

She was standing by the side of the road near a huge white station wagon from the late sixties, a tiny plain girl with a halo of ringlets pulled back in a ponytail and a battered guitar case in one hand, her thumb stuck out in the wind.

He was past her before it registered.

"What the fuck!"

She was hitchhiking.

Trevor jammed on the brakes and hauled the pickup to the side of the road. He put it in reverse and backed all the way back to her, and then put the truck in park. He never backed up on the interstate. It was illegal and stupid. Jarrett would have skinned him for it. He also never picked up hitchhikers. That was stupid, too. Jarrett had never actually made a ruling on it, but Trevor knew intuitively that that was off-limits as well.

He watched for a break in traffic and got out, then stomped up behind her.

"What the heck do you think you're doing?"

Startled, she gasped and spun towards him, her blue eyes wide. He dragged her and her guitar case out of the roadway. She shook off his hand.

"I'm hitchhiking. Are you picking me up? I didn't hear you behind me."

"Don't you know that hitchhiking is about the dumbest thing you can do?"

"Well, my car just died and I have to get somewhere."

"It can't be that important."

"It is to me. Are you going to give me a lift or not?"

Exasperated, Trevor looked from her angry face to her elderly car.

"What's wrong with it?"

"It died."

"Won't start? Won't turn over? No clicking sound?"

"I was driving along and suddenly, nothing. I steered to the side."

"Call AAA?"

"I don't have AAA and I don't have a cell phone. But I do have a place to be at 7:00 p.m.tonight, if I can get there."

"Starting kind of early, aren't you? It can't be much past 4:00 p.m. right now."

"With Esmeralda, I've learned to plan ahead."

"Esmeralda?"

"My car. This isn't a first for Essie. Do you think you can fix it?"

"No. But I've got AAA and a cell phone. We can have her towed to your mechanic."

"You'd do that? For a stranger? That's awfully nice of you, but I couldn't."

"Swell. You'll crawl into some stranger's car for a lift, but not this. Great logic."

"I don't have a mechanic. Okay? And I don't have the money for one if I did have one."

"So, what's your plan? Leave Essie up here on the interstate to be stripped—which probably wouldn't happen—or be towed away to impound, which probably would?"

"Oh, dear. I don't know."

She turned earnest eyes up to his face.

"What should I do?"

"Get in the truck. We'll figure it out later. We can't stand here on the side of the road. It's not safe."

She looked past him to his truck with its sorry, sagging rear bumper, one half of the SKI COLORADO bumper sticker still attached to it.

"Are you Ski?"

"What?"

216

"Is your name Ski?"

Trevor looked where she was looking and laughed.

"Yeah. Ski. Whatever."

She held out her hand to him.

"I'm Katie Mercer."

Trevor looked at the hand and frowned down at her.

"Just get in the truck, will ya?"

"Are you going as far as Port Charlotte?"

"Why would you want to go to Port Charlotte?"

"I have an engagement there. Are you going that far?"

"I am."

"Then I'll accept your ride. Thank you."

And she turned from him in her Walmart jeans and K-Mart tank top to get into the passenger seat of his truck. The door stuck on her. It hadn't worked properly for years. Trevor followed her and yanked it open for her. She climbed into the cab and put her guitar case between her legs, looking like a concert cellist in the rusted-out cab of his truck.

Trevor slammed the door shut on her. He waited for a break in traffic and then got in his own side, slamming his own sprung door shut.

Katie turned to him.

"Seat belts?"

"They're there somewhere. You're mighty concerned about safety for someone who was going to hitchhike."

Trevor watched for another break in traffic to get back out onto the road. Katie frowned at him.

"I had to do that. I don't have to ride without a seat belt."

She felt in all the creases of the seat, found both ends, and clicked them shut around her tiny hips.

Trevor glanced over at her.

"I'm going to Punta Gorda. Where can I drop you off? And don't say the nearest exit."

"I'm going to a place in Port Charlotte called Big Dog's. Do you know where that is?"

217

"Sure. Great burgers. Decent bar. That's your engagement? What? Are you going on a job interview?"

"There's an open mike night at 7:00 p.m. I'm playing."

Trevor realized that he was so used to seeing guitar cases in his line of work that that it hadn't registered with him.

"You play guitar?"

"Yes."

"Sing?"

"Yes."

"You any good?"

"I don't know. I'm hoping to find out."

"You were going to drive fifty miles each way in that car of yours to an open mike night in Port Charlotte, Florida?"

She lifted her chin at him.

"Yes. It's an opportunity to play. And to learn."

"Right."

"Are you going to take me or not? Because if you're not, I'll just have to hitchhike "

"Oh, no, you don't. You're staying in this truck."

Trevor slammed the truck into gear and edged back onto the roadway.

"Big Dog's, huh?"

"Yes. 7:00 p.m. every Tuesday. Upstairs."

Her teeth were gritted, and Trevor could tell she was nervous. Of the gig or of him, he couldn't say. But she was determined to go.

He drove them to Big Dog's in a rainy mist that started up as they headed south on the interstate. They were painfully early, so Trevor decided to buy them both an early dinner in the dark downstairs bar at Big Dog's.

Once they were seated in a booth, Katie daintily picked up a plastic-coated menu to read it.

"I really shouldn't let you buy me dinner."

"Why not?"

"Because I don't know you."

218

"But you'll let me pick you up on the interstate?"

"We've been over that before."

"Well, I'm hungry. I'm planning on eating. What kind of hoople would I be to eat in front of you? It's just food."

"As long as you understand."

"I do. I guess. Did I miss something?"

"Perhaps you're not that way."

Trevor was sitting sideways in the booth, keeping an eye on the crowd. He felt a little naked out in public without his brother Scott.

"Perhaps I'm not. What? What way?"

Katie folded her hands in her lap.

"I've met a lot of men who expected me to pay for my dinner. Later."

"Oh? How nuts is that? I'd advise you to eat light if you're going to be singing."

"I always eat light."

"Good for you.

Their waitress came, one Trevor didn't know. He ordered a Frisco burger, cooked Pittsburgh rare, a coke and French fries. He looked at Katie, still reading the menu.

Sensing eyes on her, Katie looked up to meet Trevor's eyes and then up again to their waitress.

"I'm sorry. So many choices. I'll have the side salad with oil and vinegar and a glass of water. Thank you."

The waitress left. Trevor frowned at his seating companion.

"Is that what you really wanted to eat or is it just coincidence that that was the cheapest thing on the menu?"

"I like salads."

"I'm just asking. 'Cause you could have had anything on that menu and what you didn't eat, you could have taken home in a doggy bag. Or let me eat. Whatever."

"I like salads."

"Well, okay then."

"You don't have to stay here with me."

219

"What do you want me to do? Go on about my business and leave you here? You'd probably try to hitchhike home."

"I'm sure someone could give me a ride."

"Yeah. Right. What are the odds that anyone's going back to Sarasota tonight?"

"You were on your way to somewhere else when we met."

"Home. I was going home."

"Well, you could still go home. Where do you live?"

"Punta Gorda. I'd rather stay and listen than go home and come back out. I'd like to hear what's out there cookin'. I'd like to hear you play."

"You'll be bored."

"Are you trying to get rid of me?"

Their food came and their anonymous waitress left. Katie placed a paper napkin in her lap.

"Of course I'm not trying to get rid of you."

"Because if you are, you're going about it the wrong way."

Trevor picked up his burger, sniffed it, smiled, and bit in. Katie widened her eyes at the size of the portions and began thinking seriously in terms of a doggy bag for her salad.

"What would be the proper way to get rid of you?"

Trevor smiled at her, his mouth full and chewing. He spoke around the food.

"Hurt my feelings."

"Oh. I wouldn't want to do that. You've been so kind."

"There you go. Want a fry?"

"No, thank you. Robbie loves fries."

"Good man. Why isn't he driving you to this gig? Is he working?"

"He doesn't have a driver's license."

"Oh. Bummer."

They chatted and chewed until it was time to go upstairs. Trevor finished the rest of Katie's salad, left cash

220

for the bill and a substantial tip. He'd been a waiter in his day. He never stiffed even the lousiest waiter or waitress.

Katie grabbed her guitar case and clunked her way out of the booth, heading for the stairs to the upper level. As he followed her, Trevor called Jarrett on his cell phone and canceled his date for dinner at the Olympia Avenue house, telling him where he was.

Upstairs, it was everything Trevor ever remembered from open mike nights at Big Dog's.

The amps were cheap and malfunctioning; the crowd not nearly drunk enough at 7:00 p.m. on a Tuesday night to appreciate the painful efforts being put forth by the current performer, a guy with a ponytail and dark mustache plucking a guitar so badly-tuned it set Trevor's teeth on edge. There was too much bass on the voice mike, so none of the words were clear. And too much nothing on the pickups of the guitar. The guy himself was a conceited jerk with a borrowed move from everyone who'd ever been in the business. Even his groupies–two fat broads in tight pants–didn't applaud very long when he ended his set, Trevor noticed.

Katie detached herself from Trevor and took herself and her guitar case gamely up front. Trevor got himself a seat in the farthest back booth, near the door, where he could see the whole room and all its occupants. The playing order had already been established, and Katie was next to last.

Gonna be a long night, Trevor thought.

And it was.

The next set was a duo of aging hippies, Willie Nelson braids and all. Their playing sucked and so did their vocals. You couldn't even tell when their pieces were over, Trevor thought. Applause was tepid.

Then came an aging rocker from New Jersey, full of false patter to the minuscule audience. You could tell he might have had some talent forty years ago, but had never grown musically since his glory days, and now was on the borderline of pathetic. Trevor squirmed in embarrassment for him, but he was clueless. He didn't even have a groupie.

After New Jersey came an unprepossessing guy with folk roots. He was better than he looked, and had a decent voice. He sang only his own tunes, the words hopelessly lost in the bad microphone. Trevor gave him a good clap for guts.

Nursing a coke, Trevor watched the whole show.

Batteries died. Strings broke. One guy brought a three-ring binder up with him and had to keep looking at it for the chords and words. It was painful. Most of them seemed to know Katie and definitely one another. Katie was the only woman playing.

And then it was Katie's turn. The guy with the three-ring binder announced her. No one noticed. She got out her guitar, nothing special, and tuned it. No one noticed that, either. Trevor had a low-grade urge to knock some heads. Even the other players were talking through her set-up. They had helped one another with volume and mike adjustments, but none of them went up to help Katie. She was on her own.

Katie hit a chair with her guitar and Trevor winced. She had no lead in. No introduction. She didn't make eye contact with the crowd and she didn't talk or joke with them. She began her piece and the sound equipment was so bad Trevor never made out a note she sang or a word, either. He could hear her guitar playing, though. She landed half off chords and hit really bad notes. But she kept on going. She was pale, sweating and tense.

This must have been what it had been like for Jarrett, Trevor thought. Stage fright and puke. Horrible to be that way. And horrible to watch.

Katie's style was derivative, her movements choppy, her talent nil. But she had heart and guts and grit. The drunks talked over her. Her fellow musicians upstaged her, poking around at the sound equipment behind her as she gamely sang on. She was appalling. Painfully appalling.

Trevor was enthralled.

In the light from a disco globe and a Coors beer sign, her Walmart jeans and K-Mart tank top showing sweat marks, she was like the walking wounded on stage. As she staggered through another song, missing notes and flinching,

Trevor found he had an urge to go up, grab a guitar and save her from her misery. He could have. He knew instinctively that he could have owned this room in three seconds flat. But he kept his seat and sipped his coke. He could do all that, but that wouldn't help Katie. It would only tick her off.

Katie's set ground to a halt and Trevor found his palms were sweating. She was awful. And she had no idea just how awful she was. She parked her guitar–not before clunking it on the same chair again–and lingered on the stage to greet the next act, another latecomer. She quietly went from musician to musician, talking and smiling. Trevor couldn't hear what she said, but the other musicians gave her back the body language of the patronizing male. She finally sat with another girl, a non-player, and courteously watched the next jackass crash and burn.

At the end, each musician had one more piece they could do. None of them shown. Katie got out her guitar for her final piece, broke two strings tuning it, and looked around helplessly. Trevor couldn't believe she didn't pack backup strings. Everyone blew an E-string, and even blowing a G-string wasn't unheard of. The guys all made gestures of denial. Nope, we got no spare strings on us. Yeah, right, Trevor thought. He felt his fingers itching to grab necks.

The New Jersey glory boy offered Katie his guitar, and probably got the shock of his life when Katie accepted it and smilingly pulled the strap over her head. It was a totally alien instrument to her, an acoustic with a wide neck and an external pickup that had been giving its owner problems all night. Katie calmly took up eight inches of slack on the strap to get the instrument within reach, and fingered the wide neck. It probably had the action of a bulldozer, Trevor thought. What did New Jersey care? He didn't finger. He strummed chords for all his stuff.

Katie smiled past the lights and into the darkened room. A drunk yowled at her. She began her final song, another unintelligible effort. Trevor watched the other musicians. They continued to upstage Katie. They talked

223

loudly with their friends through her piece. They did everything possible to make her time up on stage a living hell.

Trevor began to wonder why that was.

Katie was bad enough on her own.

But as he watched her, it began to dawn on him. These guys were intimidated by her. They were afraid of her. Afraid of her heart and her spunk, maybe. Three-ring-binder was a wannabe. New Jersey never made it in his best days. The others were jerking off. All of them played better than Katie. Most of them sang better than Katie. But none of them had her determination.

Trevor smiled, suddenly enjoying himself hugely. They all sucked. But maybe Katie sucked the least, in her way.

Katie finished and waited for her applause, which Trevor himself had to start and maintain till a few more sporadic claps sounded. She was glowing with triumph. Trevor's ears were bleeding from the assault on his senses.

Katie returned the guitar to New Jersey, enthusiastically thanking him. She said goodbye to each musician and to the girl she had been sitting with, gathered up her guitar, put it in its case and came back to where Trevor sat hunched in his corner near the door.

"What did you think?"

Trevor stood up, sliding a decent bill under his empty coke glass. He shifted his eyes away from Katie's face and nodded, not trusting his voice. It was worse than he ever remembered open mike night being. Had he been so absorbed in his own music that he hadn't noticed? Probably. Had he been as arrogant as these guys? Again, probably. Had he ever sucked this badly? No way.

Trevor opened the door for Katie and she preceded him down the creaky wooden steps and out into the wet, dark parking lot.

"Thanks for bringing me here, Ski. It meant a lot to me."

Katie shivered in the remains of the adrenaline rush of performing. Trevor wondered if it was possible to clean bad music out of your ears with alcohol and a Q-tip. What a night, he thought.

"What are you going to do about your car?"

"I don't know. It's 11:00 p.m. on a Tuesday night. What can I do? Leave it, I guess. I don't have AAA. I don't have a mechanic. I don't know what's wrong with it. And even if I did, I can't afford to get anything fixed. I'll have to leave it there. I'll take a cab to work."

Trevor shook his head as he got out his keys.

"Why don't I take you home?"

"I'm not that kind of girl."

"What? You don't live in a house?"

"Oh. I thought you meant take me home to your house. Sorry."

"Would that be a bad idea?"

"Yes."

"Okay. Then that's out. So, how about I take you home to your house?"

"That would be...I can't do that."

"Why not?"

"You might get the wrong idea."

They had reached the pick-up truck by now and Trevor had opened the sprung passenger door for Katie. She climbed in with her guitar case. Trevor leaned on the open door, frowning.

"I think I got too much amp in my head tonight. That didn't make any sense to me."

Trevor slammed the door shut on Katie and rounded the truck, getting in behind the wheel and slamming his own door shut.

"What kind of wrong idea am I supposed to be getting?"

Katie twisted her fingers. Trevor thought those fingers must be pretty tired and throbbing by now from playing New Jersey's guitar.

"You know. Sex."

"Well, I do know sex. And I kinda like it, really."

"That's not what I meant. I won't pay you back in sex."

"Oh. Okay. But about the ride. What are you going to do? Have me drop you off at the car? Sleep in the car and hope the Auto Mechanic Fairy waves a wand over that heap while you sleep?"

"I don't know."

"Get some sense, will ya? You're out of choices."

Boy, Trevor thought, did that sound familiar.

Trevor turned to her in the seat.

"Look. I've been in a jam in my time. I've had my back to the wall with no options. I got help offered when I needed it, no strings attached. I'm just passing it on. What goes around comes around. Okay?"

"Ski, that's awfully nice of you."

"But?"

"No 'but.' You're right. I have no real choice. I appreciate the help. I just want you to understand that I will not be paying you back for your kindness with sex."

"I'm not sure, but I think you just insulted both of us. I can't tell if you think I'm an animal or you just think all men are animals. It'll probably come as a surprise to you to hear this, but I'm pretty selective about my partners. I never sleep with anyone crazier than I am. I don't want to die of AIDS, so I don't jump every female that walks past me. And I'm not like whatever guy you're having a knee-jerk reaction to. Are you like this with other guys? The guy bagging your groceries? Or is all this bull and baggage reserved for me?"

"I don't like being obligated to a stranger."

Trevor nodded.

"Good. I can relate to that. We'll have Essie towed tonight. I've got AAA."

Trevor thought of Scott, and smiled.

"I know a real good mechanic, too."

"I just can't think straight. I'm all wired up. And I have to be at work tomorrow by 8:00 a.m. I just don't know what to do."

"Okay. Here's the plan. We call AAA from the car. They tow the car to Scott. I take you to work in the morning. We go from there."

"That's a huge debt. I can't agree to that."

"What choice do you have?"

Katie sighed and threw her head back against the back of the seat in frustration.

"None. I don't even have any savings."

"Don't worry about that. You can pay me back if you want. In installments. You gotta have a car that runs."

She sighed again.

"Thanks, Ski."

"No sweat. Hey. Those guys at the open mike. They were trying to upstage your act, and make you screw up. They're intimidated by you. Why is that?"

"You noticed that, did you? Well, maybe it's because every last one of them has hit on me and been turned down. I guess I'm stand-offish."

"I guess you are. Every last one of them?"

"And three of the women."

"Geez. Nice crowd. Why do you go back?"

"For the open mike."

"Well, you don't scare off easy."

"No, I don't."

Trevor started the truck and automatically turned on the radio along with the headlights. A perky voice pushed through the radio at them.

"Coming up next, Trevor Daniels with 'Guitar-Man'."

Trevor quickly jabbed another selection button.

And Katie jabbed it back.

"Wait! I love this guy."

"You do?"

"Yes. He's brilliant. And he started off just like me with absolutely nothing."

Trevor winced in the darkened cab and put the truck into gear, pulling out onto US 41 to the sound of his own voice on the radio.

"Guitar-Man, tie some feathers in your hair. Come tonight you're gonna fly..."

Katie purred into the darkness of the truck's cab.

"His voice is so dreamy."

"It is?"

"Yes. He wrote that when he was thirteen."

"No, he didn't."

"I'm sure he was thirteen."

"His dad wrote it for him and he was fifteen."

"Are you sure?"

"Oh, yeah. I'm sure."

"He came from around here. I wonder if he ever played at Big Dog's?"

"Nope."

"Are you sure? How can you be so sure?"

"It's a bar. He was underage. I don't think there even was any Big Dog's there then maybe."

"Oh. Listen, you're going to be driving all over the place to help me. Let me at least pay for the gasoline."

"Nope. Save your money for guitar strings. You're down two tonight."

"Oh, dear. I forgot. Do you know, a set of those installed costs $12.00 plus tax?"

Trevor smiled in the dark of the truck cab.

"Wow. That much?"

"Yes. It's a very expensive hobby."

"I guess. Why do you do it?"

"I can't help myself."

"You want to be rich and famous?"

"No. Not really. I'd like to be able to pay my bills on time and have something in the bank. But that's not why I play. That's why I work. I play because I love the sound. I love hearing the sounds I make."

I'm in love, Trevor thought. Then panicked.

Where had that thought come from?

"Do you write?"

"Oh, no. I have zero creativity. And a very mediocre singing voice."

"No, you don't."

Yes, she did.

"Yes, I do. But this is the only talent I have. I don't knit or crochet. I can't dance. I'm a dud at sports. But I can play guitar and I can sing a little. Other people's songs."

"You looked like you were gonna puke from stage fright."

"Yes. I've got that, too."

"Then why? You could play and sing to yourself. Why put yourself through all that to get up in front of a crowd to do that?"

"Well, I guess maybe that's my little dream."

"What? To play Carnegie Hall?"

"No. But to play at as many open mikes as I can. I'm hoping I get less queasy."

"Good luck."

"Thanks."

Trevor drove the rain-slick interstate northward more slowly than he normally would have, even given the road conditions. He found he didn't want the drive to end.

Katie babbled along about her job as a retail sales clerk in a clothing store. She told him cute and funny stories about customers and phone calls. He let her ramble on. She never asked him a thing about himself, which puzzled him. And irked him. True, he didn't want to tell her who he was, but the least the woman could do was ask, he thought.

She never volunteered any information about herself.

As he drove along in the dark, the windshield wipers slapping away endless rain and the old truck leaking water onto his sneakers from some hole under the dash, Trevor felt himself relaxing to the sound of Katie's voice.

He had the radio set to Gator Country 101.9 FM and if a song she liked came on, Katie would reach out and turn up the volume. She turned it up for his songs and sang along with some of them, doing frightening things to them with her singing voice, which was so at odds with the soft and gentle tones of her speaking voice. She turned up the volume for other artists as well, notably Steve Azar and Keith Urban.

229

She preferred ballads and she preferred male singers. Trevor found that encouraging on several levels.

They passed Essie still on the side of the road and Trevor kept on to the next exit, Fruitville Road, got off and got on again to double back. He parked behind the derelict white vehicle and pulled on his flashers, a retrofit that Scott had installed for him. He pulled out his cell phone and dialed up AAA.

He had a moment of panic and cancelled the call. No way was he giving out who he was in front of Katie to the AAA operator asking for his name and card number.

Katie frowned at him.

"What's wrong?"

He thought fast.

"Year. I'll need to know the year, make and model for Essie."

"Oh. Yes. You're right. I never thought of that."

"Well? What is she?"

"I don't know."

"Oh, come on. You've got to be kidding."

"As God is my witness, I don't know. She's a Ford. She's white. I can find her in parking lots."

"How the heck do you register her every year?"

"I don't. She's in Charlie's name."

"Charlie? Who's Charlie?"

"My ex-husband. Charlie Smallwood."

"Your husband let you drive that piece of junk? That's dangerous."

"I needed a car. He got me one. In his name."

"Give me the keys."

"Why?"

"So I can unlock Essie, go in the glove box, look at the registration and be less of a moron when I call AAA and they ask me all this."

"Oh. Okay. But it's raining."

"So? Your point was?"

"You'll get wet."

Somehow that struck Trevor as being so ludicrous it was past funny. His own truck was allowing rain to steadily drip onto his left leg where the door no longer met the frame, the seals having disintegrated from dry-rot several decades before.

He laughed, shook his head, and stuck out his hand. "Keys. Now."

Katie pulled the keys from her jeans pockets and handed them over. All of them.

"It's the one that says Ford."

"Thank you. Sit. Stay. I'll be back."

Trevor watched for a break in traffic in the rear view mirror. He found he couldn't trust that method, between black specks where the mirror backing had spotted away and the scratched and hazy back window he was trying to look through. He rolled down the side window, getting a lash of rain in his face, but a much clearer view of on-coming traffic.

Did all of Sarasota County have to be migrating south at midnight on a Tuesday?

He pre-loosened the truck door and held it at the ready. A break came, he darted out, slamming the door behind him and sprinted around Essie to the passenger side. Katie's voice came to him with bell-like clarity through the rain.

"That side doesn't work. Driver's side."

Trevor muttered under his breath as he straightened and walked between the car and the truck.

"Of course it doesn't work. No hurry now. I'm soaked. Great."

He caught a break in traffic, shoved the key in the lock as best he could, and worked the stiff mechanism while keeping an eye out for more on-coming traffic. The baseball cap he wore served only to keep ambient light from reaching his fingers. It did nothing to shield him from the rain. The wind whipped his wet hair in ropes around his arms and shoulders and finally blew the cap off.

231

The lock mechanism turned. Trevor ripped open the door and bailed into the stuffy dryness of the front seat, slamming the door behind him. He raked a hank of wet hair out of his mouth, wiped his face on his wet shirt and turned on the cell phone gripped in his left hand. It was wet, too, but the luminous green window came on and he dialed up AAA, tucking the phone between his chin and shoulder as he struggled to pull his wet wallet from his wet jeans with his wet fingers. He was beyond cursing.

"AAA. Operator Sandy. What is the nature of your emergency?"

He could have said it was a woman, but he restrained himself.

"I never get a real person. I always get a recording. Sorry. Not prepared. Don't hang up. I'm getting it."

Trevor kept babbling into the phone as he opened the glove box with his right hand and tore everything out like a dog digging for a bone.

"Got it. Okay. Here we go. Car won't start."

"Do you need gasoline or a jump?"

"Don't get me started on the really bad jokes, Sandy. I need a tow."

"You're membership number, please."

Wiping his face again and getting more comfortable in the close, dry car, Trevor gave the woman everything she wanted. Her efficient I'm-safe-and-dry voice came back to him.

"We'll have a driver there in approximately forty-five minutes, sir Please stay with the vehicle and raise the hood."

"Nope. Not gonna do that, lady. It's effing raining out here, pardon my French. Tell your driver to put the hook on the only white Ford heap he's gonna find on this road tonight. Got it?"

"Yes, sir. We'll call if there's a delay."

"Sorry about the attitude, Sandy. I apologize. Been a helluva night and it's not finished yet."

"Stay with the vehicle, Mr. Daniels, and have photo ID ready for our driver."

Sandy disconnected the call and Trevor sucked in a breath.

"Photo ID. Shit."

Before he forgot to do it all, he dialed up Scott.

It took a while to connect, but, hell, he thought, it was well past midnight on a Tuesday and they'd both worked their Daniels brothers' fine butts off on the move from The Ice Palace to Punta Gorda. Scott was probably a six-pack into a good movie, sitting high and dry in a recliner with his feet up and Carla in his lap.

Trevor blew a drop of water out of his mouth that had dribbled down from his hair as his brother answered the call..

"Scott here. What's up?"

"Bro, I need a favor."

"You'll need surgery if it involves me movin' one more darned thing tonight."

"No, no. I don't need surgery. I might need my head examined, but that's another story."

"You always needed that. Whatcha want?"

"Can I have AAA drop a car off the hook at your place tonight?"

"Why? Take it to your place. What happened? Are you okay?"

"Oh. Yeah. I'm fine. I'm in the truck. Well, actually, I'm in this car I need towed. AAA is on the way already. We're stuck on the interstate just south of Fruitville Road. I'll explain later. Will you do it? I don't know what's wrong with it."

"You wouldn't. Who's 'we'?"

"Oh. Me and a girl I met."

"Figures. What's comin' my way?"

Trevor squinted at the car's curled registration and title to refresh his memory.

"1967 Ford Country Squire."

"Jesus Christ, moron. On its best day that tank got eight miles to the gallon. It's a friggin' battleship. It's a dog."

"Not a collectable?"

233

"No. It's not. Yeah, bring it on. The neighbors are gonna love this. It's older than the clunker we borrowed off Uncle Fred for the Miami-Key West trip."

"It's white."

"Do I care?"

"I'm just sayin'."

"Make sure you dry off good after this adventure. Get your lady to wash and dry your clothes for you."

"How did you know I was wet?"

"You sound wet. Geez, Trevor, if it's rainin' in Sarasota and you're out in your truck, you're wet."

"Well, I'm past wet now."

"Send the beast to me. Get laid. Get dry. Get home. Get some sleep. Got it?"

"Yep. Got it. Thanks, Bro."

"You're welcome, moron."

Scott hung up and Trevor put the old cell phone on key guard. He bent sideways in the seat and scooped all the paperwork from the glove box up and shoved it unceremoniously back in, including the registration and title. He straightened and looked over the back of the seat to the far distant end of the huge station wagon.

Eight miles to the gallon, he thought? Jesus Christ. This girl was willing to pay in excess of twenty dollars a week in gasoline for the privilege of humiliating herself at Big Dog's? That was just not right. That was sick. That was twisted. With no talent and a queasy stomach to boot, that was just not right at all.

And speaking of being not right, he realized he was going to be getting another bath between the station wagon and the truck. He pulled his driver's license out of his soggy wallet and paired it up with the AAA card. He hoped that by the time the tow truck driver got there, he'd have had enough rainy darkness himself that he wouldn't even ask for ID.

He looked in the rear view mirror of the old Country Squire, through the surprisingly clear back window, to see the retrofitted amber flashers of his truck blinking away and a dark silhouette with a halo of light-catching curls sitting in his passenger seat.

He realized that his initial urge to conceal his identity from Katie had now become an obsession. He didn't want Katie Mercer to know who he was. Ever. He wanted to hear her ramble on freely about Trevor Daniels' singing and his songs and about her hopes for her own singing and about her semi-career in retail. He wanted her innocence and her determination. She was fresh, and sturdy, and . . .

His mind shied away from just what Katie Mercer was to him. But he wanted Ski to have the opportunity to get to know her.

Let Trevor Daniels get his own darned woman.

He tore his eyes away from the vision in the rear view mirror and turned in the seat, looking around the broad expanse of the car for anything that he thought Katie might possibly want to go with her when Essie went to Scott's house. He spied a folded beach towel and reached for it. As he did, a chunky plastic truck fell out of the folds of the towel and disappeared into the darkness of the floorboards. A car seat was revealed.

"Hm. Baby. Little boy baby."

Trevor felt his face creeping into an idiot-grin. "Cool."

He brought the towel up with him. If nothing else, he could wrap Katie in it while they waited for the tow truck. Heaven only knew whether the driver's side window on his truck would roll upwards again or not.

He gripped Katie's keys, the AAA card and his driver's license together with his cell phone in his left hand and tucked the towel under his left arm. He studied the oncoming traffic in Essie's side view mirror and gauged his break time.

He was out, the door closed behind him and shoving cell phone and keys and cards at Katie through the open truck window. She grabbed them, he jerked the door open, bounced in and landed his fairly dry butt in a huge, cold sponge of water from where the vinyl covering had worn off the driver's seat, exposing foam rubber beneath.

"Yuck."

Trevor gritted his teeth and forced a grin at Katie.

"I forgot. There's a big slit in the vinyl upholstery in this seat. I don't drive the truck much in the rain anymore. Gross. Let me see if I can persuade the window up. Here. Have a towel."

He shoved the towel at Katie. She began to wipe off his cell phone with it. Trevor struggled to grasp the slipping window with his right hand and haul upward on it while he worked the window crank with his left. He got it up to within three inches of the top before the mechanism froze.

"That's it. Not going any further up. Better than it was. Well, this is cozy. Not. AAA says the usual forty-five minutes. It's raining. There's an unlimited supply of idiots out on the road, I see. No telling how long this'll take. I phoned Scott. He'll be expecting Essie. According to the title, she's a 1967 Ford Country Squire station wagon, by the way."

Trevor paused for breath, and then shot out his question.

"Where's the baby?"

He hadn't realized his voice could sound that menacing. He was remembering what his own ex-mother had been like. Shiftless mothers didn't rate high with him.

Katie tilted her head at him.

"A friend's staying with him at the house. How did you know I had a child?"

"Car seat. Truck in the towel."

"He'll be fine. Really. She's very responsible. I cooked before I left. All she had to do was reheat dinner and help him eat. She's done this before for me. She knows his bedtime. He knows her. Why am I even explaining this to you? This is none of your business."

"Is, too. You want to call her? Let her know you'll be late?"

"We have an arrangement. She stays till I get there. I never know how long the open mikes will last. Some nights are better than others. Some nights there's a sort of jam session afterwards at someone's house and I go there."

"Oh, so you go off to some guy's house and leave your baby at home?"

"What is with you? I'm an adult. I drive there. I can leave when I want to. My son has a perfectly competent babysitter. I've made provision for him. What I do for myself is my own business. Certainly not yours."

"Well, you didn't make a helluva lot of provisions tonight, did you? Going off with a stranger in a truck. Great. Just great. You're raped and left for dead. Your son never knows where his mother is. He's thrown into foster care."

"Stop. Just stop it. Lisa would have come for me if I'd gotten to a pay phone and called her."

"Lisa?"

"My babysitter."

"Not a good name for anyone."

"I'm sorry. I don't think her parents consulted you when they chose her name some twenty years ago."

"And you'd have called this woman from where? Big Dog's? The bottom of a ditch?"

"The nearest gas station to the Fruitville Road exit."

"You were hitchhiking!"

Katie drew a breath, calmed herself and smoothed her hands down her jeans.

"You stopped. You seemed like a nice man."

"Jesus Christ."

Katie looked over at Trevor's furious face, with its long wet hair plastered to his scalp and swaying in clumps around his wet chest and shoulders. She glimmered a smile and bit her lip.

"Not quite, but close enough. You were my savior today."

Trevor's eyes went wide. His anger fizzled out. His sense of humor kicked in.

"That was a very, very good way to shut me up. Thank you."

"You're welcome."

"I'm kind of touchy about kids being left alone."

"I gathered that."

"I'm kind of touchy about anyone hitchhiking on the interstate."

"Agreed."

"You need a cell phone."

"I can't afford a cell phone."

"If you're going to continue to own and attempt to operate Esmeralda, you will need a cell phone."

"I have nothing against cell phones. I simply can't afford one at this point. I'm a very bad credit risk."

"Why?"

Katie handed the towel to him and Trevor took it automatically. Katie smiled at him.

"I think you're very, very wet. And still getting rained in on. I keep that towel in the car to dry off my son if he gets caught in the rain coming out of daycare. It's perfectly clean."

"No boy-sweat on it?"

"No. Whatever that is. It's only used once for rain and then taken into the house, washed, dried, folded, and it's back out in the car. Go on. At least put it around your shoulders. I'm sorry you got so much more than you'd bargained for tonight."

I'm not, Trevor thought. I'm not sorry at all about any of this so far.

"Katie?"

"Hm?"

"You've been up since I don't know when. You've played guitar and nearly barfed. You've spent the better part of the last six hours with a possible axe-murderer. Do you want to curl up and sleep for a while? You're working tomorrow. Right?"

"Yes. I work tomorrow. What about you?"

238

"Nope. I'm off right now. After the tow truck comes, I'll drive you to your house. What time do you want me there in the morning to pick you up?"

"Ski, I can't ask you to do that. You've done so much already."

"Can Lisa drive you to work?"

"Afraid not. She works in Sarasota but she starts at 8:00 a.m. She has to be across town in the opposite direction. I'll call a cab."

"Don't trust me?"

Katie looked at the glistening man making half-hearted attempts at drying himself while rain continued to pour onto the back of his head.

She could only see planes and angles on his face in the shifting light of passing cars' headlights. He was wet to the skin. He smelled of warm male animal and laundry detergent, and deteriorated car seat foam rubber. He had been furious with her, but she had not been afraid of him. She had spent the last six or so hours in the company of a gorgeous man whom she knew nothing about and, yet, she felt she'd known him forever.

Katie didn't at all like the direction her thoughts were taking her, and stiffened her spine.

"I am not going to sleep with you."

"What? Wait a minute. I thought we'd already discussed this. I didn't offer. I still haven't. Geez. Get a grip. I'm offering a mechanic, a ride to work and a cell phone. That's it so far. I told you. A friend in need. No strings. Don't trust me? Too bad. You're out of choices. Lookee there. Tow truck at high noon. Now we're talking. Back in a minute. Here's your towel."

And he banged out the driver's side door, heedless of traffic or rain, causing car horns to blow.

Katie held the damp bundle of the towel and watched him meet and greet the tow truck driver, walk with him to the front of Essie and personally supervise her slow journey onto the tilted bed of the tow truck.

He was getting wetter and wetter.

She watched while the tow truck driver held a flashlight to his ID and then over the clipboard while he signed his name. There were smiles and handshakes. Both men sprinted for the cabs of their respective vehicles.

Trevor yanked open the door of the truck and bounced in, highly pleased with himself, and grinned at her.

"Okay. Mission accomplished. Where are we going now?"

Katie handed him the towel. Trevor wrapped it around his head and shoulders like a monk, started the truck and squinted for a break in traffic, bumping along the side of the road in the wake of the tow truck and coming onto the roadway behind it.

Katie realized she had no idea where her car was being towed to, and said so.

Trevor answered her absently.

"My mechanic's house. He'll fix her up and get her back to you. He's real good. Real cheap. I've been using him for years. I can barely change my own oil, and don't care to anyway. Scott'll do right by Essie. Afraid he'll sell her on the black market? I'll leave you a deposit. You can get a cell phone with it. Where are we going?"

"Fruitville Road. Essie didn't get that far from home before she broke down. I already told you. I have lousy credit. I can't get a cell phone. They like a positive credit history and a contract."

Trevor thought of the spare corporate cell phone Dani wasn't using at the moment.

"Use one of mine. I've got several scattered around."

"No. I don't wish to incur further obligation to you. That's very nice of you, but no."

"Lisa's credit any good?"

"I don't know. I guess. Why?"

"Get her to get you one. Pay her."

Katie thought about that.

"Maybe. But probably not. I can't afford any more expenses. You don't understand. Between doctor bills and daycare and gasoline for Essie, I have very little discretionary income."

"Yeah, I heard. Eight miles to the gallon. And a dog besides. What was your husband thinking of to put you into such a death trap?"

Katie's face hardened.

"He was thinking I couldn't go too far in it."

Trevor glanced over at her stony face as he took the next exit, got off, got on again and began to double back.

"Well, you sure fooled him, huh?"

"Essie's the best I can do right now. I'm on a very tight budget."

"And yet you play."

"I don't do drugs. I don't drink. I don't eat much. I don't party. And I don't sleep around. I have my job, my son, and my music. That's all I can swing right now."

Trevor rubbed his finger along the side of his nose and sniffed.

"Maybe you'll win the lottery."

"I won't win the lottery. I don't play the lottery. I don't gamble."

"This from the woman hitchhiking on the interstate."

"Give it a rest, Ski!"

Katie gasped and put her hand to her mouth.

"Oh, I'm so sorry. I didn't mean that. Really."

"Sure you did. Good snappy comeback. But I'm not about to abandon you until I know the whole situation, so be prepared to tell me to shove it up my ass, too."

"Very well."

"This Charlie fella. Your ex. Is he the father of your son?"

"Yes."

"Child support?"

"He has the obligation."

"Getting any?"

"Not yet. He's countering for visitation. I'm not allowing that. We're at a stalemate."

Trevor frowned.

241

"No visitation?"

"No."

"Here we get personal. Why?"

"My ex-husband is not a proper person to have visitation with a child."

Trevor felt his jaw muscles clinching.

"Why? Is his father a fag?"

"No. His father has a history of child molestation."

Trevor's hands rocked the steering wheel of the truck and they fishtailed briefly on the interstate.

"Jesus Christ, woman! I'm drivin' here. Try to ease into stuff like that, will ya? You could have gotten us killed."

"I don't like to talk about it."

"I guess not. Small wonder. Sorry. You can't begin to know how sorry I am about that. Sorry I had to ask. Not sorry I learned that, though. Just really, really sorry."

"My son sees a psychiatrist. It costs the earth, but it's worth it to me and I'd do anything for my son."

"Good for you. Get a cell phone."

"I've told you."

"And I've told you. If not you, then Lisa. If not Lisa, then me. I will not have the single parent mother of a boy young enough to play with the truck I saw in your station wagon gallivanting around either hitchhiking or driving that frigging mothball-fleet of a car without the backup safety plan of a simple cell phone. You're getting one tomorrow because I'm getting it for you. You will keep it on you and fully charged at all times and it will be turned on for incoming calls with the key guard on. You got that?"

Katie shifted in her seat.

"Don't miss the exit."

"Screw the exit. Did I miss it? No? Good. Which way when I get there?"

"Right."

"Got it."

"Ski, I seem to always be making you angry. I'm sorry. My life is a mess right now. Things will get better. I

242

have a good job, a roof over our heads, and a wonderful little boy. We're fine. Really."

"Why do I think I hear an echo?"

"I don't know? Why do you?"

"Never mind. Cell phone. Tomorrow. It's a priority with me."

Katie chewed on her lip.

"No strings? I have to consider the baby. I have to be smart for my son. I have to think of him first. If it was just me. But it's not."

Katie turned in the seat, worriedly regarding the forceful man staring into the darkness beyond the headlights of his dented truck.

"I'll accept the cell phone. I know I shouldn't, but it's a very good idea. Thank you for that, Ski. Some day I'll pay you back for it."

"Not in sex."

"I wasn't offering that."

"Good. I wasn't accepting it. I don't want gratitude. I want safe children. I want caring mothers to have a decent chance. I'm big on safety. If you want to repay the favor, pass it on. A good deed or a kind word. What goes around comes around. It's my turn to give. Some day it may be your turn to give. When your turn comes, give. Okay?"

"You're a very strange man."

Trevor turned his head and grinned at her in the dark.

"Oh, yeah. I'm past strange. Always have been. Ask anyone."

"Right turn."

"Thanks. Got it. Where do you live? Outer Slobbovia?"

"Just short of there. I live outside of Arcadia"

"Where do you work?"

"Desoto Square Mall."

"Eight miles per gallon?"

"It's the cost of doing business."

243

"We'll be working on getting a different car. Give that clunker back to Charlie. Let him drive it around. Eight miles to the gallon. Unheard of. A limo gets better."

"And you would know this how?"

"Scott. My mechanic. Helluva mechanic. Does up a lot of fancy cars, too. But he didn't say he could get you any better gas mileage for Essie. Why Essie, by the way? Why name that beast Esmeralda?"

Katie smiled.

"It just sort of popped into my head. I looked at her, and, poof, there was her name."

"What's your guitar's name?"

"My guitar's name?"

"Yeah. Him? Her? Name?"

"Guitar. It's a guitar."

"You didn't name your guitar? You named your car, but you didn't name your guitar? Weird."

"Start looking for a pole with big diagonal strips of reflective tape on it. It'll be on the right. Turn there. Watch out for the ditch."

"Great. Thanks."

"You're welcome. When we get there, I'll put your clothes in the dryer for you, if you'd like. It's nearly 2:00 a.m. Lisa may very well be asleep. But I'll wake her up. She needs to start fresh from her own home. This is a major favor she's been doing for me."

"I'll stay in the truck."

"Nonsense. You're soaked."

"I'll stay in the truck till she goes."

"Why? Are you shy?"

"Yes, I am. Unless you've got a change of clothes in there my size, I'll be sitting around in a towel while mine dry. I don't need this Lisa person seeing that."

"But it's all right for me to see it?"

Trevor gave her a grin.

"Heck, woman, it's all right by me if you see it all, towel or not."

244

Katie punched him sharply in the arm, making him laugh.

"Whoa! Quit hitting me. I'm driving here. I'm just messing with you. Geez."

Trevor took the next turn by a dimly seen pole with stripes on it. At one time there may have been a street sign on top, but eager vandals had been busy. He bumped the truck down a county-maintained road, splashing water up through the firewall where he'd forgotten there was another hole. He thanked God he wasn't in Yankee-land with icy slush flinging onto his legs, and slowed the truck down to a lurching pace. Katie pointed through the windshield.

"Right there on the left. Watch the ditch."

"Got a lot of ditches out here to watch, woman."

"I'm sorry. I'll have to have a chat with the county about that."

Trevor grinned again in the dark.

"Yeah. That'll work. Where do you want me to park?"

"Don't block that white Chevette. That's Lisa's. There's actually a driveway here if you can see it."

"I can't, but I can feel when I go too far off it into the mud. Truck kind of shimmies. Here okay?"

Trevor tentatively pulled close to a weathered wooden porch vaguely reminiscent of his brother Scott's own pre-Jarrett home in Arcadia and wondered vaguely if Scott would know this girl or her antecedents. He shut the truck off.

"You from around here originally?"

"No. What's it to you?"

"Nothing. Geez. Just making conversation."

"Pennsylvania. My family was from Pennsylvania."

"Cool. I'm from Delaware. And New York."

"You don't sound it."

"Naturalized Cracker. And you don't sound like Pennsylvania."

"All right. I'm not. I was born in Arcadia. But my mother was very much from Pennsylvania. She insisted I not slide into the what she called the local patois."

"You done good."

"You, apparently, did not."

Trevor chuckled as Katie bumped open her door and slid out, turning to grasp her guitar case. He got out with the towel still wrapped around his shoulders and followed her up the steps in the slackening rain.

Figures, he thought. Now we're off the road, the rain slackens. Thanks, God.

Then he amended that thought as Katie pulled open a squeaking wooden screen door and turned the knob to enter her home.

Thank you, God, for everything you have ever sent my way, good or bad.

Katie flicked on a light and clutter jumped out at him. She parked her guitar case in a corner by the door and Trevor pulled off the borrowed towel and wadded it up as she closed the door behind him.

Her home was lived-in, he thought.

Dirty dishes in the ancient sink were visible beyond a pass-thru window from the living room. Plastic laundry baskets were piled high. Folded clothes in two stacks were on the sofa where a figure was stretched out, asleep.

Lisa.

Katie took the dripping towel from Trevor, whispering to him, "The bathroom's to the right, down that hallway. Let me get you a dry towel."

She pulled a frayed but clean towel from one laundry basket.

"Here. Go take off your clothes."

Trevor grinned at her as Katie shoved the towel at him, whispering back, "Dream of a lifetime. A woman who gets down to business. Ow! Don't punch that arm. It's already bruised from your last efforts."

"Just go do it. All right?"

Trevor indicated the sleeping form on the sofa.

"Not till she leaves."

Katie sighed. Trevor looked down at her.

"Is she likely to use the bathroom before she goes? I'll go hide in there."

"Yes, probably she will."

"Where else can I hide?"

"Why do you want to hide?"

"I'm an axe murderer. My picture's been seen on America's Most Wanted. I don't want some strange woman looking at me thinking I'm your lay-of-the-night. Okay?"

"Lisa's not a strange woman. You're the one who's strange."

"Live with it. I'm strange."

"This is like a cheap comedy."

"Hide in your room?"

"In your dreams."

"Maybe."

"Stop that. There's an old pantry off the kitchen. Will that do?"

"I'm hiding in a closet? Perfect. Then I can come out of the closet. Even better."

Katie punched his arm again, making him laugh.

"Ow!"

"You are so strange. Through the kitchen. Door next to the stove. Go. I need to wake Lisa so she can leave. I need to check on the baby."

"Can I help you check on the baby?"

"No. Go stand in the closet. Saints alive. It's 3:00 a.m. This is ridiculous. Go."

Trevor went, hugely tickled by both Katie and the whole situation. He opened the pantry door, entered and stood, dripping and evaporating, shoving the fresh towel in his mouth to stifle his laughter as he heard Katie wake Lisa and explain calmly that Essie had died, she'd gotten a ride and that there was a strange, shy, wet man hiding in the pantry and would Lisa like to use the bathroom or have a cup of coffee before she left?

Lisa used the bathroom, declined the cup of coffee, ignored the remark about the strange, shy, wet man hiding in the pantry and left, probably too tired between her day job and her night of friendly favor-doing to even grasp the concept of a man at all.

Trevor could hear when Lisa's Chevette started up and she pulled away. He could hear when Katie closed the front door behind herself as she came back into the house.

He waited in his dark pantry, but Katie didn't come for him. Vaguely disappointed, he opened the door himself and came out into the kitchen.

Katie was no where in sight.

He laid the clean towel on the tiny Formica and chrome kitchen table and began to poke vaguely around in her cabinets. He didn't know what, if anything, he was looking for. He glanced at the dishes in the sink. He located the dish detergent in a cabinet under the sink, and began running water in the sink till it turned hotter, meanwhile dumping soggy Cheerios into the garbage can and scraping some hamburger grease off a plate. He filled the sink with soapy, hot water and dishes and began scrubbing them with a tuffy pad he got from the mouth of a frog soap dish at the back of the sink. He wiped down the counters, wiped off the kitchen table, wiped off the stove, then rinsed and stacked the dishes in the drain by the sink and glanced around for something else to do.

Laundry.

He didn't sit on the sofa to fold the laundry, mindful of his wet butt. He stood and folded two laundry baskets full, easily able to make decisions on who's clothing was whose.

There was still no sign of Katie and he went looking for her, not wanting to startle her. He located the bathroom. Not there. He quickly peeked in another room. Bedroom. Female. But no Katie. He tried one more door quietly. A bedroom. Tiny. A night-light glowed amber in the darkness. He could make out a bare-bones room with a single bed in it. The single bed held two occupants, Katie and a dark-haired little boy. Both were sound asleep.

Trevor found he enjoyed the sight and had no wish to disturb either mother or son. He quietly closed the door.

Crossing back towards the kitchen, and getting the dry towel from the table, he opened a different door that led to a laundry room. He stripped off his clothes and tossed them all in together in the dryer, setting it for medium heat and a best guess of forty-five minutes on the time. He turned his sneakers upside down to let as much water run out of them overnight as he could. He wrapped the towel around his middle and took his keys, wallet and cell phone back into the kitchen and then into the bathroom with him. He poked in her bathroom cabinet for toothpaste and rubbed some around on his teeth with his finger, swallowing the results. He started the shower, having found shampoo and conditioner sitting at the back of the tub. Suave lavender was fine by him. He showered, shampooed, conditioned his long hair and felt much better.

Between the tired muscles from the move and the cold rain in his clothes, it had been a long day for his body, Trevor thought. Hot water felt good.

Thank you, God, for the blessing of hot water.

He remembered Katie was probably using well water, and was certainly on a budget. He turned off the shower sooner than he might have at home to preserve some of the blessing of hot water for Katie for tomorrow morning. Past 3:00 a.m? Make that today. Funny, he thought. 3:00 a.m. in this house wasn't the blues.

Trevor wrung his hair out, squeezed it as dry as he could with the towel and wrapped the towel back around his waist. He located and used the available deodorant. He went back out to the living room and snagged two more towels for himself, one for his middle and another for his hair. He wrapped his hair up in the one towel like a turban, again aware of a low-grade urge to cut all the hair off. But he was going to force himself to wait for the Locks of Love extravaganza for Dani.

He was hanging the first dry towel over the edge of the bathtub, then thought better of that and took it out to the laundry room to check on his clothes, hanging it over the edge of the laundry tub there instead. He checked his clothes and reset the dryer for more time.

The darned jeans always took ten years to dry, he thought.

He came back into the living room looking for occupation and finally settled for the sofa and the only available reading material. He slowly became acquainted with Thomas the Train and reacquainted with Dr. Seuss, an old favorite from Scott Junior's library.

He must have dozed off, because he woke with a jolt, his head tilted back on the sofa and a thin, shiny book closed with his index finger still in it. He shook himself, got up, put the book back on the end table where he'd found it and went to check on his clothes. They were finally done, and dry.

He swapped towels for clothes, saved his socks next to his shoes for tomorrow and unwrapped his hair. He hung both towels over the edge of the washing machine tub. He shook out his hair and braided it loosely to get it out of his way, walking back towards the living room sofa, turning off the kitchen lights and then living room light, leaving the door to the bathroom open a crack with the light on.

There was a faded quilt on the back of the sofa and he shook it out, wrapping himself in it to lie down. It smelled musty but clean. He put his head down on the top of a stack of clothes on the sofa and closed his eyes.

The house was quiet except for the occasional drip of rain from the roof outside and the faint mechanical click of a wall clock in the kitchen. There were the settling sounds that all old houses make. There were the distant sounds of trucks on the interstate.

He closed his eyes and relaxed into sleep with the hum of the refrigerator faintly in his ears.

# Chapter Twelve

Near 7:00 a.m, Katie Mercer stood in her bedroom door, rubbing her arms through her old chenille bathrobe. She had awakened in the early hours of morning in her son's bed and finished the night sleeping in her own bed.

The beautiful man she had met only yesterday was on her living room floor, flat on his back, his glorious hair spread out around him. He was talking to her son. Robbie sat on his butt on the floor in his pajamas, a bowl of dry cereal in his lap. The TV was turned on to morning cartoons.

Katie watched as her strange houseguest walked his fingers over to Robbie and then quickly darted them in for a tickle. Robbie giggled, but then went solemn again.

It had been the same since Charlie's assault on him, Katie thought.

She heard the warm male voice addressing her son.

"What's up, dude? You bummed out?"

Katie watched as the man walked his fingers again towards her son and Robbie watched him. Robbie was still caught off guard when the tickle came. He giggled harder and the cereal bowl rocked. The man caught it and righted it.

"Sorry, dude. I got carried away."

Robbie was back to solemn again but he was ignoring the cartoons and looking down at her houseguest. Katie watched as the man edged down the floor until his head was next to Robbie's body and Robbie looked down into his face as he looked up at Robbie, man to boy and boy to man. Robbie reached out a finger and ran it tentatively over the stubble on the man's face.

Katie thought her heart would break.

The man smiled at Robbie, a warm, open smile Katie hadn't seen from him before.

"It'll get better, dude. It always does."

How could he tell that, Katie wondered? How could this strange man tell that? Ridiculous, Katie thought. But part of her worried whether she had inadvertently exposed Robbie to another pedophile.

251

She leaned away from the door jam and came into the living room.

Trevor broke eye contact with the tiny boy beside him and watched her, chuckling to himself. Bobbi always looked gorgeous in the morning. Katie looked awful.

She came over to her son and rumpled his hair, planting a kiss on his head. Her robe fell open a little, revealing no anatomical surprises to Trevor. She pulled it closed absently. Trevor was aware of a stab of lust. Katie looked him in the eye.

"I take it you two have met?"

"Nothing formal. We're both early risers, I guess. I figured cereal was a safe bet for him."

Katie straightened.

"You figured right. Thank you. Robbie's quite capable of getting his own, but it was a nice gesture."

Still on his back, Trevor turned his head to the little boy.

"Dude. You didn't tell me you could do it yourself. I wasted a lot of effort on you."

Robbie grinned at him, and Katie watched the man's answering grin. Katie felt somehow she was out of the loop.

"Would you like some breakfast? I don't have much."

"Nah. Rob and I have been swapping spit with the cereal here. I'm fine. Go do what you'd usually do."

Katie turned sharply suspicious eyes to him.

"How did you know his name?"

"I didn't. You just told me. I already introduced myself, though. I was in his house. It only seemed fair."

Katie walked stiffly into the kitchen and began banging cupboard doors.

"You can take a shower, if you want, Ski. There's towels in the hall closet."

Robbie looked down at him, puzzled, and Trevor shrugged, whispering to him.

"That's what your mom calls me. It's my nickname, I guess."

Robbie went back to watching the cartoons, and Katie looked back from the kitchen.

"What?"

"Don't need a shower. Took one last night. Thanks anyway."

Trevor sat up, hauled his hair back out of his way and twisted the covered rubber band from his wrist into it. He drew his legs up, sitting cross-legged beside Robbie, knees touching, and reached for the cereal bowl.

"My turn."

Robbie silently handed the bowl to him, intent on the cartoon. Trevor took the bowl and watched and munched.

"Wile E. Coyote's clueless. He just doesn't get it. Bad things happen to people who do bad things. Some folks never learn that."

Katie's voice exploded from the kitchen.

"Don't sit so close to him!!"

Two pairs of male eyes looked up and over at her in astonishment. Katie ran her hand through her hair and turned away. Trevor looked down at Robbie looking up at him. He handed the cereal bowl back to Robbie.

"Here, dude. You finish up. I'll go see what's wrong."

He got up and went into the kitchen, where Katie was a tense bundle of energy and movement, slamming cupboard doors, opening and closing drawers pointlessly.

Trevor stepped into her path.

"Slow down, Katie. Stop. What's wrong?"

Katie shuddered to a halt under the influence of Trevor's calm concern. She gripped her arms around herself tightly and burst into tears. Trevor shifted restlessly.

"Geez, woman, what the heck's the matter?"

Without even thinking about it, Trevor hauled Katie into his arms to comfort her. She didn't cry pretty, he thought. She had gone all red-blotchy and swollen-eyed from the get-go.

Katie sobbed into his chest, not relaxing. Trevor set his chin on her head and just waited her out. Finally Katie gulped out her answer.

"My baby. My precious, precious baby. My ex. . ."

"Oh. That. Yeah. Rob kind of told me about that."

Katie tore out of Trevor's arms, furious.

"Told you?! How could he? He's barely four. He doesn't have the words for what that monster did."

"Katie, calm down. I don't know how I know. Rob kind of told me this morning. Maybe it's a guy thing. But I could tell..."

"A guy thing!"

"Katie. He's going to be all right. Really."

"How the hell would you know that! Are you some high-priced shrink? No! Look at you! You're a construction worker."

"I just know. A man don't want to talk about that to a woman, not even his mom."

"He's not a man! He's a little boy!"

"You're wrong there. He's a man. And I'm a man. Don't you be fooled by him being trapped inside a little kid's body right now. And don't be fooled by what you think you see in me. I'm not a lot of things I think you think I am. I'm not a pedophile. I'm not a rapist. And I don't work construction. Your baby's going to be fine. We had a chat. Not with words. You wouldn't get that. But he's going to be all right, Katie. He's going to be fine."

Katie was humming with nerves, her tears dried onto her face, and her eyes round and staring. Trevor chewed on his bottom lip.

"I can't help you so easy."

"I don't want your goddamn help!"

Trevor sighed.

"Go on and do what you'd usually do in the morning. I'll be out sitting on the couch watching TV."

Trevor turned and began walking out of the kitchen when Katie's voice sounded behind him.

"Ski? I'm sorry. You meant well. You mean well. I'm just not ready..."

Trevor froze, his back to her, then slowly turned.

"I'm not asking for that. I didn't ask you for that, did I?"

Katie shook her head and Trevor stared hard at her.

"I'm not some kind of slot machine you gotta drop coins into to get a pay-off. I'm doing what I'm doing because it's the right thing to do, and you got nobody else to do it. I don't want a payback. You don't get that. But you better just suck it up and take it, 'cause you're not going to be able to stop me from helping you. You might have before I met Rob. But you haven't got a prayer now."

Katie shivered.

Trevor continued on into the living room. He didn't bother with sitting on the couch in the living room. His nerves on the hum, he grabbed his still damp sneakers, pulled them on unlaced and left the house, carrying his socks.

He paused on the front porch.

In the gray light of dawn, Katie's house turned out to be a run-down shanty.

Trevor stuck his socks in his jeans pocket and went to sit in the wet spot in his truck and brood, waiting for Katie to finish whatever her morning routine was and bring Robbie out so they could both get on with their separate days. He realized he should have brought the baby seat from Essie with them, but Katie should have thought of that, too. It was her kid. It was her baby seat. It was her responsibility. God knew where they would have put the thing, though, Trevor thought. In the driving rain of last night, it would have had its cushions soaked in the bed of the truck, if it hadn't fallen off the back onto the interstate anyway.

Not his problem.

Trevor brooded on babies and problems and responsibility as red-gold light bloomed its way through the ancient glass of his windshield and the sound of doors closing, a front door, and then a screen door, reached his ears. He looked up to see Katie walking to his side of the truck, Robbie on her hip, wearing a dark dress and dainty heels.

"I thought you'd left. I called a cab."

"Call 'em back."

"Yes. I will."

Katie turned to go back into the house, Robbie still on her hip, and opening both doors again, disappeared into the house. Shaking off his mood, Trevor grabbed his sunglasses from the dashboard, wiped them clean on his shirt and put them on. He reached under the seat for the backup baseball cap he knew was under there, slapping dust off its faded redness before pulling his hair out through the hole in the back of the cap.

He wouldn't have to be dealing with all this hair much longer, he thought. Be a darned relief. The baseball caps would fit better, too. Didn't trust him with Robbie, huh? Took Robbie in with her to make her phone call, huh? It both angered Trevor and hurt him. His worst enemy had never seen him as a sinister monster. Now a woman-in-need saw him exactly that way, a menace to both her boy and herself. But she was taking his help, reluctantly, in spite of that, because her need was great and her baby precious to her.

Trevor sniffed and shifted on the wet spot, plans evolving in his head. He could admire the woman even while she infuriated him. But he could still do an end run around her prickles to get her what he thought she needed. A cell phone. That would be a bulldozer job. Straight ahead. A better car? Gonna have to be an end run on that one, he thought. He'd see what Scott had to say. Some sort of relief for her tight finances. Carla claimed daycare cost the earth.

Cheered by pleasant, positive plans, Trevor put his own projects at the house on Gill Street in Punta Gorda on hold mentally and faced an anticipated day of nebulous community service focused on one plain young woman and her son.

Katie came back out both doors and down the wooden steps, this time coming to the passenger side door.

256

Trevor leaned over in the cab to shove it open for her. She had her hands full with Robbie. She slid onto the seat and shifted Robbie onto her lap, grabbed the door and slammed it shut, then sat silent, looking straight ahead. Robbie lowered his head to her shoulder, but watched Trevor with owlish eyes. Trevor smiled. And Robbie smiled back.

"No purse?"

"I travel light. My car keys went with Essie. My house key is in my pocket."

"You'll need a purse."

"I own one. I seldom use it. I used a diaper bag when Robbie was smaller."

Katie turned worried eyes to Trevor.

"I forgot the baby seat last night."

Trevor started the truck with one turn of the key. Helluva mechanic, his brother Scott, he thought.

"I know. I forgot it, too."

"What we're doing now is illegal and highly dangerous."

"I'll drive real careful. Ya know, generations of kids rode in cars, on their mother's laps, before car seats were invented."

"That does not make it right. Or safe. Why will I need a purse?"

"For your cell phone."

Katie sighed, sagged, and closed her eyes briefly.

"I thought you'd given up on that. I hoped."

Katie opened her eyes and looked over at Trevor.

"No, I didn't. Do you know where you're going?"

"Heck, yeah, I know where I'm going. Do you think I was born on Mars? Desoto Square Mall. US 41 and Beneva Road. Right?"

"Yes. Thank you."

"You're welcome."

They both buckled up and rode in a more companionable silence through the rainfresh dawn along Fruitville Road. Trevor glanced at Katie.

"When should I pick you up? I'm going to be checking in with Scott about Essie, too."

"I get off at 5:30 p.m. But we have to drop Robbie at daycare before you take me to work."

"You point and I'll drive."

"Thank you."

Daycare turned out to be in a strip mall. Only in Florida, Trevor thought. The back of the whole mall faced pinewoods and was fenced. There were large brightly colored plastic forts and seesaws there, very little grass, but good shade. And safety.

Trevor pulled into the front of the place, and eyeballed the other businesses located there as Katie got out with Robbie and, setting him on his feet and taking his hand, walked him through the entrance.

There was a veterinarian in the little mall, the early morning sounds of dogs barking not unpleasant. Most of the stores were vacant. Trevor thought that was a plus for parking. There was some sort of financial service located there and the offices of an engineering firm. There were vacant lots full of jack pine and palmetto scrub on both sides of the mall that housed Little People Day Care. Potential for expansion, Trevor thought absently.

A smiling woman in slacks and a smock walked Katie back out to the front door. Katie was smiling, too. It did wonders for her plain face, Trevor thought. She was carrying a stiff sheet of bright yellow construction paper.

Trevor leaned over to help with the door again and Katie climbed in, banging the door closed.

"Oh, Ski. I've just got to share this with someone. You have no idea how special this is."

Trevor leaned over and Katie showed him a childish drawing of a house with a big yellow sun overhead, bright enough to still be visible on the yellow paper. There were clear windows and green grass and a red door. There were two stick figures outside, one in a skirt, the other much shorter. Both were grinning stick-grins.

"Robbie's?"

"Yes. Oh, yes. He's smiling."

"Heck, the whole darned picture is smiling, Kate. Sun. House. You. All smiles."

"It wasn't always so. Six months. Robbie had stopped talking at all. Nightmares. Not so many now. His pictures were dark scribbles of big black and red lines on white paper. No people. No house. Then there was just a face behind a window, frowning. The house got more detail. The windows got normal looking. He snuck in a sun but it wasn't very big. He put me in, standing outside the house. And he was inside. I think he blamed me for what happened with Charlie. I blamed myself. But, look. We're together now."

Trevor nodded.

"And everything's going to be fine. He told me so."

"Robbie drew this yesterday, Miss Marta says. She couldn't wait to show it to me."

"I'll get it framed for you today."

Katie drew away from him.

"I don't need your sarcasm. I'm sorry I showed it to you."

Trevor blinked, confused.

"What? What sarcasm? All I said was I'd get it framed for you. That's all I meant. I think it's great. No frame? Fine. How about fridge magnets? Is that all right? Tape is good, too. I understand what this means. I do. I understand what it means to you. And to Robbie. I wasn't being sarcastic. Honest."

Katie chewed her lip.

"I'm sorry, Ski. I apologize. I'm very sensitive about Robbie."

"It's okay. Thanks for sharing. I didn't mean any harm. Really."

"I wish I had brought a purse now."

"Roll it up. Here."

Trevor pulled the covered rubber band from his hair and handed it to Katie.

"It's clean. Really. Roll up Rob's picture. It won't hurt it. These things don't cut into paper the way regular rubber bands do. I use them all the time for my music and other stuff I don't want fold marks in."

Katie took the covered rubber band from him and began to carefully roll up the construction paper artwork.

"Your music?"

"Wow! Look at the time. Gotta go. You'll be late for work."

Trevor started the truck and pulled hurriedly out of the parking lot of Little People Day Care.

"Watch where you put Robbie's artwork. It's pretty nasty in this truck between general dirt and last night's rain. Do you get a lunch break where you work? No? What the heck's that all about? You gotta eat. I'll bring food. Chinese? Great."

Trevor jabbered and bamboozled his way into Katie Mercer's life as he drove her to work. She looked at him every once in a while as he drove, but apparently chalked up everything he said and did to his self-statement of being strange.

Weaving his way through traffic, Trevor got Katie to Desoto Square Mall on time and parked where he felt he couldn't possibly be seen by anyone. If Katie considered it a long hike in high heels to her job, she didn't say so.

"I never know when I'll get a break for lunch. We eat in shifts and always in the back room. Customers come first at The Sophisticated Lady Boutique. It's not unheard-of for my lunch break to come sometime after 2:00 p.m. How will you know when to come with this lunch you're planning?"

"I won't. I'll just come. Don't worry. I'll be checking with Scott. I'll be getting that cell phone. Got lots to do. Oh, yeah. Gotta sleep. Gotta eat. I'm absent-minded."

"You forget to sleep and eat?"

"Yeah. Big mistake."

Katie slid from the remotely parked truck and slammed the door shut.

"Are you really an axe-murderer? You certainly don't like people seeing you."

"Yes, I am. But I don't do women or kids. You're safe. See you later. Bye."

Trevor bumped the truck over a curb because he was watching Katie watch him leave. He didn't need to look in his rear view mirror to tell he had an idiot-grin on his face.

\*　　\*　　\*　　\*　　\*

Scott Daniels leaned back against the scarred wooden tool bench in his garage.

"So. Did you get laid?"

"Huh? What? No."

"Wake up, Trev. Or go to sleep. Whichever."

"How's Essie?"

"Who? Oh, the piece-of-shit. She'll do fine. For a live reef. Total electrical failure. Needs complete rewiring. All her connections are corroded and the wires are shot. They fall apart in your hands when you try to strip them back to get to good clean copper. She's toast. What's Plan B?"

"Huh? What?"

"Plan B, lover boy. There's always a Plan B."

"New car. Gotta be sneaky, though. Not too new. Gotta get a good story going here. How's this? My mechanic, you, found Essie is a rare and priceless limited edition. A collector wants her, real bad. Offering, I don't know, twenty thousand dollars?"

"Jesus Christ, moron. That's way too much to pay for sex. What happened to free love? You have never had to pay for sex. Heck, I have never had to pay for sex."

"What sex?"

"I don't know. But what the heck's got into you, boy?"

"Love. I think. I'm not sure. Maybe. Whatever. I'm trying to do a good deed here. Okay? But I gotta be sneaky about it. The lady's got her pride. Too much money? How about five hundred dollars?"

"For that car? Zero. For your lie, yes, I'd say five hundred might be reasonable. There's nut cases out there

261

dumber than you are. God knows someone might even pay that much for it, if it were running. But your lady can't get no decent ride for five hundred bucks, Trev. Get real."

"She'll win the car. How's that?"

"No one gives away used cars as prizes. What contest?"

"My cousin. That's it. He's in the service. Needs someone to take his car, quick. So I bought it, but I don't need it or want it. What do you think?"

"Reggie's not in the service anymore. He'd put that shackled-up GTO of his up on blocks in the garage before he'd sell it. Shoot, he'd take it with him to his grave if he could."

"It's got to be decent transportation and it's got to be used."

"Your mechanic's sellin' one."

"He is?"

"Well, he could be. Mechanics do that, ya know. Fix 'em up and sell them. We could get one off Uncle Fred at the dealership in Arcadia. One they'd usually wholesale off. Tell Katie I worked on it and I'll just charge her for what I've got in it. Make it doable as well as believable. Say a hundred and fifty bucks. Rebuilt starter. Rebuilt alternator. New water pump. Make it a good story, Trev."

"Ya think? Yeah, I like that. Let's go shopping."

"Let's have Essie towed to the junk yard."

"Auto recyclers. No, not yet. Gotta sell this to Katie. Gotta go shopping at Uncle Fred's. Gotta do lunch. I said I'd buy Chinese. Gotta go. After lunch. Okay? You free? I forgot to even ask if you were free. Sorry. I really am sorry."

Scott laughed his deep laugh.

"I'm free. I just love to see you when you're all jazzed up. Got more energy than them darned ferrets."

Trevor grinned at him.

"I'll be back. Oh, the lady doesn't know I'm Trevor Daniels"

"Who the heck does she think are you?"

"Ski."

262

"What? Ski Colorado?"

"Yes. That's it."

"Priceless."

\*　　\*　　\*　　\*　　\*

Facing the menu board of the China Star Chinese Restaurant, Trevor vacillated. He realized he'd forgotten to even ask Katie what she'd like to eat.

"Darn. Too many choices. Well, chicken then. Can't go wrong with sweet and sour chicken."

Trevor focused on the patient Asian woman behind the counter.

"I'll have a number two to go. Thanks."

Trevor paid when his order came and squelched his way back out to the truck in his wet sneakers from the night before. He was still in the same clothes he'd moved furniture in the day before as well. The same clothes he had gotten soaked in, slept in and now was going to charm a lady in.

He drove to Desoto Square Mall and pulled into another remote parking slot, adjusted his baseball cap and sunglasses. He got out of the truck, the plastic bag of Chinese food dangling from his long fingers as he loped across the parking lot.

He opened the door to The Sophisticated Lady Boutique and stepped inside. Once inside, he realized he wasn't the usual clientele for The Sophisticated Lady Boutique, but he definitely looked the part of the delivery guy for a food order. He squelched his way up to a glass-topped counter and smiled at the gray-haired female there from behind the protection of his sunglasses.

"Food delivery for Katie Mercer. Prepaid. Where do you want it?"

The woman stiffened and looked down her long nose at him.

"Mrs. Mercer is with a customer. She made no mention of a delivery coming here."

"It's a surprise. From an admirer. Leave it here?"

"Certainly not. Take it straight back and turn right. There's a small break room there. You may set it on the table. In future, use the back door."

Witch, Trevor thought, and smiled again.

It was a small shop, he mused, looking around. Excruciatingly elegant and high-end. Obviously not a chain. He wondered if the owners would be interested in selling it.

"Hey."

The woman turned cold eyes to him.

"Yes?"

"Who owns this joint?"

"I do."

"Cool."

"The back. Into the back. Now."

"Yes, ma'am."

Okay, then, he thought. He'd buy the shop, fire the witch-owner and let Katie run the place. At an increase in salary, of course, due to her new responsibilities. Perfect.

Humming under his breath, Trevor squelched his way into the back room, passing Katie in deep conversation with a patron. He ignored her, but caught her glance at him. She excused herself to the woman and followed him into the break room.

"Ski. I thought you were joking. You have to leave right now. I'll lose my job. I can't have that."

Trevor put the bag of food on the table and turned to her.

"Sorry. I'll be leaving. You got no problem with your job. Listen, I've got good news and I've got bad news. Bad news is Essie's dead. Really dead. Past CPR. Scott says so. Good news is he knows some guy who wants her anyway."

"Somebody wants my dead car? Why?"

"Flake. Who knows? Who cares? He can get you five hundred. Maybe more. What do you think?"

"I'll still need a car."

"Got that covered. Maybe. Got connections. I'll be back to pick you up anyway. I'll know more then. Sell Essie? Okay?"

264

"Yes. Okay. But leave. Please. Right now. Thanks for the food."

Katie kissed him quickly on the shoulder through his shirt and shoved him out the back door. Trevor thought foolishly that he'd never wash that shoulder again.

That was around noon.

By 1:00 p.m, he had purchased a new cell phone in Katie's name, fully charged and activated, with his cell number programmed into it by Scott.

By 2:00 p.m, he and Scott were towing Essie behind Scott's van through back roads to their Uncle Fred's car dealership in Arcadia.

By 3:00 p.m, they were heading back to Sarasota with the contents of Essie in the trunk of a metallic blue 1993 Chevy Lumina driven by Trevor with Scott following in the van.

By 4:00 p.m, negotiations were under way by Daniels Investments to purchase The Sophisticated Lady Boutique from a surprised Ruth Leasure. Simultaneously, Little People Day Care received a phone call from The Daniels Foundation for Children, announcing its intention of providing funds for a full scholarship for Robbie Smallwood on the recommendation of friends of his mother who wished to remain anonymous. When the owner declined to accept the scholarship money without the approval and knowledge of Robbie's mother, another branch of the family enterprises set about acquiring the day care facility from Miss Marta Chapman. Little Buddy Day Care was on the horizon before Scott and Trevor pulled up outside The Sophisticated Lady Boutique at 5:30 p.m, Scott now driving the newly acquired Chevy Lumina.

Trevor, finally in clean dry clothes and at least dry sneakers and a definitely better baseball cap, frowned up at the ornately scrolled sign over the door.

"That name's gotta go. It'd be a pleasure to stick the whole sign up Ms. Leasure's ass, but it's a pretty big sign and she's got a darned tight ass."

"Got any ideas for names for it?"

265

"Heck, no. What do I know about women's clothes?"

"You know how to take 'em off."

"There is that. It's probably not the clientele for Trevor's Strip Shoppe, huh?"

"Probably not. Leave it the way it is for now, I guess. Maybe run a contest. Ask all the current customers to vote on a name. I hope to God they got a decent database of customers in there. Well, Steph's people can handle all that."

"Scott, I couldn't care less if the place ever turns a profit. I want Katie working where she'll never have to be afraid she'll lose her job if she's late or food comes or she wants a decent lunch break."

The Sophisticated Lady Boutique closed its doors at 5:30 p.m, but Katie Mercer didn't leave until after 6:00 p.m. She had worked a ten-hour day and Trevor was furious.

"They do that to her because they know they can get away with it. I hate that."

"You're doin' somethin' about it, Trev. Tighten it up, Ski. Your lady's comin'."

"Hey, do you know any Mercers from Arcadia?"

"Plenty of them between Arcadia and Fort Ogden. Real common name."

"Smallwoods?"

"Nope."

Trevor opened the passenger side door of the car and stood up to watch Katie tipping across the parking lot in her tiny high heels. He thought she fit well into The Sophisticated Lady Boutique. She wore her dark dress with elegance.

As she got closer, Trevor could see faint lines of fatigue on her face, and some pain around her eyes. He tilted his head and looked at her closely as she came up.

"What's wrong?"

"Nothing. Really. I guess my feet hurt."

"Long day?"

"Yes, it was. Never mind. Where's your truck?"

"Back at Trevor's house."

"Whose house?"

266

"Trevor's. Guy I work for. That's where I stay. Climb on in. You've got short legs, so you get the center hump to straddle."

Katie got in the car and took off her shoes, sliding across the seat. Trevor got in and shut the door.

"This is my brother Scott. He's my mechanic. He works for Trevor, too."

Scott leaned over to shake hands.

"Hey. How's it goin'?"

Katie smiled at him, her hand lost in his bigger one.

"I'm pleased to meet you, Scott. Ski, does this Trevor employ your whole family?"

Scott grinned at Trevor, watched him squirm, and then answered Katie's question himself.

"He sure 'nough does, missy."

Trevor sucked in a breath.

"Well, yeah, pretty much. It's easier that way. Safer."

Scott shook his head.

"Priceless. This is gonna be priceless. I ain't had this much fun since we went mail-boxin' and hit old man McDermott's cement post."

Trevor looked around Katie to his brother.

"Yeah. You laughed all night. But I was the one holding the metal bar. I took that shock clean up my arm and into my brain."

Katie looked from one to another of the grinning brothers.

"Tell me, did you two tip cows as well?"

"Ski, I'll answer that one. No, ma'am, the cows don't much like it. It's kinda cruel. Our Daddy would have kicked our butts."

"But destruction of property was permissible?"

"No, ma'am. Restitution was duly made. And any injuries we incurred in the course of our criminal activity were best not mentioned to Daddy, or he'd add to them."

"He'd beat you?"

"No, ma'am. But you kinda wished he would after he finished laying you out with his tongue. It would have come

267

as a darned relief to the both of us to just get knocked in the head."

Trevor nodded, remembering far from pure teenage years spent getting to know his older stepbrother. He turned his head and looked past Katie to Scott again.

"You know, Bro. It's funny. All my closest friends are family or women. Or both."

"Jake."

"Yeah, there's Jake. But we're not really that close. Funny."

"Hilarious. Where are we headed, Ski?"

Trevor grinned at his brother's mock-serious face.

"Trevor's house. We're heading for Trevor's house."

"Priceless."

"Wiseguy."

Scott put the car in drive. They crossed the parking lot of the Desoto Square Mall and Scott pulled out onto Beneva Road, heading for US 41.

Katie, who had been rubbing the back of her neck as if to ease tired muscles, seemed to focus back on the conversation now.

"I think it's very nice of Trevor to let you stay at his house, Ski."

"Yes. He's a very nice person."

Scott chuckled low.

"Yes, ma'am. A real nice guy. Salt of the earth. Honest, too."

Trevor glared at his brother.

"Stay off the green side of the road, Scott. You're laughing too much."

"This is a nice car, Katie, doncha think? Trevor's got a little green MG. Got him a boat out there at his place, too. Got a whole lot of stuff."

Trevor shifted his shoulders.

"Shut up, Scott."

Scott almost purred.

"How much of the rest of the family have you met, Katydid?"

"What?"

"Sorry. Instant nickname. It's like a cricket. I forgot girls don't like bugs."

"That's darling. Thank you. I don't mind. I like it. Whose family? Ski's?"

"Yes, ma'am."

"Well, no one."

"Then quit while you're ahead, Katydid. You met the cream of the crop when you met me."

Trevor rolled his eyes.

"Scott, quit it. You're embarrassing me."

"Not like I could, Ski. I could have a real field day here."

"True. Just be gentle. Okay?"

"I specialize in CYA, Ski. You're fine."

Trevor turned eagerly in the seat to face Katie.

"Hey, Katie. This is a nice little car, isn't it? Good gas mileage. A real steal. Scott here got a thousand out of that collector for Essie. This car was chump change. Speaking of which, here's your change."

Trevor pulled six hundred dollars out of his front pocket and handed it to a stunned Katie.

"Pretty cool, huh?"

Katie looked at him as he grinned at her, then turned her head to look at an equally grinning Scott.

"What's going on here? This is my car? How could you sell Essie so quickly? You don't even have a signed title."

Trevor gave her the lie.

"The guy didn't care about the title. He's not planning on running her. Just keeping her. Up on blocks in his garage. Working on her, I guess. Maybe not. Who cares? Nice car, though, huh? This one, I mean. It's blue."

Trevor gave her the idiot-grin and Scott tried not to swallow his tongue as Katie stared at the crumpled money in her hands.

"There's something wrong here. But nothing illegal, I suppose. I need a car."

269

Scott took pity on his brother.

"Katydid, I done been over this car. It's real dependable. We got connections in the auto business. I'm a mechanic. I'm tellin' you this little car will be perfectly safe for you and Robbie. It's better under the hood than it looks from the outside. Pretty much like my baby brother here, ya know. Not much to look at, but real rock solid in the long run."

Katie rubbed her forehead.

"I suppose I should look closer here, but I'm not in a position to do so. Thank you both for selling Essie and getting me this darling little car. You've both gone to a lot of trouble for me. Scott, I appreciate your letting Essie be dropped off at your house last night and looking at her this morning. That was very sweet of you."

"I'm a daddy myself. I believe in safe transportation for my wife and baby. This whole deal is safe."

"And change back in my pocket. Just like at McDonald's."

Trevor turned eager eyes to her.

"Want to go out to dinner? Hungry?"

"We need to pick up Robbie. We need to get Scott back to his wife and baby or at least to his car. Wherever that is."

Scott passed a slow-moving vehicle.

"My van's over at Trevor's place, Katydid. Ski needed a shave and a change of clothes."

Katie turned with a gasp to Trevor.

"Oh, God, yes. You were soaked to the skin last night, you poor man, and I fell asleep in Robbie's room. I'm sorry I left you in the closet."

Scott snorted and became intensely interested in the roadway. Katie jabbered artlessly on.

"And thank you for doing the dishes. That was a big help. I forgot to thank you for that, too."

"You're welcome. Food? Eat? We can get Robbie and go over to Trevor's place."

270

"I'm tired, Ski. Really tired. I appreciate the offer, though. My boss was a total witch today. I don't think you should try to bring food again. She really didn't like that."

"That's not going be a problem for long."

"What?"

"Nothing. No food? Okay. No food. Sleep? Yeah, I could maybe use some of that myself."

"I don't wish to shock your brother, Ski, but we will not be exchanging an offer of food for an offer of sleeping together."

Scott choked and his eyes watered in an effort to control his laughter. Trevor pretended to take offense.

"Certainly not, Kate. I wasn't offering that. Exactly. When will I see you again? You have wheels now. You don't need me to drive you to work. Oh. Here. I got the cell phone, too. Forgot. See? It's in the glove box, all charged up and ready to rock. I had Scott program my number in it, just in case. Robbie's picture is rolled up on the back seat. Just so you know."

"The cell phone. You were serious about that, too."

"Of course I was. Why would you think I wouldn't be?"

"My ex. He had a way of dangling offers and then reneging on them."

"Oh. Nope. Not me. I get absentminded, but I don't forget."

Scott leaned over.

"That's the God's honest truth, Katydid. He don't forget nothin'. He don't plan ahead so good on little things, but he's got a great grasp of the big picture."

Trevor glanced at his brother, his eyes warm.

"Thank you, Bro. Now shut up."

"I'm shuttin'."

"So. Katie. When will I see you again?"

"Ski, please don't rush me. Okay? You've been everything that's wonderful. I can't believe what a difference you've made in my life in less than twenty-four hours. But please don't rush so much. Okay?"

271

Trevor bit his lip and tapped his foot nervously.

"Okay. I'm okay with that. Really. Uh, sometimes I gotta be out of town, working for Trevor. But I always have my cell phone on. Always. I'm just saying."

"Thank you. Thank you both. You're sure the collector won't want Essie's title signed?"

Trevor nodded.

"Positive."

"Because I suppose I could somehow get Charlie to sign it. He was to have transferred the title to me in accordance with the terms of the divorce. But, of course, he hasn't."

Trevor stared hard at Katie.

"Don't bother him. Don't go near him. Okay? We don't need the title."

Katie looked over to Scott.

"Scott, do you know where you're going? To Robbie's daycare? I never thought to ask."

"Oh, yeah. Ski done took me over there. Just checkin' the place out. Got an interest in daycares myself. Gonna be puttin' my baby in one, ya know."

"I just thought I'd ask."

Trevor was a bundle of nerves in the passenger seat, tapping his sneaker against the side of the vehicle and rocking slightly to some internal beat. Scott chuckled, glancing at him. The kid didn't know whether to shit or go blind, he thought.

"Priceless. This is priceless."

Katie smoothed her skirt and Trevor twitched. Scott pulled into the parking lot of Little People Day Care. Soon to be Little Buddy Day Care, he amended mentally.

Katie straightened her shoulders.

"I'd like to drive when we leave. I need to get used to this new car and where everything is located in what remains of daylight. I'll be driving back from Trevor's house to my own house in the dark."

Scott kept the car running for her and got out.

272

"Good idea, Katydid. Very smart. Slide on over and I'll help you adjust the seat. Ski, go get Robbie, will ya?"

"Sure."

Trevor opened his door and slid out, leaving his brother and Katie to adjust the seat and mirrors and locate lights and wipers. He took it as a good sign that Katie had allowed herself to be manipulated by Scott into letting him fetch Robbie. That was a step up from this morning's possessiveness.

Trevor lounged into the daycare, smiling his relaxed, easy smile at Marta Chapman.

"Hey. Nice to see you again, Miss Marta. Robbie ready to roll?"

"Yes, he is, Mr. Daniels. I can't thank you enough for letting me stay on to work here. Your offer on the business was very generous, but I really enjoy working. I'd have missed the children."

"I'm glad to have you, ma'am. I don't know squat about daycares. Maybe you'll open up another one with what you're getting for this one, but I hope you stay here, or at least help us get good people in. If this works out, I'm thinking in terms of a chain of these places. My sister-in-law tells me daycare is expensive. No offense. And that good ones are hard to find. I'd like to be able to deliver a quality service at a reduced cost, if I can. You're the lady to help me do that. I don't want any more latchkey kids or home-alone babies if I can prevent it. But I don't want me owning this place to get out. Not me personally. Okay?"

"Certainly, Mr. Daniels."

"Trev. Or better yet, Ski. My Dad's daddy was Mr. Daniels."

"Ski. Thank you, Ski. Darlene? Yes, Robbie's ride is here now. Thank you. We'll see you later, Ski."

Trevor smiled at her and took Robbie's hand, looking down at him.

Robbie looked up and suddenly that didn't seem fair to Trevor. He crouched beside Robbie so they could face one another, eye to eye, on the same level.

"I've got plans for us, Rob. Okay? Nothing bad. Nothing right away. I like your picture you drew, dude. Coming right along just fine. Everything's gonna be just fine. Come on and meet Scott. He's my brother. He's got a little boy, too. Scott Junior. He's about your age. Scott doesn't have Junior with him this red-hot minute. But you'll be meeting him soon. Scott's out teaching your mom where things are in her new car. Essie cocked up her toes, dude. This is your mom's new ride. You cool? Okay. Let's roll, dude."

Trevor stood, scooped Robbie up into his arms and settled him on his hip the way he did with Scott Junior. Robbie still had to look up to him, but not as far.

Marta Chapman watched man and boy exit together.

Trevor shifted Robbie slightly on his hip once outside.

"Hey, you all. You figured out the gadgets on that car yet?"

Scott looked over from squatting beside Katie seated in the driver's side.

"She's real tiny, Ski. I'm gonna have to take the seat out and block it up, then adjust the brake pedal higher. She can't hardly see out the windshield."

"Well, how the heck did you drive Essie, Kate? I swear to God I could barely see out of that thing myself."

"I used a booster seat."

"What booster seat?"

"The Tampa Bay phone book."

"Oops. It was four-years-ago's issue. It was on the floor and messed up. I left it in Essie. Sorry."

"I'll do fine."

"Ski, go bum a couple of blankets from that lady for Katie to sit on. No. Never mind. That won't work. You won't be able to reach the pedals, Katydid. You might be stuck with Ski again for a while."

Trevor brightened.

"Cool. Thanks, Bro."

"Chill out, Ski. We'll drive your lady home. I can do this tonight and you and I'll drop her car off at her house before she needs it tomorrow mornin'."

"By the time you adjust it for Katie, neither one of us will be able to get behind the wheel. We'll have our knees in our eyebrows. We'll look like we're driving clown cars for Ringling Brothers."

"Shoot. You're right."

Katie intervened.

"Gentlemen. Drive me to Trevor's house. That was the original plan. Correct? Scott's van is there. And Ski's truck. Scott can take my little new car home with him if he'd be so kind as to do that work. That would be wonderful, Scott. Thank you. Ski can take me home, if that won't be too much of an imposition?"

Trevor jiggled Robbie on his hip.

"Oh, I love getting imposed on."

Scott frowned at him.

"Chill, moron."

Ignoring the brothers' exchange, Katie continued.

"And after work, Ski can pick me up, if he's willing, and take me to your house, Scott, to pick up my car."

Trevor grinned.

"Willing. Oh, yeah. More than willing. Good plan, Scott. Ya think?"

"Good plan, Ski. Gets us all where we need to be, I'd guess. Got a good brain there, Katydid."

"Thank you. I don't often get compliments on my brains."

Scott frowned at her.

"Whyever not?"

"Brains aren't sexy."

Trevor bounced Robbie on his hip and grinned at him.

"They are to me."

Scott shook his head.

"Put a lid on it, Ski. Get that boy into his car seat and let's get on over to Trevor's place. I got work to do on

Katie's car tonight and a wife and child to enjoy. Plus dinner. Ski?"

Trevor answered from the back seat where he was fastening Robbie's car seat belt.

"Yeah?"

"Feed the woman, will ya? Trevor ain't got spit to eat in that house. You feed her and you and that little boy before you take her home. I swear to God, Katie. You got to watch him. He forgets to eat. He's real absent-minded."

"So I've heard."

Katie slid over to the center of the car again to allow Scott behind the steering wheel. Trevor got in beside her on the passenger side and closed his door, turning in his seat to exchange grins with Robbie in the back seat. Scott shook his head.

"Buckle up, moron. I swear. Some things never change."

"Oh. Okay. Done. Let's roll."

"We're rollin'."

He wanted to see Katie's face when she saw The Ice Palace, Trevor thought.

He didn't want to see Katie's face when she saw The Ice Palace.

Would she be stunned? Impressed? Revolted?

Suddenly Trevor didn't want Katie to see The Ice Palace at all. Ever.

"Scott?"

"Yeah?"

"Turn around."

"What?"

"Turn around."

"I can't. I'm drivin'."

"I mean turn the car around."

"What the heck's got into you?"

"The Ice Palace."

Katie wrinkled her brow and looked from Trevor to Scott. Scott shook his head.

"So?"

"Let's go over to your place. All right?"

"No. There's no point in goin' over to my place. I've got my van at your place. Your truck's there."

"You can bring me over in the morning."

"What the heck is the matter with you? I can't. You'd be stuck at my house. Then I'd have to take you back over there to get your truck, drivin' Katydid's clown car. You're makin' this thing into a Chinese fire drill. You are just so weird. Quit it. We're goin' to The Ice Palace."

Katie looked to Scott.

"The Ice Palace?"

"Trevor's nickname for this honkin' big place his first daddy left him. You'll see. Ski? You're a mess. Lean over the seat and talk to Robbie for a while. Geez."

Scott drove them down Longboat Key, Katie looking first one way and then the next as they passed various mansions.

"I've got customers who live out here. Ooh, that's a pretty house. Imagine the power bill. Oh, nice architecture on that one. Cute little mailbox. Jeepers. Will you look at that one? Frank Lloyd Wright meets Superman's Dad."

Scott nodded as they turned in at the slowly opening automatic gates.

"Yep. The Ice Palace."

"This is it?"

"Yep."

"Well, I guess the rich really are different from the rest of us. You couldn't give me this place. Well, maybe for a bed and breakfast. But no, not cozy enough at all. This is where you live, Ski?"

Trevor didn't answer so Scott filled the silence.

"No. Not really. This is where he stays when he's in Sarasota. He's got a perfectly decent house down in Punta Gorda, close to the family. One he just finished not even movin' into yet. I done busted my butt humpin' furniture into that place for nothin'. Heck, if I'd have known you wouldn't even be lookin' at it for a day or so, Ski, I could have got more troops to help with the move. Darn."

Katie's eyes roamed over the vaulted entrance and lush plantings of the Longboat Key mansion.

"House in Punta Gorda?"

Trevor shifted in his seat.

"That's my home. This is where I live. Lived. Whatever. See? There's my truck. And Scott's van. Very handy to have a van in the family."

Scott snorted.

"Yeah. Especially for apparently unnecessary moves to Charlotte County. If I'd known."

"Bite me."

"As if."

"Stephie says it's a great house for entertaining."

Katie focused back on the brothers.

"Stephie?"

Trevor nodded.

"My cousin. Our cousin. She runs all the parties."

"Parties?"

"Yeah. About one every two weeks when I'm off the road. Like now. Got another one coming up."

"The road?"

"I travel a lot for a living."

From force of habit, Scott parked Katie's car where he wouldn't block Trevor's truck or his own van.

"Ski?"

"Yeah?"

"Zip it or lose it."

"Oh. Okay. You coming in, Scott? Dr. Pepper?"

"Nah. I'd like to get started on Katydid's project here. Got everythin' I need in the garage at home. Mind you don't keep Robbie up too late playin' with him, Ski. And feed your guests. Take somethin' other than the truck, for God's sakes. You need somethin' with more room in it and less drafts. Move on up to the twentieth century at least."

Trevor opened the passenger door and got out, keeping it open for Katie.

"Will Mary's old Beemer do, your highness? Got enough room in that?"

"As long as it holds you, your lady, and the car seat for Robbie, I'm happy."

"Peachy. Aw, look, Scott. Rob's asleep. Cute."

"Yeah. They are cute when they're asleep. Let Katie get him. You get the car seat. Those things are heavy."

Trevor came around to Scott in the driver's seat. He stuck his head in the open window and bumped his forehead into Scott's solid shoulder, grinning at him.

"Thanks, Bro. I appreciate. I really do."

"I know, moron. Try to do the right thing here, will ya? Quit screwin' up."

Robbie slept in his car seat though much of what Trevor considered to be his second date with Katie Mercer. Scott had driven off in Katie's car, leaving Trevor a bundle of weak nerves and fumbling hands. He'd given Katie a tour of The Ice Palace, which was even more impressive and oppressive without the lightening effect of his family portraits and Buddy in residence. Mary and Jarrett were keeping Buddy at the house on Olympia Avenue until he got used to his old home area again and Trevor arranged for a cat-door to be installed in the Gill Street house.

"Got a housekeeper, too. I don't have to do jack. Well, I do my own dishes and laundry, of course. I'm not a pig. Want a Dr. Pepper?"

"Yes. Thank you. Why do I feel as though I'm invading a mausoleum? Is it just me? This house is creepy."

Trevor grinned.

"Nah. You're not nuts. I feel it, too. Let me snag those Dr. Peppers and I'll show you my favorite part of the house."

Trevor bent his long frame into the white refrigerator while Katie stared around her and up to the lofty ceilings. He clutched two cans of Dr. Pepper, nudged the refrigerator door closed with one hip and grinned at her.

"Come on, Katie. Shove that sliding glass door open, will ya? We'll go sit out on the deck."

Katie complied, picking up Robbie in his car seat, and Trevor led her to the teak lounge chairs with their green and white-striped cushions. He flopped into the one he considered to be his and grinned again as Katie carefully lowered herself onto the other massive piece of furniture after setting a sleeping Robbie beside her on the deck. Trevor popped a can of soda for her and handed it to her.

Dusk was falling and the night was quiet with only the sound of the nearby water lapping and a slight breeze rustling the palm fronds. Light from the house lit the deck area slightly as well as solar lanterns glowing a dull yellow around its perimeter. There were stars coming out overhead. Trevor took a sip of his soda and let his head fall back on the cushions.

"This is my favorite part of this house. Outside."

Katie leaned back and looked up to the stars.

"This house is Trevor Daniels' house. I read his name on the gate post."

"Yep."

"What do you do for Trevor Daniels?"

"Anything that comes along."

"Scott said this was your place."

"We think of it that way. Scott and Carla spent a sort of honeymoon here. We consider it to be in the family. Available for whatever. Stephie really likes it. I wonder if her husband Ed knows just how much she likes it. Do you like your little house in Arcadia?"

"It's shelter. It belongs to Charlie. No transfer of deed yet. He's pretty much ignoring the divorce decree but I'm not pushing it. I have neither the time, the money, nor the inclination to push unless it's to push back."

"Good. I'm kinda laid-back myself about some things."

"You couldn't prove it by me. And here you are, helping me to solve yet another problem. Dragging your brother into my mess. And you'll be sleeping on my sofa again. I'll cook you breakfast."

"I'll try to remember to bring a change of clothes. I always seem to be sleeping on couches in dirty clothes. Flashbacks for me."

Trevor shook his head at himself, remembering sleeping on Jarrett's old plaid couch, and further back to the rented floral ones his former-mom had preferred.

Katie turned her head to watch his profile.

"You won't have to sleep on my couch any longer, Ski. I'm deeply appreciative of what you and your brother have done to help me. And to help Robbie. I wish..."

"Yeah?"

"Hm. Never mind. It's a funny life."

"Hilarious. Are you feeling any better about being around me?"

"Oh, yes. You're the sweetest axe-murderer I've ever met. Very thoughtful. I'll miss you."

"Miss me? Why? Where am I going?"

"Back to Trevor."

"Oh. Yeah. Forgot. Good old Trevor. But not until after I take Robbie to daycare and you to work. And then, after work. I've got one more night. Maybe."

Katie sighed and looked over the trees, watching the moon begin to rise.

"What a beautiful night, Ski. My world is turning around. I'm going uphill now. I'm so very tired of going downhill. You've given me a wonderful start. And hope. It's so great to be sitting here with a gorgeous man, enjoying the night air and feeling safe."

"I'm gorgeous?"

"You know you are."

"Oh. That. Yeah. I guess."

"That's very invigorating for me. Charlie had just about destroyed all my self-esteem. I've never been pretty."

"Stop."

"It's true. You make me feel pretty. But Charlie tried very hard to make me feel ugly and stupid and undesirable. Also inadequate, sexually."

281

"Am I hearing this right? I have never in my life had a woman tell me things like this. Geez. I'm not sure I want to hear much more."

Katie laughed softly in the darkness.

"That's pretty much it, Ski. I promise. He wowed me. He was flashy. He was a musician."

"Swell."

"He was after the money he thought my mother would leave me when she died. He got the poor branch of the Mercers confused with the rich branch. He cheated on me."

"Jesus Christ."

"I'm still alive. I would have left, but I had nowhere to go, I thought. Silly me. But I left when I found out what he'd done to Robbie. I called the police. It was a nightmare. Robbie and I lived in a shelter for a while. Then we got food stamps. Welfare. Paperwork and pity and patronizing voices talking over our heads, deciding our futures. I was so glad to be out then that I took it. But now I don't have to take it. A car and money make a huge difference. They shouldn't. I shouldn't be so shallow. But I have to be shallow and take it, for Robbie's sake."

Silence drifted between them. Trevor broke it, finding it easier to speak of personal matters while looking up to the stars.

"Do you hate men?"

He heard Katie sigh.

"No. I guess not. I'm even past hating Charlie, I suppose. I'm afraid of Charlie, and he disgusts me. But hate? No."

"Good. That's good."

"I have no desire to date, though."

"Huh?"

"I don't want a relationship with a man."

"Oh. But you've got a relationship with me. Don't you? Kind of?"

"Oh, that's different."

"Different? How?"

"You know."

"No, I don't. I'm totally clueless."

"Never mind. I like sitting here with you, relaxing in the darkness. Robbie's asleep. My feet have stopped hurting. This is bliss."

"Yeah."

They finished their sodas in silence and then went back in.

Trevor drove Mary's BMW through the drive-thru at Arby's and fed his troops per Scott's orders, splitting an order of mozzarella sticks with Katie, who fed pieces of roast beef to Robbie over the back seat of the car. He easily threaded his way through Friday night traffic, his mind on a pleasant tomorrow of waking up in Katie's house and spending time with her and Robbie on their way to work again. He'd found out she only worked till noon on Saturdays.

Katie wiped her fingers clean and turned on the radio, tuning it from 104.9 FM, Mary's favorite station, to WIKX FM, broadcasting out of Punta Gorda.

"This is KIX Country 92.9 FM with today's hot country and your all time favorites. Next up, Trevor Daniels with his recent hit, 'I'm Free'."

"Oh, Ski. I love this song."

"You do? Good."

"He's a very talented man."

Trevor listened uneasily to his own voice coming from the radio.

"I lay on the banks of the Pontchartrain,
My backpack tucked under a tree.
I lay down in wonder under the sky
And watched the stars flow over me.
I'm free now.
I'm free."

Katie sighed gently in the darkened car.

"This had just come out when I left Charlie. Robbie and I spent a few days sleeping out in the palmetto scrub. It was good weather, thank God. We were safe and we had each other. I pulled Robbie into my arms and looked up through the jack pines to the sky and I sang that song to him. 'I don't mind sleeping out in the rain 'cause I can. I've had fancier homes in my life, but I ran.' I was free. It was as though Trevor Daniels understood exactly how it felt to be trapped and then to be free."

"You want his autograph? I could get you that."

"No, silly. I appreciate his talent. I love to hear his voice. It's beautiful. And the words of his songs? Well, as I just said, sometimes they've been an inspiration to me. He sounds as if he's suffered and understands what it means to overcome great odds. To fight and win. To struggle and try and lose but to keep hope."

"No autograph?"

"I'm not into that. That has no appeal for me. The man is no way as important as his music or his message."

"I just wondered. Like to meet him?"

"No. I'm very much afraid the reality would be a disappointment to me."

"Oh. Okay."

Trevor huffed out a breath.

"So. You don't want to meet Trevor Daniels?"

"No. I do not."

"Why?"

"I've already told you. I feel it might be a disappointment to me. I might discover he has feet of clay. He might be a jerk. He might have sweaty palms. Any number of things that would destroy the illusion for me. He might turn out to be a very ordinary person completely."

"This would be a problem?"

"To me he's almost god-like. He's larger than life. Maybe he drools when he talks."

Trevor shuddered at Katie's image of him drooling.

"Maybe he can't swim well. Maybe he's susceptible to chest colds. Maybe he has asthma."

"Maybe he can't. Maybe he is. Maybe he does. That would all be very disillusioning for me."

"Swell."

"I'm sorry to insult your friend. And employer. Perhaps I wouldn't like Trevor Daniels at all."

"Perhaps."

"Maybe he's obsessive."

"You have no idea."

"And I don't wish to have any idea. He's my hero."

Trevor just groaned.

Katie hummed along with the rest of his song, her humming not nearly as bad as her singing. Maybe when she sang for Robbie, her voice wasn't as bad as it had been at Big Dog's, Trevor thought. Then again, maybe Robbie wasn't much of a critic.

"I'm sorry you had to sleep outside, Kate. That can suck."

"We were fine. I'm glad I don't have to do it anymore."

"Good."

Trevor had turned off Fruitville Road at the striped pole and was bumping his way down the rutted county lane. He turned into Katie's driveway and pulled the BMW up close to the front steps, putting it in park and turning off the engine.

The house was dark but the moonlight was full and kind on the old house. Trevor looked over the back seat.

"Robbie's asleep. How about you get the door and I'll get Robbie in his carrying case?"

"Thank you. As he gets bigger, I begin to appreciate male muscle more and more."

Trevor brightened.

"Cool."

When Katie flipped on the lights this time, the house was immaculate. Trevor's jaw dropped. No dirty dishes. No baskets of laundry. No folded clothes on the sofa. No clutter.

"Wow."

Katie chuckled.

"Yes. Nothing like a little money ahead to improve your self-esteem and to make you look around at your life and decide you don't like what you see. Lisa helped me."

"You were at work all day. I know. I took you there. I brought you lunch. I picked you up. Well, Scott and I did."

"Silly. Lisa got off at 3:00 p.m. She called me at work because she said she remembered me saying something about a man in the closet. I told her about you. She said she'd come over and pick the place up for me. She's really just hidden it all. You did the dishes. And folded the laundry. The clutter is probably all stacked in my room. Or Robbie's. But she dusted for me and picked up and threw away. She's a great friend. We met in the Food Stamp office. Sometimes I baby-sit for her little girl."

"Is she happy where she works? Is her daycare all right? Married? Divorced?"

Katie laughed at him.

"Put Robbie down before your arms fall off."

"I'm fine. His bedroom? I could get him at least that far."

"Yes. Thank you. I'll take it from there, Ski. Lisa? Lord, yes, she loves her job. She uses a daycare closer to her home and her job. She's married now, but she wasn't when we met. Being a single mom is no picnic. I baby-sit Jasmine so she can go off on a date with her husband once in a while. Romance is important, too. Cup of coffee?"

"Oh, no. No caffeine this late, thank you."

"Yes. How silly of me."

"No, it wasn't. Lots of folks drink coffee after dark. I do myself if I want to stay awake. I don't want to stay awake that badly tonight."

"Well, make yourself at home while I put Robbie to bed. We'll get back on a schedule of post-dinner showers once I get the car back tomorrow from Scott and I can get myself back on some sort of schedule as well. Watch TV if you want."

Katie disappeared into Robbie's room and Trevor took off his sneakers and flopped down on the sofa on his back to stare at the ceiling overhead and smile to himself. The clock in the kitchen ticked. The sofa felt good.

He was asleep before he knew it.

286

## LITTLE BOY

Little boy sitting on my knee.
Who'd have thought that heaven
Was a little boy to me?

Got my arms around him.
Listen to him talk.
Take his tiny, little hand.
Take him for a walk.
Big eyes now are looking
Up at me.
When he does that, what's he see?
Smooth his hair back with my hand.
Help him grow into a man.
Who'd have thought that heaven was a son?

I was once a little boy like him,
But my future then was very dim.
God, believe me, I will try
To keep the tears out of his eyes.
Who'd have thought that heaven was a son?

Katie woke in the night to a faint strumming of a
guitar from Robbie's bedroom. It was low and muffled, a
cheerful four-four beat with basic major chords. But it was
toe-tapping music and she felt her head nodding
unconsciously to its beat as she got up and padded quietly in
the darkened house towards Robbie's door.

Where had Robbie gotten a radio, she wondered?
Maybe Lisa had brought one over for him. She could make
out a man's voice singing lyrics.

"Here comes the big one
Right behind the tow truck
Churnin' up the surf on Marion.

If I want a quick hit
I'll go down to Nesbit.
Surfin' in the streets of Punta Gorda."

Katie smiled. She remembered this silly song. Marta Chapman at day care had a copy of it, along with the newly released two CD boxed set of Trevor Daniels' entitled 'Lullabies'. Its cover was a stark black and white photo of a beautiful, haunted little boy with long, dark hair. The first of the two CDs was a wonderful collection of traditional lullabies full of old imagery and nonsense. The second CD contained songs that Trevor Daniels was said to have made up to sing to his baby nephew. This silly song about surfing lizards was one of them.

Katie pushed open the unlatched door to Robbie's room.

Her houseguest sat cross-legged on the floor with her guitar in his hands, using the pad of his thumb to sound the chords and rocking slightly with the gentle beat of the song as he sang. Robbie was smiling sleepily from his bed, one foot keeping time under the covers.

Robbie saw her standing in the doorway and his smile broadened.

Her houseguest froze over the guitar, his hands abruptly cutting off the flow of sound and turned his head, slowly looking up at her through the curtain of his long hair. His voice was a whisper.

"I'm sorry. I know better than to borrow another person's guitar without their permission, but Rob had a nightmare. It was all I could think to do."

"You're fine. I'm glad you borrowed it. I don't mind. Obviously Robbie is better now. Thank you. I thought he had a radio in here and I wondered how he'd gotten one."

"Nope. Just me."

"I didn't even know you played."

"Yeah. I play. A lot, really."

Katie moved to leave.

"You two carry on. Robbie'll be asleep again soon. I didn't mean to disturb you."

"I didn't mean to disturb you, either."

"You didn't. Good night, boys."

Katie backed out of the room, closing the door to where she had found it. After a while, the gentle playing and singing began again. Katie enjoyed the sound as she walked back to her own room. It rocked her to sleep.

## SURFIN' IN THE STREETS OF PUNTA GORDA

I'm a tiny lizard.
I live in Lizardville.
That's right down on Gill Street
Up a tiny hill.
When it gets to rainin'
Mama lets me scamper.
I grab my board and head for Marion.

Here comes the big one
Right behind the tow truck
Churnin' up the surf on Marion.
If I want a quick hit,
I'll go down to Nesbit.
Surfin' in the streets of Punta Gorda.

I'm just a tiny lizard
But I can climb real good.
You can find me on your car
Sitting on the hood.
If I know the hour
I'll climb the old Clock Tower
But surf the streets is what I love to do.

There's a boy who lives down my same street.
When he goes out walkin', then we meet.
He puts me on his shoulder.
I can see to Boulder.

He puts me in his hair
And all I do is stare.
But when it starts to rainin',
I grab my twig surfboard.
I climb up on it, waitin',
And Lordy, Lordy, Lord.

Here comes the big one
Right behind the tow truck
Churnin' up the surf on Marion.
If I want a quick hit
I'll go down to Nesbit.
Surfin' in the streets of Punta Gorda.

## Chapter Thirteen

The next morning Trevor drove Katie to work, dropping Robbie off at Little People Day Care on the way. When he swung by Scott and Carla's rented house to check on Katie's car, he found Scott out in the garage. His hands restless, he picked up a screwdriver and began tapping it against his leg.

"Well, ya know, I think I'm off to a good start here with this relationship. I've insulted the woman. I've worried her. I've lied to her. Have I missed anything?"

"Worried is good."

"Not if it's whether or not the guy's going to molest your child."

"Jesus Christ, Trev. How the heck did you do that?"

"Being male, I guess. That one I couldn't help."

"If that's so, you ain't the only one with problems. What insult?"

"I think I labeled her a whore. I'm pretty sure I called her an irresponsible parent. I was ticked off."

"Wonderful. I've seen Katie with Robbie. How'd she earn that irresponsible-parent insult?"

"Being a woman, I guess. Looking tiny and feminine in her smart little dress and heels and make-up didn't help. But I gave her that bad-mom insult when she was still wearing jeans and a tank top."

"Trev, there's eight-year-olds with better social skills when it comes to women than that. This ain't your usual smooth pickup. This makes me suckin' in my gut and grinnin' at Carla look smooth. What's got into you, boy?"

"Love. I think. Maybe. Maybe not. Can't tell."

"The wonder is this woman don't show you her back bumper and go on down the road."

"She has no other choices, Bro."

"Well, that can't be much of a help. So now, instead of no choices, she's got Ski."

"She's divorced from the child molester. No visitation. No child support. She hasn't said much about her

291

marriage to the guy, but she's said enough. She's got a shaky job. I've handled that. She had a dead car. I've handled that. She had expensive day care. I've handled that. All anonymously, you understand. She's got her pride."

"So now she has a safety net, but still no choices. Well, that's better. Her only choice now is to get along with this moody, insulting, pushy guy Ski Colorado?"

"Yes."

"And you're sure she has no idea who you are? 'Cause if she did, that would make some sense at least."

"No idea. Not unless she's a whole lot better actress than she is a singer."

"If she knew you were Trevor Daniels, she could be a barracuda. If she thinks you're Ski Colorado, she still could be allowin' you to stay in touch with her for the goodies you at least manage to arrange. A car. A mechanic. That cell phone. Back off the goodies, moron. See if she sticks. Let her work her job, drive her new car, pay for her own day care, and work these open mikes. You know how to find her. She knows how to find you. Back away from her and see what happens. You know the drill. The barracudas always leave if they don't get the goodies they want. Money. A career boast. Jewelry. Sex with the dumb and famous. Inside gossip to sell to the tabloids. Cut off the goodies, and they swim away."

"It won't be the same for me, Scott. It's me wants the goodies this time."

"You ain't admitted wanted somethin' for yourself since it was Tom Petty's autograph. This could be serious."

"I'm sayin'. I want to be around her. I want to be around Robbie."

"You gotta be sure she's no 'cuda."

"Okay. You're right."

"If she's a 'cuda, she'll swim off. You'll get over it."

"Yeah."

"If she's not a 'cuda, and you finally break cover, you're dead meat."

"Yeah."

292

"You best talk to Daddy."

"Back off, huh?"

"Yep."

Trevor sighed and shrugged. Scott took the screwdriver away from his brother and gave his shoulder a nudge.

"Get back on track, Trev. Run. Eat. Sleep. Go on down to Gold's Gym. That was a great idea. Ain't had no bad repercussions there. Run it off. Sweat it off. You know all that stuff's good for you. For God's sakes, take an interest in your house down there in Punta Gorda. Move into it. There's that Gold's Gym in Charlotte Harbor in School House Square. Remember? Go to it. This woman ain't the world. You gotta get a life. You go into rehearsals again soon. Stephie's parties. Tour comin' up again. Live while you can."

Trevor looked up at his brother in misery.

"Not the world? She might be the world to me."

Scott nudged his brother again.

"To the gym. Run. Back off. Live. Wait and see."

"Okay. Done."

Scott handed Trevor a rag and a bottle of Armor-All.

"Here. Do somethin' useful. Help me clean out the limo. You take the back. I'll clean out the front."

Trevor opened the back door of the limo and slid in. He began spraying down the leather upholstery. Scott crumpled up a hamburger wrapper from the floor of the front seat and shoved it into a garbage bag.

"So, what do you think of that book of Margaret's, rat boy? I hear Carl Palermo's gonna be carryin' it at Banyan Tree Books in Fort Myers."

"Ferrets. They were ferrets. 'The Trevor Daniels Story'? I don't know. It reads better if I think about it as being about some other guy."

"It is. Margaret don't know jack about you."

"Dani does."

"And I'm bettin' not even pillow talk'll get that out of her to Margaret."

"It just reads so hokey."

"Oh, that. Humble beginnin's. Soarin' talent. Upward struggle. Not to mention vauntin' ambition and charitable urges."

"Don't mention them. Darned Bachelor Auction Stephie's trying to crowd me into."

"That book's a love story for your fans, moron. Who wants to read the truth?"

"Who the heck knows what the truth is? I don't. Not anymore. It's just kind of creepy reading about myself. It's embarrassing."

"Not nearly as embarrassin' as Margaret could have made it."

Scott stuffed another hamburger wrapper into the garbage bag he was using.

"I hope you know when I call you a moron, I don't mean nothin' by it."

"I know."

"My momma used to tell me I was stupid."

"That's not the same thing, Scott. I know you're not stupid. You know you're not stupid. Carla knows it. Dad knows it. Mary knows it."

"I get the picture. But it still hurt, when I was a little kid, and I believed her. What did I know? Maybe I was stupid. I just want to be sure you know I don't really think you're a moron."

"I know. Really. Listen, I got plenty of people outside the family telling me I'm brilliant, I'm a genius, I'm a legend. Blah, blah, blah. You all keep me grounded. I like that. I can get fawning adulation anywhere. I gotta come to my nearest and dearest to get insults."

"You're sure? I been real mindful of that insult thing since we been havin' problems with Junior's speech. Ya know? 'Dumbie'? All that."

"Kids his age are already saying things like that?"

"Nope. Older kids."

"I swear to God. Why is it people can't leave other people alone?"

"Hand me that rag a minute, Trev."

Trevor did and Scott wiped the Armor-All rag over the backseat upholstery.

"I notice you ain't been in a tearin' hurry to introduce Katie to Carla. Why is that?"

"Nothing personal. I swear. I love Carla. But I know darned well she wouldn't go along with the Ski thing. She'd bust me for sure. I'm not ready to bleed to death yet."

"Got a point there. Carla says Junior's small muscle control is underdeveloped. Whatever. She's draggin' in a speech therapist for him. Can't hurt. Here's your rag back."

Carla had been in the house but now came looking in the garage for her husband. She slid onto the front passenger seat of the limo next to him and snuggled close. Trevor looked up at her from his cleaning.

"Carla, am I a fairly likeable guy?"

Carla looked at him as if he'd lost his mind.

"Well, of course, you are. Why?"

Scott looked up from under the front seat where he had begun fishing out coins.

"He's afraid his new girl friend don't even like him."

Carla looked from Scott's grinning face to Trevor's blank one.

"Trevor. What have you done?"

Scott chuckled.

"Done lied his sorry butt clean off, Carla. Ain't got no more butt left at all."

Carla looked at Trevor in puzzlement.

"You have a girlfriend and you're lying to her? Why?"

"It makes it easier."

"How in the world does lying make it easier? Lying about what?"

"Who I am. I didn't lie about Scottie being my brother."

"A minor caveat, Trevor. Again, why?"

295

"I'm in love with her and I'm afraid I'll lose her so I've been letting her think I'm this other guy she likes. Maybe likes."

Carla's mouth dropped open and she looked over to Scott. Scott shook his head.

"Ain't he a piece of work?"

Carla closed her mouth with a snap.

"Trevor, this is serious. Why would you even want to be anybody other than who you are? You put years of misery into being Trevor Lane and years of joy and hard work into becoming Trevor Daniels. I thought you were proud to be Trevor Lane Daniels. You're betraying yourself and insulting your family name as well as deceiving this woman. You are dooming yourself to disaster."

Stunned, Trevor slowly put down the bottle of Armor-All and the rag he was holding and faced his brother.

"I'm sorry, Scott. I didn't mean any insult. I am proud to be a Daniels. We all worked hard so I could be a Daniels."

"Trevor, my wife done took one of them Yankee-serious pills. Don't you take one, too. I know you ain't spittin' on our good name, but you sure enough got a problem now. 'Fess up and take your licks, boy."

"I'll lose her."

Carla threw her hands in the air and slid from the front seat.

"I've had enough of this nonsense. I'm going for a walk."

Both Daniels men watched her leave.

## AM I REALLY WHO I WANT TO BE?

I look into the mirror
And looking back I see
A nose, two eyes, a mouth
And all around me
A car, a boat, a house.
Responsibility.

296

But who am I inside myself?
Am I really who I want to be?

Who am I when trouble comes to call?
Am I strong or do I take the fall?
Am I to be trusted?
Are my morals rusted?
Am I really who I want to be?

Stranger in the mirror,
You have my first name.
When I look for meanings
I just see your frame.
Angles, planes of camera light,
Keep the real me out of sight.
Am I really who I want to be?

Change the mirror.
Look another way.
Am I still the me of yesterday?
I can point the mirror high or low.
I can shrink me down or make me grow.
Am I just reflected light?
Will I pass into the night?
Am I really who I want to be?

I look into the mirror
And looking back I see
A nose, two eyes, a mouth
And all around me
A car, a boat, a house.
Responsibility.
But who am I inside myself?
Am I really who I want to be?

Trevor actually stayed away from Katie Mercer for more than a week.

He got back into his routine of eggs, juice, fruit and coffee in the morning. But he got back into it at the sunny house on Gill Street in Punta Gorda. The rooms with their wonderful light and glowing walls warmed him, cheered him and relaxed him. He fine-tuned some problems. Sticking doors. Details of caulking.

He went over to his old home on Olympia Avenue and hung out with Mary in the garden or helped Jarrett wash the most recent of the pickup trucks he'd acquired, this one a little Toyota Jarrett jokingly referred to as his "rice-burner". He had allegedly purchased it for Mary's benefit but Mary had yet to drive it.

Trevor played guitar with Jarrett, tossing scraps of melody at him and bouncing ideas for lyrics off him. He worked with Mary on some of Shawn Lane's old fragments, trying to get a feel for what direction his birth father would have wanted a particular piece to take. Mary had history on her side, but he had instinct.

Mary and he forged steadily ahead on Shawn Lane's scribbled fragments, Mary on the baby grand piano and himself still on his favorite instrument, the guitar, using the Martin twelve-string Shawn Lane had bequeathed to him. Sometimes he took a turn at the piano while Mary was on her violin. He loved the sound of the violin but had never mastered playing it. Working on Shawn's efforts helped him with his own. He and Mary hoped to have a CD out later in the year with these never-finished bits of Shawn Lane on it, arrangements by Trevor Lane Daniels, Trevor Daniels on guitar, Mary Buck on violin, backed by musicians who performed with the Charlotte Symphony Orchestra, which always needed money and now would receive it from the sale of the CD. Pre-release interest was keen in certain quarters. Hence the bi-weekly Stephie parties when he was off tour.

Trevor relaxed into his life in Punta Gorda, connected with his roots, and nudged his music into two directions at once.

It was heaven.

But get Katie Mercer out of his head? No way, he thought.

*　　　*　　　*　　　*　　　*

It was a Saturday.

Trevor, unable to stay away from Katie Mercer any longer, punched up her number on his cell phone and shifted from foot to foot waiting to connect.

The call went through.

"Hey. It's Ski. How's the car?"

"Oh, Ski, I can't talk right now. I'll call you back."

Click.

It was like a dash of cold water on his soul.

Okay, he thought. My timing's off. What's new about that, romantically speaking?

His cell phone rang and he almost dropped it in his haste to answer it.

"Ski here."

"Hi. It's me. I'm in the back room now. I gave the customer I was working with to Darlene. How are you? Where are you? I thought I'd never hear from you again."

Trevor felt the smile roll up his face from his toes.

"Fine. I'm fine. Robbie?"

"Wants a play date with Scott Junior. Remember talking about that? I want a play date with Scott Junior's uncle. I've missed you. I've missed Scott, too. I played Big Dog's again and kept looking in the audience for you. Silly me."

"I forgot. What was I doing Tuesday night? I don't remember. Probably nothing. Do you want me in the audience to hear you on Tuesday nights?"

"Of course, I do. If not for you, I wouldn't be there."

Trevor didn't respond to that, thinking that, musically, he might have a great deal to answer for to the world if he was the reason Katie Mercer was still playing open mikes.

"Sure. I'd love it."

My ears will fall off, he thought. And I can feel my nose growing, too.

"Does that witch you work for let you out on time yet? Want to eat food with me? And Robbie, too, of course."

Katie laughed into his ear, sending shivers down his body.

"Of course she does. The Sophisticated Lady Boutique is now Keturah's. Keturah's is employee-friendly. We have new owners. Ms. Leasure is out. I'm in. I'm manager. I have an assistant. I got to name the shop. This is great. And I've got plans for the place. I want to talk to management about that."

Trevor felt his internal joy cloud over.

'Cuda in the water, he thought, and felt his heart contracting in pain.

"Sure. Glad to hear it."

"I wanted to call you and tell you, but I guess I chickened out. I didn't know if you'd want to be bothered with me any more."

The bands around his heart loosened a little.

"Sure. I want to be bothered. I love being bothered. Tonight? Food?"

"I'd be delighted. Robbie keeps singing that little song about surfing lizards. I can't get him to stop singing it."

Trevor smiled.

"'Surfin' in the Streets of Punta Gorda'?"

"Yes."

"Singing doesn't bother me. Bring him on. After work? I'm living in Punta Gorda now. I'll be using a different vehicle to get up there to you. Mary's Beemer is still out at The Ice Palace. My own car's kind of small, but I might be able to borrow my Dad's latest truck. I don't feel my old blue Chevy pickup is all that safe anymore."

"Whatever you want to do. Wherever you want to go. It'll just be so great to see you again. Thanks."

Trevor smiled and curled his toes.

"Cool. 1:00 p.m? Desoto Square Mall?"

"Yes. Do you think you could park a little closer to the shop? Maybe next to my car, if there's a spot?"

"Sure. I could do that."

"Because I still have to wear heels to work, so my feet still hurt when I get off. The last time it was a long walk to you in your truck."

"I'll park closer this time."

"Thanks, Ski. I'll see you after work."

She hung up.


Mary, sitting on the old plaid couch in the house on Olympia Avenue, put down her needlepoint, cocked her head and looked over at Jarrett in his recliner.

"Jarrett?"

Jarrett was reading the Charlotte Sun-Herald and looked up.

"Huh?"

"Do you hear something? I mean, out on the streets somewhere?"

"That whoopin' sound?"

"Yes."

"Yep, I hear it. Sounds like Trevor to me."

"Is that normal?"

"With Trevor? Or with the general population?"

"With Trevor."

"Oh, my, yes. If he's really excited about somethin', he'll be whoopin' and runnin' and jumpin' and turnin' in circles. I ain't seen much of that. Less still as he got old and mature on me."

"Oh, yes. I remember that sound. Shawn when he learned Lisa was pregnant with Trevor. Oh, my God, Jarrett. Has he gotten some woman pregnant?"

301

"I shouldn't think so, honey. Real serious about protection, that boy. I guess we'll hear all about it when he's ready to tell us."

## LOVE

I stretch my arms over my head.
I feel every muscle and sinew.
I run with the wind,
My hair flying back.
People ask me, "What's gotten into you?"
I answer back,
"Love".

There's sun on the woodwork.
There's sun on the floor.
There's sun on the front porch.
There's sun on the door.
Sun on my fingers
Sun on my feet
Sun on my shoulders
Sun glowing deep.

Love.

How can I bleed and have it drip gold?
How can I twist and still smile in my soul?
One little woman did this to me.
Caging my heart, she's setting me free.

Love.

\*     \*     \*     \*     \*

The next Tuesday night at Big Dog's, Katie danced from the stage, all smiles. She hadn't been queasy the whole time and hadn't missed any chords. She bounced over to the back booth where Trevor sat, sunglasses and baseball cap on.

"Come on, Ski. Play. I know you know how."

"No."

"Oh, come on. Are you shy?"

"No."

"Then what?"

Her face was aglow. Trevor picked up her hand and slowly raised her curled fingers to his mouth, smiling mischievously at her. She watched him, her eyes focused on his sunglasses in the dark but darting nervously down to his mouth.

He slid her index finger into his mouth and bit slowly and gently down on it, still smiling. It distracted her, as it was meant to. He pulled her finger out of his mouth and kissed her knuckles.

Katie pulled her hand away.

"Ski, I don't think that's appropriate behavior."

"Oh. Okay. Sit and share a coke with me? My waitress is going to starve to death on the business she's gotten from me so far tonight."

Katie slid into the seat opposite him.

"I was so glad to see you in the back here. I was afraid you wouldn't come."

"You asked me to come."

"Yes. But I didn't know if you would. Why won't you play?"

Trevor sighed. Katie hadn't stayed distracted for long, he thought.

"I don't want to play."

"Why?"

Trevor looked at her from under the brim of his baseball cap. He removed his sunglasses in the dark bar.

"Katie, please."

Katie bit her lip and wrinkled her brow.

"I can't imagine you with stage fright."

"You're right. I don't get stage fright."

Trevor looked at her earnest, puzzled face.

"Kate, if I borrowed your guitar, went up there on that stage, sang and played, our relationship would change forever. And maybe not for the better. Knowing that's the way I feel about playing here tonight, do you still want me to go on?"

Katie gnawed on her bottom lip.

"You make it sound so serious."

"It is serious. To me."

"Then it's serious to me. I don't ever want to hurt you. You have your reasons for what you do. I'll respect your reasons."

"Sometime, Katie. Maybe not here. But sometime. God knows I hope it'll all make sense sometime."

"I never enjoyed Taco Bell as much as I did when the three of us went there last Saturday."

Trevor smiled wanly at her and slid his sunglasses on again.

"Then we'll have to do that again."


LIVING A LIE

Sometimes I do things
And I don't know why.
Sometimes they hurt people.
I've made folks cry.

I've got my secrets.
I've got my demons.
I've got my sore spots.
I've got my reasons

God, I hate secrets.
God, I hate lies.
Tearing my friends up.
Causing good-byes.

Help me, my loved ones,
To fight off the night.
Shake off my nightmares

And walk in the light.

Sometimes I do things
And I don't know why.
God, help me, forgive me.
I'm living a lie.

*　　　*　　　*　　　*　　　*

Trevor met Katie and Robbie on Sunday. The vote on
food had been for Taco Bell again, so they had met there.
Now all three of them were standing in line to order, Robbie
on his own two feet. Watching Robbie scan the pictures of
choices on the menu board suddenly struck Trevor as unfair.
A kindergartner was now being more of a man than he was
being. He touched Katie's arm to get her attention and began
to blunder his way into a confession once she looked over at
him.

"Uh, I told you I don't work construction. I told you I
work for Trevor. He lets me play with his stuff. You know
I've been staying at his house."

"Don't do this, Ski."

"What? Don't do what?"

"Don't lie to me. You don't lie well. You shuffle
your feet and avoid eye contact."

"Oh."

"I don't care what you do for a living or how you
live. I especially don't care that this man allows you to drive
his vehicles and live in his houses. I really don't want to
know about all that. You've been wonderful to me and to
Robbie. I apologize for any misunderstanding there might
have been. It won't happen again."

"You do? It won't? What misunderstanding?"

"About your relationship with Trevor Daniels. I'm
perfectly fine with that. I understand. You have no cause for
shame."

"I don't? Good. I guess."

Trevor sighed and chickened out on his confession.

305

"Listen, do you want to come over to The Ice Palace again? With Robbie, of course. There's a great swimming pool there. I can snag Scott Junior for a buddy for him. Scott and Carla won't mind. I do it all the time. It'll be fun."

"You're sure this man won't mind my being there? I mean, it's one thing for you to be there. Or you and your nephew. But guests?"

"Oh, no. He won't care. Get some use out of the pool. God knows I don't use it much. You'll find out later why that is. Rob got trunks?"

"Yes, he does. Both of us are set with that."

"How about today? Trevor's got sunscreen and towels. I'll go snag Junior. Where do you want to meet? Unless you don't want that. I was trying to save you a drive, ya know, out to Longboat Key. But if you'd rather have your own car?"

"That's a wonderful offer, Ski. I'm not at all familiar with Longboat Key. I'd probably get lost trying to find The Ice Palace again. And I'm still trying to conserve money. Would you believe it? With the new position, I've been able to start a small savings account for Robbie. Letting you pick me up somewhere will save gas money, and wear and tear on Cheyenne."

"Cheyenne?"

"Oh. Yes. I named the new car you helped me to get Cheyenne."

"Girl or boy?"

"Girl. Why?"

"I'm just trying to keep the competition down."

"Oh, Ski."

Katie laughed at him, a carefree laugh that warmed his heart and stirred his loins.

"You are just so nuts."

"Oh, yeah. Ask anybody."

They arranged to meet in two hours in the parking lot near Keturah's. Trevor had no problem picking Scott Junior up from his parents. As he'd told Katie, he often did so simply to go off with Junior and play with him. Junior liked

306

trucks. Trevor liked Junior. So Trevor played trucks with Junior.

He hit a technical difficulty after he'd popped Junior into the car seat he kept solely for the purpose of picking up Junior. He realized there was no way four of them were going to be able to jam into the cab of either his old blue pickup truck or Jarrett's more recent one. The MG was down in Punta Gorda and out for the same reason—not enough space. Mary's BMW was down with a flat tire. The play date began to look problematical due to available resources in the family carpool.

Trevor grinned when inspiration struck. He made sure he was at Keturah's well in advance of the agreed-upon time and lounging against the fender of his ride when Katie pulled her Lumina up beside him, frowning.

"A limousine? Ski, are you sure about this?"

"Well, yeah. I'm sure it's a limo. It's got too many windows to be anything else."

"You know what I mean. Would this man be upset to find grubby children in his limousine?"

"Junior's not grubby. Well, he was earlier, but I cleaned him up. Some. Nah, Trev won't care. Junior's ridden in it before. He kind of likes it. Plays with the buttons in the back. Two kid seats weren't going to fit into the pick-ups or my car. They're all too small. The Beemer's got a flat."

"They'll fit in Cheyenne."

"I thought you were saving money."

"Not if it jeopardizes your employment."

"It won't. I told you. Trev won't care. Scott will. I'm going to have to drive real careful, 'cause if I mess up the limo, Scott'll kill me."

"Scott? Your brother Scott? Why would he care?"

"He drives it. And he keeps it running. It's kind of his pet. Not his dream car, mind you. That's our cousin Reggie's shackled-up GTO. Need a hand with Rob? Come meet Junior."

The play date with Scott Junior was hilarious. Robbie didn't talk much, but Scott Junior never shut up. His speech

307

was largely unintelligible, so his occasional 'Unka Trev' passed unnoticed. Robbie and Scott Junior bonded on sight and crashed trucks around the pool deck while Katie swam and Trevor sat on the side talking to her and keeping an eye on the boys. Katie was wearing a sensible swimsuit in basic black. So was Trevor. She swam past him, smiling up at him.

"This is wonderful. I love pools, but I'm glad I don't have one."

Trevor couldn't have cared less if she liked watching snuff flicks and smoking cigars. He just wanted to watch her and hear her talk.

"How come?"

"Look at the expense. And the maintenance. This much water in captivity in one place can't be water-wise."

"Oh. Cost of doing business. Pool service. Local employment boost for out-of-work accountants. Do you like hot tubs?"

"Junior's sneaking towards the edge of the pool. Doesn't Trevor have a barrier fence? Oh, no, what was I thinking? He'll never need one."

"Why not? He might have kids some day."

"Right."

"It could happen. Well, he won't be carrying them exactly, but having kids isn't ruled out. If you think we need a barrier fence, we'll get one. Done. A phone call away."

"Stop. You're teasing. I know I'm teasing. Next time, I'll plan ahead better. I can always put noodles in Cheyenne's trunk. I'll be better prepared another time. If there is one."

Trevor swung his feet in the water and idly watched Junior pop the hood of his vehicle and look inside. Just like his daddy, Trevor thought.

"Why wouldn't there be a next time?"

"Is Robbie all right?"

"Oh, yeah. He's watching Junior do a tune-up on the Tonka. Can he swim?"

"No. Not yet. Not really. I used to take him to the YMCA for lessons, but that's out economically. And, no, I don't want to hear I've suddenly gotten a scholarship to the Y for Robbie from the Swim Fairy. No offense."

"None taken. Who would do that?"

"You would. You're like my personal wish-genie. I have to be careful what I wish for in front of you, or, poof, it's there. Can Junior swim?"

"Good enough for his age. Scott likes to fish, so Junior grew up in the gross slime in the bottom of a fishing boat. He's got his own little life jacket. I'm the one you'll have to save if I fall in the pool."

"I noticed you were sitting, not swimming."

"I'm allergic to embarrassment."

"Who isn't? I won't tease you then. I'm enjoying myself."

"Me, too."

"Robbie and Junior get along."

"It would seem so."

"They're too young for putt-putt golf."

"Maybe. I'm not, though. You into working out? I've got a membership at Gold's Gym. Free guest."

Katie rolled onto her back and floated past him, making his stomach muscles contract.

"Not really. I'm trying to think of another play date for the boys."

Trevor tried hard not to think about his own idea of a play date without the boys. Or water. Or clothing of any sort.

"Uh…"

"McDonald's has a play land."

Good God, he thought.

"Perfect. When and where?"

"Are you sure your brother and his wife won't object?"

"Positive. I'm broadening Junior's horizons. He's a helluva kid. I like kids. I like Robbie."

"I'm partial to him myself. Don't you ever work? I never see you work."

Trevor grinned.

309

"Ha! 'Money for nothin' and your chicks for free.' Recorded by Dire Straits. I work. I'm off now. Soon enough to go back. This double dating with toddlers is going to put a strain on the limo. Can you imagine the limo pulling up at Mickey D's? I can. No low profile there. I think Trevor needs a van. I hate to keep borrowing Mary's Beemer, too. She won't mind, but Scott will. I just know that nail in the tire is going to be my fault."

"That's not fair."

"I'm the younger brother. It's always my fault. Of course, it's Scott's fault if I get into a position where it becomes my fault. Sometimes you can't win with Dad."

"Your whole family is close."

"It is. You wouldn't believe. We work hard, we respect one another and we like each other as people as well as sharing the love. I'm blessed."

"Yes, you are. It's marvelous to hear a man say that."

"It is? Cool. I'm blessed. Do I get sex now?"

Kathie laughed at him and splashed him with water, making him laugh, too.

By the next play date, Trevor had acquired a late model Chevy Suburban. In his usual baseball cap and shades, Junior on one hip and Robbie on the other, with Katie's hand in the crook of his elbow, he attracted no attention at McDonald's Playland whatsoever because he wasn't where anyone would think to find him, nor doing what anyone would think the fifth most eligible bachelor in Sarasota County would be doing.

## Chapter Fourteen

"I hear you kidnapped Junior from his mother again."

"I needed him, Bro."

"To front for you?"

"Yes. He had a play date with Robbie. It was cool."

"You're usin' my kid to get sex? That's low."

"Worse. It didn't work. And I think I'm in even deeper doodoo."

"Is that possible, Ski?"

"I didn't think it was, but now I suspect it is. First she wouldn't have anything to do with me because she thought I was a child molester. Then maybe because of what that ex-husband of hers has done to her head about men in general. Now I got real problems. I was going to tell her who I was. Kind of. I was creeping up on it, you know."

"A cluster-fuck. I swear to God. "

"I told her I worked for Trevor Daniels and he let me use his stuff. You know. The MG, the limo, the house, the pool. Creeping up on it."

"And?"

"She apologized to me."

"For what?"

"For, I guess, having maybe some lustful thoughts about me. I didn't know I'd gotten as far as her having lustful thoughts about me. She don't have 'em no more, I guess. She's real relaxed around me now. No tension at all."

"That's good. She apologized for havin' lustful thoughts?"

"Sort of. She mentioned a misunderstanding and said it wouldn't happen again. I got confused. But I'm pretty sure she thinks I'm Trevor Daniels' homosexual live-in companion."

"You are so fucked. Or not. This is priceless, moron. Your nookie is backin' further and further up. You might not ever see it now. You can hit on her all you want. She won't mind. She won't think you're hittin' on her. Priceless. Swear to God."

311

"Well, what do I do now?"

"Tell her the truth."

"No."

"All right. This relationship has about as much chance of takin' off as a penguin does of flyin'."

Trevor considered this.

Hm. Penguins.

\*　　\*　　\*　　\*　　\*

For his next visit to Keturah's, Trevor opted for a polo shirt and Dockers, part of his respectable-collection from J. C. Penney. His hair was back in a ponytail and carefully banded down his back in three places. He had abandoned his baseball cap, but had his sunglasses tucked in his shirtfront for quick access in case of need. He was idly checking price tags while he waited for a chance to talk to Katie. The place was busy, he noticed.

Katie came up to him as he was fingering a men's plaid bathrobe and he smiled at her.

"Hey, Katie. This bathrobe is pretty cool. Feels like flannel. I like flannel. How much is it?"

Katie held the tag up to him, giving his thrifty nerves a jolt.

"Jesus, Mary and Joseph! Some bathrobe."

"It's 100% wool by Worthington."

"My former-mom liked their sweaters. Now I know why. Three hundred dollars?"

"Don't forget the sales tax."

"Darn. Nobody's worth a three hundred dollar plus sales tax bathrobe, myself included. Listen. I got a job to do for Trevor. But I need your help. Okay?"

"Certainly. If I can. What is it?"

"I need a date. Well, he needs a date. We need a date. I'm him. I need a date. To go on this date with me. Cocktail party and sit-down dinner. Black tie at The Ice Palace. You game?"

"I don't even understand what you just said. Or asked. What did you ask?"

"Oh. I asked if you'd be my date at a cocktail party at my, at Trevor's, house while I do what I do for Trevor."

"All right. Oh, I get it. This man really doesn't want people to think the wrong thing so he wants you to bring a date. Duh. I can be so dense. I apologize for that, Ski. Certainly. How should we arrange this?"

Trevor gritted his teeth until he thought they would crack.

"I'm Trevor."

"I beg your pardon?"

He chickened out again.

"That's my job. I play Trevor. I go to parties and sub for him. We kind of look alike."

"Oh. Like a stunt double? So that's how he's able to be at all those media events. He's not really there. You are."

He should have told Katie the real truth right then. But he didn't.

Katie moved a hand to his arm and studied his face.

"Well, now I can totally and completely understand why you've been living at that huge house on Longboat Key, and why you're missing so often. Totally and completely. The wonder is you have time to go down to Punta Gorda at all. I just thought you were nuts, but now it all makes sense."

"It does?"

"Yes. I always wondered why you were so nervous in public, as though you actually were a suspect on America's Most Wanted. Trevor threw a party last weekend. Only, it wasn't Trevor, was it? It was you."

"Stephie made me do it. She's in marketing. She insists on giving these stinking, little parties. They're no fun. Part of the job."

"So, you do the stinking parties instead of Trevor. Lucky Trevor."

"Yeah. Lucky Trevor."

"Scott came by the shop last week. We talked. I never knew the real reason behind Trevor canceling out the

313

balance of his East Coast tour. He's very sickly. I had no idea. I think it was a smart idea to sort of divide up the work load."

"Yeah. Good idea. Sickly?"

"Trevor does the music part and you do the guest appearances and, I suppose, all the Stephie-stuff. Brilliant. It's very convenient that the two of you look alike."

"Yeah. It is. Hard work, too. You going to do it?"

"Of course, I will. You never ask me to do anything for you. I'd be delighted. Black tie? Hm. We sell items in the shop that would be appropriate for me to wear."

Trevor whipped out his wallet and fingered out several big bills.

"Here. Cost of doing business. Trev'll reimburse me. Gotta have the right dress. Short notice. Shoes?"

"No. I think my black pumps will be all right. I don't think Trevor's date would drive herself to the Longboat Key house in a Chevy Lumina. Where do you want me and when?"

Trevor stood before her, a quivering bundle of nerves.

Right here, right now, he thought. And sucked it up.

"6:00 p.m? The parking lot here? I'll have to be at the party real early, greeting guests and all. Scott'll be handling security. Well, actually, he'll be driving the limo and Jesse'll be left in charge of security at the house. I'll get to ride in the back of the limo with you."

"Why wouldn't Trevor already be at the house he lives in?"

"Prior engagement. Running late. Besides, I want to ride in the back of the limo with you."

His prior engagement was signing autographs at a charity function in Clearwater.

Katie nodded.

"Very sensible. You better clean the sand out from the boys."

"Scott already did. He's real anal about the limo."

"Then I'll see you tonight at 6:00 p.m. I'll have Valerie close the shop. The privilege of rank and seniority."

"What about Robbie? I forgot about Robbie."

"The new owners of the daycare are wonderful people. They have a division that screens babysitters and one of their ladies can take Robbie home with her. I'll contact them and make the arrangements. I won't need all this money for a dress, Ski. I get an employee discount at Keturah's. But this babysitter is also the cost of doing business for your employer, so I'll simply apply the money to that. Will Trevor want a receipt?"

"Can't hurt."

"I'll see you at 6:00 p.m. I'm so glad to be able to do something useful for you after all you've done for me."

*    *    *    *    *

Scott lounged on the white satin coverlet of the bed in the master bedroom in The Ice Palace. He watched his nearly frantic younger brother fiddle with his black bow tie, rub his patent leather evening shoes on the legs of his tuxedo trousers and fidget with his cuff links. There was a sheen of sweat on Trevor's handsome face. Scott was hugely tickled.

"You done messed it up ever better, moron. I didn't think that was possible. Are you suicidal? One slip and you crash and burn in front of a hundred and fifty people. Better yet, your lady is goin' out with you as a favor. And you won't even get a favor-fuck out of the deal, because you're gay. Priceless. Got any other bright ideas?"

"Not at the moment."

"You don't sweat this much at awards ceremonies."

"I don't sweat this much in full sunlight in August in Florida. I could always barf on her shoes. That might work."

"Can't be any worse than this. How'd this happen?"

"I asked her out on a date."

"Bull."

"Okay. I wanted to flaunt it a bit."

"You're gonna. It's the usual set of penguins that Stephie likes to work towards."

"Maybe seeing a non-starlet-non-famous woman with me will help. Stephie says this demographic prefers the artist to be married or committed, not single and wild."

"And you'd do anythin' to satisfy the demographics."

"Certainly."

"Bull."

"I'm seeing how Katie'll fit in."

"Bull."

"I'm desperate."

"Agreed. And so totally clueless. You ready, Ski?"

"Shut up and drive the limo."

Scott slowly rose from the bed, watching his younger brother's wired and jerky movements.

"Priceless. Just priceless."

Trevor turned back to his brother as they went down the stairs with Trevor in the lead. "I'm so fucked, aren't I? I'm never getting her. I'm never getting any of it."

"Will you calm down? I've never seen the likes of you for messin' things up for yourself. Get back to the basics, for God's sake."

"Center. I need to center."

"Yes, you do. Who you are and what you want."

"I want Katie. I'm me."

"There you go."

"Hi. I'm Trevor Daniels. I want you. I'm not a fag."

"I think I might have got you out of the fag-thing problem, Trev."

"Yeah. Thanks for that."

"No problem."

"Hi. I'm Trevor Daniels. I want you."

"Not bad."

"Jesus Christ."

"Not by a long shot."

Stephie's party this time was a sit-down dinner for a hundred fifty people at fifteen hundred dollars a couple. She had no vacancies.

Katie worked the receiving line with Trevor. She seemed relaxed and at home with what Trevor considered the unnerving formality of Stephie's parties.

Katie greeted one gray-haired matron by name, extending her hand with a smile.

"Mrs. Baxter. Nice to see you again."

"Katie? I didn't know you knew Trevor. Smart girl, hiding that from me."

"We've only just met."

"He's a prime piece of real estate, Katie. My advice is to always buy land. When that dress I ordered comes in, just give me a call. Trevor? Let me introduce you to my husband Walter."

And so the evening went.

Katie did indeed know many of the wives because they were customers from Keturah's. The wives dragged their husbands to charity events and the husbands opened their checkbooks.

Tonight's gathering was to benefit the American Cancer Society, but it was doing double duty by promoting Shawn Lane's music by way of Trevor. Mercifully, no one asked him to play this night, he thought, but Stephie made him pay for that concession and for her part in going along with what she considered his harmless hoaxing of Katie.

After the caterers had removed the last elegant dish, Trevor had stood to make his rehearsed plea for funds as well as his brief mention of the anticipated Shawn Lane CD.

As he sat down, Stephanie Norton had gracefully snatched the hand-held microphone from him.

"And to help out the cause this year, I'm proud to announce the participation of Sarasota's own Trevor Lane Daniels in the Sarasota Bachelor's Auction."

Stephie whipped the crowd's enthusiasm with her smile and her bold use of gesture. She had learned drama from Trevor. She flipped off the hand-held microphone and

317

leaned down to Trevor, delighted with her cornering of him. Trevor smiled his idiot-grin for the crowd as he stood up again from the head table to acknowledge the applause, muttering under his breath to his cousin beside him.

"I'll kill you for this."

"Shut up, Ski. You owe me."

"Does Ed know you lust after The Ice Palace?"

"*Touché, mon cousin.* And bite me. Your lady won't care. It's for charity. And if she does, so much the better for you."

Trevor broadened his smile and nodded again to the applauding crowd before sitting down.

"It's official. I'm in hell."

\*  \*  \*  \*  \*

The guests were gone. A smug Stephie was gone. But Katie was still very much there, and up in his face.

"You're a fraud."

"Shawn Lane was my father. I consider his music to be a sacred trust. I want to finish his fragments and get them out to his following. He's like Chopin or Greig to these people. I cannot fulfill the promise of these pieces as Trevor Daniels, honky-tonk hero. Shawn Lane's followers aren't fans. Trevor's fans shout and stomp. Shawn's followers sit quietly and nod. It's just different. I'm straddling a fence here, but it's my choice to do so. If you don't feel comfortable doing this, I'll accept that. I appreciate your trying to help me on this one."

"I don't know what I feel. I have no problem meeting these people or helping you promote your father's music. I think the problem may be with you. Suddenly you're not the good ole boy you were when we first met. I have no problem being introduced as Miss Keturah Mercer because that's who I am. I think I have a problem with who you are."

"I'm the guy hustling Shawn Lane's music. He's dead. He can't hustle his own work product anymore. Aunt Mary usually comes up to help me. She lets herself be conned by the attendees into playing one of his short pieces on the violin or a fragment on the piano. Mary's a celebrity in her own right with the classical crowd. I can play short parts of his work, but his talent was massive and his works were for full orchestras. I can only do his early stuff. But I look like him, so it helps to sell his product. It's not about me. It's about him, and his music."

"There's something missing here, but I'm too tired to try to figure it out. Can I take my shoes off now? My feet are killing me."

"Sure. Just be careful not to slip on these marble floors. They're cold, too. Want a pair of socks? I've got the kind you get in hospitals with, like, griptape on the bottom. Want to take your clothes off? No offense. Hot shower? Hot tub? Foot rub?"

Katie shook her head, heaved a sigh and then chuckled at him.

"All good offers. I'll stick to taking my shoes off. And maybe these pins out of my hair. I think the cigar smoke gave me a headache."

"Take a shower. Wash it all off. I usually do."

"Don't even think about offering to shower with me."

"Kate, I'm shocked. I would never do such a thing. I'd much prefer the hot tub and a bottle of the really excellent Asti we served tonight. Let's get out of this house and onto the deck. Watch some stars. Not just me and my dad."

Katie was rolling her head on her tired neck, her eyes closed. Trevor slid a hand to the back of her neck.

"Katie?"

"Hm?"

"You're fading fast. No kidding. Go take a shower. Let your hair down. There's fluffy big bathrobes in all the bathroom closets. Up the stairs, hang a left, third door. I've tried that shower. It's a good one. I'll be using the shower in the master bathroom. Scott's gone off to get Robbie from the babysitter. Jesse's locked down the grounds. The caterer and the string quartet have left. We're alone. I'll meet you out by the hot tub."

"I have no swimsuit here."

"Check out the closet in that room."

Katie's eyes came open wide.

"You keep women's swimsuits here?"

"Cost of doing business. See if you can find a two-piece. I'm gonna scare up some candles. We both need to relax."

"I may fall asleep in the shower."

"Then I'll come and get you."

"Okay. I'm awake now."

"Got a really neat sound system here. I'll put on some of Shawn's tunes. Come dance in the dark with me."

Katie sighed and stepped out of her shoes.

"Tempting. Very tempting."

"Do it. Shower, swimsuit, hot tub, me. Champagne, candles, music. What the heck?"

Katie smiled at him.

"What a wonderfully romantic offer. I hope I don't chicken out. Or fall asleep."

"I'll come for you if you do either."

"Maybe I'll feel better about this if I see you out of that tuxedo."

"Really? Cool. That's a done deal."

Trevor began hastily shucking off his shoes and simultaneously pulling at his bow tie. Katie punched him playfully in the arm.

"You wiseguy. Quit that. Go take a shower. I'll meet you in the hot tub."

## DANCE IN THE DARK

The baby's asleep.
The guests are long gone.
You drag your feet. You're tired.

We glittered and chattered
As if it all mattered.
The sprinklers start up on the lawn.

We climb the stairs and yearn for sleep,
But it's our time to finally be free.
Won't you dance in the dark with me?

Your makeup is off now.
Your hair is combed out.
You've never looked better to me.
I smell like cigar smoke
And too much cologne.
Won't you dance in the dark with me?

Little gestures and touches
By kind candle light;
Little sighs and releases
Complete our own night.
My eyes may be gritty;
My back stiff and sore,
But, God, you are pretty
As you close the door.
Won't you dance in the dark with me?

\*      \*      \*      \*      \*

It was Jarrett on the phone in Punta Gorda calling
Trevor in Sarasota. Trevor smiled with the phone to his ear,
picturing the big man and falling in love all over again with
him.

"Dad, I just love you so much."

"Son, are you all right up there in Sarasota? Why
ain't you livin' down here in your house in Punta Gorda?
What's goin' on?"

"Love. I'm in love."

"Well, that explains an awful lot. Explains why
you've got a brand new house you ain't hardly moved into

yet. Explains why the family now owns a dress shop in Sarasota. And a day care. Vertical integration. Women need these things. Doesn't maybe explain why you gave a lady a car older than last week's news. If you're tryin' to wow some lady with a car, I'd suggest somethin' newer and shinier than a 1993 Chevy Lumina, son. But what's all this you've been shovelin' to Stephie?"

"Oh. That. Yeah. That's all become a problem."

"Who the heck is Ski?"

"Me. I'm Ski."

"Ski Colorado?"

"Yeah. Long story. I think I'm in trouble."

"I know darned well you are, but not the trouble you apparently want to be in."

"You been talking to Scottie?"

"I talk to both my babies. You two babies and Mary is all I care about, son. Stephie's puzzled. Scott's amused. When do Mary and I get a vote?"

"Well, Dad, here's the straight skinny. She doesn't know I'm Trevor Daniels. She thinks I'm Ski. She's met my brother Scott. She knows about you and Mary and Punta Gorda."

"What's missin' in this story, son?"

"I think she thinks I'm Trevor Daniels' homosexual kept-boy."

There was a long pause at the other end of the phone.

"Dad?"

"And would she be right, son?"

"Dad! You got a brain tumor or something? I'm me. I'm Trevor Daniels."

"You ain't been you for awhile, son. You were starting to get your true self back what with seein' Dr. Panjikaran and comin' to terms with that Chris tape. Now you've lost ground again. What you got goin' right now is one helluva lie. You are doomed with this woman. Tellin' her the truth may not save you now."

"Well, what is the truth?"

322

"With you, who knows? You've been on that tour bus and in that life so long now you've become paranoid. You don't let your guard down to anyone. You don't mingle, really, at parties. Stephie sees it. You put on a plastic smile and press flesh. You've become your own legend. You hide behind your baseball cap to cover your hair and your sunglasses to cover your face. You don't have a life outside maybe six adult people, tops, a fifty-mile radius and eight notes on a scale. Maybe you are Trevor Daniels' kept-boy. At this last shindig, you had Stephie treat you as though you were Trevor Daniels to your guests and Ski playing Trevor Daniels to your date. You're stressin' your cousin out, boy. These smooth little parties she shoves you into are for the benefit of Trevor Lane Daniels' serious instrumental work and Shawn Lane's unfinished gems, and you're runnin' some sort of college prank on these fairly influential people and on your lady. If you're tired of your career, get off the ride. Don't kill the driver."

There was silence on the other end.

"Son?"

"Yeah?"

"I didn't mean to rant at you, boy. I'm worried about you. I thought you were back on track when you began takin' care of yourself, eatin' right, exercisin', gettin' back to your roots. Followin' your heart. Now, I don't know. Come home, son. Come back to who you are. Bring your lady with you."

"If she'll come."

"Why wouldn't she?"

"I don't know. I'm all messed up, I guess."

"Why'd you lie to this woman?"

"I was doing my anonymous thing, you know. Driving down the interstate. Then I just kind of fell into it. I guess I wanted to see if she'd like me without all the fame and fortune stuff."

"So when did you stop being Ski, a regular guy, and begin to be Trevor Daniels, legend?"

"I'm not to the legend part yet. But darned close."

323

"So I hear from Stephie. Does your lady like you any better when you're playing Trevor Daniels than when you're playin' Ski?"

"I don't think so. I can't tell."

"Maybe you're not her type."

"As far as I can tell, she still likes men. In spite of her ex. She likes Trevor's music. She doesn't mind Ski hanging around her. She let's me play with her little boy now."

"Bring her down here, son. Let's see what it is you ain't got."

"She's prickly as bougainvillea, Dad. Pretty as sunlight and blue water. I called Bobbi and told her goodbye."

"You're toast. Got words for this one. Bring her over. Let Mary and me see what kind of woman's been givin' our little boy a hard time."

Trevor relaxed into the beloved sound of his father's voice. That voice rumbled on in his ear.

"Trevor, I want you to think about somethin' else. I ain't real sure how to go about sayin' all this. You remember when you was a kid and your Aunt Mary first popped back up in your life?"

"Yeah."

"You didn't want her."

"Yeah."

"But you wanted her badly. You wanted her in your life. You wanted her love."

"I thought she'd screwed me over as a kid."

"And your mom did."

"Yeah."

"You ain't had what I'd call a long-term relationship with any female ever except for Mary, or maybe Dani."

"Dani's special."

"She is. In many ways. But she doesn't represent a potential threat to you. You were never gonna fall in that kind of love with Dani. She was never gonna mess you up emotionally."

"I don't think I'm following all this."

"You remember what you did with your Aunt Mary? You tried to drive her away with every trick in your book. But only tricks that were easy to see. Tricks that were real obvious. Because you really didn't want to drive her away. You just thought you did. You thought she was a threat, but deep down inside you felt she wasn't."

"And?"

"I guess I maybe see this same pattern with the way you're handling this little gal. Maybe you're scared of this little gal. Maybe you're tryin' to drive her away 'cause you see her as a threat to you for wantin' her so much. Maybe you really know deep down inside that she's not a threat."

"What a mess."

"Maybe. But only if you let it be a mess. Drop all the foolishness, boy. Just lay it on the line."

"I'm doomed. She's told me she doesn't even want to meet me if she had a chance to. I'm her hero. I'm god-like. I'm dead meat."

Trevor clunked his forehead against one of the sliding glass windows of The Ice Palace. Jarrett bit back a smile on his end, hearing the sound.

"Son?"

"Yeah?"

"Time to 'fess up to her."

"Past time. I'm screwed."

"It can only get worse, son. Believe me. You might be havin' a change of heart about hidin' your identity from this woman, but she hasn't had a change of heart about not wantin' to meet the real Trevor Daniels and she's told you so. She is gonna be right mortified to know she done told you that but you cannot keep buildin' your house on a foundation of sand. It will not stand."

"She has no interest in me. Even in me as Ski. She's never even asked what my last name is. She's written me off as a fag and a friend."

"Do it and die, boy. Come clean."

"I told Bobbi goodbye."

# EGRET IN THE SKY

I watch an egret leap into the sky.
White wings across the mangroves, flying high.
I think about the beauty in goodbye.

We helped each other up in our careers.
Goodbye can be so pretty, no harsh tears.
We'll see each other often through the years.
The beauty of goodbye we'll enjoy here.

The beauty of goodbye.
An egret in the sky.

I hope you find the one you need.
I hope your love outshines your greed.
I hope the one to make you plead
Ends goodbyes, so you won't bleed.

The beauty of goodbye.
An egret in the sky.

\*     \*     \*     \*     \*

Less than a week later, Trevor was back on his courtship routine. Robbie was out with Katie's friend Lisa and her little girl. Trevor had opted for a day with Katie simply sitting outside The Ice Palace and looking down the long dock to the water, trying to relax himself. He was seated in one of the Adirondack chairs while Katie sat in one beside him, her hands clenched in her lap.

Trevor glanced at her face now, trying to read her mood.

"Kate, I have a confession to make."

"If it's about the car, I already know. Your brother's a worse liar than you are. Either his wife or his conscience was pricking at him to tell me the truth. We spoke a few days ago on the phone. I've been waiting for you to catch up."

Trevor shifted his weight uneasily.

"You needed a decent car."

"I've put the 'change' you gave me into Robbie's savings account. I am very grateful for the car. Embarrassed but grateful."

"There's no obligation. I swear to God."

"And I believe you. I wouldn't have believed that at the time."

Trevor drew in a deep breath.

"There's more. The day care."

"Little Buddy Day Care? Ms. Marta said the new owners don't wish to be known."

"They don't. I don't. Corporate may own it, but the bottom line is I own it. Also a woman's dress shop. Renamed by you Keturah's."

"You own Keturah's? You're lying."

"No. I have been lying. Now I'm telling the truth. My name is Trevor Lane Daniels. I own a day care and a dress shop."

"You're lying. You are not that man. You look like that man. I know how the rich operate. They need tax write-offs. What better than a day care and a dress shop? They've poured  thousands into both operations between decreased fees at Little Buddy and increased staff and salaries at Keturah's."

"Yeah, they're tax write-offs. For now. But that wasn't why I bought them. They were like the car, only on a bigger scale. That's all beside the point. Kate, I'm Trevor Daniels. I am. Look. Long hair, toothy grin. See?"

Katie twisted her fingers together in her lap.

"You're delusional."

"No."

"I understand. Living in his shadow, forced to eat crumbs while he gorges himself."

"I never gorge myself. Well, there was that first Christmas. Too much turkey. Who knew? I barfed and I was fine."

"I do have a bone to pick with him. You play the role of Trevor Daniels and the best he can do for you is that old truck"

"I love that truck. Dad gave it to me."

"What a horrible person he is. You do all the hard work and all he does is sing and fly around the country and sign autographs."

"That's hard work. You have no idea."

"Sleeping with models and actresses. At the White House."

"I've never slept with models at the White House."

"Fast cars. New cars. His own jet."

"Yeah, the jet's kind of cool. Scott won't let me fly it. He says I could get a speeding ticket in outer space."

"Look how you're forced to dress. Holes in your jeans. Holes in your shoes. Holes in your shirt. It's disgusting."

"Wait. I like this shirt. The jeans are finally soft enough. And the sneakers are finally comfy."

"He keeps you in his houses like some sort of charity-case houseguest. He's rich and you're struggling."

"Kate. It's me."

"I am furious with him."

"Not like you will be."

"There's more? Now you couldn't give me his autograph if you paid me to take it. I told you I didn't want to meet him. I've changed my mind. I wish he were right here in front of me. I'd punch him in the nose."

"You would? That's sweet."

"Bring him on."

"Katie. It's me. I'm Trevor Daniels."

"Delusional. No wonder. Playing The Ice Palace for him. Even your cousin Stephie didn't blink an eye when she was introducing you to all those people. What a fraud he is. And she's in on it. I liked her, but if she's aiding and abetting Trevor Daniels to defraud his fans, I'll have to rethink that."

"Stephie's doing her job. Her job is to promote Trevor Daniels. Jesus Christ, I am delusional. I'm talking about myself as if I were another person. It's Stephie's job to promote me. I'm Trevor Daniels. Punch me in the nose."

"Prove it."

Trevor raked his fingers through his hair and looked wildly around. Wasn't there something left at The Ice Palace to prove who he was? He patted down his body. No wallet. Where the heck was his wallet anyway? In the truck?

"I'm doomed. I don't even have my driver's license with me, I guess. What if I could find someone who knew me? Would that work?"

"Get real. Half of Sarasota thinks you're Trevor Daniels. Certainly the half you and Stephie lied to. She runs a 'Play-The-Ice Palace' every two weeks. God knows how many people think you're Trevor Daniels. I've been reading up on him."

"Oh, God. None of those books are authorized editions. Margaret's working on one approved by me and the family. I can get you the proofs to read."

"There were photos in the books. You do look like him, in a superficial way. I think it's the hair."

"The hair again. This hair has so got to go."

"But you are not that man. So, just stop that 'I am Trevor Daniels' thing. I'll go along with it because so many people would be shocked or angry or hurt to learn they've gotten a signed photo from a fraud. And you do work hard for the man. But, between us, just drop all that silliness, Ski. Be yourself."

"I am. I'm trying. Really."

"There's a superficial likeness to the photos. That's all."

"Doomed. I'm doomed."

"I can see how it all came about."

"You can?"

"Certainly. Based on how much effort you put into his life, he can't possibly do it all. Neither of you can let that be known. He's in Orlando right now. At a dinner."

"He is? I am? What dinner?"

"Some charity. I forget. But he's expected to attend. It's being televised."

"Steph didn't say anything about that. She usually faxes me my schedule. Are you sure?"

"Yes. Well, let the real Trevor Daniels work that crowd. You're here. Too late to get to Orlando."

"Maybe not. I'll call Stephie's cell. I swear to God she sleeps with it turned on. If I were Ed, I'd be ticked off."

Trevor pulled his cell phone from his belt and punched up his cousin's number. It connected and Trevor's worried look abated somewhat when Stephanie answered.

"Trevor? What's up?"

"God, I'm glad you keep that thing on. Am I supposed to be in Orlando for a dinner or something?"

"No. You bought tickets. Why?"

"Katie's waiting to see if I'm in Orlando on TV when I'm here in the flesh."

"As Scott would say, priceless. If you want to go, and take Katie, I can have two of the tickets delivered to you by courier. Oh, drat. No, I can't. I gave them away. Sorry, Trev."

"I don't suppose you could tell Katie I'm me, could you?"

"Why should she believe me? I'm the one who called you Ski one minute and Trev the next. She knows I'll lie."

"Doomed. I am doomed. Well, say hey to Ed and the kids. Love you."

Trevor clicked off his cell phone and faced Katie.

"My name isn't Ski. In fact, the only Ski I know is what you do on snow in Colorado."

"My grandfather had a friend whose nickname was Binkie. No one ever figured out why."

Trevor put his head in his hands, rubbed his face.

"You never even asked what my last name is."

"I figured it was Daniels."

"It is. My name is Trevor Lane Daniels. Let me go find my wallet. I think I left it in the truck."

330

Trevor stood up and slowly ambled across the well-manicured lawn to where he had parked his old blue Chevy pickup in the shade of the front entrance way.

He found his wallet tossed carelessly on the seat, as worn and battered as the rest of his favorite possessions. He brought it back with him, pulled out his driver's license and handed it to Katie.

She took it and held it between two fingers, sticking her arm out straight and sighting down her arm to the photo. She held it next to Trevor's face.

Trevor gave her a hopeful toothy grin.

Katie glared from photo to face, then squinted at the address on the driver's license.

"This is a California driver's license. Isn't this address near OJ's old house? Pretty fancy neighborhood."

"I was staying with Aunt Cass the summer I turned eighteen. Perfect neighborhood for Prince Charming's castle."

"That's Cinderella's Castle from her prince. The jury's still out on you being Prince Charming."

Katie shoved the driver's license at him.

"This could be a fake ID, you lying, arrogant bastard."

Trevor slid his license back into his wallet and stuffed the wallet into his hip pocket. He sat calmly back down on the Adirondack chair.

"Not a bastard. My parents were married before I was born. A liar, yes. I've just confessed."

"Why?"

"Why what?"

"Why lie? Why confess?"

"I wanted you to have stable, decent employment. And how much fun could it have been for customers to have Ms. Leasure wait on them? I'd have gone screaming out the door. Keturah's now provides a soft, fuzzy outlet for Shawn Lane's and my serious work to the end-user most likely to make the purchase—women of taste with money."

"You bastard."

331

"Son-of-a-bitch. I prefer the technical term."

"Scott and Carla? Stephie? Your family's in on this?"

"Not from the start. Can't blame them for that. Carla stopped talking to me completely when she heard. This lie was totally my fault."

"Why?"

"'The Prince and the Pauper.' You thought I was Ski. I was driving incognito anyway. I often do. It's restful. It gives me a break. Anonymity, Kate. Can someone love me for who I am, not what I do or what I have? Can someone love me for who I am, not who I am? As God is my witness, I have never bought a store and a day care for a woman."

"Cars?"

"Oh, my, yes. Newer cars. Faster cars. Why is it that the smaller and faster a car is, the more it costs?"

"Don't try to pull that red herring past me."

"No, ma'am."

"You're unrepentant."

"Yes. But not about the lie."

"Yes, you are. You'd do it again. I can tell."

"I had my reasons. They were valid reasons at the time. The problem came when it was past time for the reasons, and I did nothing. That I do regret."

"What am I going to do about you?"

Trevor gave her a weak, toothy grin.

"Marry me?"

"Very romantic."

"Last ditch effort of a desperate man? Katie, I did no harm."

Katie shook her head and turned away from him.

Trevor leaned around to see her face.

"Kate?"

"You did the greatest harm."

"How? I don't get it. I've told you the truth."

"You really don't get it, do you? You should have told me the truth sooner. A lot sooner. I'm the one that doesn't get it. I've seen you in public. You accept your fans.

You even court them sometimes. When a fan comes up to you, asking for an autograph, you never blow them off."

"I wouldn't."

"No, you wouldn't. But you blew me off."

"Katie! No."

"You'll smile and give that patented 'How's it goin'?' to total strangers. I was a total stranger to you. You don't try to hide who you are once someone spots you. You hide from me more than from a total stranger. That hurts."

Trevor straightened his shoulders.

"I had more to lose with you."

"And now you've lost it."

"No. I won't accept that. Rant at me. Call me names. Whatever you want to do. Just don't leave me."

"I was never with you."

"Don't say that. You know more about Trevor Lane Daniels than any fan with my autograph."

"What if I suddenly told you my real name was Anna Bollenger and I was a runaway heiress?"

"I'd ask if you were married. I'd be puzzled about the name thing. Why bother? Or are you beginning to understand why I did bother?"

"Well, I'm not married and I'm not an heiress. In romance novels, they always lie to escape arranged marriages or for freedom."

"Close enough. The family once hoped I'd marry Stephie, but neither of us were having any part of that. Freedom? Yeah, freedom's always been a big thing to me. In this case—your case—freedom for me to be Joe Schmo, regular guy, take it or leave it."

"There's nothing even remotely regular about you."

"Well, I was trying to be."

"I have to think about this. I'm not sure how I feel about this. I'm still not sure I believe you. You still could be like a stunt-double, or a famous person look-alike."

"Can I keep on being Ski then? I kind of like Ski. Simple guy. Loves his woman. Loves her baby. Drives a

333

beat-up old truck. 'Made mad, passionate love 'til the candles guttered out and the dawn crept in the window'?"

Katie's eyes flew wide open and she gasped.

"You bastard! We never did any of that."

Trevor cringed and then shrugged.

"That's what Trevor does for a living. He makes things up in his head. He writes music and he writes songs. He sings and he plays."

"You're lying."

Trevor buried his face in his hands again.

"This is getting to be hysterically funny and completely frustrating. How about we call up Dad and Mary? Mary's got all these scrapbooks full of stuff about me."

"She could be just a really devoted fan of Trevor Daniels'."

"She is a devoted fan. She's got tons of stuff. Articles from magazines. Candids from when I was a kid. That tabloid article about me being a cross-dresser really ticked her off, but Dad convinced her that ink was ink, good or bad. And then Elvis was spotted and I was back out of the spotlight again. And I did not, nor would I ever, sleep with Liz Taylor. Yuck."

"You're all delusional. Your whole family. I can't handle this."

"But I'm not dead yet. Right? You haven't actually killed me. You can keep on calling me Ski."

"You seem to be harmless, if demented. This is just too much for me to process right now."

"Want my autograph?"

"Why? I'm sure it matches."

Trevor shook himself like a dog.

"Yeah, it does. You're right. Not good enough proof."

"Now, if you could get me in backstage to meet someone really famous, like maybe Dalton Struthers."

"I outsell him! I can show you the numbers."

Katie had an introspective scowl on her face.

"No, that won't work. As Trevor's stand-in, you would know a lot of famous people."

"Yeah, that won't work, will it? I'm fucking doomed."

Katie brightened.

"I've got it! Get him to let me sing on stage with him."

Trevor paled.

"No. No can do. Even I don't have that kind of pull with him."

Disaster averted, Trevor grasped at a straw.

"I'll tell you what. Since I'm his stand-in, and I've got all this stuff to go to—openings and parties and signings—you come along with me. Trev'd be real appreciative."

"He's seen with women."

"Yeah, but not one woman all the time. He's been real careful about that. I've been real careful about that, even playing Trevor Lane Daniels. Me. Playing me. And you're not some model or actress. You're like Cinderella. Yeah. Cool. That'd work. What do you think?"

"What would my name be?"

Trevor groaned and Katie giggled.

"Oh, yeah, never mind. I forgot. I'm me. It's you're the one with the false name. Sorry."

"Fine. It's fine. I'm fine. I am such dead meat."

## TILL WE MEET AGAIN

We made mad passionate love
'Til the candles guttered out
And dawn crept in the window.
Now you lie in my arms,
My beautiful one,
And I know it's a sin
To wake you up.
We must get up.
The sun is up.
Another day

Is rolling in.
I will keep you in
My mind.
'Til we meet again.

Cars and travel
Will unravel
Our nerves,
Drain our reserves.
I must drink the joy from your lips
To live.
Please forgive
All the heartache that I've brought
Anytime that we have fought.
I have prayed right from the start,
From the bottom of my heart
That we would never part.
I will keep you in
My mind
'Til we meet again.

\* \* \* \* \*

Trevor stood on the doorstep of the Olympia Avenue house. Jarrett frowned down at him.

"What do you mean Katie don't believe you?"

"She doesn't frigging believe me. She still thinks I'm Trevor's stand-in."

Trevor stomped up the steps and came into the kitchen. Jarrett followed him as he headed for the couch in the living room and flopped down on it.

"You ain't got no stand-in."

"Do you think I don't know that?"

"What the heck's the matter with you, boy? You can sell ice cubes to Eskimos."

"But I can't convince the woman I love that I'm me."

"Gotta be a way around this, boy."

336

"I think she's in shock. In denial. But she hasn't killed me. God help me when she finally does believe me."

"Amen to that. Scrapbooks?"

"Reflected glory, Dad. We covered that base. She asked to sing in the band."

"Your next concert?"

"I will not have that woman singing on stage with me. She's bad. Really, really bad."

Jarrett ran a hand through his hair.

"Turn her mike off. They say Paul McCartney used to have to do that with that wife of his."

Silence.

Trevor sucked in air through his teeth.

"I might have to do that, Dad. Both the on-stage and the off-mike."

"She drives a hard bargain, son."

"If I was Elvis, I could be seen in two places at once. Did you ever try–really try–to prove you were who you are? It sucks."

Jarrett's deep chuckle soothed some of the nerves out of Trevor.

"Calm down, Yankee. Let a southern man think on this. Katie a fan of Trevor's?"

"Of his music, yes. Seemed to be somewhat up on biographical details. I'm talking about myself in the third person. This is creepy."

"Calm down. How come she's not some teenage girl with one of your posters up over her bed?"

"God only knows. My face is everywhere else in the known universe. Just last week I saw a bobble-head doll of myself in Sam Goody's, for Christ's sake. She's said all along that the music is more important than the man. She didn't want to meet me or get my autograph even back when. Maybe she intentionally never wanted to know what he looked like. I mean me. Geez."

"Then I guess I'll have to go hire us a Trevor Daniels stand-in. Maybe run a contest for it. Yeah, I like that."

"If you run this contest, do you think Ski should enter it? Katie might make him enter it. Ski better darned sure win this contest."

"Trevor, get a grip. You can't enter and win the contest. You have to be there to award the prize to the winner. Right?"

"Yeah. Right. This is messing up my head."

"We'll get the PR people on it. Katie still got her cell phone?"

"Yeah. And a AAA membership, just in case. She's practical enough to not reject either of those."

"Good. Give me her number."

Trevor did and Jarrett programmed it into his own cell phone.

"Is your cell number in her cell phone?"

"Yeah."

"Make sure she has that cell phone with her at all times, charged up, and turned on. All right?"

"Yeah. Sure. You up to something?"

"Oh, my, yes. Don't you worry, boy."

\*　　　\*　　　\*　　　\*　　　\*

The Trevor Daniels Look-Alike Contest hit the local airways two days later. It started on the local Charlotte County stations. From there it went north, south and east to every radio station from Naples to Tampa and out to La Belle. Stations from Tallahassee to Jacksonville, out the Panhandle and down to the Keys carried the details.

Then it went national.

Mini contests were set up in major cities.

The finals would be held in Punta Gorda. Jarrett booked the Charlotte County Auditorium and alerted the Tourist Development Council and all the major tourist beds in a three county area. The date was set for two weeks before Trevor's next concert tour began, the winner to open with Trevor onstage in Dallas, complimentary tickets for accommodations and backstage passes for friends and family of the winner, and round trip airfare included. Trevor saw his own face grinning back at him from magazine covers more than he saw Tim McGraw's or Kenny Chesney's. And forget about Blake Shelton.

Trevor commuted happily between his newly acquired Sarasota family and his established Punta Gorda family. He had Charlie Wagner of Slot A Slot B Furniture assemble two-story rustic playhouse/forts for Robbie at Katie's house as well as at The Ice Palace. He had a pool fence installed around the pool at The Ice Palace.

Energetic and edgy songs of freedom and love poured out of him, music and lyrics full-blown. They were great, singable tunes. Karaoke music. He was high as a kite on love and loving every minute of it.

### FUN, FUN, FUN (calypso beat)

Fun, Fun, Fun.
Come and get me.
Fun, fun, fun.
You'll never catch me.
Fun, fun, fun
'Til the day I die.

Look what's comin' over the hill now.
Look what's comin' to give me a thrill now.
Fun, fun, fun,
'Til the day I die.

I can watch my two feet a-shufflin'.
I can feel my body jumpin'.
Fun, fun, fun,
'Til the day I die.

Mr. Trucker, give me a ride now.
I'll play songs. You'll smile for a while now.
Fun, fun, fun,
'Til the day I die.

Mr. Cruiser, don't you arrest me.
Jailhouse food just don't impress me.
Fun, fun, fun,
'Til the day I die.

Fun, fun, fun.
Come and get me.
Fun, fun, fun.
You'll never catch me.
Fun, fun, fun,
Till the day I die.

## Chapter Fifteen

Trevor knocked on the door of the house on Olympia Avenue and walked in, his arm possessively around Katie Mercer's shoulders.

"Mary? Dad? This is Katie."

Jarrett looked lazily up from his newspaper to find his son glittering a two hundred-watt smile and holding a really very ordinary-looking girl clamped to his side. Jarrett almost did a double take and then caught sight of Mary's mouth hanging open.

From behind the girl's jean-clad legs peeked a shy toddler. Jarrett felt his face relax into a smile.

"Son?"

"Yes, sir?"

"Turn down the volume."

"Oh. Okay."

Jarrett watched Trevor make a concerted effort to contain his bright energy and drive. If the lady was as shy as her little boy was, Jarrett thought, no wonder Trevor scared her.

"Missy? You got a little tadpole clingin' to you there. That tadpole got a name?"

The girl's wooden face relaxed.

"This is my son, Robbie."

Jarrett slid off the couch and lay on the floor on his back, turning warm eyes toward Robbie.

"Don't get me wrong, Katie. I'm pleased to meet you. But I'm real pleased to meet Robbie. You like trucks, Robbie? I got me a lot of trucks we could play with."

Robbie detached himself from Katie and came to stand looking down at Jarrett. His face was serious as he dropped to the floor and sat cross-legged within reach of Jarrett.

"Trucks."

"Yep. Got plenty of them. Son?"

Trevor turned from gazing fondly at Katie.

"Yeah?"

341

"Did you teach Robbie to sit like that?"

"No, sir. Not that I know of."

Katie ducked out from under Trevor's arm and knelt on the floor by her son.

"Yes, he did, Mr. Daniels. Robbie never sat like that until he met Ski."

Jarrett glanced over to his son and Trevor shrugged.. Mary gathered her scattered wits together and, rising from the couch, extended her hand down to Katie.

"I'm Mary Daniels. Perhaps we should let the men bond over trucks. Do you like to garden? I could show you my hibiscus. I'm rather proud of them."

Katie rose from the floor and extended her hand, letting Mary's gentle flow of persuasion carry her away from her son and out the side door.

They did nothing much throughout the long afternoon. Mary and Katie pulled weeds. Jarrett and Robbie and Trevor played with trucks and Legos on the braided rug in the living room. They ate tuna fish salad sandwiches for lunch. Mary played part of one of Shawn's fragments on the violin for Katie, who had seen the work in progress on the coffee table. Then Katie spotted Jarrett's guitar by the fireplace.

"May I?"

"Go right ahead, missy."

Katie began beating out "Blowing in the Wind" on Bessie. Jarrett turned his back on her and faced Trevor, sucking in air and whispering.

"Whew! She's really bad."

Trevor laughed and rubbed his eyes. He looked at his fingers to make sure his eyes weren't bleeding.

"Yeah, she is."

After Trevor and Katie and Robbie left for Sarasota, Mary turned sparkling eyes to Jarrett.

"Oh, Jarrett, our little boy's in love. Isn't it wonderful?"

342

"With a plain-faced gal who can't even croak out 'Blowin' in the Wind'?"

"She's meeting some need of his, Jarrett. He's the strangest I've ever known him to be. He wasn't this strange in high school. Or college. He wasn't this strange when he was on drugs. He's moody and up and down and all over the place."

"He's hangin' around that gal with a line of drool comin' off his lip. It's disgustin'."

"Love, Jarrett. He's fallen in love."

"I like that little boy of hers."

"Maybe he'll have a sibling soon. This isn't Trevor's usual pick-of-the-beauties. I've seen him doing things today I've never seen him do before, not to mention yardwork, which he hates. He was down on his hands and knees beside her in that front flowerbed, pretending to enjoy digging with the trowel while she set out three flats of Mexican heather for me today. It could only be love, Jarrett."

The next Saturday, Mary expressed a desire to go shopping in Sarasota. Jarrett nodded. Trevor was up in Lakeland at a mall opening. Keturah's closed at noon. Mary was there at 11:30 a.m, persuading Katie to pick up Robbie from her friend Lisa's house and come back down to Punta Gorda with her for the day.

Jarrett reported the results to Trevor on the phone.

"Mary had her out giving her the Daniels standard test."

"Mary had Katie doing Bondo work on your truck?"

"No. I ain't got so much as the thought of a scratch on that beauty. You're the one's got the heap. Gardenin', boy."

"Oh, my God. Is Katie all right?"

"You moron, Mary wouldn't have her out in the sun for four hours with a shovel. She ain't got your mean streak."

"What then?"

"Just a little weedin' and chattin'. I'm Bondo. You and Mary are gardenin'. Mary seems to feel there ain't much you can't tell about a person if you garden with 'em. I don't know about that. But Mary done give her a clean bill of health."

"Not a barracuda?"

"Not unless she's got Mary fooled, too. After years on them concert tours of hers, jauntin' all over the world and kissin' cheeks with people and talkin' in thirteen different languages, I'd say it'd be hard to fool your hard-headed aunt. It appears the lady is what she seems. A single mom just out of a lousy marriage. A good-hearted woman who can't sing or play worth a lick. A concerned parent."

"How about a beautiful woman who can't get enough of me?"

"Darn, boy. You gotta do some of the work yourself."

\*     \*     \*     \*     \*

Mary was up in Sarasota again, this time helping Carla make new curtains. Trevor had driven his MG from a mall opening in Lakeland to Fort Myers for a live-on-radio appearance. Now he was back in Punta Gorda at the house on Olympia Avenue, helping Jarrett put groceries away.

Jarret broke open a bag of peaches and began lining them up on the kitchen window sill to ripen.

"There's somethin' about this gal that makes her special to you, Trevor. Maybe she brings out the man in you, wantin' to protect her and her little boy."

"Maybe you're right. Maybe I love the boy so much I think I love the mother. Who the heck knows?"

"Well, then separate them, son. Talk her into leavin' Robbie with Mary and me. Katie likes us well enough. Get her off by herself without the boy. Just the two of you."

"I'm telling you, Dad. She won't be alone with me. Time was she'd at least ride in the truck with me. I haven't made progress. I've lost ground. She keeps the boy with us. Much good it'd do her if I was a jerk. She keeps us in crowds of people, or even with Scott. She's fine then. But alone, together? Not a chance. I swear to God, Dad. I have never

344

given her cause. I can't even touch her hand now. I can't brush past her. Nothing. You'd think I had the plague or something. Intimate? Personal? Cozy? I got her into the hot tub at The Ice Palace after one of Stephie's parties. We were making progress. I thought. Now? Zip."

"You're gettin' wound up."

"Damn right I am! This sucks. What the hell am I gonna do?"

"Find out why."

Trevor had been pacing the small room, his hair flying behind him. He stopped now.

"What?"

Jarrett shook his head.

"Find out why, Trevor. There's got to be a reason. Real or in her head. You remember a little boy afraid of hugs?"

"Yeah."

"There were reasons for that."

"You were always so calm and patient."

"Bein' calm and patient ain't easy for you, Trevor. You're all fire and lightnin' now, but you weren't when we first met. You had genuine fears. Once you got free of your fears, you flew. But you weren't free when we met. You need to help your lady. You done helped little Robbie. I didn't see any shadows in him."

"She was scared to death I'd be like her ex with Robbie. But that passed. I was surprised she didn't think it of you. I was holding my breath. But she was fine. She gets on fine with you. And Mary. It's me."

"It's hard not to make comparisons, son. Real hard. In the beginnin', you were always comparin' me to your mom. Lucky for me we were worlds apart. I'd guess you couldn't be farther apart from her ex, but there may be things she sees in you that were a problem in him. Not your fault. She may not even be aware of it. You got to go slow. Easy for me to say. I ain't the one hurtin'. Could be your smile. Maybe not. Could be your eyebrows. Who knows? Try to remember what it was like for you when we first met,

345

Trevor, and go slow. Lay your cards out on the table. 'Katie, it bothers you when I try to hold your hand'. Tell me why that is.' Don't ask her questions she can answer yes or no. Be as neutral as you can and get her to tell you why. You may still never win your lady. She may wake up one day and move on from you. But she's important to you, Trevor. You're gonna have to be selfless. That's a hard thing to do, son. You're gonna be takin' a lot of cold showers."

"I'm going back on tour soon, too. I'll lose her."

"Find her some job in the organization, son. One that pays a salary so huge she won't be able to say no to it, for Robbie's sake. One that puts her in daily contact with you, especially in the bus or hotels. Mary and I can take care of little Robbie, if Katie's agreeable."

Trevor glimmered a smile.

"The Ben Daniels Agency is now head-hunting retail sales clerks?"

"You've got clever people in your organization. Find one that can sell it, son."

"She'll hate me if she ever finds out."

"You ain't gettin' nowhere now. What have you got to lose? Plead the diminished capacity of the lovelorn."

"God, that's revolting."

"Close to the truth, though."

"Yeah. I'm desperate. I'm forgetting the words to songs I've been singing for years."

Jarrett nodded, his face perfectly somber.

"You owe it to your fans to help solve Katie Mercer's problems."

Trevor looked up into his father's face and chuckled.

"Why do I feel like I've just been hosed?"

"Son, accordin' to what you've told me, Katie says her ex-husband was a charmin' liar, correct?"

"Yeah. That's the bottom line. At best."

"Well, you've lied to her and you're a charmer. That's two good reasons right there for her to give you a wide berth. And she has. But she's still there, son. Maybe in spite of herself. And in spite of you and your truly pathetic efforts to either win her love or drive her completely away."

Jarrett reported his findings to Mary when she got back from her Sarasota curtain-making activities.

"Our baby's in love."

"How can you tell?"

"He's all edgy."

"He's always been edgy."

"Not like this. A Daddy can tell."

"You're sure it's not anything serious?"

"Of course it's serious, honey. It's love."

\*     \*     \*     \*     \*

Not a week later Jarrett and Trevor were sitting in the emergency room of the local hospital, Trevor with a clean towel held to his face.

He'd been up on his own roof, gotten absent-minded, missed his footing and slid down the roof to crash into a bougainvillea bush. He was all right, but he had numerous bleeding and festering cuts all over his face and arms.

Jarrett had calmly driven him to the emergency room of the nearest hospital when he turned up at the house on Olympia Avenue.

Trevor shifted the towel to a new surface.

"I don't care if my face is messed up. Tell them to leave it alone."

"No can do, Trev. Gotta have a way to keep your eyeballs from fallin' out. Gotta have a nose to prop your sunglasses up on."

"It doesn't have to be pretty."

"Well, no. They ain't that good here, son."

Trevor laughed, but tension took over again.

"Stop it. I don't want to laugh."

"I know it. You just want to feel sorry for yourself."

Jarrett rested a hand on Trevor's shoulder.

"Gotta have a face, boy. It might as well be your own. You come out lookin' like Brad Pitt, I ain't gonna be able to recognize you on the street. Be sendin' a battered-up Chevy to the body shop for a paint job and get back somebody else's Rolls Royce? I don't think so. Darn it, if I send in my Chevy, I want my Chevy back."

"Katie says I scare her, Dad."

"Heck, you been scarin' me for years."

"Not like that. Quit joking, Dad. This is serious. I'm serious."

"What scares her, boy? Your pretty face? Is that what this is all about? Don't tell me you threw yourself into a bougainvillea bush on purpose to mess up your face."

"No. I slipped. Yeah, my pretty face is part of it. We worked out a deal. This is nuts. I can hug her and kiss her and hold hands with her if I'm pretending to be Trevor at one of Stephie's parties. But any other time? No. This is surreal. I can't live like this. I need her touching me. The real me."

Jarrett began massaging the tense muscles he found in Trevor's shoulders.

"The lady's got some issues, Trevor. This really can't be all about you and your pretty face. You ain't that pretty."

Trevor drew a shaky breath.

"What the heck am I gonna do? I'm past the age where I should be asking my dad for help with my sex life."

"And I ain't givin' you none. This ain't about sex, Trev. Not for neither of you. It's about closeness. Seems like your lady's drawn to you, but just can't commit. That said, I'd guess you would scare her. She scare you, boy?"

"No. I just want. I just need."

"You let me know when you can 'fess up to bein' scared, Trevor. Then we'll talk again. Meanwhile, do for your lady what I had to do for you when we first met. I had to treat you like a stray dog that's been beat. I just had to keep the love flowin' out to you until you stopped shiverin'. Just go from your heart, Trevor. Give her what she'll take, even if it seems goofy to you. And take what she can give."

Trevor nodded and leaned back into Jarrett's hand at the back of his neck.

"Why does life have to be so darned complicated? I seriously don't have time for this."

"You'll make time, Trevor. This is important to you."

Jarrett let his hand drop from Trevor's neck and bumped shoulders with him, getting a brief smile back. He bumped shoulders with Trevor again.

"Best not let Mary see your face for a few days. Somehow or another it'll be my fault you fell off your own roof."

"Why? I did it. Cheap sneakers with no treads. I got to thinking about Katie and didn't watch what I was doing. My fault."

"It's a dad-thing, son. Dumb stuff is always the dad's fault."

"I feel like a idiot."

"The press'll probably claim you got road rash from layin' down your Harley."

"I don't have a Harley. I don't have any motorcycles. They make my insurance company nervous."

"You'll have one by the time the press finishes. Maybe broke your heart over a woman."

"Please."

"Lighten up, boy."

# Chapter Sixteen

When Trevor had gotten Katie's cell phone for her, he had had Scott program his own cell phone number into it. Katie had never initiated a call to him, but he still considered it to be a link to her.

His cell phone rang now as he sat on the floor in his house on Gill Street, nursing his shredded face and forearms away from the public eye and playing fetch with Buddy. He pulled the phone off his belt now, absently answering it as he flipped another small, wadded ball of paper to Buddy.

"Yeah?"

"Ski?"

He straightened his spine as Buddy ignored the ball of paper and curled up in his lap for a pet.

"Yeah."

"It's me. Katie. I really hate to bother you, but I've got a problem."

"So? What's the problem?"

"I'm the homeless now again. Charlie owned the house. Remember? I got home from work today and all my things were out on the front lawn. All Robbie's things, too. The locks were changed. There's a For Sale sign on the front lawn. And two policemen are here to arrest me."

Trevor slid Buddy off his lap and stood up from the floor.

"What for?"

"I don't know. Breaking and entering maybe. Apparently there's an alarm system in the house now. My key didn't work but I set off some sort of silent alarm."

"Where's Robbie?"

"He's here with me. Oh, Ski."

"Is one of the officers willing to get on the phone? Find out."

Trevor heard muffled voices in the background and remembered being a fifteen-year-old boy in the Port Charlotte Town Center Mall, pursued by mall security.

He didn't have Jarrett Daniels' cachet to help him here, he thought.

Or did he?

He heard the phone exchange hands.

"Deputy Stafford here. Who's this?"

Trevor sucked in a breath.

"This is Trevor Daniels. I understand Miss Mercer has a problem. I can't have one of my people and her little boy out on the streets. I'd like to send the limo for her. Where should the driver go?"

He swallowed.

This was major balls, he thought.

"Ms. Mercer is being arrested, sir, for breaking and entering. She'll go to the Sarasota County Jail until her arraignment or until she can make bail. Her son will be put into foster care."

With a jolt, Trevor came out of his shell.

"Who filed these charges?"

"A Mr. Charles Smallwood."

"That's her ex-husband, the bastard. She uses her maiden name. This is a domestic dispute that guy's dragged you all into. I'm sorry for that. Where can I send the limo?"

Trevor gripped the phone hard while he heard more muffled voices and hoped his name carried sufficient clout. When the deputy came back on the phone, Trevor could hear the change in his voice.

"Ms. Mercer confirms what you've said, sir. She should have told us all this right off. She says she'll wait here for the limo, Mr. Daniels, but between you and me, I'd just as soon you sent a truck or van for her belongings, too. They won't be worth much if they stay outside all night. My partner and I will stay with Ms. Mercer. She looks pretty shook up."

"Thank you, Deputy Stafford. I'll take your advice. I'll send a couple of our men down with a pick-up truck on this. I appreciate you staying with Ms. Mercer."

Trevor hung up, limp with relief. He hated dealing with cops. Old habits died hard, he thought.

351

He phoned Scott and Jarrett, briefing them on Katie's problem and asking for their help. He gave them directions to Katie's house.

Part of him wanted to roll up in the limo to impress the cops. The other part voted for the Chevy pickup as being more practical.

He pulled on a better T-shirt–one with no holes in it– and dragged a cleaner baseball cap over his hair. He grabbed two of his latest CDs and a short stack of backstage passes to an upcoming event, grabbed the truck keys and he was on the road, doing his usual ninety miles an hour up the interstate.

When Trevor arrived, Scott was standing with Katie and Robbie, making small talk. The two Sarasota County sheriff's deputies were over by their patrol car, arms folded across chests, sunglasses on.

Trevor slid his own sunglasses on and parked behind Scott's van. He brought the two CDs in their cases and the backstage passes with him when he joined his brother and Katie. Robbie was up in Katie's arms, his head resting on her shoulder. Robbie smiled at him and he smiled back. When Scott took the CDs and passes from him and wandered over to talk to the deputies, Katie began to move a hand toward his bougainvillea-shredded face but then stopped herself.

"Ski, what happened to your face and arms?"

"Uh. Cut myself shaving? Actually I fell off my own roof."

"Are you all right?"

"Yeah. I guess."

"Ski, I appreciate the help. I never thought to tell them Charlie was my ex. My mind just froze."

"No problem. I'm glad you called me. I'm glad to help out."

"I have no one else, Ski. I just couldn't drag Lisa into this."

"I understand. It makes the choice harder when you don't have a choice at all. Dad's coming, too. He just doesn't drive as fast as I do. We'll get all your belongings into

Scott's van, Dad's truck, my truck, and your car. The Suburban's over at Scott's house, but we'll make do."

Scott walked towards them.

"Trev, you got some work to do. Officer Stafford asked me for your autograph."

"Okay. Got a Sharpie marker? Which one's Officer Stafford?"

Scott slid a Sharpie marker to him from the front pocket of his shirt.

"The guy on the right."

Katie shifted Robbie in her arms as Scott walked off to begin loading his van with some of Katie's bulkier items.

"Both officers became much friendlier after they spoke to you on the phone."

"The benefits of power."

"I am extremely embarrassed."

"Why? You're the victim here. Let me go take care of business. Hey, Officer Stafford. How's it goin'?"

Smiling a relaxed, sociable smile, Trevor walked towards the two uniformed men.

By the time he finished with them, and watched them drive off, Jarrett was pulling up in his newest truck. Scott had already begun to load the back of his van with assorted boxes from the front lawn, one of which looked like it held a Christmas tree.

Trevor smiled at a forlorn-looking Katie as he positioned himself at her side.

"Want to do your own packing? I can hold Robbie."

Katie slid Robbie from her arms.

"Robbie's a big boy. He can stand on his own."

"Can I hold his hand? I have a tendency to wander off. Ask anyone."

Jarrett and Scott between them made quick work of loading Katie's larger pieces of furniture. Her bed, bureau, TV and Robbie's bed went into Scott's van.

Jarrett came up, rubbing his hands.

"Hey there, Katie. How's it goin', Tadpole? Gimme five."

Robbie grinned and gave Jarrett a high five.

"Best move it, Katydid. You'll know how or where you'll want all those clothes and shoes and stuff."

Katie turned stunned eyes to Jarrett.

"Where will I go?"

Jarrett hoisted Robbie up into the crook of his arm. They were now eye-to-eye and grinning at one another.

"What's that, Katie? Where will you go? Why, to Trevor's place in Punta Gorda, of course. Where else? You can't live out at The Ice Palace. People will talk."

Trevor, Jarrett, Scott and Robbie all looked at her as if she were softheaded and simple. Katie huffed out a breath and began to pull clothes off the front lawn and stuff them into trash bags.

Trevor glanced at his companions and went to help her.

Flustered and overheated and tired and distressed, Katie muttered under her breath as she worked. Trevor gave her space, mutely grabbing what he felt was safe to grab, and leaving extremely personal items alone.

"Ski, I don't know my way."

"Sure you do. 'Second star to the right and on to morning'."

"That's 'Peter Pan', Ski."

"Oh. Right. Okay. Over the Peace River, hang a right at Best Western. That's Retta Esplanade. It's the house on the corner of Retta and Gill. You can't miss it. Really. It's big and yellow. Dad and Mary live right around the corner. You'll be fine."

"When I called you I didn't know what I was thinking."

"I'm glad you called. Maybe you were thinking, 'Here's a guy I can trust to help me when I'm down.' I hope so."

"If it weren't for Robbie, I'd have never called you."

"I know."

"I have to consider Robbie. I could live in the woods, but Robbie can't. Not again."

354

"There is no reason in the world for either of you to live in the woods. I'm here."

"I'd be in jail if not for you."

"Nah. Eventually you'd have remembered to tell them it was your ex playing stupid games. Maybe they just needed to hear it from Trevor Daniels."

"I'd rather live in the trees than in a shelter. Drugs and alcohol and disease. I'm trying to protect Robbie from all that."

Trevor stuffed a big box onto the back seat of Katie's car, the sweat of exertion running into his scratches.

"Will you give it a rest? You're not sleeping in the trees."

Katie turned on him, tears and fury in her eyes.

"I'm not sleeping in your bed, either!"

Trevor set his hands on his hips and looked at her, totally exasperated now. His face was throbbing painfully from the bougainvillea scratches and his conscience was still digging him in the ribs about his recent deceptions..

Why did he have to fall in love with this, he wondered?

"No. You're not sleeping in my bed. You haven't been invited. Got it? We've had this conversation before. I distinctly remember having this conversation."

"Then where am I sleeping?"

"In your own room. In your own bed. Robbie gets the nursery."

"The nursery?"

"Figure of speech. Small bedroom at the top of the house. Great view of the Peace River. Look all the way to Heaven through the skylights. Great room. Real small, though. Perfect fit for Robbie."

Katie began jamming more clothes into a trash bag. Trevor looked at the worn clothes and wondered why she even bothered. The homeless were better dressed. She threw clothes in with plastic plates, tying off the bag savagely.

"Why are you doing this?"

"Because you asked for my help."

355

Katie threw the bag into the car and burst into tears. Trevor moved quickly towards her and she moved just as quickly back.

"Don't touch me."

"Katie."

"Don't touch me, I said. I'm fine. I'll be fine."

She was shivering and gulping and holding her arms around herself. Trevor put his hands in his pockets.

"Yes, you will be. You'll be fine. You have your health. You have Robbie. You have hope. You've got friends. Okay?"

Katie snuffled and sucked it up, wiping her eyes with the backs of her hands. Trevor smiled at her.

"You look a mess, Kate. You'll worry Robbie. You don't want that. Neither does he. Take what comes, Katie. Nothing bad is coming. I promise."

Katie rubbed her face and shook back her short curl of a ponytail. The tendrils of her naturally curly hair framed her face. She should have looked awful, but to Trevor she looked like an angel.

I'm toast, he thought. Stick a fork in me. I'm done.

Katie straightened her shoulders.

"Well, that's all I've got. I'm done."

Trevor shook himself.

"Let's roll then. We'll do a convoy."

Jarrett lounged over with Robbie still up in his arms. Robbie had his arms around Jarrett's neck, his head on Jarrett's shoulder, and was looking at his mother with owlishly sleepy eyes.

"You all best put Trevor here in the back of the convoy. If he leads, we'll all be left behind. Can I keep Tadpole with me? Got that car-chair-baby thing? You'll need to concentrate on your drivin', Katie."

Taking Katie's silence for consent, Jarrett pointed his chin from Scott to Katie's car and Scott went to remove the baby seat and install it in Jarrett's truck.

"We'll put Scott in front. He's real steady. I'll follow. You can follow me. You'll be able to keep an eye on me that way, with this precious cargo onboard. Trevor can bring up the rear. About time he did. He can make sure we don't lose you."

Katie found she was nodding her agreement before she even thought about it. Trevor smiled. Jarrett had that effect on people. He was so smooth and reasonable. God knew it had worked on him many a time, Trevor thought.

Scott and Jarrett retreated to their respective vehicles, Jarrett settling Robbie into his car seat. Katie zombied to her car, then turned back to Trevor, holding a glossy dark green shopping bag with KETURAH'S printed on the side of it in gold.

"I don't like doing this."

"Can't live on the streets, darlin'."

"I could. But I have to think of Robbie."

"Lucky for me you've got him, then. Lucky for me you've got him anyway."

"Are you making fun of me?"

"No, darlin'. But, I'm looking at you standing there with all your most important stuff in a shopping bag and I'm remembering me doing the same thing a long time ago. I'm sorry your place is gone. I'm sorry I'm your only choice. I'll never take advantage of that. I've had that done to me and I didn't like it."

Katie got in her car. Trevor closed the door, then leaned his scratched arms on the frame of the open window, lowering his chin to his arms so that his currently scratched and puffy face was lower than Katie's and he was looking up at her profile.

She glanced defensively over at him.

"What?"

"I may have to tell you a great deal more about myself than I had planned on. So you won't be so afraid of me."

"I'm not afraid of you."

"Sure you are. You've got a right to be."

They did the convoy thing out Fruitville Road and up onto the interstate, heading south. They passed exit after exit

357

to familiar roads and stayed closer as the exits came for Englewood. And then Port Charlotte. Trevor would have taken the King's Highway exit–old Exit 31 where he had been mugged and raped by the Spath boys so many years ago. He liked to remind himself of the cosmic nature of even horrific events. But taking the Route 17 exit just across the Peace River was quicker and made more sense.

Trevor wondered if Katie was looking for the right-hand turn at the Best Western he had told her about and smiled. Going this way it would be down Marion Avenue and a right turn onto Gill Street. She'd never even see the Best Western. God only knew what nefarious plot she'd make out of that.

Once in Punta Gorda, Scott led the convoy to the Olympia Avenue house first, parking on the street far enough up to allow his father into his own driveway and for Katie and Trevor to pull in behind him on the street. Robbie was put down for a nap in Trevor's old bedroom after a quickly consumed dinner of fish sticks and French fries.

For the adult population, Mary served the baked grouper and rice pilaf she had had time to prepare since receiving Trevor's call. The five of them sat around the kitchen table with an added straight chair from the master bedroom. It was awkward, but Trevor was happy enough to sit on the same side as Katie, leaving Scott facing him and Mary and Jarrett at either end. Jarrett said grace and then opened the needed discussion as he stabbed at a spinach salad laden with blue cheese dressing.

"You gotta have a decent place to stay, Katie. I can understand your reluctance to impose on strangers. But we ain't that strange."

Scott bypassed the salad and headed for the fish.

"Trevor is. I can understand Katie not wantin' to live with him at all."

Mary watched Katie and Trevor and said nothing for the moment.

Trevor nudged Katie.

"Katie, eat."

Katie picked up her fork but seemed unable to understand its function. Mary entered the conversation now.

"Kate, is there some friend or relative we could contact for you? I know you called my nephew for help, and he and we are more than happy to help, but I sense that you may be regretting your initial impulse."

Katie looked up from her untouched plate.

"I've never had anything like this happen to me before."

Trevor munched away at his salad.

"Sure you have. You bugged out with Robbie and slept in the scrub. This is much better than that. You still have all your stuff. Or most of it. Right? I don't see any problem."

Katie turned to him.

"This is different."

"I don't see that."

Katie laid her fork down and put a hand to her forehead.

"The last time I left, I chose to go. I took my precious baby and left to protect him. I didn't care about my belongings. I still don't, really. Maybe Robbie's pictures. I didn't see them out there in the grass. Perhaps they're still inside the house. Maybe they're thrown out. I don't know."

She gathered her shattered nerves together again.

"I had no preparation for this. Mentally. Emotionally. It was out of the blue. I couldn't think straight. I just called for help. Now I'm in a worse predicament and I've dragged all of you into it, too. I'm mortified to have this happen. I am so ashamed."

Trevor finished his salad and attacked his rice next.

"Got nothing to be ashamed about. I liked getting your call. Not 'cause Charlie threw you out. I liked knowing you thought enough of me to feel I'd stand your friend if you needed help. Remember? What goes around comes around. Just passing the favor on."

Katie straightened her shoulders.

"In answer to your question, Mary, no, there isn't anyone else to call. My friend Lisa lives in a two-bedroom apartment with her new husband and her little girl. My parents are both dead. While I was married to Charlie, he effectively cut me off from any of my former friends."

Scott waved his fork.

"I expect Carla and I could squeeze Junior into our room and you and Robbie could move in with us."

He received a kick on the shins from his brother's foot under the table and a slight scowl. He grinned.

"Or maybe not. Got the same problem your friend Lisa has. I guess your best bet is to bunk in with Trev. He's got the biggest house at the moment."

Mary cleared her throat.

"For tonight, perhaps the least upheaval the better. For Robbie's sake. Jarrett and I are able to accommodate Robbie in Trevor's old bedroom, but we gave the other beds in the house to Habitat for Humanity years ago. When we have out-of-town visitors, we put them up at the Best Western. We have no rooms set up as guest bedrooms. Scott is right. The Gill Street house is the best choice at the moment. Jarrett and Scott can set up your bed there, Katie, and move any items of furniture in that you want. The rooms are still mostly unfurnished. Scott can borrow the MG to drive home, leaving the van for you to unload at your leisure."

Katie was still doubtful.

"Mary, that would be wonderful. All of you have been so kind. But I feel badly about imposing."

Trevor moved to get out of his chair.

"Well, I'm done. Scott, stop eating. Dad?"

"Set your butt back down there, finish your meal, and let your lady relax and eat. Katie, some of us here at this table should have more sensitivity about your plight. Some of us should remember when the shoe was on the other foot. I know it hurts your pride to ask for help, but it shouldn't. Bein' the target of spite or the victim of cruelty does not reflect on you. If you have the slightest problem over there at

360

that Gill Street house, I will undertake personally the grave duty of rectifying that problem."

Jarrett fixed a chilling eye on Trevor, who subsided mutely into his baked fish.

Katie picked up her fork to eat.

"Thank you, Jarrett. You make me feel better about all this."

"Glad to help. Mary? We got any dessert with this meal?"

After dinner, all three Daniels men convoyed the vehicles over to the Gill Street house. Jarrett and Scott moved heavy pieces into the bedroom upstairs that faced the Peace River and would be a step away from the stairs leading to what Trevor referred to as the nursery. Buddy, commuting between the house on Olympia Avenue and the one on Gill Street, supervised.

Millie Crawford's cats headed for the bushes again.

Trevor carried the trash bags and smaller boxes and pillows and cushions and lamps, running up and down the stairs and dodging around the bulk of his brother and his father. Katie stayed back at the house on Olympia Avenue with Mary, helping with dishes. When Katie drove her Lumina over to the house on Gill Street to unload it, Mary stayed with Robbie, still asleep in Trevor's old bedroom. Trevor, still full of energy, helped Katie unload the remaining boxes and bags.

It was getting on towards midnight before they were finished moving the bulk of what furniture Trevor had in the house out to the detached garage and Katie's in. Katie was drooping with fatigue. Scott was stretching his back muscles and Jarrett was fondling Buddy's ears. Trevor was still upbeat and focused.

"We'll need more stuff. I'll go shopping tomorrow. Give me a list, Kate."

Jarrett shook his head.

"Son, here's how it's gonna be. Katie's gonna take a shower and go to bed. You're gonna let her. For breakfast, she can eat whatever you've got in the fridge and go on to

361

work. Mary and I'll take care of Robbie tomorrow. One less thing for you to worry about, Katie. You get your head on straight. Have your mail forwarded, but don't have it forwarded to here. You understand? I hate to be the cloud on your horizon, but somethin' set your ex-husband off and made him do this. Ain't any one of us know what that somethin' was. I don't want him turnin' up down here messin' with you, or your boy, or my boys, or any of us, either. You forward all your mail to The Ice Palace address. We'll get it down here to you. Call up to disconnect your phone and all your utilities, if they're in your name. Don't go back over to that house for nothin'. You got that?"

Katie sagged against a door frame.

"Oh, dear God, I hadn't even thought of that. I was so stunned. Of course, he did it for a reason. Merciful heaven's, what have I brought down on all of you?"

Jarrett stood up and Buddy went to rub up onto Trevor's legs.

"Nothin' we can't handle, missy. When you're more rested, you can make lists of what you need. Curtains, toys. There's got to be a lot things. That's no problem. Does this ex of yours know where you work?"

"No. I got the job after I moved out and divorced him."

"Good. He won't be able to bother you at work unless he's been spyin' on you and followin' you from the house. You need a lawyer?"

"No. I've let Charlie do what he wants."

Trevor looked up.

"Not about visitation, you haven't."

"No. But I was simply answering his attorney."

Jarrett slid his hands into his pockets.

"Don't you worry, missy. We'll lawyer-up for you. This all looks like it's got the potential for gettin' ugly. We'll just be nippin' that in the bud. We got lawyers with the feedbag on all the time. Might as well work 'em."

Katie came away from the door frame to hug Jarrett and lean into him briefly.

"Thank you for all you're doing to help me."

She went to Scott who folded her into his arms and rocked her back and forth slowly. Trevor scowled.

"Hey. Don't I get a hug?"

Scott grinned at him.

"Heck, no. You ain't done squat."

Jarrett smiled knowingly at Trevor.

"And you ain't leavin'. Katie's givin' us a goodbye hug, son."

"Oh, well, that's okay then."

Scott released Katie and patted her shoulder.

"I'll see you when I see you, Katydid. Get the moron there to do the heavy work. I'll take the van back when you're done with it. Good night, you all. I'm outta here. Give my love to Mary. I got your keys to the MG, Trev."

Scott ambled out the back door. Jarrett looked pointedly at Trevor as he walked past him to follow Scott.

"Do the right thing, boy."

And he was gone.

Trevor faced Katie in the quiet of the barely-furnished house. He should have felt joy. What he felt was the awkwardness of a virgin bride on her wedding night. He imagined Katie felt worse.

"My family's right. Move in with me here. At least until you get your feet on the ground. I've got a cat. You've got Robbie. There's about a million rooms in this house. Save up some more money for first, last and security. Try it for say three months."

His face got an odd expression on it and Katie shifted her feet.

"Three months is a long time."

"Yeah. You're right. It is. I ought to know."

"You've done this before?"

"Yeah. So to speak. I guess I never thought the shoe would be on the other foot. I wonder about life's ironies sometimes."

"What happened when you did this before? I don't suppose you'll tell me the truth."

363

Trevor chuckled and shook his head.

"Why not? I left. After the agreed-upon three months, I left. I never regretted not going back. I never regretted not staying. I was free. You will be, too. But you're right. With the deal I made, it didn't take me three months to know I'd made a bad deal. How about no stipulation on length of time? I hope we're both past the point of not being able to stand one another as human beings."

"What do you get out of this?"

Trevor smiled.

"It's a pleasure doing business with you, Kate. I suppose in the short run I get the feeling of doing something nice for someone when they really need it. That's the very short run. Next, I have way too much house for one man and I get lonely in it. I won't bug you, but it'll feel good to have someone else in here. I'll get to play with Robbie."

"And?"

"The possibility of love."

"I'd rather sleep in the trees."

"Not sex. Believe it or not, I can and do get all the sex I can handle, or want to handle. Love is different. It's too soon to plan on love. But it's not too soon to hope for it. I need love."

Katie's mutinous face was still scowling at him.

"What would I have to do? Clean? Cook? Organize your file cabinet?"

"Breathe. Keep going to your job in your car. Keep taking Robbie to Little Buddy Day Care. Maybe pet my cat, Buddy. If he'll let you."

Trevor indicated the gray tabby tomcat currently flopped across his feet.

"This is Buddy, by the way. I can't remember if you were ever formally introduced. Be a mother to Robbie. Play with him. Sing to him. Well, maybe not sing. I suppose if you were to meet some man and fall in love, I'd expect you to move out and let him be the one to take care for you."

"And what about you?"

"What about me?"

364

"I'll be going to my job, raising Robbie and getting a life. What will you be doing?"

"I'll be going to my job, playing with Robbie when you're there and hoping to get a life. I'll be hanging around the two of you as much as I can and as close as I can."

"Damn you to hell."

"Been there, did it, done it, got the T-shirt. You can't trust me? Fine. I don't blame you. You won't trust me? Fair enough. It's too soon. What will it take to make you feel safe with me?"

"You in another house."

"Nope. Not gonna happen."

"A lock on my door."

"Done. There's one there now. The key's over the frame."

"Why? Why me?"

"If I told you, you wouldn't believe me anyway. Oh, you mean why Charlie did this? Who knows?"

Trevor watched Katie's face. She was still looking for options, he thought. He knew how that felt. He knew she was frightened.

"Kate, you have no choice. No real choice. Because of Robbie. I will not hurt you. Or Robbie. Ever. Not ever on purpose. But you don't know that. I hate that you have no choices. I'm talking a sort of partial employment here."

"As what?"

"Be my escort of choice to social events. Deal?"

"I have my job."

"Quit it."

Katie chewed on her bottom lip.

"I will not quit my job. I'll be your escort and your friend. When do I officially start?"

Trevor allowed himself a smile.

"Darlin', you started when you were up on the interstate the first day we met. I swear God has a sense of humor. This is going to be priceless. You get to be me. I get to be either Jarrett Daniels or one Christopher de Nunzio. What a funny, funny world."

365

"I don't know what you're talking about. You're nuts."

"Oh, my, yes. Totally and completely nuts. Don't let it bother you. I've always been nuts. Ask anyone."

## LOVE'S FINE BY ME

I was young
And a man
Said, "I'll show you love."
And he did.
I said to myself, "If this is love,
Then love's not for me."

I was old
And another man
Said, "I'll show you love."
And I ran
But he caught me
And taught me
All about love.
I said to myself, "If this is love,
Then love's fine by me."

Here you stand.
Now I'm the man.
I said, "Let me love."
And you ran.
"I've had love, Lord above,
And love's not for me."
I understand.

Let's get this straight.
Sex isn't love.
Love isn't sex.
Though sex is great,
Let's stick to love

'Cause, Lord above,
Love's fine by me.

\*     \*     \*     \*     \*

Katie moved into the house on Gill Street somewhat hesitantly. She kept her job at Keturah's and drove the extra miles to and from it in her Chevy Lumina. She kept Robbie in Little Buddy Day Care. Her friend Lisa helped her replace the items she'd lost when she'd been thrown out of her home. Robbie's artwork was the only thing she felt was irreplaceable, but Robbie soon replaced it with new efforts.

As it turned out, Trevor wound up moving back up to The Ice Palace temporarily anyway because it was more central for most of the events Stephie had planned and faxed to him.

Jarrett drove up to Sarasota to check on him, knocking on the door. Trevor opened it to him and Jarrett frowned at Trevor's feet.

"Nice socks, boy."

Trevor looked down at his feet and laughed.

"A side benefit of my stay in that Virginia hospital. They've got treads on the bottom. They keep my feet warm in here and they don't slip on the marble floors."

"Darned expensive socks."

"Amen to that. Come on in. Why do you bother knocking anyway?"

"I guess it's this house. It feels real formal."

"Yeah. It does. Well, come on in."

Trevor led his father into the kitchen.

"This Charlie jerk's got to go."

"Trevor, we simply can't have the waters off Florida stackin' up with dead bodies like cordwood. We got to pace ourselves. One every ten to twenty years or so ain't bad. Two in one year is risky. Charlie'll have to live. Or someone else'll have to get him."

"What scum. Throwing his own kid out. Not to mention Katie."

"Well, yes, son, this Charlie does seem to be shapin' up to be scum. He know about you?"

"No. I don't think so. Why?"

"Well, now, he might, on top of everythin' else, be the jealous kind. You might be messin' with what he considers to be his lady."

"His? They're divorced. He's scum. What?"

"Love and hate do not make sense, Trevor. You, of all people, should know that. Katie started the divorce. Right?"

"Right."

"Maybe Charlie Smallwood don't consider himself divorced. Maybe that's his wife you're messin' with. You just watch your backside."

"Then why throw her out then? She's really bound to love him for that."

"Throwin' Katie out narrowed her choices, son. Maybe he felt she'd snuggle back up to him to keep a roof over Robbie's head. She might have, if she hadn't had us to turn to. She'll do just about anythin', I'd guess, for that boy. Maybe this Charlie just didn't bargain on her havin' anyone else to ask for help. She sure didn't want to ask for help. I could tell. I'm hopin' he don't know she's got you to turn to. Even from ten feet away, I could tell she was ticked at herself that night for askin' for your help and real defensive."

"She was ticked at me, too, Dad. One of the Sarasota County deputies asked for my autograph. Maybe she finally believes I'm Trevor Daniels. Whatever that is. Or maybe not. Maybe she's just going along with it because she needs us right now. I know she thinks I'm nuts. She's said so."

"Well, I'm glad all that foolishness you were pullin' is over with. Women don't seem to see the humor in some situations. Mary and Carla both been goin' around mutterin' about men takin' advantage of naïve women. We're still gonna be doin' the Trevor Daniels Look-Alike Contest. We're locked into that one now."

"I'm not taking advantage of the woman. I wouldn't. I've been there myself, Dad. I'll not be a Chris. I'm hoping

368

to be a Jarrett Daniels. You're a tough act to follow, you know."

"Go with your heart, son. Be kind. Be patient. I'd tell you to be honest, but you got a problem there. And I don't just mean Ski. If you are truly serious about this woman being your life partner, you're gonna have to let down your guard and let her in, son. That's hard for you. This could still all blow up in your face. Try to put yourself in second place. You're a good man, son. Let your goodness lead you."

"I want to be with her all the time, Dad. I want to just sit and watch her breathe."

"Stay out of that house on Gill Street, son."

"What?"

"You heard me. Move on back up here to The Ice Palace permanently until Katie finds another place to stay."

"I can't."

"Why not?"

"Katie'll be down there in Punta Gorda."

"That's the point, boy. Give her her freedom, son. Don't sit there on top of her watchin' her breathe like you was a darned cat watchin' a canary in a cage. Don't make her feel the walls of her prison any more than she'll feel them herself. Move up here to The Ice Palace."

"I hate this place. I moved to Punta Gorda to get away from it."

"Be selfless, Trevor."

"This sucks."

"You've got my advice. Do what you want. Try a lot of things. I did. You were skittish. Katie's skittish, too. Robbie's fine."

"I'll see if we can try it there in Punta Gorda first. I don't want to be away from her, Dad. Now's my chance."

"No breakin' wings, Trevor. No jerkin' chains."

"No. I'd never do that. That's not me."

"You ain't never been in love before, boy. You don't know just how low a man will sink to get what he wants if he's in love. You just keep a tight rein on your selfishness and pray you don't screw up."

# Chapter Seventeen

His face healed of its bougainvillea scratches, Trevor was back in Punta Gorda from a short gig in Tampa at the University of South Florida. He hadn't bothered to drag the band out with him or the tour bus. He'd just grabbed Blondie and driven up to USF in the MG to play a mixed collection of his and his father's pieces to a largely acoustic college following. He'd finished off his day signing autographs in a local bar frequented by both the college students and their professors.

He felt relaxed and natural on college campuses with his near-peers. He'd been a college student himself. He felt just as relaxed in red-necked bars. He was one of them, too. It was Stephie's and Mary's crowd of stiff penguins that left him edgy and uncertain but he was getting better there, too, he thought.

He decided to hang out with Jarrett at the house on Olympia Avenue because he couldn't resist the magnetic pull of closeness with his father, and saw no reason to resist it. He was throbbingly aware of the house on Gill Street and its proximity.

He parallel parked on Olympia Avenue and cornered Jarrett on the sidewalk as Jarrett was carrying a load of groceries in from his truck. He grabbed a bag of groceries himself.

"Dad, am I arrogant?"

Jarrett chuckled and shook his head.

"Trevor, when you was a little boy, arrogant was about the only coat you had against them cold Yankee winds. Maybe you don't need that particular coat no more? Who called you arrogant?"

"Katie."

"Figures."

"Why?"

"Well, you wouldn't give a darn if it was some guy. And guys don't usually use the word arrogant. That's a chick thing."

"Actually she called me an arrogant bastard."

"And you said?"

"I told her I wasn't a bastard. But I'm arrogant? Right?"

"Trevor, if it bothers you or you think you've earned the title, make it right. Did you hurt her feelin's?"

Trevor frowned.

"I don't know. Maybe. I guess."

"Well, in my time, that's what I've been called after I've hurt some gal's feelin's."

"Okay. Yeah."

"Well, then, take them perfect manners of yours up to her and apologize to her. It weakens them. Puts 'em off balance."

"Works, huh?"

"It works. So, what crime did you commit or not commit to earn you this title?"

Trevor shifted his feet.

"Uh, I pretty well took over her life and choices and ran all over her with the money. Or so she says."

"Smooth move, Ex-Lax."

"I guess. That used Lumina I bought her? She was suspicious at the time."

"You're an idiot."

"It was a used car."

"Better than she'd had?"

"Yeah."

"You're an idiot."

"I didn't want her breaking down in that bucket of bolts she had. It was older than dirt."

Trevor fixed a grim eye on Jarrett's face.

"I didn't want her hitching on the interstate."

"Katie was hitchin' on the interstate? Jesus Christ, Trevor. Did you tell her why that bothers you so much?"

"Heck, no. I'm not easy with people knowing about what the Spath boys did, Dad. And I don't want her pity. Or her gratitude."

371

"It would appear you ain't never gonna get nothin' at all."

"Yeah."

"You messed up, boy."

"Yeah. What do I do now?"

"Like I said before. Take them perfect-manners out of storage and go snivel some. Apologize to her. Trevor, how would you feel if someone gave you a car?"

"Grateful! I loved it when you gave me your old truck. And I tried to hide from her that it was me doing the giving. I wasn't trying to cash in."

"This woman's got a lot of pride, Trevor. Don't be steppin' on it. When you and I first met, you were so needy you'd done lost your pride. You got it back before you met Mary again. Try to remember how you felt about the money from your dad, when you first heard."

"It ticked me off."

"There you go. Maybe you are arrogant, Trev. Run some internal diagnostics there. And check yourself out for the seven deadly sins. You ain't no glutton, unless it's for punishment. You're no sloth. But you best check up on the other five."

"What are they? I forget."

"You go look 'em up on the Internet. You got another problem here, too, son. A problem with commitment to a woman. If you scare Katie and make her run, you don't have to worry about commitment."

"You're right. I can barely say the word commitment."

"You not bein' able to commit with a woman? Who couldn't have seen that comin'?"

"Me. I couldn't."

"Heck, Trevor, look what bein' committed to a woman did to me back when. And Scottie with Tiffany. Look what it did to your dad. Look what it did to you. You loved your mother. All babies love their mothers. Sex, now, that's different. You can get all the sex you can handle. The looks-decent truck didn't pass you by. You're right pretty."

372

"Thanks."

"Keeps your juices from backin' up on ya. It ain't love, though. Grab another bag of groceries. You got two arms."

Jarrett led the way into the house.

"Dump them bags on the kitchen table and then come on in here to the livin' room and sit down on this old couch. My legs are tired."

Trevor sat down on the couch and Jarrett did too, leaning his shoulder into Trevor's. Trevor's face smoothed out and he got just the hint of a smile on his lips. Jarrett nodded.

"Can you tell how you feel right now, Trevor? Can you feel that warm relaxation come over you? Get that feeling of aahhh?"

Trevor's face spread a grin.

"Yeah."

"Well, that's true love. That's what true love feels like. When you get that aahhh, you'll be able to commit. You won't be able to stop yourself. 'Course, if you get a taste of that aahhh, and then can't get no more, it's gonna make you real edgy. You'll do anythin' or say anythin' to get that aahhh and keep it. But your time ain't come yet. You can't hurry it. You just gotta wait it out."

"You're right. I've never felt anything like this with any of the women I've been with, not even Dani. I didn't feel edgy afterward, either."

"Gotta have both, Trevor. Gotta have both a need and a fulfillment. The lady has to feel the same way."

"Geez. It's a wonder the human race gets ahead at all."

"Lots of folks don't hold out for the aahhh. They get the edgies and settle. Don't settle, Trevor. You've seen what happens from that. I'd say me and Mary have got the good stuff."

373

# WHEN DID IT ALL GET SO DIFFICULT?

I want you.
I love you.
I need you.
Please have me.
These words stay in my head.

Please touch me.
Don't touch me.
You scare me.
Please have me.
These words are all in your head.

When did it all get so difficult?
When did love really go blind?
When did our problems become my fault?
Will I go out of my mind?
Hug me.
You fear me.
I'm harmless.
Please kiss me.
These words stay in my mind.

Hold me.
I'll hold you.
I'm frightened.
You're fearless.
These words stay in your mind.

When did it all get so difficult?
When did love really go blind?
When did our problems become my fault?
Will I go out of my mind?

After he and Jarrett finished putting the groceries away, Trevor drove over to his house on Gill Street, parked the MG on the bricked area behind it, and calmly let himself into his own house. It was late on a Saturday afternoon. He figured Robbie and Junior were with Scott and Carla and Mary and Katie, doing Sun Splash Water Park in Cape Coral as planned.

He followed vague sounds he heard up to his bedroom, and found Katie kneeling on his bed, her face buried in Buddy's fur.

She was laughing.

As he stopped at the doorway to the room, Buddy looked up at him reproachfully. The old tomcat was having the time of his life, Trevor thought, back feet kicking out into Katie's hair, front claws tangled up in it, too.

Katie was laughing and rumpling his fur, completely unaware of Trevor's presence.

Trevor quietly entered the room, and rounded the bed. He sat down on the floor by the bed, looking over the width of the California king separating them. Katie hadn't yet spotted him.

He watched jealously her carefree play with his cat. He brought his arms up over the top of the blue coverlet scattered with glow-in-the-dark stars, his house-warming gift from Mary. He folded his arms and lay his head in his arms, his hair falling forward to hide his face.

Katie must have sensed him, or looked up, because all movement ceased. He heard the distinctive sound of Buddy jumping from the bed and padding downstairs.

Silence.

He drew in a breath.

"My cat gets better than I get. Tell me why, Katie. Please tell me why. If you could see your way to maybe just touching the ends of my hair? Just a friendly gesture?"

He sighed and slumped against the bed. He felt Katie's weigh shift on the bed.

"It's not you. It's me."

"Please tell me why. I'll understand. I promise."

375

"Charlie was a charming man. He played guitar."

Trevor groaned but Katie continued.

"It wouldn't have mattered if he'd been a politician. He was gorgeous and charming. He was also on drugs, a thief, a liar, and mean-spirited. You already know what he did to Robbie."

"I'm none of those things. Well, I do play guitar. And I am a liar. I quit the drugs."

"I know you're not like him. I've watched you. But I'm so scared. I thought I was in love with Charlie. I had bad judgment. How can I trust my judgment again?"

"I'm not... What can I do to help? What would it take?"

"Be patient. Let me get used to you. Let me get used to being around you."

"You won't be around me. You run from me."

"You're frightening to me."

Trevor shook his head, the waves of his hair moving in the light.

"How? I've never..."

"You really don't know, do you?"

Trevor shook his head and Katie inched her way closer to the shining mass of Trevor's hair.

"You're larger than life. You're all energy and power and glitz. You have a natural magnetism that can grab any room you walk into. You turn heads."

Trevor shook his head and sighed.

"It's just me. If you only knew. I'm not mean. I was never mean in my whole life. Well, I was mean one time and I apologized to Mary for it. I don't lie. Well, except to you. I don't take drugs. I quit. What else can I tell you? What can I do to help you? If not for me, then for some other Joe Schmo. I can't even touch your hand any more. Why is that?"

Katie drew a careful breath.

"I'm afraid that even that touch of hands with you will suck me in and I'll be lost. You're very appealing. Even when I thought you were just a down-on-his-luck construction worker, I found you irresistible."

"You're resisting just fine. Forget I said that. What can I do to help you?"

"I don't know."

"If you touch my hair and I don't jump you, will that prove anything?"

"I don't know. It might."

"Please...?"

Katie reached out a tentative hand to a long strand of Trevor's hair, pulled it slowly towards her on the bed and toyed with the end of it. Trevor could literally feel the sensation down into his scalp, and then further out through his body.

"When I was in the hospital, as a kid, Dad came and washed my hair. He took forever, cleaning the crud out of it, combing the tangles out. I thought that was the most incredibly comforting and soothing sensation I had ever felt in my whole life. I still do. My grandmother used to play with my hair. She'd look at it and tell me how pretty it was. God, I miss her...Sorry."

"It's all right. It's like that with me. Just one touch, and I get the whole avalanche of feeling. I just can't cope with it."

"I miss tenderness. I'm on the road so much. I miss my home. I miss my family."

"You're wonderful with Robbie."

"He's a great kid. He'll be fine. Really."

"I know. I can tell. He loves you. He loves your parents."

"My parents want to keep him for you when you go on the road."

"Why would I go on the road?"

"You'll be getting a job offer. A really great one. From me. You'd have never known it was from me. I was going to lie. But a lie's never a good idea. Take the job, Katie. It's a good job."

Katie withdrew her hand and her voice chilled.

"What was this job going to entail?"

"I don't know. I don't care. It was just so you'd be with me."

"Well, you just lost your bargaining chip, didn't you?"

"Yeah. So much for honesty. Hair feels good, though. Thanks."

"You haven't jumped my bones."

"Not going to. Still want to. But not going to."

Katie sighed and reached again into his hair, sending off shock waves in Trevor's body.

"You do have beautiful hair. You are absolutely gorgeous. A stunningly beautiful male animal. You scare me."

"I don't see myself the same way you see me."

"What do you see?"

"I see a scared little boy in a lot of pain. I don't see any power. I don't see any glitz."

"You can't be unaware of your impact on people."

"Parlor tricks. Showmanship and good timing."

"You didn't use parlor tricks on me. It's part of who you are."

"Then I guess I can't help it. I'm screwed."

Katie chuckled.

"You're dropping all your pretences."

"I'd have dropped them sooner if I'd thought it would work."

"You still scare me."

"I know. Especially when you catch me talking to Robbie."

"I thought I'd done it again, you see. Used bad judgment."

"Can we negotiate to holding hands again?"

"Why me?"

"I have no idea. It's driving me nuts."

Katie edged closer and laid her head down next to Trevor's. He could feel her warmth through his scalp and eased his head closer to her carefully.

378

"I understand about being scared to love again. I'm not scared of this, Katie. This feels right. It feels good. I'll just wait for you to catch up. I hope you catch up."

"I don't want to take your job offer."

"I'll be on tour. I won't have you there. I'll miss you."

Trevor dragged up from the bed, his face averted, and stumbled out the door. Katie, concerned, got up to follow him down the stairs.

"Trevor? Wait."

She caught a brief glimpse of Trevor as he vaulted into the MG parked behind the house. She heard the sound of the MG start up. Then Trevor revved the engine, popped the clutch and shot out into the street, his hair flying behind him.

Katie ran out onto the bricked back area.

"Ski! Stop!"

When he ignored her, Katie ran back into the house and dialed Jarrett.

"Jarrett, Trevor's driven off in the MG like a madman. I don't know what he's going to do!"

"Goddamn it. Been taking those Yankee-serious pills again and done gone from high-strung to completely nuts on us again."

"It's my fault."

"Darned straight it's your fault, missy. I told him to be patient; to find out why you couldn't accept his love. Well, I guess he blew it. As long as I've got you on the phone anyway, why the heck can't you love my boy? Is he so horrible? Is he such a terrible person?"

"No! I do love him."

"Well, Jesus Christ. Can't you just tell him? You're killin' him."

"If he doesn't slow down that MG, I may well have."

"Oh, he always drives like that. He'll burn off his crazies. He always does. Either that or he puts them into music. But can't you give him a little somethin'?"

"He was negotiating for hand-holding."

"Good for him. Can you give him that?"

"Yes."

"Well, good. The boy needs somethin' to keep goin'. And take the darned job."

"You know about the job?"

"And I knew he never could abide lyin'. That's part of what's got him all strung out. I knew he'd tell you about the job."

"I will not take this job from him. I am still so angry with him for deceiving me. I am so embarrassed. Did you know about the car?"

"Not till just recently, missy. He and Scott cooked up that gift of a car between the two of them. Hard to tell who did what there. They are a pair. They knew better than to come to me with that story. I'd have told them to 'fess up long ago. They both had good urges to do a good thing by getting' you that car, Katie. They just fumbled the ball badly. Don't hold it against either one of them. You needed a reliable car. My boys are proud to be able to help folks out. It was a selfless act. Did I know about Trevor callin' himself Ski? Again, not till recently."

## <u>I'M CHOOSING YOU (3/4 time)</u>

I've chosen my freedom.
I've chosen my future.
I've chosen my life-style.
I've chosen my path.
I've chosen my lovers
And I've chosen badly.
I'm choosing better
'Cause I'm choosing you.

Freedom is scary.
The future is here.
My life-style is empty
But one thing is clear.
All of my loves
Prepared me for you.

You are my present
'Cause I'm choosing you.

Choices have meaning
Far down the years.
Bad choices haunt you;
Good ones are dear.
All of my choices
Led me to you.
Choose me, my darling,
'Cause I'm choosing you.

\*      \*      \*      \*      \*

Trevor was down from Sarasota again, making
another of what he considered to be his lame attempts to woo
his lady. Katie had moved his couch to face the fireplace in
the house on Gill Street where his huge family photographic
portrait hung as it had hung over the fireplace in The Ice
Palace. Katie was sitting with him on the couch. They had
negotiated handholding, so Trevor was holding her hand and
absently playing with her fingers while he relaxed into her
physical nearness.

"Trevor?"

"Hm?"

"You're still lying to me."

Trevor stared at their joined hands.

"Give me till this Locks of Love gig. Okay? I'm
coming clean then. I'll spill it all then. I promise. I swear."

"You're still determined to get me into bed, aren't
you?"

"Yeah. But only if you want to."

"What if I never want to?"

"Friends. We'll be friends. You can never have too
many friends."

"What happens if you find a willing partner?"

Trevor smiled, raised her hand to his lips and kissed
her knuckles.

"You've been here two months. You see how I live. Have I even been looking for a willing partner other than you? Where would I look? On the road? At Stephie's parties? This is one heck of an admission, but I haven't even wanted sex with anyone else since I met you. The tabloids sure would laugh about that. All or nothing. I've been handling the problem myself, so to speak. There won't be another coming in to boot you out. But don't you be bringing in any men. I'll not have that. Got it?"

"You've known me now for the same two months. Do I strike you as a wild woman wanting to bring in men?"

"No."

"Then I guess we've moved up to being friends."

"Geez. I thought we were friends two months ago."

"We were acquaintances. Part of that time you were using an assumed name."

"You live here, for God's sake."

"By your grace. Because I have no where else to go."

Trevor unlinked hands with Katie and stood up to walk to the fireplace where he stared at the huge photographic portrait.

"Don't go. Just don't go. Or at least just don't run off and disappear. I hate surprises. Okay?"

Katie folded her hands in her lap.

"Do I strike you as a woman who'd sneak off in the middle of the night? Is this how you see me, Ski? As a floozy who'll bring in men and leave you without a word and disappear for good?"

Trevor bit down hard on his bottom lip, an image of his former-mom springing to his mind, her excellent figure encased in a snug dress, her acrylic nails tapping restlessly against any hard surface available, her restless energy driving her to excess.

He turned from the fireplace to face Katie.

"No. Dammit. Dad's right. He always is. I don't see you that way, Katie. That's the woman I loved who abandoned me that I see. That's my secret fear. Not so secret, I guess. Dad knows. He always did."

382

Katie was watching him, puzzled. Trevor licked his lips.

"Abandonment. I'm coming clean, Katie. Worst fear. Abandonment. Don't go. Please don't go."

"The woman you loved was a floozy who brought in men and then abandoned you?"

Trevor nodded.

Katie stood up and stepped to him. She put her arms around his middle, pulling him in tightly to her and snuggling her head against his chest. Trevor brought his arms around her, rested his chin on her head, and closed his eyes. Katie smoothed his back.

"You've been acting so strangely. Now it all makes sense."

"I am strange. Ask anyone."

"That was horrible for you. That was worse than what Charlie did to me. I'd stopped loving Charlie. I was left with rage and hurt, but not rejected love. Oh, Ski."

Katie moved her hands up and down his back, making the shivering within him shift subtly from cold fear to warm anticipation.

Trevor sought to distract his body.

"Katie?"

"Hm?"

"You woke up Santa Snake. His intentions are friendly, too. But different."

"Santa Snake?"

"Scott and I got a little crazy in our rambunctious teens around Christmas time one year:

Santa Snake with his little red hat
Comin' down your chimney and unloadin' his sack.
Bringin' all his goodies to little girls and boys
Not just toys.
Santa Snake knows when you're good.
Santa Snake knows when you're bad.
Santa Snake don't mind the beefsteak,
But it's fish he'd rather have.
Santa Snake is comin',

Santa Snake is comin',
Santa Snake is comin',
All over town.'"
Katie giggled briefly.
"That's filthy."
"That's why it's never been recorded. Good drinking song. Good bus song. Good for karaoke. It's a Daniels' family standard now."

Trevor rambled on, revealing more of himself to Katie as he looked fondly into his sunnier, more recent past.

"We all get together here at the Best Western Water Front for Christmas, if we can. Some years I can't make it. Mary takes pictures and Uncle Richard shoots videotape and they send it to me ASAP on tour. I always call Dad and Mary on Christmas Eve and they call me on Christmas Day. God bless cell phones. Yeah, we got some pretty strange Christmas traditions."

"No, you don't. That's sweet."

"The kids overheard us singing 'Santa Snake' one year. Like I said, a real good tune. Easy to learn. Easy to sing. They must have been awake, whispering under the covers, taking notes. Now even Stephie's little one, Phaedra, belts it out. God only knows what her day care workers think."

"I suppose if a child sang it, it wouldn't sound the same."

"It doesn't. But when Phaedra stood up and sang the whole thing for us at Christmas Day dinner that first year, well, I can tell you, my eyes were about ready to bleed. I just kept smiling at her and hoping my relatives wouldn't blame me somehow for it."

"Did they?"

"Nah. Like you said, it sounds different from a four-year-old than it does from a raunchy teenager with a leer in his voice."

"Just like 'Little Pussy'?"

Trevor shook his head, chuckling.

"Oh, my God. I'm dead meat now. How'd you hear that one? It hasn't been recorded either. It's only been done on tour. We've been testing it out. I've been fine-tuning it. I swear to God, that's not out there."

"I found it on the kitchen counter one morning after you'd been in the kitchen. Next to the orange juice."

"That's a double whammy, me leaving work-product all around the place and not putting the orange juice back in the fridge after I used it."

"It was hard to make out. You have really bad handwriting."

"Don't I know it."

"And you don't write notes the way I'd think you would."

"Old habit. Tablature. I learned real music later in life. If I'm running hot and I'm in a hurry, I revert. So, what do you think?"

Katie released him and clasped her hands behind her back.

"It's filthy, too."

"Is not. You just ask Buddy. He's done all that and gone back for more. He loves it. How bad could it be? Wanna try?"

"No."

"You don't want me to clean your ears?"

Katie shivered, but giggled again.

"No."

"Just a nibble on your neck? Can I give your nose a peck, Little Pussy?"

"Do you think in rhymes?"

"Some days."

"Quit that, Ski."

Still vaguely uncomfortable with the trend of Trevor's hints, Katie playfully punched his arm and went back to sit on the sofa.

Trevor followed her helplessly and sat down beside her, capturing her hand again.

Katie gripped it absently.

385

"Listen. I've got this great idea. 'Keturah's Closet'. This is prefect. The ladies that buy clothes at Keturah's are really, really wealthy. There's just so much you can buy and use. They buy clothes not because they need them, but sometimes just because they're bored. Most of them have never worked in their lives. Some of them do volunteer work for local hospitals because they're bored out of their skulls, and volunteer work at a hospital is socially acceptable. They don't get any flack from their husbands or children about that. They come to Keturah's more for fun and stimulation than they do for clothes."

Trevor watched Katie tune him out as she pitched her idea. He rested back on the sofa. He found he no longer cared one way or the other if she was a barracuda in the water or not.

Katie rattled on.

"The women from Keturah's wear a dress once and give it to charity. Goodwill, Salvation Army, others. Some clothes they never wear at all, and when the next season comes, they can't possibly be seen wearing last season's clothes, so they give them away, too. What if? Are you listening to me?"

"Yeah. I'm listening. Why wouldn't I be?"

"Well, I tend to ramble on. Charlie just tuned me out or ignored me completely."

Trevor straightened on the sofa.

"If you're drawing comparisons, quit now before you insult me. Okay?"

"Oh. Yes. Okay."

"You were about to make a point."

Katie gazed into his clear gray eyes and fell in love with him.

She gasped when she realized what she'd done. Trevor frowned at her.

"Are you okay? You look funny."

"Oh. Yes. I'm okay."

"Katie?"

"What?"

"Keturah's Closet?"

"Oh. Yes. Second-hand shop. Consignment."

Katie shook herself.

"Well, not all the clothing sold at Keturah's is appropriate for what I have in mind, but those pieces may work at a different shop. I haven't thought that far ahead. Interview clothing. Employment clothing. In the Food Stamp office, talking with others, especially with Lisa, we discovered we had a common need that wasn't covered anywhere we could find. We could get training for employment—nurse's aide, culinary arts, cosmetologist—but if we already had a marketable skill and could get our own employment, we still needed help with getting appropriate clothing. I had retail sales experience, but no longer any wardrobe suitable for an interview, let alone employment. Lisa loaned me clothes. It was just dumb luck that they fit. Luckily I'm tiny. I could take them in. Lisa helped me. When she got her job, she needed work clothes, too. You need the clothes to get the job. You need the clothes to work the job. And sometimes you don't get paid for several weeks. When you do, there's more pressing needs than clothing. There's gasoline and electricity. Suddenly, your new job is a curse, because now, on paper, you make too much money to qualify for some of the programs or your benefits are greatly reduced. You're kind of a niche baby."

Trevor had been listening, remembering back to his friend Darryl's mom. Some of what had drifted past his young ears matched what Katie was saying.

"So. A demonstrated need. And you have a solution."

"Yes. How succinct. You have a wonderful mind."

"Don't suck up. Give me some details."

"Mrs. A buys a dress. Wears it, doesn't wear it, whatever. Crowded closet. Time to drop it. She brings it to Keturah's Closet as a donation and gets a tax receipt. Or puts it into Keturah's Closet on consignment. Working-women-in-need come to Keturah's Closet. The really needy get their clothes for free. The better off get such a deal. What do you think?"

387

"Doable. We can have corporate check it out. They'll know best how to set it up. Got scads of lawyers. Never keep a dog and bark yourself. I'll make some phone calls later and get them started on it. How about Robbie. How's he doing? I'm sorry about his artwork. All ruined when Charlie cleaned house, huh?"

"I was furious, but I'm over it now. I would have liked to have kept that one I showed you. The yellow one with the yellow sun and the two of us smiling, but Robbie's done others since. I started an art gallery for him. I hope you don't mind. We're not using pins or tape. We won't hurt the walls."

"I couldn't care less if you used roofing nails and an air gun. Where's your art gallery? I'll swear it's not on the fridge door. I'm in and out of the fridge often enough. I'd have noticed. Well, you got one of Robbie's pics there, too. I've seen that one."

"That's his picture of you."

"Me? Heck, I thought he had a girlfriend."

"It's the long hair."

"Darned hair. A picture of me? Wow."

"He likes you."

"I like him."

"The gallery's on the walls of the stairs leading to his room."

"I haven't been up those stairs since you moved in. Robbie's room, you know."

"Ski, I haven't truly been afraid of you being around Robbie since the night I found you in his room at my old house, playing guitar. He was in his bed and smiling. You were sitting on the floor. Music woke me up, not screams of terror."

"He didn't scream, Katie. You'd have heard that. It was more like the sound of a little boy trying hard not to make any sound. I recognized that sound, so I went in. Sure enough, there he was under the covers, hiding. That's when I grabbed your guitar and started playing. It worked, too, and it worked pretty fast. He came peeping out real soon.

Mother's love and a good shrink had him on the right track. He'd just hit a little speed bump, I guess. Might even have been having me in the house that was his speed bump, but we reached an understanding. He knows I don't mean either of you any harm. He's cool with it."

"Well, he certainly seemed cool with it that night. And now you rate pictures. Of course, so does Buddy. Don't get a big head, Ski. Let me just throw the meatloaf we're having for dinner into the oven and I'll show you the art gallery."

Trevor followed Katie into the kitchen to watch her dinner preparations. Then he followed her upstairs.

She showed him the art gallery.

There were dozens of curling and scrawled sheets of construction paper covering his discreetly pinstriped yellow wallpaper. Reds and blues and greens. Yellow and purples and the odd lavender shade only construction paper comes in, as well as the not-white white one. Crayon drawings of cats and houses and trees. Stick figures in dresses and curly hair. Stick figures with long hair, some holding brown pickaxes.

"It's a guitar, Ski."

"Oh. Brings a whole new meaning to the slang term 'axe', doesn't it?"

"It's difficult to get detail with a crayon."

"It is? I didn't know that."

"You never crayoned? Come on."

"No. I never did. I was all music. You've seen my handwriting. I can't draw a straight line. Is Robbie an artist, do you think?"

Katie laughed at him.

"No. He's just a sunny, little boy expressing joy. Finally. I've finally got my sunny, funny baby back."

"You make a great mother."

"That's not what you thought at first."

"I'm kind of touchy on that subject."

Trevor ran a hand over one of the pictures with a car on it. It wasn't Katie's blue car. It wasn't a truck.

389

"Whose car is this?"

"I think that would be the car that Robbie and Junior are planning on owning when they grow up."

"Already? Junior hasn't even started real school yet."

"I think they've bonded."

"Trucks. Or, in this case, cars. Just like Scottie and me."

"You bonded with your brother over trucks and cars?"

"Heck, no. I can barely pump my own gas without dribbling the gas onto my sneakers. We bonded over women. We were men when we met."

"How old?"

"Scott was sixteen."

"Men?"

"Well, look who's planning on owning a bright yellow Volkswagen."

"I think it's meant to be an orange Cougar, but I could be wrong."

"Muscle cars. That's my boy! Oops. Sorry."

Katie smiled at him as he continued to smooth his hands over the bright efforts of Robbie's crayon pack.

"Wow. Buddy looks like a dog. Or a rabbit. Could be either."

"At least it's not a ferret."

"Who knew they were so lively? If they hadn't gotten out of my room, it would never have come to anyone's notice. But, no, some moron, me, had to forget to close the door to their cage. They're real agile. Real clever. Like raccoons. They were illegal to have on campus. Who knew? So I moved off-campus. My landlady didn't appreciate them, either. My frat brothers were more understanding, but they let Frick and Frack drink beer and tequila. That had to stop and finally I wound up giving them to the local elementary school, fully equipped. I'd been dating an elementary education major and she took them off my hands. They were great guys, but too much for a college kid to handle."

"I like to hear Scott tease you about them."

390

"He's got his skeletons, too. But they mostly involve me, so I've got no call to tease him about them. I'm very impulsive. And sensual. The ferrets looked cool and their fur felt great. I'm not much on short-term planning ahead. Let me tell you, sensual and impulsive is one helluva combination in a young single male some two thousand miles from home."

Katie laughed up at him.

"Did you give your daddy gray hair?"

"Is it gray now? Then I'm the one who did it. Scott never would. I'm giving Scott gray hair now."

Katie had been progressively leading Trevor further and further up the sunny stairs as she pointed out pictures and Trevor was heedlessly following her, absorbed in Robbie's work-product and remembering his own youth. There had been no crayons and paper for him, he thought, but he hadn't needed them. He'd had the music he heard in his head to amuse him.

Katie looked up at him through her lashes, but Trevor, intent on Robbie's work-product, never noticed.

"Ski, I've got to show you something else. Robbie won't mind, I'm sure. Come on up."

Katie opened the white door at the top of the stairs and stepped into the tiny room that was windows on all four sides and a skylight above. It was the widow's walk and had a panoramic view of the Peace River and also of greater Punta Gorda in the other direction. The windows started at the height of an adult's waist, so there was plenty of wall space for a bed and nightstand with lamp, a desk and chair, and short shelves for toys and storage. A hump-backed chest held Robbie's small collection of clothes.

Katie reached into a corner made by intersecting windows and brought out a stick with string wound around it lengthwise. She smiled and held it out to Trevor, who took it carefully in his hands.

"Bow? As in bow and arrow?"

"No. Guitar. As in play guitar."

391

Trevor's face went from puzzled to stunned to joyous.

"He plays guitar?"

"Not well. It may be the instrument."

"Geez. I never thought. He likes to hear me play. God, I remember trying to make my own guitar. What a bust. Can I get him a guitar? Will that be all right? Nothing special. Maybe Toys R Us or a hock shop. We'll see. But could I?"

Katie nodded. Trevor grabbed her and gave her a big kiss right on the lips. He froze when he realized what he'd done and released her.

"Sorry. Sorry. I got carried away."

Katie blushed.

"Yes, you can get Robbie a guitar. There must be ones around somewhere that are small enough for him. I've watched him. He doesn't do like the other children do at day care. He doesn't take a stance like Mick Jagger or pretend to slam out chords like Elvis. He sits down on the floor, cross-legged, and makes little chord movements with his left hand while he fingers the strings with his right."

"He's mimicking you, Katie. You play guitar."

"He's mimicking you, Trevor. You play guitar."

"Oh, my God. Thank you."

"For what?"

"The loan of your son."

Katie moved into him, putting her arms around his waist and sliding her hands up his back.

Stunned, Trevor moved into her, his eyes closing. He nuzzled his chin gently into the area between her neck and her collarbone, inhaling her scent and breathing warm air softly onto her skin. Aware he had a stubble of beard on his face, Trevor replaced his chin with his tongue and felt Katie shiver.

He bathed her neck with his tongue.

He bathed behind her ear.

He became so engrossed in the minute sensations of her hair against his forehead and her cheek against his, that when Katie's hands slid down to his butt, Trevor jumped.

He backed off from her then, laughing softly to cover his embarrassment.

"I guess I watched 'Cats' one too many times."

"It was beautiful."

"Yeah. I liked the original Broadway version best."

"Not 'Cats', silly. You. What you just did. That was so beautiful. Can I do that back to you?"

Trevor pulled further away, a flicker of fear deep within him.

"Uh. Maybe not."

"What's wrong?"

"Nothing."

"Yes, there is."

Katie dropped her hands to her sides, looking at him. Trevor broke the eye contact first.

"You're nuts. Hey, look at the time. Is the meatloaf done yet?"

"Stop it."

"Let's go check on the meatloaf."

"Trevor?"

Trevor pushed past her, hiding his erection. He was down the stairs before Katie could even gather her wits.

In the kitchen, he kept up a nervous, babbling monologue on local efforts to preserve Punta Gorda's historic homes in order to avoid having to explain to Katie a reaction that he couldn't explain to himself.

After dinner, he walked hurriedly over to the house on Olympia Avenue, went up the back steps, through the kitchen and into the living room, flopping onto the old plaid couch, a bundle of weak nerves.

Jarrett loomed over him, looking down.

"What's wrong now?"

Trevor flopped back on the couch.

"I caught myself being Chris."

Jarrett had to shake himself loose from the image that brought.

"You best enlighten me right now about how you managed that."

"Forcing someone to do something they don't want to do."

"You? How? You don't force. You charm."

"Well, okay. I didn't force this time, either."

"This is about Katie."

"Yeah. I was moving in on her. She's asked me not to. I broke my word."

"She have a fit about this movin' in?"

"No."

"Maybe she's changed her mind. How far did you get? Never mind. I don't care to know. Was she strugglin' and battin' your hands off?"

"No. As a mater of fact, she grabbed my butt."

"Get back over there and finish business. Trust me, she's changed her mind."

"I'm scared."

Silence.

Jarrett nodded.

"So, we've finally come to the crux of the matter, have we? Not the lady's vote. Your vote. Do you love her?"

"Yes."

"Then of course you're scared. Sex is easy compared to love. I'm sayin' the lady voted yes for the sex. How's she feel about the love?"

"I don't know."

"I feel like a darned marriage counselor. Grab your lady, spill your heart, and get on with it. Where's the TV remote?"

"On the table next to you."

"Right."

"Just do it, huh?"

"You can only crash and burn once, son."

"Yeah. Well, I'll be seein' ya, Dad."

"Good luck, son. Keep me posted."

Trevor heaved himself off the couch and left.

Mary came quietly out of the master bedroom after he had gone, sat down on the couch and folded her hands in her lap. Jarrett looked over at her and grinned.

"I ain't had this much fun in years."

"He's our baby."

"He's a darned cartoon to me right now. Daffy Duck and Elmer Fudd. It's hysterical. I done give him my best advice. Can't do it for him. This is one of those painful things he can look back on with fondness years from now. I don't want to spoil so much as one minute of his agony right now. He'll do fine once he gets his courage up."

## <u>LITTLE PUSSY</u>

I'm a lean, mean, nasty old alley cat.
If I beat up a rat
Will you give me a pat,
Little Pussy?

You're a kitty.
I'm a tom.
Can I give you a lick, Little Pussy?
Can I groom your right ear?
You got nothin' to fear, Little Pussy.

Let me pull on your tail.
Let me scrape with my nails.
Let me kiss your sweet nose.
Let me nibble your toes.
Let me polish your fur.
Just listen to me purr, Little Pussy.

I'm a lean, mean, nasty old alley cat,
But if you treat me real sweet
I'll follow you down the street, Little Pussy.

Let me tug on your whiskers
And give you a kiss here, pussy.
You can scratch up my back
Just like that, Little Pussy.
Let's sun at high noon or
Howl at the moon, Little Pussy.

You're a kitty.
I'm a tom.
Can I give you a lick, Little Pussy?
Can I groom your right ear?
You got nothing to fear, Little Pussy.
I'm a lean, mean, nasty old alley cat.
If I beat up a rat,
Will you give me a pat,
Little Pussy?

## Chapter Eighteen

Trevor laid down tracks of his own singing to be mixed later with back-up singers' tracks. He good-naturedly let himself be auctioned off several times for various charities. He wrote, he ran, he worked out, he ate, he slept. He kept close to his family. And he wedged in a few hours with Katie when he could factor it into a schedule that made the road look like a rest cure.

He did promos and appearances, interviews and photo shoots.

He did them in Dallas.

He did them in Boise.

He did them in LA.

He did them in every major city west of the Mississippi and south of Maryland. He left everything north and east of those vague parameters to Trevor Lane and his birth father's following, and worked those areas just as hard under his old name of Trevor Lane.

When he was with Katie, he was often jumpy and hollow-eyed from too much caffeine and too little sleep. But he found even the few short hours he spent with her both relaxed him and refreshed him. He felt badly that he couldn't take her anywhere. He wanted to take her everywhere. He resented the trip to and from Sarasota only because it wasted a precious hour in each direction that he could have enjoyed better with Katie.

Sometimes their date was simply Trevor staggering up the back steps of his own house in Punta Gorda to fall on his own couch and crash out to sleep with his head on Katie's lap.

She never complained about it.

Robbie was currently up in Sarasota visiting with Scott and Carla and Junior. Trevor had his head in Katie's lap this Sunday, too. They'd progressed to touch. Katie was drifting her fingers over Trevor's brow and into his hair, making him smile the half-smug smile of a happy tomcat. He was getting more from what Katie could give him and

397

that he could accept than he had from any other non-related female he could remember.

He had his eyes closed his eyes now, enjoying Katie's gentle, caring fingers on his skin. Katie whispered softly to him.

"Ski?"

"Hm?"

"Where do you see yourself five, ten years from now?"

"At the pace I'm going now? Dead. I see myself dead."

Trevor frowned, hearing himself, and snapped his eyes open.

He'd given that answer once before in his youth. That was not a good answer.

"I didn't mean that."

"Maybe you did. Maybe I should be asking a different question."

"Maybe you should be. You've got my attention now. I was drifting."

"I know. I like to watch you while you drift. I like to watch you, period."

"That's fair. I'm a spectator sport for millions of people. Why not you?"

"I like to touch you."

Trevor let his heavy lids fall shut again.

"Good. Did I forget to tell you how much I appreciate that? I get a lot out of your touch. That was a major good thing when we moved up to touch."

"Trevor's supposed to be a really good in bed."

He was so tired his brain was blurry, so he missed the obvious implication of Katie's statement.

"Been reading the tabloids again? Can't be anything current. I swear to God I haven't even seriously kissed anyone since slightly after the Richmond cancellation. That's the truth."

"I like touch. You've been very patient. You've never shown me a side of you I don't like or can't

398

understand or at least sympathize with. I might enjoy something more intimate."

Trevor's eyes snapped open and he looked up to search Katie's face.

"Don't toy with me. You're not a cat and I'm not a mouse. Kill me and eat me or let me go. Don't play with me."

"I'm not."

Trevor reached up a hand to touch Katie's face. Katie smiled down at him, then turned her head to plant a kiss on his palm. She sighed and looked back down into his eyes.

"Can I touch your face?"

"Why would you want to do that?"

"You just touched mine."

"And?"

"It felt good."

"Good is good. Can we do Monkey-see-monkey-do?"

"What?"

"You touch my eyebrow. I touch yours. Maybe you touch my nose. I get to touch yours. You get to lead. I get to follow."

"Maybe."

"Kate. The lights are on. Robbie's out on a date. I don't even have curtains on the windows downstairs here yet. Absolutely nothing gross is going to happen here on this couch in front of the fireplace. We may not even get around to main body contact. That's your call. I want you. I want you to be mine. But I want you to feel safe. Always."

Katie reached out a finger and gently touched Trevor's right eyebrow where it started near the bridge of his nose. She drew her finger slowly over the hairs of it to the tail, then lifted her finger away, searching his face.

Trevor lifted his hand and slowly ran the pads of his fingers over Katie's right eyebrow, ending on her cheekbone and leaving his hand hovering over her face there. Katie licked her lips and leaned her face into his fingertips, moving so that they trailed across her cheek and wound up going

399

down the bridge of her nose. She closed her eyes and nudged her lips under his fingertips.

Trevor watched her and yearned to hold her and kiss her, but forced himself to concentrate on the minute sensations of her soft facial skin under his rough hands. She reminded him of Buddy, soliciting a pet and smoothing into his hand for affection.

Trevor ran his fingers into the hollow at the nape of Katie's neck, and smoothed the pad of his thumb over her closed eyelid at the same time, so small was her head and so long his fingers that he could reach both areas simultaneously. He brought his other hand up, the calloused fingers of his chording hand, and cupped the air just short of her face, letting her feel his warmth there before he touched her, allowing her time to protest, if she wanted to.

Katie hadn't touched him again since the one time on his eyebrow, her hands gripped now in her lap. She released them and touched the hair on his forearm with her left hand, setting his body to shivering. She moved her hand to his shoulder, smoothing lightly.

Trevor resisted the urge to do the same, allowing Katie time to explore. But the nerve endings on his skin, always sensitive, were screaming at him for more, and his shivering became shuddering.

"Trevor, are you cold?"

"A hug would help."

Katie moved her body in closer to him and he sat up straighter. She snuggled her head against his chest, causing the breath to back up in his lungs. He was left with his hands out in mid-air like some department store mannequin, unsure of what to do.

"A hug? Is a hug going to be okay? Just a hug. I swear."

Katie nodded and Trevor slowly wrapped his arms around her and relaxed into her warmth.

"Oh, God, this feels good, Katie. Thanks."

Katie turned her head to kiss his bicep and smiled. He kissed her hair and held her closer. He closed his eyes and relaxed.

"Aaah. This is great."

Katie nodded her agreement.

"That trip from Sarasota to Punta Gorda and back? I worry about you on the road like that. Speeding and all. I know you do."

"Yeah. I do. You worry about me? That's nice."

"I worry about my friends."

"I'll take friend. So, you're not, like, scared of me anymore?"

"No. I guess I'm not."

"Could I come home? Please?"

"Home? To here?"

"Yeah. To my home. To my house."

"Well, of course, you can. If you're serious, there's meatloaf for dinner again. Truth to tell, the house has seemed rather large and dead with you living in Sarasota. We've missed you."

"Missed me? You've missed me? Sweet."

Trevor pulled out of Kaie's arms just far enough to grin at her.

"I forgot what we were doing. Home. I'm just so glad to be coming home. Thanks."

"You are so strange."

"Oh, yeah. Don't let it bother you. Kiss? You were looking to kiss me?"

"I'm not sure now. I feel as though I've been under some sort of spell, and now the spell is broken."

"No, no. Spell's not broken. Give me a minute."

Trevor carefully released Katie and stretched out on his back with his head in her lap again.

He closed his eyes and slowly relaxed his body, snuggling his head into her lap, inhaling her scent and enjoying her warmth and softness. Katie ran her fingers into the hair at his brow line.

"Why do you do it?"

Trevor felt his bones melt and a smug smile of contentment curl his lips.

His cat Buddy to the life, Katie thought, as Trevor seemed to purr.

"'Cause I like your scent."

"Stop that. I mean why do you work so hard? You don't have to work this hard."

"I've got responsibilities."

"You say yes to every offer that comes your way unless it's a double booking. No is an answer, too."

"I don't take what I've got for granted. It could all be gone tomorrow. You ever heard of Melitza Korjas?"

"No."

"There you go. Coloratura soprano from the twenties. Or the thirties. I don't remember which. I think they called her the Swedish Nightingale. See? Glorious voice. Toast of Europe. Gone and forgotten."

"You can not outrun death. Fame is fleeting. You're not stupid. You know both of those things. Stop lying to me."

"It keeps me tired and distracted. Happy now?"

"Distracted from what?"

"Sex."

"Sex?"

"I'm a young, healthy male. I want sex. I need sex."

"Then get some."

Trevor groaned.

"Mary says men don't need love to enjoy sex. She might have a point there. I've certainly had sex without love. Some of it I enjoyed. Some of it I didn't. I don't want sex with just anyone now. I want sex with you."

"I haven't had sex since before I divorced Charlie."

"I figured that. I haven't had sex since the day I met you."

"Bull."

"No. Really. First, I was too busy. With you. Then I wanted sex with you. Then I didn't want sex with anyone but

402

you. Go figure. So, here I am. Tired and wired and sexless. But happy. I'm happy."

Katie kept absently smoothing her hands over Trevor's brow and hair, and Trevor closed his eyes again, letting himself relax more and more into the sensations. Occasionally Katie's hands would stray to his shoulders or upper arms, but no lower. He enjoyed what she could give him.

And what he would let himself accept.

"I need your love, Katie. Don't ever stop loving me."

Trevor stiffened in Katie's lap.

He hadn't meant to say that out loud.

Katie just kept smoothing her hands over him.

"I like touching you. It does tingly things to my insides."

"Mine, too."

"You're a very sensual creature. I've watched you enjoy the sun on your skin. You enjoy the wind in your hair. You stretch and enjoy your body. It's wonderful to watch."

Trevor chuckled.

"You're leaving me so many openings to say really lewd and lustful things when you talk like that."

"You're also a wiseguy."

"Oh, my, yes. But seriously. I really do enjoy your hands on me."

"Let me explore a little bit more."

"Oh, yeah. Explore all you want. You've got a safe pass. I won't jump you. I want to. But I won't. No. I'm telling a lie. I don't want to jump you. I never want to jump you. I want to soothe you, and smooth you, and hold you and snuggle you all up. I want to kiss behind your ear and nibble your neck and run my hands up over your breasts. Darn. I'm turning myself on."

Katie giggled and even that sent splinters of lust jabbing into Trevor. He opened his eyes again to look up into Katie's face.

403

"Kate, maybe you better stop touching me. It's moving to the next level. I'm loosing control. I'm not tired enough."

Trevor started to sit up and Katie restrained him with her hands.

"Let it be. Let's see how brave I can be. Do you mind?"

"Oh, heck, no. I'm dying here anyway. You're killing me."

"Silly. I don't suppose this is the best time to bring up comparisons?"

"It's not. What the heck. Bring 'em on."

"Charlie always wanted darkness. He always wanted to be on top. He'd just grab me and do it."

"Red-neck foreplay. 'Spread 'em'. Huh."

"Yes. And he wasn't even a redneck. He was from Chicago."

Trevor watched Katie's face. She was watching her own hands on his body. It was hugely erotic for him and he tried to fight it.

"I'm light, Katie. I'm air and sunshine and joy and happiness. I'm totally consensual. I want to watch. I want light and to have my eyes open. I want to see your face. And your body. I want to know what you like and what you don't like. I'll tell you what I like. I like tender. I like slow. I like comfort."

Katie licked her lips, still carefully moving her hands on him. Now one hand ventured down to his chest, making Trevor's stomach muscles contract and his breathing go ragged. Katie watched her effect on him, slowing her movements cautiously.

"Charlie was my first."

"Figures. What a bastard."

"He didn't want Robbie."

"Then he should have used protection."

"I wanted Robbie."

"Consolation prize?"

"Sort of. I knew what I was doing. I stopped my pills and bided my time. Eventually it worked. I hid my pregnancy from him as long as I could. Past any deadlines. Just in case. I only grew huge in the last month. Robbie was very small. He still is."

"He'll grow. Don't sweat it."

"I don't. And I don't regret a thing I did to achieve my goal."

Trevor grinned up at her.

"Ruthless, selfish witch."

Katie smiled back.

"Yes. And I'd do it again."

"Just so you know, with me you won't have that problem. You won't have to rape me to get pregnant. I love babies. Every nine months would be fine with me."

"Well, since I plan on being married, when and if I remarry, for at least fifty years, I don't really feel that nearly fifty children would be practical."

"I can afford them. But remember, there's a limit to functional childbearing years for females. The number of babies might have to drop to, say, twenty or thirty, disallowing for any tabloid freak occurrences."

Katie punched him in the arm and Trevor protested laughingly.

"Ow! Quit that. No violence. I'm not into violence."

Katie bent and kissed the red mark she'd left on Trevor's skin, making him squirm.

"Oh, geez, woman. No lips on my skin unless you're serious. I'm struggling as it is."

"Stop struggling. Let me explore. Charlie never did."

Katie flushed while Trevor relaxed his muscles and reached his hand to her fingers.

"I'm guessing here. You're a functional virgin. Never seen a naked man in broad daylight?"

Katie shook her head, her color growing redder. Trevor smiled at her.

"No sweat. Take your time. It's just a body. Eventually we'll get it naked. It's pretty much like yours.

405

Well, no breasts to speak of. Got a cock. But I feel what you feel. My body feels what your body feels. Okay?"

Katie nodded and closed her eyes. Trevor nudged her.

"Hey. No hiding in the dark. You can't see with your eyes closed."

"It may be scary."

"What? Santa Snake? Dodge around him. Ignore him. I do. Well, I'm trying to. If things get too difficult, I'll take care of Santa Snake. You just go exploring. My cock and I are cool with that. We'll handle it."

Katie gnawed on her bottom lip and blinked. Trevor smiled wanly up at her.

"Word of a Daniels. I'll just lay here and enjoy. Do what you want. No pain, though. I'm not into pain."

Trevor closed his eyes to give Katie some privacy. And to allow himself to focus on inner control. He felt Katie slide her warm kitten fingers down over his chest, sending flutters through his stomach muscles and making him tense slightly in her lap.

She paused.

Trevor relaxed himself again and Katie trailed one hand down his arm from shoulder to elbow and then from elbow to hand. That was safe territory for both of them and Trevor got his breathing under control.

Katie laid a hand on his hipbone and he thought he'd go nuts. His cock swelled and tightened his jeans on him. Katie brushed her hand over the bunched front of his jeans and he jumped with the sensation, trying to relax again as she moved on to his jean-clad leg.

"I'm not really naked, you know. Got my jeans on. Got my shirt on."

"I know. It's enough for me."

"Never seen guys in swim trunks?"

"Never touched them."

"Geez. Okay. This is fine."

Katie brought her hands back up his pant legs, around his bulge, slowly up his ribcage and then under his shirt and over his stomach, making him suck in his breath sharply and causing him to tremble.

Katie's soft voice whispered to him.

"Am I hurting you?"

"No. Oh, no. I'm fine."

"Your skin is so warm. And soft. I never realized."

"Soft is good."

"Yes. It is."

Katie slowly moved a hand up over his chest.

"You have hair around your nipples."

"I'm a guy."

"Yes. And quite beautiful."

"Thanks."

Katie ran a finger down his mid line and left him helpless.

"I gotta turn over now. Gotta turn over."

Trevor struggled to organize his limbs and flopped on to his stomach, his head in Katie's lap.

Katie lifted her hands from him.

"What have I done?"

Trevor mumbled into her lap, driving himself crazy with the increase in her scent he found there.

"Nothing. You've done nothing bad. I've got it handled. Go on. Do your thing."

Katie massaged his neck muscles and Trevor moaned into her lap. His cock was getting serious now. She played with his hair, bringing tears to his eyes. She smoothed her hands over his back and shoulders, relaxing him.

She ran her hands over his butt and drove him wild.

"Gotta go. I gotta go now. Right now."

Trevor struggled to gain his footing, rolling off the couch onto his knees and staggering up. Bent double, he pounded clumsily up the stairs, heading towards the bedroom he had allocated to himself for sleepovers when he was too tired to drive back to Sarasota. He was trying to simultaneously unbutton and unzip his jeans as he went. He ricocheted off the stair rail and again off the doorframe of the bedroom before he made it inside and kicked the door closed behind him with one foot.

He was fully aroused and clawing to get free of his jeans. Released, he fell on the bed on his back across the star-spangled coverlet there and went to work with his right hand, seeking further release. His brain was so fried with lust he never heard the bedroom door open.

He sweated and jerked and lurched and shivered and shouted and mumbled his way to a climax, his body heaving and contracting as he ejaculated. He hadn't even grabbed a pillowcase to catch the cum. He finished and lay spread-eagle, his right hand sticky, his jeans wide open and covered in spume.

It had been a fast, furious fight.

Katie's soft voice sounded from the doorway.

"Goodness."

Trevor groaned and opened one eye. Katie stood in the open doorway, her arms around herself. Trevor closed his eye and groaned again.

"Well, this is romantic."

"It is to me. I had no idea. Well, I did. But I've never actually watched."

"Yeah. Hard work. Sweaty, hard work. Feels great, though. Not as good as the real thing. Well, sometimes. Sometimes better. It depends. I'm probably gonna fall asleep now. I'm not being rude. I'm just saying."

"I did that?"

"Yep."

"We didn't do anything."

Trevor opened his one eye again.

"Nope. Just you and your killer hands on me. I was passive."

"Would you like a towel? Or a washcloth?"

"Washcloth. Warm water would be the kindest. Soft dry towel. Tender area."

Katie nodded, and Trevor closed his eyes again, drifting. He heard water running and the muted sounds of expensive cabinetry opening and closing. The water shut off

408

and a slight weight dipped the bed. It felt somehow right when a warm wet washcloth surrounded his penis and he could feel tiny fingers on the other side of the cloth.

Katie cleaned up his mess and carefully placed a soft dry towel over him. She picked up his lax right hand and carefully cleaned all the stickiness off his fingers and between his fingers, much as she would have cleaned barbeque sauce off Robbie's fingers.

Much as Jarrett had cleaned away blood stains and dirt so many years ago, he thought.

Trevor smiled to himself. Katie kissed the side of his mouth and he drifted off to sleep.

His cock knew it before he did.

Katie was in bed with him, playing with him. He lay as still as he could, fighting the urge to roll her into his arms. Her head was next to his hip, her curls tickling the sensitive skin there. Her fingers were in his nether curls and one finger was experimenting with stroking his cock softly back from tip to base.

It was great.

It was hell.

She was getting results. Trevor wondered if there was any baby oil in the house. He foresaw a need to jerk off again if Katie kept it up.

She did better.

Katie kissed the side of his cock, sending his eyes wide open and arching his cock considerably.

"Kate?"

"Hm?"

"Could I take my jeans off?"

"Certainly."

Trevor sat slowly up and began shucking his jeans off, letting them drop to the floor before he glanced over at Katie, not wanting to disturb her in any way. She sat with eyes averted, wearing one of his T-shirts.

And nothing else.

"Jesus Christ, woman. That's no way to help me keep a lid on it."

"I thought I might perhaps wish to participate more fully this time. I'm not perfectly sure."

"Okay. Just don't flaunt anything. All right? My imagination's been giving me problems enough. The reality might kill me."

"You're so silly."

"It was meant as a compliment."

"Thank you then."

"So. Where do you want me to be this time? On my back? On my side? Face down? What?"

"You're very obliging."

"I have experience being a passive bottom."

Katie reached out a hand to touch Trevor's shoulder as he pulled his shirt off over his head, still hiding the scars on his back from her.

"There's something painful about this for you. I don't like the way your face looks right now."

"Flashbacks. Not your problem."

"Yes, it is. I care about you. I don't want to cause you pain of any sort."

"Being passive is scary. I wouldn't have a problem if I could touch, too. Give me parameters. Legs? Arms? Nothing central, so to speak?"

"Agreed. I think we should remove this coverlet."

"You comfy in this bed? I've got an idea. It might solve some problems for both of us."

Katie sat back on her heels, pulling Trevor's T-shirt easily over her knees and tucking it around her feet like a tent. Trevor propped himself up on his elbows, easy with his nudity, and let her carefully questing eyes look their fill. Even her gaze on his skin left feathers of yearning for him to deal with later.

"Here's my idea. Hot tub. You can keep the T-shirt on if you want. I'll go naked. I'll feel all soft and slithery to you. I won't weigh as much if you decide at some point you want me to sit on your lap."

"Why would I want that?"

"Who knows? It's been done. I'm just saying. And all that hot water will keep Santa Snake less active."

"All right. I'm game."

"Good for you. Come on. We got total privacy. I made sure. Well, actually, Dad made sure. I can be pretty oblivious at times. There are no sight lines for people or cameras at all."

Trevor stood easily up and extended his hand down to Katie on the bed. It took a moment for her to respond and he reminded himself to go slow.

"Want me to cover up?"

"No. This is fascinating for me."

"Glad to oblige."

"You have a tattoo."

"Yeah. I've been a wild one in my day. I'm hoping my wild days are over."

"I don't want you to see my body."

"I won't be able to see squat in that T-shirt. Well, outlines and structure maybe, once you're wet. No details. Come on."

Katie took his hand and came off the bed to stand next to him. In her bare feet and his T-shirt, she seemed like a child to him and he frowned at the truckload of responsibility that illusion brought to him.

Trevor squeezed her hand, then raised it to his lips to kiss her knuckles.

"Word of a Daniels. Nothing you don't want to happen. Nothing I don't feel you should even get into yet. Okay?"

Katie licked her lips and swallowed. "Okay."

Trevor led her slowly from the room and down the stairs. Katie kept her hand in his, her face turned towards his face.

"There were a lot of two-piece swim suits in that closet at The Ice Palace. Lots of different sizes."

"Like I said, a wild one. Some of the suits were there for use, just in case. Some got left there just because. Tons of condoms in nightstands. Back-up toothbrushes. It used to be a pretty well stocked house up there. And a wine cellar. Now the caterers bring it all in for Stephie and then take it all away. There used to be drugs. I quit that. Dad and Mary helped me with that. I've been to hell and back. I don't want to go there again."

Trevor shoved open the sliding glass door from his kitchen onto a small lattice-surrounded deck with a hot tub, then paused.

"You want a Dr. Pepper? I'm kind of thirsty. Sex is thirsty work."

"Yes, please. I'd like that."

Trevor let go of her hand to open the same white Kelvinator refrigerator that Millie Crawford had had when the house was hers and extracted two cans of soda from it. Katie quietly admired his rear view and wondered about the line of scarring she saw going down the back of his right leg.

"You're being very honest and unpretentious with me today."

Trevor grinned over his shoulder at her and shoved the refrigerator door closed with his hip.

"Hard to be pretentious when you're naked."

"I like that. Maybe I wouldn't be so scared if I was naked."

"Don't rush it, Kate. I'm guessing you might be more scared. Keep the T-shirt on. You'll know if and when you want it off. Might not be today."

"Okay. I'm glad you understand."

Trevor sighed.

"I understand more than you know. Come on. Let's try out this hot tub."

Trevor pulled the cover off and Katie helped him to fold and stow it by the side wall. He turned on jets, tested chemicals following Scott's detailed, written instructions, and declared the hot tub perfect for use. From a shelf stacked with towels, he picked up a large banana clip and wound his hair up in it.

"The chemicals play havoc with my hair. It gets all snarled up and the ends split. Margaret has a fit. That's my hairdresser. This is easier. If I'm trying to look sexy, though, I don't bother with a hair clip. Sexy it ain't."

Katie laughed at him, and considered this odd creature before her.

"On you, it's sexy. A bag over your head would be sexy. Anything would be sexy."

Trevor grinned at her.

"It's a curse."

Katie rolled her eyes and shook her head.

Trevor helped her up the steps and over the lip into the hot tub. Once she was in, his big T-shirt that she wore billowed up with a wet bubble of air from the jets, making her giggle. Trevor swung his legs easily over the side and slid in.

"Ow! Shit. This motherfucker's hot."

Trevor hauled himself back out and sat on the lip.

"How can you stand this? I might have to sit on the edge for the rest of the night."

"It feels fine to me."

"Chicks. Santa Snake's sacks don't much like this. Well, no getting pregnant tonight. I just heard the rest of my sperm scream and die a horrible death."

"Silly. Turn down the thermostat."

"It'll still take a long time for the water to cool off."

"Then I'll just play with your toes."

Katie tickled Trevor's arch and sent him laughing and thrashing, then massaged his leg muscles, apparently fascinated with his leg hair.

Trevor watched her silently.

Katie would wet his thigh and watch the water flatten and darken the leg hairs there and then watch as they sprang back up as they dried. Trevor enjoyed the physical contact and watched Katie's wet T-shirt billow out and then suck back in to her tiny body. It was an oddly lustless pleasure for him.

413

The hot tub finally cooled enough for him to slide back into it and he insinuated himself under Katie, easing her onto his lap. They were closer to eye level that way. Closer to lip level. Katie gripped his shoulders for support and Trevor curved his arm around her back to hold her. He could feel her rounded bottom against his cock. And he knew she could feel his cock against her rounded bottom.

They gazed into one another's eyes and Trevor gave her a slight smile.

"Want to play some more Monkey-see-monkey-do?"

"Yes."

Katie moved a hand over his shoulder; Trevor moved a hand over her shoulder. She snuggled into him; he snuggled into her. She touched his face. He touched hers. She traced his lips with her finger. He did the same, showing her how her movements felt to him by the way they felt to her–never initiating, but no longer totally passive. He used restraint, but not rigid control. He caught her smiling as she traced his cheekbone with her finger and he traced hers back.

"What?"

"It tickles."

"A little more pressure. Yep. You got it. Fine line there."

Katie kissed the side of his mouth. He kissed her back, letting his lips linger there, keeping his breathing slow and steady and the contact between their faces light and airy. He smoothed his cheekbone gently against hers. He ran his nose up and down her face, closing his eyes.

"Ski?"

"Hm?"

"Where are you?"

"I'm in la-la-land. Come join me."

Trevor felt Katie slightly tense in his arms and brought himself back to reality, cursing himself mentally.

Selfish bastard, he thought. You broke your word.

"Sorry."

"It was beautiful. I've never had a man get lost like that with me. I wish I could go to la-la-land."

Trevor opened his eyes, smiled ruefully at her, and gently kissed her on the lips.

"Someday you will. I hope it's with me."

"Who else would it be with?"

"I don't know."

Katie put her arms around Trevor's neck and buried her face in his shoulder. He brought his arms around her, cupped the back of her head and lightly kissed her hair. He was the only one of the two of them who realized how ironic the situation was. Katie was him as a little boy, sexually abused and yearning for love and closeness. He was in the position of being either the evil opportunist of a Christopher de Nunzio or the patient goodness of a Jarrett Daniels.

He chose goodness.

"Katydid?"

"Hm?"

"There's a limit to how long a body should be in a hot tub. Let me get out and get us both some robes. I don't want you catching a chill from that wet T-shirt."

## TIMING ALWAYS SEEMS TO PLAY A PART

You touch me and I melt.
It's more love than I have felt
From any woman
In my life.
Please be my wife.

Is there such a thing as fate?
What if I had been too late?
Or gone too fast?
Had hurried past?
Timing always seems to play a part.

Are you holding out a loving heart?
Will I look and find you gone?
Did you wait for me too long?
Timing always seems to play a part.

Evil in the past has left its scars.
We stand, walking wounded, from our wars.
Can we learn to trust again?
Will love be a bust again?
Timing always seems to play a part.

I move forward; you retreat.
You grow cold while I feel heat.
Stop, please stop, your moving.
I will stop pursuing.
Please put down the sword you wield.
I'll put down for you my shield.
Timing always seems to play a part

\*       \*       \*       \*       \*

Having gained Katie's permission to do so, Trevor
moved quickly from The Ice Palace and into the sunny spare
bedroom on the second floor of the house on Gill Street
before Katie could change her mind. Afraid to leave the turf
he had gained unguarded, he called Scott and persuaded him
to toss the few belongings he still kept at The Ice Palace into
his van and any leftover food out into the woods for the
raccoons.

He hovered over his newly won prize like a hawk
over a freshly caught fish, greedy and nervous and very, very
careful. He had a fax line installed in the spare bedroom and
tossed a cheap machine on line quickly, alerting Stephie of
his change of fax number and location so there wouldn't be a
break in the flow of his schedule. Stephie made the necessary
adjustments for the change in traveling distances.

The date for the Texas tour was approaching.

The date for Locks of Love was approaching.

Trevor gathered the warmth of his sunny house and
his growing bond with Katie to himself jealously.

He did everything he loved to do. He ran. He played
with Robbie and Junior. He kept up with his workouts at
Gold's Gym. He hung out with Jarrett and Mary. He
followed Katie from room to room in the Gill Street house,
helping her clean or straighten.

He helped her fold laundry.

Anything to be with her.

### WHAT WILL IT TAKE

What will it take
To make
You feel safe in my arms?

Can my hand brush your cheek?
Will you wince?
Will you ever believe
I'm your prince?

Let my lips kiss you brow.
Are you trembling now?
Is it passion or fear
Any time I am near?

If I let you touch me
Will that work?
Can you see me as me,
Not that jerk?

Touch my hand. I am warm,
And I mean you no harm.
Touch my lips. They are soft.
You're my light. I'm the moth.
You think I'm a tease
But I'm asking you, please,
What will it take
To make
You feel safe in my arms?

We climb the stairs.
I touch your neck.
You aren't easy
With me yet.
What will it take
To make
You feel safe in my arms?


It was another Sunday morning. Robbie was in Sarasota with Scott, Carla and Junior again. And again Katie and Trevor were in bed together. But this time it wasn't Trevor after jerking off and Katie crouched in a T-shirt beside him.

They were in Katie's room in Katie's bed and Katie turned warmly to him, snuggling into his side.

"I was brazen last night."

"Yes, you were. I loved it."

Katie's eyes went wide.

"I did, too. Oh, my God. I enjoyed sex."

"With me. You enjoyed sex with me."

"Yes, I did."

"Good. I just wanted that clarification. I don't share."

"Are you the jealous type?"

Trevor sat up in bed., a puzzled frown on his face.

"It appears I am. This is new for me. Don't press our luck. I've never been in love before. It's doing strange things to me. Jealousy is new to me, and not very pretty. I'm just warning you."

"Could you be violent?"

"I don't know. With you? To you? No. Not ever. But to others? I have been violent. Not often. But, like I'm saying, this jealousy is new to me. I can see some changes going on in me. I'm going to have to watch it."

"You are so funny. I love you."

Katie put a hand quickly over her mouth. Trevor grinned.

418

" 'Oops'? I know the feeling. Said too much? You can't take it back. You love me?"

Katie slowly took her hand from her mouth.

"Yes, I do. How did you do that?"

"Being clever and manipulative? Being goal-oriented and focused? Being dumb and lucky?"

"I'm serious."

"Yes, you are. I'm not. What a world. Usually I'm the one who's too serious. You bring out the kid in me."

Trevor sobered.

"You bring out the man in me. Marry me. Quick. Before you have time to think about it."

"No."

"Shit. Too late. You had time to think about it. Agree to marry me?"

Katie blushed slightly.

"Yes."


## <u>ARMS AROUND ME</u>

Arms around me in the middle of the night.
Who wouldn't think that wouldn't be all right?

Who had a dream
That arms around me would make it all right?
Me.
Who got more than he bargained for that night?
Me.

Arms to hold you and keep you warm.
Arms to keep you away from harm.
Arms can bind you up and hurt you bad.
Arms can pin you down and make you mad.
Arms around you often make you bleed.

When we met, I didn't want your arms.
Yes, I did.
Arms to hold me up when weak.

Arms to rock me back to sleep.
Arms to give me comfort.
Arms to give me strength.
Your arms brought the world to me.
Your arms taught me to be free.

Arms around my middle hold me tight.
Jarrett's arms and Scottie's arms.
Mary's arms and Robbie's arms.
Arms around my middle hold me tight.

Arms around your middle in the night
Hold you tight
If they're right
And you might
Find arms around you is where you want to be
To be free.
Loving arms around you hold you tight.
But no tighter.
Loving arms around you help you fight.
If you're a fighter.

Let my arms come round you now, my love.
They're just my arms, not a cage, my dove.
Put loving arms around each other.
Right?

## Chapter Nineteen

The temperatures dropped. The wind picked up. People began to cover their plants against the promised freeze.

Trevor got worried.

"The homeless, Dad. People will die tonight. What can we do?"

Jarrett considered the earnest face.

"I've got several answers for you, Trevor. First off, people are gonna die tonight regardless of what we do."

"I understand that, but what can we do for some of them at least?"

"Hard to find 'em, Trevor. They don't like to be found. They darned sure don't like official notice, so to speak."

"They're out there. I was one of them. I didn't even know where to go to get help. I was a kid. I didn't want official notice, either. A blanket. I could have used a blanket. Maybe more than food on a night like this."

"You got the money, boy. You can do it. We got the troops. You and me and Scott. Maybe Dani, Margaret. Carla, Mary. Katie's at work. I don't much like sendin' the women out by themselves. It can be a pretty rough element at times. Bein' homeless don't make you a worse person or a better one."

"I agree. Who would know how to find clusters of the homeless?"

"Cops."

"Oh, geez, no. They'd run. I'd have run."

"Jack and Jay would know, I'd guess. I been out of the business too long."

Trevor licked his lips. Except for Jarrett, members of law enforcement still made him nervous.

"Can you call them? They're your old buddies more than mine. Get locations and head counts? Get an idea of where we are with this? The girls can buy up the blankets on their credit cards. I'll bet they can con stock boys into helping them load vehicles. Maybe even store managers. If we're talking enough targets, we'll rent U-Haul trucks. What do you think?"

Jarrett nodded.

"I'll call Jack Tatum."

The numbers stunned Jarrett.

The locations weren't as big a surprise.

Carla took Scott's van to Bed, Bath and Beyond. Dani and Margaret covered the Walmart in Punta Gorda. Mary took Big Lots. Jarrett reported his numbers to Trevor, who rented two pack trucks for them and they split up, Trevor going to the K-Mart in Murdock, and Jarrett to the Super Walmart there.

Trevor chewed on his lip, considering the distribution problem.

"We can't cover Englewood, Dad. We don't have enough drivers."

"We'll do what we can, son. If we have time, we'll cover Englewood, too. I'll get maps and flashlights. Cell phones on all around. Scott and Carla in their van. Carla drives. Scott can do the tossin'. Mary and I'll take one of your rental trucks. Mary'll drive. Scott and Carla get Punta Gorda and out Rt. 17. You've got out past El Jobean. Mary and I'll take US 41 in Charlotte Harbor. I guess you're flyin' solo, boy. I don't feel so edgy about Dani and Margaret goin' off together. They can take US 41 from Forrest Nelson north to the county line. There's two of 'em. Dani drives, and you can tell Margaret that from me. Dani looks like prey. Margaret never has. And you watch your backside out there, too, son. Let your big head do your thinkin', not your heart."

Jarrett set up round-trip patterns for them. They phoned one another back and forth, checking on one another's safety.

Store managers, noticing the huge sales, got curious and helped load cartons into the trucks along with stock boys. Carla maxed out the van before she maxed out her credit cards and told Scott she was leaving a few blankets in the store for regular customers. Everyone was buying blankets tonight.

Dani and Margaret did their short run with the load they could wedge into their van. Margaret didn't grumble over who drove. They were already back home when inspiration hit Trevor, and he phoned to Jarrett from his U-Haul truck, heading out past Murdock with his load.

"McDonald's coupons. Or whatever. What do you think?"

"Doable. Might have to do it tomorrow, son. Blankets first. Food next. Comin' up for a coupon won't be as hard to sell in daylight when you're takin' it from the hand of the same person who gave you a blanket after dark the night before."

"Yeah. Comin' up on the Ranger's Stadium."

"Go straight. You ain't even close yet."

Scott, weaving a pattern of dark back roads off Rt 17 between Punta Gorda and the Desoto County line, shoved cartons out in areas known to have populations of the homeless. He wrote "Free Blankets" with a black marker on the sides of the cartons and shouted in the direction of the woods.

"Free blankets! Got free blankets here! Anybody hearin' me? I'm leavin' now. Ya'll come on out and get these things, ya hear?"

Scott would close the back doors of the van and Carla would drive them to the next known site. Scott never saw a soul come out for the cartons as he watched the darkness and hoped his eccentric brother hadn't wasted his money.

Jarrett had Mary drive their U-Haul truck slowly through the back roads of the sector Jarrett had chosen for them while Jarrett tossed blankets in their plastic wraps out the open back overhead door from an open carton, spacing one blanket every four feet or so and shouting into the frigid darkness.

"Free blankets. Come and get 'em. We'll be back tomorrow with food coupons. Free blankets. Come and get 'em."

Jarrett flung with one hand, his other hand deep in the pocket of his ski jacket for warmth, thinking about the year that Trevor had been the homeless. Yankee winters were much worse than this.

"Free blankets. My son's givin' away free blankets. You need a blanket? Got a blanket here for ya. Food tomorrow."

Dani and Margaret had simply driven to designated areas and Margaret had tipped the cartons out. They had driven soundlessly away, the heater in their van blowing fiercely.

Jarrett worried the most about Trevor's sense of survival.

By Jack Tatum's calculations, they covered the known populations of the homeless and then some.

As far as Trevor was concerned, there was no such thing as too many blankets.

"I'd rather more than not enough. If there's a blanket hog out there, I want more than enough to cover the rest. We'll cover the same areas again tomorrow. If there's unclaimed blankets, we'll move them to another location. I'm hoping I never get a single blanket back, but if we do, we'll just give 'em to charity anyway."

Trevor had the longest haul out to his destination. He was unfamiliar with the roads in West County. Punta Gorda and Port Charlotte had been his old stomping grounds.

He was edgy as he drove. Was he too late with too little? Why hadn't this idea come to him earlier?

He turned the heater off in the truck and unzipped his ski jacket. Fair was fair, he thought. He had a jacket. And a blanket. He smiled to himself in the dark.

In his youth, he'd lived outside in the winter. He'd been the one to wear the jacket he'd gotten in one of his barter-with-sex deals and Blondie had been the one wrapped inside her black plastic garbage bag beside him, his arm around her as he slept, his right hand gripping her neck, the blanket over both their heads as sleep claimed him. He'd wake up with the first light of dawn, his fingers cramped

424

from cold and pressure, but Blondie would still be with him, not stolen from him in the night.

He'd avoided staying with others like himself, both adult and teen. He'd been too small to protect either himself or his possessions. Blondie, traveling incognito in her black plastic garbage bag, had still been as attractive to others as his backpack and his body had been.

He sobered now, realizing that he would never probably be able to find and reach the ones like himself–the small, defenseless, solitary travelers falling off the radar screen on purpose. He thanked God grudgingly for the Spath boys. Without them, he truly wouldn't be where he was today. Or tonight.

As he drove the dark roads, his music machine began to turn and to give him snatches of songs and nebulous ideas to go with those flitting melodies.

Cold.

And bricks.

The world of his first winter on his own had been filled with cold bricks and cold exterior walls and cold galvanized trash cans and cold concrete. Much of it was an endless blur of day into night and into day, his lungs clogged up with what must have been asthma, and running a fever. His fingers had been stiff and cramped from the cold. Even Blondie's strings had been cold to the touch. He hadn't had a tip jar then. People, creating drafts, walked too briskly by him in the cold weather to worry about a tiny boy playing guitar and sitting cross-legged with his back to a wall.

But occasionally money had fluttered down to him. Playing guitar didn't pay well then. But sex for money or goods was doing just fine. Sex was indoors with the heat on. Sex often produced a meal afterwards or at least a handful of peanuts or candy stuffed quickly into his pockets while the john's back was turned. He hadn't considered it theft. He'd considered it in the nature of a tip for a job well done.

As he'd worked his way steadily southward, first in the city and then through New Jersey, sex was what had put meat on the table, so to speak. Music was what filled his

425

soul. He'd often played for himself, becoming engrossed in his music and drifting away from his surroundings, surprised when he found coins at his feet or a loose clutter of dollar bills between his legs as he sat and played.

When he got to his dream destination of the country, he had found out what hungry was all about. Life in the city had only been a warm-up for the real game. Out in the country, there was cold, too. And less available food. And a lot less johns. He discovered the true meaning of hardship and loneliness. In the country, he was too much alone.

He discovered the interstate and things got better. On his compulsive quest for south, he discovered hitchhiking.

And truckers.

And truck stops.

Here, his music began to be appreciated, and his body less of a commodity. He played for food. He played for rides to amuse the truckers and to help them stay awake, often being passed from one trucker to another by way of the network of truckers frequently running the same routes. He found himself at family dinner tables in Omaha and sleeping in Kenworths in California. Heading south often got a detour to it. He never did Mexico and he never did Canada. He never did Alaska and he never did Hawaii, but he was all over the contiguous lower forty-eight states.

Trevor chuckled, remembering the good times, his music machine working away within him.

Near his target area, his cell phone rang and he answered it, a smile in his voice.

"Yeah?"

"Mary and I are done here, son. Scott and Carla took another load out. Dani and Margaret have packed it in. Where are you?"

Trevor squinted at a signpost.

"Coming up on the light at Sailors Way and 771. There's a Publix there."

"Got it. Pull over, son. Mary and I'll be out to help you."

426

Trevor smiled more broadly into the phone and into the darkness of the chilly cab.

"Thanks, Dad. I'll just do a short section here and then park it."

"Stay safe, son."

"Thanks, Dad."

He disconnected the call, warmed from within by the love.

Grit and God's good grace had kept him alive as a boy on his own, he thought. The Spath boys had ended his career as a homeless prostitute. Jarrett Daniels had shown him love and hope. And Mary had brought him his roots.

Trevor drove the truck past the Gulf Cove Publix at the intersection of Sailors Way and 771, turning right finally at Sunnybrook to turn several more times through the dark back streets, but then thought better of his original plan.

Things had changed since he had been a boy on his own and he had even then avoided populations of the homeless. A younger Trevor would have thought nothing of going off into the boonies alone and dragging cartons of blankets off from the back of a truck. But he was older now, and, he hoped, wiser. He had a decent regard for his own skin, and a vivid memory of what it was like to be out in the boonies and be attacked.

He drove the U-Haul back to the Gulf Cove Publix shopping center and parked it and his sorry butt under a good light in the parking lot, turning on the radio and listening to the music of his fellow artists on Gator Country 101.9 FM while he watched in the dark for another U-Haul truck to arrive.

When it did, Trevor felt his whole body relax. He knew he would never get over the blessing of family. He rolled down his window and shut off the radio as the other truck pulled in, driver's side to him. He grinned into his father's eyes.

"Dad."

"I see you've finally got some sense to you, boy. I thought you might go wanderin' off on foot to deliver them blankets in person. Glad to see I was wrong."

"You gave me the boonies on purpose, didn't you?"

"Darned straight I did. I knew it'd take you a while to even get out here. It's just not possible to speed in a rental truck. I knew Mary and I had a concentration of the homeless so we could be finished sooner. I knew Scott would do double. I knew Dani and Margaret would do fast and turn in. I know my troops. But you? God knows what you might do. Glad you did the smart thing, Yankee."

Trevor chuckled.

"We go together? We toss together? Mary drives?"

"Yep. One truck after another. This here Publix is as good a place as any to park your truck until we empty this one. Shut her off, son. Lock the cab, but just leave the back as is. Worst case scenario? The truck gets robbed of all the blankets and we got one less load to disperse."

Trevor nodded and rolled his window up. He followed Jarrett's directions and came jogging around to the passenger side door of Jarrett's truck. Mary slid over; Jarrett slid out the driver's side. Mary got behind the wheel and Jarrett rounded the truck and got in, leaving Trevor sandwiched in the middle and grinning.

Jarrett hunched closer to him.

"Darn, boy. You're cold as ice. Somethin' the matter with the heater in that truck you've got?"

Trevor grabbed his aunt's face and kissed her enthusiastically on the mouth, making her squeal.

"Trevor, get those icy fingers off my neck right now!"

"I love you both so much. Nothing wrong with the heater. I just didn't think it was fair for me to have heat when other folks didn't."

Jarrett shuddered.

"You are so nuts, boy. Mary, let's get on with this, shall we? And you, moron, will just have to figure a way to get portable heaters and kerosene out to the homeless, because I'll be darned if you'll turn the heater off in this truck."

Trevor threw back his head, laughing, as Mary bumped the big truck out of the parking lot.

"This is just like going to Boca Grande in the old pick-up truck. Remember that? Right down 771 here. It was my first time ever seeing the Gulf."

"I remember. I let you drive some. Scared the daylights out of your aunt. She ain't been the same since."

"It was beautiful. Just like now."

"Trevor. It's cold. It's dark. We ain't goin' to the beach, God forbid. Just thinkin' about water makes my bones ache. This is not beautiful."

"Sure it is. I'm sitting between the two people I love most in the whole world. I'm alive and happy. It's just like then."

"You are so nuts. Mary, turn here. Trevor, quit bouncin' on the seat.

Mary pulled to the side of a vacant back road as instructed and stopped the truck.

"Jarrett Daniels, you old grouch, he's seat-dancing. Do you want to ride in the back?"

"No, ma'am."

"Then just quit picking at the boy and the both of you start flinging blankets and shouting."

Trevor and Jarrett opened cartons and flung blankets and shouted out across the cold, dark pinelands as Mary slowly drove the maze of back roads that skirted Rotonda.

"Free blankets. Here by the side of the road. Food coupons coming tomorrow. Free blankets."

Mary drove them back to the Gulf Cove shopping center, they switched trucks and began again in another sector, the area between Gulf Cove and Placida.

Jarrett blew on the cold fingers of one hand as he flung blankets with the other.

"You might want to rethink this food coupon thing, son. Can't be shovin' no coupons off a truck. Folks might not come up at all, being afraid. And it's a darned long walk to Mickey D's from some of these spots."

"Food. Food is important. I promised food."

"Then make it food, son. Make it canned food."

"It's frustrating to have a can of tuna and no way to get into it. I know."

"Make it food with them pull-back tabs. Make it baked beans. Whatever. Heck, make it Spam. Whatever the homeless don't get, the raccoons'll feast on. You'll make somebody happy."

"Yeah. Maybe that. You're right about the coupons."

"What would you have wanted to get, son?"

Trevor sniffed, his hands thrust into his armpits while he thought.

"Rule out pizza. That was like a wet dream. I would have wanted portable. Easy-access opening. Able to last a few days, if possible. Rule out anything perishable. It spoils. You eat it anyway and then get sick. I know."

"Them cheese and cracker packs? Graham cracker and peanut butter packs? I don't think them things ever go bad. Raccoons'll like 'em, too."

"Good deal. Sam's Wholesale Club?"

"Good plan. Tomorrow. Not tonight."

"Oh, no. I would never do that."

"The hell you say."

"Well, I don't think they're open this late anyway. And I owe the family big time. Scott and Carla. You and Mary. Dani and Margaret."

"No tuna fish."

"As if."

"I'm just sayin'."

Mary bumped the truck over a concrete curb in the parking lot.

"Oops."

"You drive like Trevor," Jarrett grumbled.

"I do not," Mary retorted, "Take us all out to dinner, Trevor. Bring your lady. Just a little family get-together. Let your lady see what your life is like–the good and the bad."

430

Silence.

"You think about it, Trevor."

Mary gave Trevor a hard stare in the darkened cab of the truck.

"Full frontal nudity, Trevor. Your core people interacting with you. Crowds. Potential for fan recognition. Out of the closet."

Trevor groaned.

"Big Dog's? Not on a Tuesday night."

Jarrett glanced uneasily at Mary, trying to read her intentions.

"Of course not, son You're not an amateur. We're talkin' downstairs for food where the lights are better. Tomorrow's Friday. There should be a good crowd out for food."

On his way back into Port Charlotte with his rental truck, Trevor called Katie on his cell phone and invited her to go out flinging food with them the next day, too.

"It's going to be sort of like Mardi Gras with cheese packs. Mary drives and Jarrett and I fling. You fling, too. Or keep Mary company in the cab. Whatever. Robbie? Sure. Him, too. We can bring him with us or set him up with Junior and Scott and Carla. Yeah, they'll be flinging in Punta Gorda. We'll be doing Port Charlotte and Englewood. Your job? Oh. Yeah. Darn. Forgot. After work? You'll come eat with us all? Yes, Robbie, too. Should I come get you, or do you want to drive over? Drive? Sure. Big Dog's. Say, 7:30 p.m? Downstairs. We'll have the tables in front of the rock wall. It's about the only place they can put us all together. Cool. I'll see you then."

Trevor was fine the whole day, going to Sam's Wholesale Club in the U-Haul truck and, when it opened, cleaning them out of cheese packs and peanut butter crackers. He got the big combo packs and munched on some of the bright orange-colored cheesy crackers in the cab as he drove to the house on Olympia Avenue that would form their

431

base of operations, getting orange-colored crumbs on his shirt and orange-colored dust on his lips.

Flinging food was a breeze after tossing blankets. They all hit the same areas again in daylight, keeping in contact by cell phone. There were scattered areas where some blankets, still in their wrappings, could be found on the shoulders of roads. Trevor ordered that they be left for one more night at least. They'd be safe in their wrappings. They could always be retrieved later if they were still there.

Junior had a real blast, Trevor thought, and Trevor found he missed not having Robbie there to enjoy. Robbie was with Katie's friend Lisa in Sarasota and her little girl Jasmine. He saved a box of assorted packs back for Katie and Robbie. The Lord only knew what Katie's opinion of actually throwing food off the back of a truck was, he thought. Maybe she didn't believe him at all about doing it. She didn't believe a lot of things about him.

Scott and Carla went back to Mary and Jarrett's house after their food-fling to relax and tempt a wound-up Junior into a nap on the big bed in the master bedroom. Mary took a soaking bath and joined Junior there. Carla took the single in Trevor's old room. Jarrett took his recliner. Scott took the old plaid couch.

Trevor went back to his own house, wired and tired, and full of edgy energy. He braided his hair back, pulled on a hooded sweatshirt from Gold's Gym and ran down Retta Esplanade, up Shreve Street, down Virginia Avenue and back up Marion Avenue, a familiar sight to many residents.

My town, he thought. This is my town.

Trevor dropped the hood back from his head and let his braid swing free. It was still cold enough to see his breath. He hadn't put on his sunglasses, getting ready for tonight. No baseball cap. No sunglasses. Like Mary said, for him, full frontal nudity. But this was his town. His hometown. If you had to pretend to be someone else in your own hometown, well, there was just something wrong with that.

And with you.

432

At Big Dog's that night, Dani was in high spirits, her sparse hair tucked up under a bright red ski cap.

"You should have seen! This scrungy-looking guy came right up. I was driving slowly along. Margaret was in the back, dumping off blankets. I heard him come right up to the back doors of the van. 'What else ya got in there, babe?' he asks. I jammed on the brakes. Silly me. I should have hauled ass with the van, but, duh, I didn't. Margaret was great. 'It's free blankets, asshole', she says, 'Not free sex.' 'Gimme your money, bitch'. Margaret whipped out that gun of hers. 'Gimme your gonads, bastard, and get off my back bumper'. Well, he backed off then. We dumped the blankets and vamoosed. Wasn't Margaret great?"

Jarrett looked down the table to Margaret.

"That would be your old Colt revolver? The one you got from your granddaddy? The one you never got around to gettin' a carry permit for?"

Dani cut in.

"Oh, pooh, Jarrett. Don't get her started on the constitutional right to bear arms."

Jarrett nodded, a smile in his eyes.

"Well done, Margaret."

Margaret nodded once in acknowledgement. Dani was still bouncing.

"I'll bet that man took all the blankets. I'm sorry, Trevor."

Trevor leaned around Katie.

"You did the right thing. Both of you. Maybe there'll be someone bigger and meaner than he is to take all the blankets away from him. I'm sorry you had to have that happen."

Then Trevor grinned over at Margaret.

"It probably only happened because it was two women out after dark. Now, if there'd been a man along, too."

Margaret lifted her eyebrow and Trevor cracked up.

"Margaret, you can't shoot me. I'm the meal ticket."

Dani giggled and leaned into Margaret.

"Don't bet on it, Trev. We'd be talking justifiable homicide here. We'd collect from your estate for back wages from your date of death till the end of time or when the case was settled, whichever came last."

Jarrett leaned forward to address Trevor.

"You gonna feed us, boy? Or you just gonna entertain Margaret with her plans for your demise?"

"Eat. We're going to eat. This place is busy tonight, Jarrett."

"Where's that sassy waitress of ours? Mary, get out a pen and a piece of paper. Everybody, read them menus or just write down what you want and pass the paper around the table. Katydid? What you want to drink? I know what everybody else likes."

Flustered by the direct question, Katie looked up from her menu.

"Oh. Sorry. No liquor for me, thank you. I'm driving. A coke, please. And one for Robbie?"

"Sure thing. Any changes in the usual for the rest? No? Fine then. I'll go around to the bar for mine and Scott's and Mary's drinks. Trevor?"

"Yes, sir?"

"Hustle up the water and sodas, boy. Carla? You're in charge of that food list. Put me down for a Frisco Burger, three-quarter pound, Pittsburgh rare. Them Yankees know a thing or two about beef."

Jarrett stood and ambled into the bar.

Trevor stood and went to snag a pitcher of water and a stack of plastic glasses from a cart. He wove his way back between tables, smiling. He liked restaurants and had fed his college preoccupation with discount beer and condoms by working in a succession of them for tips and the opportunity to play guitar and sing.

Katie watched a lady with a cane nudge his ankle as he scooted past.

"Trevor Daniels?"

"Yes, ma'am. Well, hey, Mrs. Mercer. Nice to see you."

"I didn't think you'd recognize me. It's been years since you mowed my lawn."

"Sure, I recognize you. I didn't want to interrupt your dinner. How's Earl?"

"Dead."

"Oh, geez. I'm sorry, Mrs. Mercer. When?"

"Going on six years now."

"I'm real sorry. I didn't know. He taught me how to tie a tie. Dad didn't know how. I still tie my ties that way. When I wear one."

Eloise Mercer patted Trevor's arm.

"No reason for you to know about Earl's death. You were out on tour. Your folks probably missed the obit. Thank you for that memory of Earl. That was very nice of you. Go on and join your party, Trevor."

"You want to come join us?"

"No, thank you. It's very nice to see you again, Trevor. You grew up taller."

Trevor chuckled.

"I couldn't get much shorter."

"I've been through twenty-five more lawn people since you, Trevor, and not one of them has stayed as long or worked as hard as you did."

"Thanks. I like to hear that."

"Go on. Get back to your table. Is that curly-haired gal with the baby your lady? She's been watching us. I hope she's not the jealous type."

Trevor laughed and looked over at Katie. She was indeed staring at him. He blushed.

"I better go."

"Good for you, Trevor. God bless."

"You, too, Mrs. Mercer."

Trevor continued back to the table. Jarrett was already there with the alcoholic beverages. Carla was handing him the food list.

He turned to Trevor as Trevor set the pitcher on the table.

"Pour the darned water, Trev. You make a lousy bus boy. There goes your tip. Sodas next. I'll grab our waitress and give her the food list."

Trevor nodded and began pouring water into the plastic glasses. Scott took them and passed them around and across the table. Dani abandoned Margaret to pull rolled bundles of utensils in paper napkins from a basket by the cash register. Carla and Mary chatted about the Chesapeake Bay area. Robbie and Junior exchanged stares and the secret signals and sounds of toddlers and other pre-schoolers.

Katie considered the gruff Margaret.

"Have you known him long?"

"Trevor? Oh, yeah. Goin' on a lifetime now. I remember when he first blew into town. Women were fallin' all over themselves to get a piece of that. Dani, too, I guess. I'm older than they are. Not by much, but enough."

"You don't like him."

Margaret compressed her lips.

"Can't say. What's it matter to you? Doesn't have a thing to do with you."

"I'm trying to get to know him. I can get all the rave reviews I can find. You're the first person I've met that seems to feel differently."

"Well, now, I see him as competition for Dani's affections. I'm jealous of what they share. I shouldn't be, but, there it is."

"But Dani's with you. Anyone can see that."

"I didn't say it was logical or fair. You asked me and I told you. Why don't you like him?"

Margaret fixed a chilly eye on her and Katie had to stop her first instinct, which was to hotly deny it. She pressed her finger to her lips.

"I'm not sure."

Margaret scowled at Trevor's back as he went to return the water pitcher to the cart by the kitchen.

"He's about as full of shit as a goose, but there's no real harm in him."

"Maybe it's the shit."

Margaret nodded curtly.

"Maybe it is."

Their flustered and apologetic waitress came up to the table, a tray full of food on one shoulder.

"Jarrett, darlin', I'm right sorry. We're so darned busy right now. Cook called in sick. Dishwasher never showed up. We got the day manager cookin'. Food'll be fine, but the wait staff is washin' its own dishes. Well, at least the bus boy's been helpin'."

"Throw Trevor back in there to do prep work or wash dishes."

"I can't. We don't have a big enough hair net for him."

"Your loss. Here, gimme that tray. Go get another one. I'll pass the food around. I ain't goin' in the kitchen for it, though."

Trevor and his hair were beginning to attract attention. Katie watched as eyes slid to him and then narrowed, or furrows appeared on brows. One woman nudged her dinner companion and leaned forward to whisper across the table. Katie watched, fascinated, as heads began to turn.

Jarrett handed around food. Trevor came back with another pitcher of water. Scott leaned over to Carla.

"It's about this time I'd be callin' for a puppy bag and gettin' Trevor out of here."

"The natives are restless?"

"The cows are about to stampede."

"Here?"

"You just watch. Katydid? Best move yourself and Robbie out of the way. Come on over here to me and Carla. Mary?"

"Yes, Scott?"

"Got a Sharpie marker with you?"

"Always."

"Good. We'll make do."

Trevor sat down next to Katie, picked up his burger and bit into it, beaming into Katie's face. Katie scooted her chair away from him and then moved Robbie. Trevor looked puzzled. And then the storm broke.

"Trevor Daniels?"

"Trevor Daniels…"

"Trevor Daniels!!"

Trevor looked up from his burger, dazed by the ring of eager faces suddenly around him. He set his burger down. Mary slid the Sharpie marker to him as he plastered his idiot-grin onto his face and attempted to stand.

"Hey. How's it goin'?"

Placemats, notebooks, shirts, baseball caps, hands all waved and crowded around him, causing a tight warmth around his seated body. He felt hands on his shoulders, hands on his hair and in his hair.

Hands elsewhere.

He tried to shove back his chair, but got little distance from the move.

Jarrett and Scott moved the line of tables down and he stood up, shedding a few of the more tenacious hands on him. He felt a slight pain at his scalp and realized one eager fan had literally pulled some of his hair out.

He looked wildly around for Scott, his eyes worried but his smile still in place as he made signing motions with his Sharpie marker over endless surfaces and for faceless faces.

He looked for Katie and couldn't find her.

Scott moved into his bubble of air and simply expanded his body backwards, easing the press of humanity. He saw Carla with Junior on her hip. He saw Jarrett with a stack of Styrofoam containers and their waitress waving away his credit card and urging them to leave. He saw Mary with her sad smile of sympathy. He saw Dani heading for the door and Margaret's stony stare. But he couldn't see Katie or Robbie.

Scott expertly moved him towards the door.

The crowd, satiated, began to thin, but remaining there would only have set them off again. Or they might even be calling in more people with their cell phones. Or reporters. Or TV.

In Sarasota, the crowd for Trevor Lane Daniels, serious composer, was very low key and passive. In Punta Gorda, he was just the Daniels boy, the younger one. But in Port Charlotte, he might as well have been in LA.

Jarrett came to walk beside him across the cold, dark asphalt parking lot. The last fan had given up and gone back inside.

"Sorry to break up your party, son."

"I wanted it to happen, Dad. I knew what I was doing when I chose Big Dog's. I wanted her to see."

"Well, she saw, son."

"Where is she?"

Jarrett leaned carefully into Trevor.

"She left, son. Took Tadpole with her. I'd guess she's gone on back to the house in her little car."

"Was she all right?"

"She seemed fine to me."

"Why would she leave?"

"I don't know, son. Just what were you expectin'?"

"A feeding frenzy from the fans. Got that. Scott's really good at that crowd control, isn't he? That getting me out of a jam thing?"

"He is. But your lady?"

"I guess I expected to look in her eyes and see reality. She never believes I'm real."

"And that back there was gonna prove to Katie that you were real? That's the least real I've seen you up close in three years."

"I don't think she really believes I'm Trevor Daniels. I don't think she believes I'm me."

"Got two separate and distinct people there, son. Got the guy flingin' blankets into the freezin' darkness on back roads in Charlotte County. Got the popular icon scribblin' his name and wearin' the idiot-grin."

439

"They're both me."

"Maybe she don't like one of them. Maybe she don't like you the same way you like her. You ain't gonna be the first guy in this world that got rejected by a woman."

"Well, it's new to me."

"Darn, boy. Maybe the lady's right. Maybe you are an arrogant bastard."

"Son-of-a-bitch. I prefer the technical term."

"Son-of-a-bitch, then. You just might be. You done stomped a butterfly with a combat boot here, boy."

"Kill it or cure it."

"Be careful what you wish for. Here. Take this box on home with you. You can reheat the burger. Buddy'll like the fries. Never did get my beer drunk. Oh, well. Our little waitress said the meal was on the house. She was glad enough to see us go."

"Helluva price for a free meal."

"I'm sayin'."

\*    \*    \*    \*    \*

The media took the blanket story and ran with it. Trevor groaned his frustration to Jarrett.

"I didn't do it for the publicity. I did it so folks with nothing much could have a blanket and a meal."

"Don't forget the raccoons."

"Them, too."

"Be happy it's good ink and pretty close to the truth. 'Eccentric young singin' star'? Who are they kiddin'? You ain't young no more."

"Amen to that. And getting older by the minute."

"Had a darned fine victory celebration while it lasted."

"And lost Katie. What part of me and my life couldn't she swallow? The lies or the truth?"

"Who knows, boy? Can't never figure a woman out."

\*    \*    \*    \*    \*

440

It was the night of the Trevor Daniels Look-Alike Contest.

The Charlotte County Memorial Auditorium was packed.

Katie decided she'd never seen so many lean and darkly handsome men with long hair in her life. It was like an ad for Chippendales with clothes on. They crowded the small stage of the auditorium, over a hundred and fifty of them, posing and preening, flinging hair back over their shoulders. Some carried guitars. Some had feathers in their hair. One had a plush toy cat around his neck. All wore Trevor's signature white shirt and blue jeans. Half of them were barefoot.

But none of them looked like the life-size cardboard cutouts set around the edges of the hall.

Katie felt her mouth go dry.

Her cell phone rang and she plunged her hand into her beaded evening purse to answer it, glancing at the incoming number.

"Jarrett? Where is he? What's happening?"

"He's down at Airport Road."

"Why? He doesn't have a flight out tonight."

"He ain't at the Charlotte County Airport, Kate. He's at the jail."

"Doing what?"

"Five to ten, for all I know. Jack Tatum called me, but I'm with Mary up in Atlanta. You'll have to take Scott and the limo over and see what you can do."

"What can I do?"

"Bail him out."

"I don't have any money."

"Trev will."

"Well, send Trev then," she snapped waspishly into the cell phone. "Ski works hard for him. Tell Trev to get off his fat ass and come judge this beauty contest or get Ski out of jail."

"No can do. It's all on you, Kate. Go get your man out of jail. Gotta go. Bye."

Katie stared at the cell phone with its incessant dial tone. She disconnected the call and phoned Scott in the limo, walking swiftly to the exit as she spoke, the black crepe of her long skirt swirling around her ankles.

"Scott, meet me out front. Do you know where the jail is? Good. We're going there."

Katie hung up and banged her way out the front glass doors of the auditorium as Scott pulled the limo up. She opened the front passenger door and got in before Scott could get out and come around to open the door.

"Drive. We'll worry about speeding tickets later."

Scott drove.

Katie called up directory assistance on her cell phone and got the number for the Charlotte County Jail. She opted for the additional charge to have it dialed for her.

"Charlotte County Jail."

"Do you have a prisoner there by the name of Ski...?"

Katie turned frightened eyes to Scott who smiled back at her wickedly.

"Colorado?"

She narrowed her eyes at him.

"...Trevor Daniels."

"Yes, we do. He's been arrested on an outstanding warrant for speeding."

"He would be."

"Will you wish to make arrangements for Mr. Daniels' bail?"

"Something like that. Yes. We should be there in approximately. .. ?"

Katie turned questioningly to Scott, who thoughtfully provided her with the answer.

"Five minutes."

"Five minutes."

"We've started the paperwork, Ms. Mercer. Jarrett Daniels phoned ahead to let us know to expect you."

Katie hung up the phone and refused to either speak to Scott or look at him.

When they got to the jail, Trevor was sitting on a metal and gray plastic stack chair, his posture defensive.

He was just another gorgeous hunk of lean, darkly handsome male animal, Katie thought. Just another chiseled profile with long, flowing hair wearing a Trevor Daniels shirt and blue jeans. She'd seen way too many of them in the past hour. For a wonder, he had socks and shoes on, his favorite battered house-brand pair of sneakers from Walmart.

Trevor looked woefully up at her from the straight chair. The harsh florescent lights and the echoing emptiness of the huge building made him seem small and fragile somehow. Katie stopped walking when she got to his chair.

"Your father is such an asshole."

"Yeah."

"You really are him, aren't you?"

"Yeah."

"Oh, Ski."

"Can we leave now? I don't like jails."

"Then pay your speeding tickets."

"I did! I do! I was framed. It was Dad's old buddies Jack and Jay. They took me away in handcuffs!"

"Like I said, your father's an asshole."

"Yeah. Can we get married?"

"Maybe I'll like one of the other hundred and fifty yous back at the Auditorium."

"Shit! The contest. The concert."

"That's right. That's why I'm here. To bail your sorry butt out of jail so your loyal fans don't get stiffed buying tickets for a concert where the talent is late or never shows up at all. God, I hate that."

"Me, too. Let's go."

"Jarrett said you'd have the bail money. God knows I don't."

"Oh, yeah. I got it. They just wouldn't release me on my own recognizance. Repeat offender, ya know."

"Speeding? Why am I not surprised."

"I've never lost my license."

Trevor handed the clerk on duty his credit card and Katie stared into the distance.

"That's a very good likeness of you on your driver's license, by the way."

"I thought I looked pale."

"You look pale now."

"I hate jails."

"Stay out of them."

"Dad's asshole friends."

"I am furious with you."

"I know."

"And I don't give a rat's rear about the fame."

"I know."

Trevor collected his credit card and scribbled his name wherever the clerk pointed on the paperwork. He smiled at her.

"Thanks, Pam. Say hey to Bill. Sorry you won't be in the audience."

"It's okay, Trev. I can always catch you down at Gilchrist Park. Why pay when I can get it free?"

"Excellent point."

Trevor shoved his wallet into his hip pocket and turned to Katie.

"Scott and the limo?"

"Out front, engine running."

"Okay then. Let's burn some rubber."


Brian Carpenter, a bass player in a band from Port Charlotte, won the Look-Alike Contest. His girlfriend jumped up onto his hip after running, screaming, on stage. His family and friends joined her and they surrounded him in a grinning, jumping mass. The audience howled and applauded. Brian jumped all over stage, turning in circles and hugging his fellow contestants, who slapped him good-naturedly on the back. He was young. He was a fan. He worked days for a local electrician. His girlfriend had talked him into entering the contest.

Trevor, wrapping an arm around the young man's restless shoulders and making sure his face was pointed at least a few times towards the clicking cameras, eyes open and mouth shut, could completely relate to him. Who knew better than he did what a man would do to please the woman he loved?

Trevor stayed until the last fan left and the last camera clicked.

The echoing emptiness of the hall buzzed at his ears.

Scott sat on the edge of the stage, swinging his legs, his walkie-talkie in his hand. Carla sat beside him. Junior and Robbie ran all around the empty hall, whooping with glee.

Katie stood back and to one side, hugging herself.

She had watched Trevor's easy charm and good-heartedness flow steadily from him as he posed for fans with instamatic cameras and scribbled his name with the ever-present Sharpie marker on everything from CDs to shirt backs. He'd been up since 4:00 a.m, been arrested, released, played an intimate acoustic concert for two hours with no break or backup, and was still cruising along on a flow of energy some eighteen hours later, having accommodated his fans and a number of well-wishers he knew locally. He'd had no lunch or dinner and might not even eat again until the next morning.

Katie shivered, and wondered what she'd gotten herself into.

Trevor capped his Sharpie marker, stuck it in his pocket and flopped up on the stage beside Scott. He grinned at his brother and began swinging his legs, still all restless energy.

"That went well. Ya think? What nice people Brian Carpenter's got rooting for him."

Scott nodded.

"They'll have the time of their lives in Dallas, stayin' at the Hyatt."

"Did you see how happy they were for him? I feel great."

Carla shoved an open can of Dr. Pepper at Trevor and he took it gratefully.

"Thanks, Carla. Do I hear wild Indians?"

"That would be Junior and Robbie."

"Cool. Nothing like running around when you're that age."

Carla smiled.

"Voice of experience. Last year. Maybe even two days ago."

Trevor laughed and sucked down some soda.

"Jesse and Becky?"

Scott shifted tired shoulders.

"I done sent them home earlier. Jesse and her'll be halfway to Georgia in the tour bus by now. They'll have picked up the band in Tampa. Meet us all in Dallas at the Hyatt. It's just us six here now. Daddy and Mary are still up in Atlanta. I figure me and Carla and Junior'll go on over to the house on Olympia Avenue. Sleep in. Change the sheets and wash the towels tomorrow morning before we leave. I'll be parkin' the limo out to the airport again tomorrow. I'm just leavin' it here tonight in the parkin' lot. We ain't but a couple of blocks from home. We can walk it."

Trevor took another sip of soda.

"You up for dinner? We could catch some sushi from Tony at Amimoto's. Maybe some hata or some ebi-ten."

"Be more like real early breakfast, moron. It's past midnight. You want us to take Robbie with us? Them boys'll be all wound up."

Trevor glanced uncertainly at Katie. She was still hugging herself and hadn't joined their group. He gnawed on his bottom lip.

"Katie? What do you want to do?"

Katie came away from the wall, walking slowly, her arms still hugging herself.

"I want to kill you."

Scott shifted uneasily. Carla smiled. Trevor winced.

"Uh. I meant what would you like to do about letting Scott and Carla take Robbie for the night?"

"That was a very beautiful concert."

"I like playing my hometown. I know about every third person in the audience. It's an easy sell. They like me. It feels good to play to an audience predisposed to like you."

"There was new material."

"Some was part of Dad's old efforts. Did you know he once did this? A long time ago. He had some pretty stuff stored away. He and I have been working on it. Heck, we've been working on some of it since I was fifteen years old. I'm getting it out there now. He's like you, Katie. He gets queasy and barfs on stage. But he deserves credit for what he's done."

"If Scott and Carla are agreeable to taking Robbie, so am I."

Scott slid off the edge of the stage.

"Don't kill the paycheck, Katydid. I'd hate to have to actually work for a livin'."

Katie's mouth twitched in a brief smile.

"Who are you kidding, Bro? You work the same hours Trevor does."

"Well, at least I don't have to smile so much. I got others can do my job if I'm sick or feelin' lazy. We ain't found an adequate stunt-double for the moron here yet. Don't let Brian Carpenter's looks fool you. He don't play or sing Trevor's style."

Trevor continued to sit on the stage and watch his feet swing and feel his heels bump the back of the stage.

"His girlfriend's happy though."

Carla slid off the stage and leaned over to give Trevor a kiss on the cheek.

"Food. Bed. Sleep. We'll see you out at the hangar tomorrow around 10:00 a.m. Okay? I'll handle all the healthy snacks for the flight. Junior's grandmother is taking him for the duration of the tour just like before. Katie knows where Martha's house is on Marion Avenue. We'll leave Robbie there, too. Goodnight, sweetheart. Helluva concert. As usual."

Carla hooked her arm around Scott's waist and walked him slowly past Katie. Even Scott's feet were dragging. Carla smiled sympathetically at Katie

Seeing his parents moving as a unit toward the exit, Junior skidded to a halt and then dashed over to them, Robbie following his lead.

Katie watched her son trail off with what had become for him a functional extended family. She knew he'd be well cared for and happy. He liked Scott and Carla and Junior. There would be no nightmares.

At least part of that was due to the man left sitting on the empty stage behind her, she thought.

Just another lean, darkly handsome man with long hair.

Just another man.

Trevor was still watching his feet as they swung back and forth, seemingly absorbed in the rhythm.

God only knew what was going on in his head, Katie thought.

Sensing her eyes on him, Trevor looked up and glimmered a brief smile. He sighed and slid off the stage, stretching to get some of the kinks out.

"Time to go. Midge Curran needs to close up. I don't like to be thoughtless. She'll be retiring soon. I'll bet her feet hurt."

Katie turned and began slowly to walk towards the exit. She could hear Trevor's sneakers scuffing behind her and stopped to let him catch up. He didn't reach for her and she didn't reach for him.

An older woman with frizzled salt and pepper hair, wearing a navy blue skirt, white blouse, and navy blue jacket was lingering near the top of the stairs as they left the main floor of the empty auditorium. Trevor, hovering close to Katie's elbow, looked up and smiled.

"Hey, Midge. How's it goin'? Finished that restoration on Joanne's painting yet? Sorry we took so long."

"You didn't. Stay safe on that airplane of yours, Trevor. You and Scottie both. I don't want to hear about

448

another Ricky Nelson or the Leonard Skynyrd band all over again. Reba McIntyre had a real close call, too. You hear?"

"Yes, ma'am. Or, no, ma'am. Midge, I'm so tired, I don't know what I'm saying."

Midge Curran patted his shoulder as Trevor walked past her.

"Say goodnight, Trevor."

"Goodnight, Trevor."

Her chuckle followed him outside into the clean, fresh darkness of the front steps of the auditorium. Both he and Katie heard the doors lock behind them and then be rattled to make sure they were locked. Midge, it seemed, had parked in the rear.

Trevor scuffed his way across the parking lot, his hands jammed into his jeans pockets.

"This place never seems to change. It's looked the same since I first got here. Midge looks the same. Illusion. Nothing's ever the same."

He trailed under the stained gray concrete of the Gilchrist Bridge as it crossed the Peace River, following the path that connected the auditorium parking lot to the back of the Best Western Waterfront, avoiding the danger of crossing US 41 South on foot. Katie paced silently with him. Trevor glanced at her.

"This isn't where I was born or raised. Unless you count raised from my teens on. But this is my home. My hometown. My friends and family and acquaintances. It's where I want to live. And die. Certainly where I want to retire to."

Trevor scuffed his way diagonally across the parking lot of the Best Western, passing the strange Peter Toth statue of an Indian carved from an old banyan tree.

"I remember meeting my Aunt Mary for the first real time here. I tried hard not to want her in my life. The Indian's still here, I'm still here, and Mary's still here. Are you going to still be here?"

Katie hugged herself and remained silent.

449

Trevor sighed as they came out onto Retta Esplanade and walked under the arching branches of the banyan trees.

"Gilchrist Park. My first exposure to Charlotte County music. Charlotte County's first exposure to Trevor Lane's guitar playing. I still suck at harmonica. I'm never going to be Bob Dylan. Or Uncle Milt on banjo. Dead now, God bless him. Not Dylan. Uncle Milt. Dad hadn't adopted me yet. I was still a Lane. Whatever that meant. When Mary came, I found out what it meant to be a Lane. Dad taught me to be a Daniels. Scott came later for all of us. My strong right hand. I needed strength and love around me. I still do."

Katie caught up with him as they neared the house at the corner of Gill Street and Retta Esplanade. Automatic timers throughout the house and grounds kept it lit inside and out until dawn, or until they were manually turned off.

Katie slipped a hand through Trevor's arm, slowing him.

" 'Scream in Pain' was probably my first exposure to your work. After that, I went looking for more."

"I've mellowed some from there."

"Your 'Dance in the Dark' is beautiful. And I cry every time I hear 'Guitar-Man'. I don't know why. It's a very beautiful, hopeful song."

"My dad wrote that. My second dad. Jarrett."

"I know. But it's your voice singing it. I've never really liked other artists' covers of your work."

Trevor kicked at a pebble.

"You don't even know who and all's been playing and singing my stuff."

"No, not that. I mean the songs you yourself perform. The ones I associate with you. You already know how I feel about 'Free'. Junior Suggs brought absolutely nothing to 'Little Pussy'. Your original version was teasing and playful and innocent. His was lewd and suggestive."

"Same words and music."

"But definitely not the same message. When his version comes on the radio, I just turn it off."

450

"Seems you're not in the minority. He hasn't done too well with that one. Would it surprise you to know I wrote 'Hump Her' for Junior? And 'Girl, Remember What Your Knees Are For'?"

"Yes."

"Well, be prepared to be surprised. I've got stuff in me even I don't much care for. I don't think I'd do well covering Junior's versions of my own songs."

"No. You wouldn't."

"And I do a nice little trade in instrumental under another label, using my old name that I got from my first dad. Trevor Lane. It surprises the heck out of me that no one's ever put two and two together there, but they haven't. I'm rather proud of 'The Snowy Egret Suite'."

"I can't say I've ever heard it."

Trevor opened the front door for Katie. He never locked his doors in Punta Gorda.

"Come on upstairs. I'll toss an Orpheus label into the CD player and we'll chill out on the bed with Buddy."

"We will?"

"Sure. 'The Snowy Egret Suite' is chilling out music, not 'Hump Her'. I need a shower and bed. Maybe some food."

"It could be stalk-her-and-pounce music."

"No. I write that for Darren Chalmers."

"Get out."

"Yeah. You coming or not?"

<u>COME IN TO ME</u>

We stand before each other,
Naked to the skin.
You complain to me
That I'll not let you in.
Come in to me.

You're right, you know.
I've hidden in the dark.

Scared of love,
I've never shown my heart.
By letting go, I gain much more.
I'll let you in and we can soar.
Come in to me.

Sunny clouds and warm sweet air,
Flying high with wings to spare.
Such release, such freedom.
I've let go. We'll be one.
Come in to me.

You're my life.
Make me whole.
Become my wife.
I'll be your world.
Come in to me.

## Chapter Twenty

Trevor did a whirlwind tour of Texas, starting in Dallas at the Cotton Bowl.

Brian Carpenter was on stage with him there. Brian's family and friends were backstage with their passes, a grinning collection of tears and nerves and awe.

"Hello, Dallas! How's it goin'?"

It was a time of sweetness and innocence for the Carpenter clan and affiliates. Trevor left them still enjoying the amenities of the Hyatt and moved on to his next engagements.

"Hello, Fort Worth!"

"Hello, Houston!"

"Hello, San Antonio!"

"Hello, Lubbock!"

"Hello, Amarillo!"

"How's it goin'? Goin'? Goin'?"

Roadies rack it up.

Band on.

Trevor on.

Band off.

Trevor off.

Roadies break it down.

Drive through the night to the next honky-tonk or the next big city.

Over and over and over again.

He played his own music, dropping in new ones to get crowd reaction. To the hard-core country crowd of Texas, he played the hard-core country music written by Jarrett Daniels. Jarrett's tunes were toe-tapping and upbeat, his lyrics often puns on puns. The crowds loved it. With its steady four-four rhythm, it was dance-hall music, tongue-in-the-cheek flirtation and feel-good all around. It kept Trevor from falling down the pit of his own worries.

The tour bus was rolling. Trevor was sitting on the padded seat of the kitchenette, his elbows on the table, his face tight. He tapped the side of his cell phone with the palm of his hand, and then shook it.

"Is this thing dead? Does it need a new battery or something?"

Scott looked up from his doodling.

"Nope."

"Darn."

Trevor slid the cell phone back onto his belt. Scott filled in the tires of the GTO he was drawing.

"Wonder is that thing works at all."

"It's done fine all these years."

Scott glanced up at his brother's face and then down again.

"Manny's in heaven out here. He's been lookin' for good beef and he swears these Texans know a thing or two about beef."

"Glad to hear it."

"He's got a source for fresh trout, too."

"Good."

"Crowds are likin' Daddy's music."

Trevor's tight face softened.

"Yeah. I'm proud to be able to do that. Time was I never thought my voice would fit around his music. His voice always seemed deeper than mine. More like yours."

"Don't insult the man. I can't sing."

"You know what I mean. I can hear my voice. Darned if I'd pay good money to hear it. Dad's, though? Yes, sir, I would pay to hear that deep rumble.

'I'm country.

Ain't ashamed of that.

I'm country.

Got my cowboy hat.'"

"They sure did love you in that big white Stetson."

"I looked like an idiot."

"I'm sayin'."

"'I'm country.

Got my pick-up line.

Just get in the truck, honey,

You'll be mine.

I'm country.'"

"We'll be home soon, Trevor. It'll be all right."

"Katie hasn't called. Not once. Maybe she lost her cell phone."

"Maybe."

"Yeah. I know. She could go over to Mary's and Dad's and use their phone. What's happening, Scott? I told her the truth. Finally. We were getting along. I thought. Even that last night, after the contest."

"Don't give me no details."

"I wasn't going to. But I thought it was forward progress. What happened?"

"You cannot control other people, Trevor. You did the best you could."

"My best sucks."

"Then it's still your best. Live with it."

Trevor groaned and put his head down on the table. Scott filled in another tire on the GTO.

"You wanna get laid?"

"No."

"Drunk?"

"Maybe later. After the next show. I want to go home to my woman and baby. I want rid of this stupid hair. I can't wait for Locks of Love. Try to keep scissors out of my reach, will you? I'm tempted to hack it all off myself."

"I try to keep sharp objects away from you anyway. I'll admit that Stetson would have looked better to me if you didn't have all that hair. I half expected you to be in the barrel races on a pony with pink and purple ribbons on the bridle."

"Thanks."

"Don't mention it."

"I don't know how the married guys do it."

"Drugs."

"Well, I'm not going there again."

"The rest either cheat on their wives or jerk off or drink too much. Out of deference to the feelin's of others, Carla and I have been abstainin' durin' the tour."

Trevor looked up from his folded arms and twinkled a smile at his brother.

"That sucks."

"Tell me about it."

"Well, you've finally found a way to make me feel better. Thanks."

"Glad to oblige."

Trevor idly watched Scott filling in details on his picture.

"You draw. You're an artist. I guess I'm so used to seeing you do that, it never dawned on me. Robbie draws pictures. Great pictures."

"Junior does to."

"Trees. Houses. People. Trucks."

"Yep."

"He drew me."

"Good for you."

"Next town we hit, I'd like to pick up some coloring books and a pack of crayons. Maybe one of those packs with like sixty-four colors. And a pad of construction paper. Or pack. Whatever."

"Branchin' out?"

"I never did it as a kid."

"Get out."

"No. Seriously. I never did."

"This I gotta see. Trevor Daniels colorin' inside the lines."

The Texas tour was too tight to allow for trips to Gold's Gym, but the basketball and hoop came out. Trevor bought his crayons and coloring books and construction paper. Scott picked up a traveling version of Battleship.

"Hello, El Paso! How's it goin'?"

"Hello, Del Rio!"

"Hello, Paris!"

"Hello, Laredo!"

456

"How's it goin'?"

Trevor was hunched over a coloring book, intent on covering ground. Scott was watching him.

"Just how much of your childhood did you miss anyway?"

"All of it. No, that's an exaggeration. Say anything from about age two to twelve. How's that?"

"Darn, boy. That is your childhood. No wonder you're so crazy. You got all this lost time to make up."

"I've been trying."

"God knows that's true. I had no idea."

"Red's pretty cool. I like the different shades of red I can make."

"What was your favorite toy?"

Trevor grinned up at his brother.

"Santa Snake."

"Wiseguy. I meant when you was little."

"I didn't have one."

"I liked Matchbox cars."

"After the Virginia fiasco, Dad got me into Legos. I like Legos. Junior got me into trucks."

"And Robbie inspired you to artwork?"

"Yep. This is harder than it looks. There's a skill and a technique to this."

"What the heck'd you do in school? Sleep?"

"We moved a lot when I was a kid. I missed a lot of school. I was sick a lot. Probably with asthma. Who knew? Or busted up. Couldn't let anybody see that, so she kept me indoors. Really, really indoors."

Scott shifted.

"Like Chris did?"

Trevor chewed on his bottom lip, carefully coloring darker at the edges of his drawing.

"Yeah. Like Chris did. Chris was better."

"Yatztee? Risk? Checkers?"

"Nope. Sit and shut up. Later on, change the beds, do the laundry, clean, cook, sit and shut up."

"I had no idea, Trevor."

457

"It's wonderful to watch what you and Carla do with Junior. What you both and Katie do with Robbie. Just wonderful."

"Junior and Robbie don't exactly come back emotionally scarred from a visit with Uncle Trevor. You do fine yourself."

Trevor looked up and smiled, his eyes crinkling in fun.

"Thanks."

"You're welcome. Gimme a blue crayon, will ya? And a sheet of that construction paper. Make it a red one."

"Why do they put black construction paper in? You can't color on it properly. Well, a white crayon maybe, but who wants that?"

"Good at Halloween for makin' masks. And Billy-Bob teeth. 'Course, if ya get it wet, ya get black stuff on your teeth. Mom's don't much like that."

"Why not? No harm done."

"I'm sayin'."

The brothers colored and dribbled and dunked and Battleshipped their way across Texas in the wide southern arc of the tour and finally headed home, hitting a few pick-up gigs on the way, faxed to them by the ever-diligent Stephie.

They dropped Manny off in Tampa, along with Jake and assorted members of the band, and then the balance of the personnel in Sarasota. Jesse headed them down the interstate and Trevor felt his shoulders relax as the familiar exit names of home flashed by. River Road. Toledo Blade Boulevard.

The Lear jet was still in Dallas. Eventually, Scott would fly out on a commercial carrier and fly it back. The tour bus went into the hangar at the Charlotte County Airport and everyone still on it drove themselves home to family or friends. Scott and Carla planned to give themselves the balance of the day to rest and recuperate before picking up Junior. By tacit consent, the brothers' crayon artwork stayed, for now, on the tour bus.

Scott and Carla drove off in their van.

Jesse was met by Becky, who drove away with him in her Kia.

Trevor climbed into the cab of his old blue pick-up truck and just sat there.

Katie hadn't called him once in the two weeks he'd been on the road. He didn't know whether he wanted to go home to his house or not.

Finally he just curled up on the seat, pillowed his head in his arms, and drifted off to sleep in the warm Florida sunlight.

*     *     *     *     *

There was a tapping on the glass of his truck window. At first, groggy from heat and sleep, Trevor thought it was a trapped bottle fly and sat up to let it escape out the window or door. His grainy eyes fixed on his sister-in-law's concerned face beyond the scratched glass of the truck's side window.

"Trevor? Are you all right? Let me in. The door's stuck."

Shaking his head to clear it, Trevor hauled up on the door handle and put his shoulder into shoving the door open. It popped open with a deep creak of rusty metal and he shoved it wide, sliding to the edge of the seat, his long legs touching ground.

"Hey. How's it goin', Carla?"

"What are you doing here? Didn't you even go home yet? Where's Katie?"

"What? No. What are you talking about?"

"Scott and I went to pick up Junior after we'd crashed and rallied. Martha said Katie picked up Robbie about a week ago. She hasn't seen her since, which is odd, because, at least on weekends, Robbie and Junior play together."

"Katie?"

"Wake up, Trevor. What's happening?"

"I don't know. I haven't been home. I never got around to it. She didn't call me on tour, Carla. Not once. Gone? She's gone?"

"I don't know, Trevor. Maybe. Scott and I swung by your house after we picked up Junior to ask about Robbie. Your truck wasn't there. The house was locked. You never do that when you're home, or when you just go out somewhere. We got concerned and just started to follow your backtrail. And here you are. Why didn't you go home?"

Carla was searching his face and smoothing her hand down his arm. Trevor looked up to find Scott standing behind her, a worried frown on his face, his huge bulk shading the glare of the sun.

Trevor tried for a smile that never quite appeared.

"I didn't want to go home to an empty house. I guess on some level, I knew Katie'd be gone."

Scott stepped around Carla.

"Come on, kid. Come on back home with us."

Trevor shook his head.

"No. Maybe I better not drive, though."

"We'll get the truck back to you. You know the drill. Shower. Eat. Sleep. Survive. Okay?"

"Yeah. Okay."

"We'll sort all this out later. Olympia Avenue or Gill Street?"

"Gill Street. Thanks."

Scott guided a limp Trevor into the back of his van, where Trevor rolled onto his side and curled mutely up. Scott didn't bother talking to him and, angry to the roots of his placid soul, didn't attempt conversation with his wife, afraid his rage would find an inappropriate outlet.

Nobody messed with his little brother.

Carla retreated from the brothers and simply watched.

When Scott pulled the van into the bricked back area at the Gill Street house and parked it, she averted her eyes from the sight of her husband helping Trevor up off the floor of the van and into the house.

460

It was more than half an hour later that a grim-faced Scott came back out to her and climbed silently back behind the wheel of the van. He started the van, but didn't put it in gear.

"We'll be checkin' on him in another hour. We'll be stayin' here in Punta Gorda for a while. At least until Daddy and Mary get back, or Trevor snaps out of it. I'll walk over from Olympia Avenue next time. I want to stay close to him, but he needs his privacy, too."

"Of course. Whatever you want to do."

"He's my brother."

"He'd do the same for you."

"Yes, he would. He has. I didn't handle it well when Tiffany ran off with another man and left Junior and me. Trevor's done a lot for me. You have no idea."

"Love."

"Yep. It's a witch."


## SURVIVING

I was down on my luck.
Didn't have a buck.
Surviving.

Play the guitar;
Work the tip jar.
Surviving.

Then bad times got worse.
I started to curse.
I bartered my body,
And I sold my soul.
Surviving

Fate picked me up
In a dark green truck.
Surviving

Devils on earth.
It could not get worse.
Surviving.

It's funny how just
When you think you're all through
God comes along
And smiles down at you.
Surviving

I'm doing fine now
And I'll do my share.
God helped me along
And I think fair's fair.
If you're down on your luck,
I'll give you a buck.
But you'll work for it, boy.
I ain't nobody's toy.
Play me and lose
And you'll sing the blues.
Do what is right
And I'll help you fight.
Surviving.

I was down on my luck.
Didn't have a buck.
Surviving.

Play the guitar
And work the tip jar.
Surviving.

\*     \*     \*     \*     \*

Katie didn't call and Trevor didn't call her.
He went into rehearsals, and then back out on the
road, this time touring the Midwest.

He was curiously repressed, and focused, but not depressed. It was as though he had suddenly, and finally, grown up.

If he caught himself slacking, he straightened his spine and rolled his shoulders. If he caught himself staring out the window of the tour bus, he worked on a crossword puzzle, or his music. He ran. He ate. He went with Scott and Manny to available Gold's Gyms. He performed steadily and adequately. He arrived early. He left late.

But something inside him had died.

He found, though, that he could pick up the pieces and go on.

Trevor's next CD had the driving anger of rock in it and the beauty of plaintive ballads. He included complex instrumentals as well. The CD itself didn't do well, but individual tracks did surprisingly well in surprisingly different markets.

Trevor couldn't have cared less.

He pulled the scabs off old wounds and unleashed anger he'd forgotten he even had. He brought to life the story of Darryl's grandfather playing guitar. He brought to life the confusion of drugs. He brought to life hunger and despair. He wove in wonder over music and stars and running with the wind in his hair. And love.

He sent Katie an autographed copy of the CD, to his own house, hoping she had a forwarding address and hating himself. When he still didn't hear from her, he briefly hated her. Then he accepted what appeared to have been the truth. He was the only one of the two of them who had fallen in love. He'd been dancing in the dark all by himself. Then he felt foolish. And then he didn't care at all.

He channeled it all through the music machine.

He got a polite little note back from Katie thanking him for his kindness to her. He shoved it in a drawer, unable to throw it away.

# FACE THE DAWN

Come lay with me and help me face the dawn.
All my life for you I've waited long.
In the morning light I'll see
Beauty shining up at me.
Come lay with me and help me face the dawn.

It's 3:00 a.m. The roads are flashing by.
Bus, train or plane, I stare into the sky.
Glistening darkness all around.
Not one good thing to be found.
Come lay with me and help me face the dawn.

Some men yearn for beauty.
Some men live for gain.
Some men seek out glory.
Some men want to maim.

I want you beside me
Tender through the years.
I want love to guide me.
Kiss away my tears.
I'll take away your hardship.
I'll make your sorrow pass.
Gentle in the partnership,
I'm strong enough to last.

Come lay with me and help me face the dawn.
All my life for you I've wanted long.
In the morning light I'll see
Beauty shining up at me.
Come lay with me and help me face the dawn.

Back off tour again and rattling around in the house on Gill Street–now devoid of even Robbie's art gallery– Trevor decided to meander over to the Olympia Avenue house. Buddy trotted beside him, Tonto to his Lone Ranger again.

Watching the fluffy cat-fur trousers precede him, plumy tail held high, Trevor smiled. Unconditional love. He got it from Jarrett. He got it from Buddy. He gave it unconditionally back to both. He'd never been totally easy about love with Mary. And it seemed he'd been wrong about love with Katie. Not Robbie. He loved Robbie. Robbie loved him. He could tell.

Trevor cut off his train of thought before a pit could open at his feet and suck him in.

Gray tabby cat trotting down the sidewalk. Clear lungs. Sun on his shoulders. Life was good, he thought.

That steadied him as he bounded up the back steps to his old home, following Buddy in.

There was classical music coming from the stereo, a weeping fall of violins. He should have known that Jarrett wasn't home. He followed Buddy through the kitchen and watched him jump up beside Mary on the couch. She put down her needlepoint to stroke his fur and looked up.

"Hello, darling. Come on in. Jarrett's out fishing with Scott and Junior. You know I abhor that. Carla's taking a well-deserved break with Becky. Dr. Pepper? You know your father. I'm sure there's quite a collection of it in the fridge."

Trevor smiled wanly and doubled back for a can of Dr. Pepper. Skirting Jarrett's recliner, he sat down next to Mary on the old plaid couch, Buddy between them, and tapped the top of his can before opening it. It was an old habit he'd picked up from Jarrett. A meaningless one, he thought, but ingrained.

He sucked down a mouthful of soda, concentrating on the sharp, bubbly goodness to keep his mind from wandering to dark places.

Mary tilted her head, considering the curiously blank profile beside her.

"You're going through a difficult time."

Trevor smirked and sucked down more soda.

"Nice phrasing."

"I'm trying to be diplomatic."

"Waste of time. I'll get over it. Well, I guess I'll shove off. Thanks for the soda."

"Sit."

Trevor frowned over at his aunt.

"Okay."

"Maybe we need to talk."

Trevor groaned and rolled his eyes. Mary gave the back of his hand a brief tap with her hand.

"Stop that. I'm not Jarrett, but I love you and I'm worried about you."

"No need to. I'll be fine."

"You've never been comfortable in Shawn's world, have you? My fault."

"No, I haven't. How does it get to be your fault, Mary?"

"I was the one who introduced you to that world. I should have done a better job."

"Not your fault. That world is a very serious world. They take their music seriously. And Shawn's. And mine. I just never warmed up to all that seriousness. I like to have fun. That's not a very fun-loving crowd, Mary."

"They have fun in a different way, Trevor."

"There you go. Not my style. I can fake it for short periods of time, but I can't hold it together for too long. Gotta run. Gotta romp. Gotta laugh."

"So like your mother."

Trevor frowned and drew back from Mary a little.

"Hey. No need to insult me. Has Stephie had any complaints about my behavior? I tighten it up for the sake of the music."

"No insult intended, darling. Your mother had her good points. She was very fun-loving, too."

"You couldn't prove it by me."

"And, no, I've heard no complaints about your behavior when you're playing Trevor Lane Daniels."

"Lisa was fun-loving, huh? You couldn't have said anything to make me change my ways faster."

"I didn't intend that, Trevor. I'm far from forgiving Lisa for what she did to you. She is a very warped, self-centered, unhappy person. But to give the devil her due, she did have some good qualities. She just had everything to excess."

"Like me. No limits. Swell."

"Do you not see essential differences, Trevor? Spirit? Intent? The soul, if you will? Satan is often depicted with wings, as a fallen angel. Some fly upward, Trevor. Shawn did. You did. Lisa flew downward. There is nothing essentially wrong with your fun-loving ways reminding me of my sister in her better days. Your fun-loving has never been evil, or harmful to others."

"Okay. I'm glad. You had me worried there for a while."

"Lisa was a fallen angel, Trevor. A blight to you. A curse to herself."

Mary reached across Buddy and picked up Trevor's hand, sandwiching it between hers. Much as his Grammy had done when she had wanted to get his undivided attention, Trevor thought.

"Trevor, you are beset by well-wishers and good advice. I've tried to stay out of the advice category, but I'm worried about you. You say you want this relationship with Katie, but I never saw any signs of it."

Trevor shook his head as though to clear it.

"What? I'm going nuts here. I've told her every secret I could think of. I've made it possible for her to have a secure, sufficient income and all that stuff. I'm more than pleased to know Robbie, and to have gotten to be a part of his life. She didn't even call me on the Texas tour, Mary. She didn't call me on the Midwest tour. Scott sucks in his gut, grins at Carla and they fall in love. It wasn't this hard to get

467

you and Jarrett together. And you don't see any signs that I want a lasting, loving relationship with Katie?"

"No, I don't. I see Lisa with her johns giving her gifts."

"Katie's not like that. You gave her a clean bill of health as a barracuda yourself."

"Not Katie, Trevor. It's you I see the Lisa in."

"What?"

"Not the giver of the goodies, Trevor. I see you as the recipient of the goodies. Lisa would take and take and never give back. Maybe she was a black hole. I hope you aren't."

"Black hole? Can I get a translation here? I'm lost."

"You, like Lisa's johns, have been very generous. You, being Trevor though, never sought to buy your lady with goods. Katie is not Lisa. Katie is not a barracuda. Katie gives you back what she can, and what you will let her give. Her love. The love of her son. Her body. Her soul. She gets back stuff, Trevor. What is the one thing that Katie wants to receive? What is the thing that Lisa would or could never give?"

"I give love to Katie! I love her."

"Self, Trevor. You will not give of your self."

Trevor's mouth was hanging open in shock.

"I've told her everything now."

"Verbal stuff. Material stuff. You will not let her inside you. Maybe you're not capable of it. I thought you were with Jarrett. Never with me."

"Mary! I love you."

"I still remind you just enough of your mother that you don't open up to me, either. Maybe it's women, Trevor. Maybe only women you want opening up to you. Maybe it's any person you think you love. But I could swear it's different with Jarrett. With Jarrett, I could swear you have no limits or barriers between the two of you."

Limits, he thought. Barriers?

"Tell me what to do."

"I don't know, Trevor. Do you feel you're open with Jarrett?"

"Yes."

Trevor smiled to himself, remembering even the physical feel of relaxing into total trust and love.

"Oh, yes."

"Try to find that feeling within yourself again, Trevor. What made you open up to Jarrett?"

Trevor chewed on his bottom lip.

"Fear. No. Not fear. Need. Desperation. My need was greater than my fear. I literally felt I had nothing to lose because I felt I'd lost everything already."

"Not fear, then. A liberation so great that it surpasses basic survival instincts. Jumping out into space and trusting the air will hold you aloft. Pure freedom."

"So. I have to be even more desperate than I think I am now, huh?"

Trevor sighed and slumped. Mary shook her head.

"You've made progress somehow, darling. I feel that if Katie would agree to marry you now, the two of you could manage a perfectly adequate union for the duration. But is that what you want?"

"Jarrett told me never to settle for less than edgy cancelled out by aaaah."

Mary chuckled.

"How very like him."

"I refuse to be like Lisa. I'm not having it."

"Then give Katie the one gift she really wants. Give her you. You had a miserable childhood, Trevor. Years of it. But you've now had even more years of the best emotional support and love that Jarrett and I could possibly give you."

Mary leaned over to gently kiss Trevor's hair.

Buddy stirred and got down, drifting unobtrusively out his cat door to cat pursuits.

Mary gripped Trevor's hand.

"Trevor, what Jarrett calls your 'sugar tanks' still run frighteningly low at times. I was never the one you came to to have your sugar tanks filled up."

Suddenly Trevor swept Mary into his arms and onto his lap, surprising her both with the suddenness of the move and with his physical strength. He gripped her shoulders firmly and looked her fiercely in the eyes. He couldn't remember a time when they had been this physically close before.

"Try now. Try to fill my sugar tanks. I'll try to let you."

Trevor put his arms around Mary, engulfing her small frame. Mary put her arms as far around Trevor as she could and felt him make a concentrated effort to relax. She smoothed his back and that seemed to help.

He mumbled into her hair, "I'm not Lisa."

"No, Trevor. Neither you nor I are Lisa. If this struggle is what Katie feels when the two of you are together, no wonder she worries about what's going on inside your head."

Trevor relaxed more and felt better about it. Every time he got a jolt of fear or uncertainty, he shoved it ruthlessly down mentally and tried for the inner psychic bond he felt when he was with Jarrett.

When it finally hit, it was like a warm rush of air and he let it take him up into clouds and sunshine. He felt his face relax into a smile and a chuckle worked its way up from his toes.

"Sugar. I can feel sugar."

Mary gripped him tightly.

"Oh, Trevor. This is the way you felt as a baby. A glowing ball of sunshine in my arms. You haven't lost it. I can feel you opening up to me the way you did as a baby. Not missing-in-action any longer, darling. You're found. You're home. Oh, sweetheart."

Mary's face was streaming with tears. Trevor was still soaring on the warm updraft of love.

"Got my sugar tanks filled. How are yours, Mary?"

"Filled. Filled to the top. Wonderful. Thank you."

Mary pulled out of his arms, wiping her face on the backs of her hands.

"What a mess I must look. I feel like an idiot."

Trevor kissed her enthusiastically on the cheek.

"No crying. That's illegal. That's cheating. I can't handle crying women."

"Neither can Jarrett. Lock on those sugar tanks, Trevor. Internalize that feeling of release and joy. Bring that to your lady. There's nothing in the world like shared love."

## EVERY LOVE SONG ALWAYS SOUNDS THE SAME

Every love song always sounds the same.
This is just another. It sounds lame.
Holding you fills up my heart.
I loved you right from the start.
Every love song always sounds the same.

Be my bride and raise a family.
I'll crawl to you stripped naked, cheerfully.
Pull me from my hermit's cave.
Let me lay down in your grave.
Every love song always sounds the same.

Lean on me.
I'll lean on you.
We'll lean together through the years.
I'll feed your soul.
With me grow old.
We'll take the laughter with the tears.
Every love song always sounds the same.

I love you. Please love me.
You love me? Can it be?
Every love song always sounds the same.
Every love song always sounds the same.

# Chapter Twenty-One

The following week, it was Jarrett on the phone to Trevor.

"Son? Are you all right?"

"Oh, yeah. I'll do. I'm in neutral. Chugging away in neutral, but I'm not going Ferndale over this. I guess I conned myself. I miss her, but I got an education about myself."

"That's my boy. Spin that straw into gold. Carla's pregnant."

"No shit! That's great. Babies. We're gonna have babies. I love babies."

"I know, son. A new chance every nine months. Scott and Carla make good parents. They've got the knack. And we've had a new name added to the waitin' list of people wantin' to go on tour with the band."

"Who now? Bill Clinton?"

"Keturah Mercer."

"Suit yourself. Any relation to Mrs. Earl Mercer? The lady I used to cut lawns for?"

"Wake up, son. It's Katie."

Jarrett heard the pause.

"Katie? Our Katie?"

"Yep."

"What the hell now?"

"I couldn't say, son."

"Suit yourself. Bump her up in line, but let her have the standard interview. She giving me as a reference?"

"Nope. We just been passin' the list around so the rest of the team could cross off anyone they knew was an obvious dud or circle anyone they knew was okay. Margaret's the one who tumbled to it. Sure enough, on her resume she lists Keturah's as her current employer, putting herself as manager."

"She's still there?"

"Apparently so. Keturah's is runnin' a profit. She's gettin' good ink for Keturah's Closet. Sales of your longhair

472

music is steady from up there. Looks like she might have made better use of Stephie's parties for the family business than you did. Her address isn't The Ice Palace, though."

"I know. She sent me a note thanking me for my kindness in letting her stay there and at Gill Street."

"Ouch."

"Yeah. Do what you want. If you don't think she'll be able to hack it, don't hire her. If she's looking to switch jobs, there's plenty to do in the organization that doesn't involve the romance of the road."

"Stephie liked her."

"Let Stephie hire her."

"Son, she didn't apply for a position with Stephie's group. She applied for one that'll put her under your feet 24/7. And she didn't try to use you to get it."

"Prideful witch."

Jarrett chuckled.

"Takes one to know one."

"What about Robbie? A mother's job is to make a home for her son."

"We'll make a point of askin' that in the interview."

"Do what you want. I'm fine either way."

$$*\quad*\quad*\quad*\quad*$$

It was the truth as far as Trevor knew it.

He was wrong.

He caught some bad road rash when his heart lost its balance and fell all over again in love with her. He channeled that, too. Into work. Into running. Into the gym. Into the music. Channeling and draining and discarding the excess emotion.

Jarrett and Mary agreed to take over the care of Robbie for Katie during the upcoming tour of the upper Midwest.

Katie was nervous and Trevor was aloof.

Katie moved back into the Gill Street house temporarily. Free housing was part of her job benefit

473

package in the newly created position of Trevor Daniels' personal assistant-in-training.

They faced one another over breakfast, Katie playing with her now empty glass of orange juice.

"You're absolutely gorgeous."

Trevor shrugged.

"Well, this is a new tactic. Get real. Nobody's absolutely gorgeous."

"You are. It scares me."

"White bread scares you. Geez. Listen, how I look is an accident of birth. Yeah, there's times I'd rather not look like me. I guess we all have those days. Too bad. This is it. Take it or leave it. I can't change it. I won't change it. At times, I've considered the merits of wearing a bag over my head. Today isn't one of those days. Deal with it."

Trevor slammed his glass of orange juice down on the table, exasperated male radiating from every inch of him.

"As to the body, I worked hard to get this body, dammit. And I work hard to keep it. Not as hard as Scott works at keeping his. I'm not into pain. How would you feel if I told you I'm scared of you? Huh? Well?"

"You are? Oh, Trevor."

"What? What did I say? Geez."

Katie slid her unfinished eggs over to Trevor. She knew he hated waste.

Trevor shoved them back at her.

"Eat 'em yourself or feed 'em to Buddy."

"Dani came over with more prototypes for costumes."

"Dani's out of control. I'm beginning to feel like a Ken doll. She bring anything that doesn't make me look like a fag?"

"There was a fairly nice vest."

"Describe."

"Medium brown suede, long fringe on the bottom and at the yoke, front and back. There may have been some beads, very small, black and white. That might have been a trick of the light. She was moving very fast."

"That's Dani for you. Always fast."

Katie picked at her eggs.

"I understand men consider that a virtue in a woman."

"Very funny. Anything else? Vest sounds good."

"Why are you being such a witch today?"

"Witch? I'm being a witch?"

"Listen to yourself."

Trevor dropped his forehead onto the table and then bumped it twice.

"Katie. Maybe my nerves would all go away if you'd just sleep with me again. Whatdya say?"

"What I've said before. No. Thank you. It's not considered maybe even legal to sleep with your employees, Trevor."

"There was a time you wouldn't sleep with me before I was your employer."

"I didn't know you well enough."

"Do you know me well enough now?"

"Not really. And now you're my employer."

"I may be destined to be a witch for a while."

"Go get laid."

"God knows I'm trying."

"Not me, silly. Some willing floozie."

"Thank you for that description of my partners of consent."

"I know a man has needs."

"And you don't? Isn't this some sort of reverse chauvinism?"

"So just go get your needs met. Or have a friend over."

"It's not quite a choice between a whorehouse or a slumber party. This is ridiculous. I'm going running. I need a good run."

"You run?"

"Like the wind."

"I've never seen you run."

"Well, that's kind of the point. I slip out and run. Then I slip back in and work."

"Oh. Jogging. I've seen jogging."

"Maybe you've seen Scott jogging. You'll never see me doing any jogging. I run."

"Can I come watch?"

Trevor frowned at her, puzzled.

"It's not like an Olympic event or anything. I go out. I come in. End of story."

"Where do you run?"

"Wherever I am."

"When you're here, in this house, where do you run?"

"Oh. I get it. Parks work out best for me. Lots of underbrush to crash through. I love that. Uneven terrain. I drive over to a park and run. I ran on Longboat Key once, but someone called the cops, saying there was a fleeing felon in the neighborhood. You know, long hair, running too fast. So I stick to parks."

"Can I come?"

"Why would you want to?"

"To watch you run."

"Knock yourself out. Well, then. Are you ready?"

"For what?"

"I thought you just said you wanted to watch me run. For whatever reason."

"Yes."

"Well, come on then."

Trevor stood up, guzzled his orange juice, washed, rinsed and set his glass to dry in the dish drainer.

Katie feverishly did the same with her egg plate and fork and juice glass.

"Aren't you going to change clothes?"

"Into what?"

"Running clothes."

"Please. I got dressed this morning. This is pretty much it for me for today. Grab a book to read. You might get bored."

476

Katie grabbed a book.

They took the pickup truck, a vehicle, Katie reflected, that must have annoyed the Longboat Key neighbors to no end.

Trevor drove his usual full throttle to Kiwanis Park in Port Charlotte and jerked the truck to a stop under some trees.

He was out of the truck almost before it stopped, leaving the door open and the keys swinging in the ignition. Katie watched open-mouthed as he tore across a partially cleared area and crashed gleefully into a wall of underbrush, thrashing out of sight.

The truck engine clicked and cooled. The keys finally stopped swinging and Katie leaned on her own door, shoving mightily on it to force it creakingly open. Deep in the woods, she could hear thrashing and an occasional whoop, followed by cackles of laughter.

No wonder the residents of Longboat Key had called the police, she thought.

Katie climbed onto the hood of the truck and opened her book. She had read more than twenty pages, her ears growing used to the distant sounds of thrashing, when Trevor burst from a nearby clump of palmetto, making her jump.

He was sweating, panting, grinning and covered in twigs and leaves, his hair wild.

"Wow! What a run! Get off my truck. You'll scratch the paint."

Katie frowned at him under her brows.

"What paint?"

"Okay. It's a little oxidized by the Florida sun."

"A little?"

"A lot. You'll have paint dust on your butt. And red primer dust, too. Get off there, woman."

Katie slid to the ground, using the sagging front bumper to ease her trip. Trevor leaned on the hood, dripping sweat onto his precious paint job. His elbows and forearms came away white with oxidized paint when he stood up again, hands on hips, lifting and bending one leg after the other.

Katie tucked her book under one arm.

"Leg cramps?"

"Some. Great run, though. I love this park. Heck, I love all parks."

"You should live near one."

"I should. Good idea."

"I didn't get to see you run."

"I told you it wasn't much of a spectator sport."

"I could hear you, though."

"Gotta be quick to catch me running."

"What do you do now?"

"Well, I like doing cartwheels, but I'm too winded right now."

"No, silly. Do you get a Swedish massage or something?"

"No. Maybe a shower. There's that change of clothes you wanted. If I'm hungry, I eat. I drink lots of water. If it's shaken me loose, I write. If I'm still all wired, I might slap on the rollerblades. The neighbors don't mind that. It's civilized. Jumping jacks are good, too. Got a punching bag out in the garage. Scott likes that. Me, I'm pretty much a pussy about messing up my hands, so I just bounce around for a while."

"You could get a trampoline."

"My insurance agent would have a fit. Never mind my homeowner's insurance company. No, I'll stick to running. No special equipment needed. Ready to roll?"

Trevor slid into the cab of the truck again.

"Listen. I apologize for being a witch earlier. I was. I'm sorry. Glad you pointed it out. That's when I knew it was time to run. You told me to listen to myself, and I did. Thanks."

"You're welcome. You're the strangest man."

"I've heard that before."

Trevor slammed his door and started the engine.

Katie scrambled in, half afraid Trevor would pull out of the park without her.

"You had a swimming pool in Sarasota."

"Yep."

"I've never actually seen you in it. You sit on the side with your legs dangling in."

"The pool came with the house."

"You don't like swimming pools?"

"They don't like me. You think I look gorgeous? You've never seen me swim. Did you bring a swim suit when you moved back in? Good. We'll go for a swim. That oughta put paid to this gorgeous thing."

Trevor slammed the truck into reverse and then into first, bumping unconcernedly over a concrete barrier he had forgotten was there.

"Oops. Sorry. Forgot."

"For months you've been trying to get me to like you."

"Yep."

"But today you've been trying to get me to hate you, or be afraid of you. Or whatever. And now you're trying to prove you're not even good-looking. What's with that?"

Trevor paused briefly to glance right and left before turning onto Midway Boulevard.

"Well, I figured I tried to woo you. That didn't work. Friendship didn't work. Gratitude didn't work. I've run out of positive attributes. You don't like what you've seen so far, so, I figured, what the heck. You might as well see witchy. And cranky. And wired up. Oh, and speed demon. Well, you're still here. I'll tell you, speed demon has scared its fair share of people off."

"Why? You're just whooping and crashing and running around."

"That seems to be the main complaint. That I'm whooping and crashing and running around."

"You're not harming anyone."

"Nope. Doing myself a world of good."

"Then the heck with those people."

479

"So, since you don't seem put off by speed demon, we'll try drowned rat next. That ought to get a giggle. It's hard to be gorgeous if women giggle at you."

Trevor turned to Katie, biting his lower lip.

"You're seeing the me most people never see. How do you like it so far?"

"I like it better than the other one."

Trevor smiled and nodded.

"Cool. When I take my shower, you can loofah my back."

"That's not in my job description."

"If I solemnly promise not to jump you, will you loofah my back? Not my front. Not my butt. Just my back."

"Trevor, you're scaring me."

"Oh, never mind then. I'll take a quick shower, change into my swim trunks and try for a pity fuck. Fair enough?"

Katie caught herself laughing at him before she realized she really wasn't afraid of this open, boyish Trevor.

"You know, Trevor, what you do isn't who you are. What you do is because of who you are. Who are you?"

At US 41, Trevor waited for a break in traffic before turning right to head back to Punta Gorda.

"I'm Trevor Lane Daniels. All of them. Clown. Idiot. Liar. Musician. Composer. Sometimes whore. On many levels."

"You run. Like no one I've ever seen or heard about. You enjoy. Again, like no one I've ever met. You go to extremes all the time. Emotional. Physical. Why is that? Who are you? Why do you do the things you do?"

"I run to stay sane. I figured that one out a long time ago. I won't stop running. I can't. It's physiological. I didn't know that word when I was a kid. I just tumbled to what worked. Periods of physical inactivity literally drive me crazy. I cannot and I will not stop running."

"I'm not asking you to. Why would you think that I would? I'm just trying to understand. Extremes?"

"Limits. No limits. Trying to find the limits. Trying to set up the boundaries. We've been here before."

"I'm not trying to make you angry. I'm trying to understand why you feel you have to always test the limits. Of your music? That I can understand. Of your body? Why?"

"It's mine. In the world I grew up in, it and my mind and my imagination were all I had. I needed to know where my limits were. I've found my imagination has no limits in any direction. That's been a curse at times. I can scare myself. I don't need anything outside my own skull to scare me. I've already done it. My mind? Okay. I'm bright enough. Sometimes too bright. Sometimes dumb as a rock. It depends. Got a weird mind, but I know its limits now. Body? That's the weakest. Can't fool the lungs. God knows I've tried. I'm locked into a minimum of two medications twice a day for the rest of my life plus a third one I carry in my pocket for emergencies. I'm working on the rest of my body piece by piece at Gold's Gyms. Even on tour."

"What about your emotions?"

"What about them?"

"They were significantly missing in that last dissertation."

"Weakness. Got a weakness for emotions. Extremes. Can't rein it in. I've tried. You try."

"Why would you want to rein your emotions in? It's beautiful to see you diving headlong into something. A flower. Rust spots on the truck. Me. Why rein it in?"

"Because it hurts. You've seen the positive emotions. You haven't seen the negative ones. Hate I've got under control. Outrage? Working on it."

"What's missing, Trevor?"

"Fear. Loneliness. Got no limits. No bottom. I've looked down into that well. I've been down that well. It's deep, and dark, and it has no bottom. I cannot go into the well safely. Hence the shrink. Dad taught me tricks to use long ago. They work. Most times. We used to help one another out of our own personal wells. It's easier to help someone else than do for yourself. I'm an emotional cripple."

"Trust?"

"Goes with the fear. Flip side, so to speak. I told you once my worst fear. Didn't believe me? Too bad."

"I don't mean to make you defensive and angry. Abandonment? Yes, we discussed that. The woman who left you?"

Trevor gritted his teeth and narrowed his eyes.

"Was my mother. After a decade of abuse, sensory depravation, and starvation for love, affection and common decency as well as food. This is not a pretty world when you're young and defenseless. If I do what I do and it harms no one, and it helps me, I'll be damned if I'll quit it, even for you."

"Let me in."

Trevor blinked, reminded of Mary's almost identical words.

"No."

Katie's face turned an unbecoming red at the blunt refusal, her cheekbones shiny. Her tiny body vibrated with her fury.

"All right. You're a great one for the bottom line and the straight skinny. Here's mine. I will not become involved with a man who is a liar. I've had that. I will not do that again."

"There were reasons I lied to you. They were important to me at the time. Then it all got out of hand."

"Did you just hear yourself, you arrogant bastard?"

"Son-of-a-bitch. The technical term. Remember? Do you want an explanation? Maybe if you hear it, you'll even see this as amusing."

"No, I don't want an explanation. Whoever you are. Trevor Daniels. Ski Colorado. Got any others?"

"No. Didn't you ever read the 'The Prince and the Pauper'? 'Cyrano de Bergerac'?"

"You're not a prince and you're not ugly. That's fiction, Mr. Whoever-you-are! I'm real. You lied to me, not to someone else. I take that personally. You want me to listen to an explanation? You listen to me. Are you listening?"

Trevor drew a careful breath.

"I'm listening."

"How would you feel if I had been the one to lie to you?"

Katie was quivering with rage, tears shining in her eyes. Trevor finally put the shoe on the other foot.

"Betrayed."

Katie nodded.

"Humiliated."

She blinked. Trevor continued.

"Foolish. Heartbroken."

Katie's tears spilled over. Trevor felt his throat squeezing tight.

"What can I do to make it right?"

Katie flung her arms wide.

"I don't know. Maybe nothing. I want you to feel what I'm feeling."

"I am. I was wrong. Stupid. Then chicken. I never meant to do you harm."

"It doesn't matter. I got harmed. Again."

"Don't blame yourself. You weren't gullible. Katie, I'm not Charlie. I'm not after your mom's money. I would never knowingly harm you. Robbie? I would never, never, never. I can't even say the words for that in the same breath as his name. I just would never ever. I lied to you to protect myself."

"Protect?"

"If I explain, you'll call me arrogant again."

"I'll call you an arrogant liar."

"If you thought Charlie was after your mother's money, how do you think I feel about anyone I think might be after mine? It's a Daniels family tradition to hide the money. Not from the IRS, but from opportunists. Anyone I meet, unless they're wealthier than I am–and sometimes

483

that's not even a qualifier–has the potential to be an opportunist after the money."

"That's so much bull."

"Protection, Katie."

"Carla didn't go through all this."

"Scott isn't Trevor. In many ways. Scott doesn't have a problem with trust. I do."

"You don't trust me? Me? You're a liar."

"How could I know? You were some stranger on the highway. 'Hi, I'm Trevor Daniels. Want a lift?' Would you have believed me?"

The redness was fading from Katie's face and her eyes were no longer swimming in tears.

"No. Probably not. You could have been Ski then. I can understand the practical side of that. But later?"

Trevor shifted.

"When?"

"You're back to excuses now. I can tell. I can always tell."

"Well, I'm not much of a liar."

"Yes, you are, if volume counts."

"I don't lie well. I don't lie efficiently or effectively. It bothers my conscience."

"Not enough to make you stop."

"Fear outweighed the soul. Katie, do we have a future? Am I wasting both our lives over this? Am I wasting time? What can I do to make it right? Do you want a future together?"

Katie squared her shoulders, her face still stormy.

"I want the real Trevor Daniels. I don't want the actor. I don't want the showman. I don't want that stiff in a monkey suit."

"They're me, Katie. They're all me."

"I'm not sure I've met the real you yet."

"That guy on the interstate. That's me."

"Not for long, it wasn't. If at all. By 8:00 p.m. that night, you were certainly lying to me."

Trevor felt his anger rise.

484

"At Big Dog's. Yes. How could I tell you who I was there? You saw what happened when we were just downstairs for food. Upstairs on Tuesdays is all about music and musicians. 'And introducing now, amateur musician, Trevor Daniels.' Swell."

"You were hiding."

Trevor lashed out.

"Yes. And I'd do it again."

"But you didn't have to hide from me."

"Yes, I did. How could I tell if you were a barracuda or not?"

"And that model? Bambi?"

"Bobbi."

"She's not a barracuda?"

"She is. But both of us know it. We had an arrangement. I told you the truth. I haven't been involved sexually with anyone since the day we met. I gave Bobbi my goodbyes by phone a week after you and I met."

"I haven't been involved sexually with anyone, either."

"Maybe you're used to it. I'm not."

Katie sucked in her breath, her eyes going wide.

"Bastard."

"Son-of-a-bitch. I keep telling you. Get it straight."

Katie screamed her rage, and planting her hands on Trevor's nearest shoulder, gave him a huge shove, surprising him into swerving the truck.

Afraid of an accident, Trevor pulled the truck quickly to the side of US 41 and threw it into park. He grabbed Katie's wrists before she could do anything further and squeezed just hard enough to get her attention.

"So. You're the physically abusive one. Not me. You're another tiny witchy broad with a bad temper. I hate tiny witchy broads with bad tempers that get physical. Do you beat Robbie when he ticks you off? Do you backhand him across the room? Does he cry in a closet in the dark, starving while you go out? Do you tie him up? Do you sell his body?"

Trevor snapped himself off, aware that Katie had gone oddly still under his hands. He tried to steady himself. He glanced away from her, then concentrated on looking out the windshield. Katie scarcely breathed.

"Trevor?"

Trevor glanced over, then away again. Katie didn't struggle.

"Let me in, Trevor."

He shook his head. Katie sat very still.

"Then let me go."

Trevor bit his bottom lip, and shook his head again. Katie relaxed.

"It's not about being a barracuda, is it?"

Trevor shook his head again. Katie sagged.

"You're afraid of women? No, that can't be. Physical intimacy? No, I don't think so. Closeness. Oh, Trevor."

Trevor released her hands then, but still wouldn't look at her. Katie folded her hands in her lap.

"You were telling me the truth. You were lying to protect yourself. And you lie badly. But I'm very gullible, so it took me longer to catch you at it."

"I was coming clean after Locks of Love."

"We'll never know now whether that's the truth, a lie, or wishful thinking."

"What do you want to know?"

"Nothing. I can read the biographies."

"They're not complete. Margaret's won't be, either."

"I don't want facts and figures. I don't want history."

"History has a way of repeating itself."

"Does it? Am I destined to fall in love with charming, lying men? Am I destined to fall in love with sadistic, cheating pedophiles?"

"Neither. I'm neither. You control your own destiny."

"And you? Do you see yourself as marrying only tiny women who are abusive? Or ones who want your money, power and fame?"

"I hope not."

"Do you want the Chevy Lumina back?"

"Of course not. Do you think I want to see you hitching on the interstate again? That was a voluntary gift. You were never ever to know where that came from. You never would have, except that I couldn't stay away from you."

"Do you want a prenuptial agreement? Should we ever part, I only take with me what I brought into the marriage? I'll agree to that."

"No. What nuptial?"

"You've asked me for sex. I'm your employee now. You've asked me to live with you. I will not shack up with you. I have a child to consider. We only ever slept together when Robbie was out of the house. You asked me to marry you."

"I didn't think I was still in the running for any of it."

"Don't lie to me. Don't cheat on me. Don't hurt me or my baby."

"Don't cheat on me. Don't hurt me or your baby. Never leave me. Never hide Robbie from me."

Trevor paused.

"Can we define sex?"

"Cock, internally. Consensual pleasuring."

Trevor licked his lips.

"Mouth?"

"Agreed. What about your money?"

"What about it?"

"Don't you want that in the agreement somewhere?"

Trevor gave her a sudden cheeky grin.

"Heck, no. You're agreeing to never leave me. The money's not going anywhere. You're not going anywhere."

"I could spend you blind."

"You? It'd kill you to own two pairs of black shoes simultaneously. I'm not worried about the money."

"So, it was never about the money?"

Trevor shifted, his grin fading.

"Not really. It was about safety. We Daniels men seem to have a real weakness for choosing the wrong kind of lady for our first wives. My first dad did, too. If I get what I want in a wife, she can have all the darned money."

"What do you want, Trevor?"

He could hear his deceased grandmother's voice in his head. *'What do you want this bright beautiful day that the Good Lord has given us?'*

"I want love. Compassion. Warmth. Touch. Respect. Safety. You?"

"I want love. Compassion. Safety. Honesty. Kindness. Respect. Marriage."

"I think we've got a deal."

"I think we do."

"I'm still psyched up to come clean after the Locks of Love."

"There's more? My God, Trevor."

"I want you to see the real Trevor Lane Daniels. No one has seen this person since before even Stephie was born. This is before Jarrett. You'll never find any of this in those biographies. And it certainly won't be in Margaret's. You'll know things that Jarrett doesn't know. You'll know things that my birth mother, wherever she may be, doesn't know. Not to mention Aunt Mary. You'll be the one woman who knows it all."

Katie risked a hand up to Trevor's arm. She could feel the energy pulsing through him. Trevor brought his clear gray gaze defensively to her face. She put her other hand up to his cheek, just brushing it with her fingertips.

"Please don't be afraid of me, Trevor. I'll never intentionally harm you."

"I'm nuts. Everyone knows it."

"Please don't try to chase me away again."

Trevor glimmered a brief smile.

"Busted."

"We agreed that mouths are okay, didn't we?"

"Oh, yeah. I distinctly remember mouths as being okay."

"I don't want you to clean my ears right now. But I'd like to work up to that again."

"Oh, yeah. Bed's good for that. Horizontal. Private. Kiss? Maybe a little fondle?"

Katie slid over on the seat to him.

"I thought we were going swimming."

"Oh, yeah. That's right. I'm trying for my pity fuck."

Katie shoved his upper arm and then kissed it.

"We seem to conduct a lot of business on the sides of roads in your truck. Maybe we should move on now."

The house on Gill Street didn't have a swimming pool, but the Best Western Water Front across the street on Retta Esplanade did. It was a Daniels family tradition to use it, with the permission of the manager. Trevor felt a certain sense of *deja vu* when he pulled on his black swim trunks and a worn University of Delaware T-shirt with the arms hacked off. He and Jarrett had packed fried chicken into a cooler with some Dr. Pepper and spent the day at the pool when he was a boy. Jarrett had tried to teach him how to swim. He'd never advanced past survival in the water. He loved water. He just couldn't seem to swim in it.

Katie met him downstairs in a tank top and Daisy Duke cut-offs. They walked the short blocks to the pool, carrying sunscreen and towels, both with sunglasses on, Trevor with his hair braided down his back.

The green and yellow canopy around the hotel hadn't changed. The cabana with its palm-thatched roof was the same. The lounge chairs were new, or re-webbed, a glistening white. The hot tub had been filled in and planted with bushes, mulched and edged.

Trevor chose one lounge chair and tossed his towel down, toeing off his sneakers. He grinned down at Katie from his towering height.

"Sunscreen? I'll do your back if you'll do mine."

"I'll pass. Keep your shirt on."

"Okay. Just offering. Well, here goes. Prepare to be dazzled. No woman not related to me has ever seen me in a swimming pool."

Trevor walked to the far side of the pool and jumped in feet first. Katie came to watch him. Trevor surfaced and began to dog paddle towards her, his chin well out of the water, his dark braid a wet tail behind him. Katie sat down on the edge of the pool, swinging her legs.

Trevor paddled up to her and grabbed the edge of the pool, clinging to it and moving his legs. Katie smiled at him.

"That's adorable."

"No pity fuck, huh?"

"Whatever for? You're cute when you're wet."

"It didn't seem to be so cute when I was wet at age fifteen and dog-paddling."

"Fifteen year old boys are so sensitive."

"And fifteen year old girls are so insensitive. A giggle could slay me back then."

"You do look like a drowned rat, but you're still gorgeous."

"Darn. No gains there. You coming in? I know you know how to swim."

Katie slid into the pool beside him.

"I float."

"Swim. Float. Whatever."

Katie moved into his arms. She placed her lips against his chest and felt him shiver.

Trevor gripped her elbows.

"If we're going to get personal, tow me into the shallow end of the pool."

Katie did so and then put her arms around his waist and they drew one another closer together, Trevor tucking her head under his chin and closing his eyes.

"Oh, yeah. This feels great."

"Kind. We will be kind to one another."

"We'll be a lot of things to one another, but kind will definitely be one of them. Do you think it would be possible to buy off your ex-husband?"

Katie kissed Trevor's chest again.

"What in the world are you talking about?"

"Cash money. I'd like to get title to Robbie over to the Daniels family."

"He's not a car. He's a little boy."

"Sorry. Traditional Daniels family terminology. Would Charlie be open to the idea of relinquishing his fatherhood? For suitable recompense?"

"Probably. There's your true barracuda."

"Done. It might be amusing to hook him up with my former-mom."

Kate lifted her head to look at him.

"I'm not sure I want to marry Trevor Daniels. I like Ski better."

Trevor sighed and his shoulders slumped.

"It's a package, Katie. I can't separate the two."

"Won't."

"Won't. Can't. What's the difference? They're both living in the same body. You get the whole package, warts and all."

"I don't mind the warts. I deeply resent the dishonesty."

"I came clean. It just took me a while."

"You lie to yourself."

"And who do I hurt but me?"

"Me. You hurt me. Because I love you. You hurt your family. Because they love you."

"I hurt my family? How? Tell me when. I'll make it right."

"You can't make it right, because you can't stop yourself, or won't."

"What is it? I'm clueless. Tell me."

"You shut yourself off emotionally from those who love you. That hurts."

"I don't do that with Dad. I haven't in a very long while. That's no bull."

"Agreed. And you don't hurt Jarrett with your silly games because he knows you so well. He knows your reasons, I'm guessing. You don't hold back with Robbie or

491

even Junior. But Carla or Stephie? Or Mary or me? Yes. You hold back with us."

"What? What hold back? From what? With what?"

"Tell us why you do the crazy things you do. We love you. We're living with your quirks, but I for one would like to know why you hide yourself so much."

Trevor froze. He felt naked and cold now. It was sunny, he was in swim trunks, but he might as well not have been.

"Mobs. I hate mobs. Mobs of people. Closing in on me. I hide from the mobs."

"That's practical. And it begs the issue. That's physical, not emotional."

"I don't hide from Scott. Not anymore. But you're right. I used to. You ask him. He won't tell you why. But he'll tell you. Carla I hardly know. Stephie I hardly know. Mary? I don't hide from Mary. Not anymore."

"Yes, you do. And it hurts her. I can tell."

"I don't."

Trevor shifted, remembering.

"Do I?"

"When you have problems, you go to Jarrett."

"He's my dad."

"You never go to Mary."

"I get dad-problems."

"That's sexist. You go to Jarrett because he and you share a base of secret knowledge about what motivates you. You know you can go to Jarrett because he understands you and what makes you tick even when you don't understand it yourself."

"So?"

"What terrible secret are the two of you hiding? Is the secret so terrible? Or is it just that you've both hidden it for so long, you think it's terrible?"

Trevor blinked, his mind sending him flashes of his birth mother, flashes of Christopher de Nunzio, flashes of the Spath boys. Flashes from that span of time on his own, on the road. Flashes of secrets. Flashes of horror. He licked his lips.

"Secrets."

"Yes. I can sense them."

"Scott knows some. Most. Not all. Jarrett knows all. No. I know all. No one else. Jarrett knows the most. Maybe my shrink. Did I tell you I've got a shrink? Surprise. I've got a shrink."

"Well, I should hope so."

"I keep things from Mary. Jarrett and I both do. We're sheltering her."

"You're lying to her. She senses secrets and it hurts her."

"No. I never meant to hurt her. I never meant to hurt anyone."

"Then come clean, dammit."

"I don't want Margaret to know."

"Fine. I can see your point. Margaret knows she has issues with you. She's dealing with it."

"She is? She does? Wow."

"We talked."

"You talked to Margaret? When? How?"

"Big Dog's. The night of the living dead. I can understand your concern for your physical well-being. And what I thought was Scott's obsessive protectiveness of you now makes sense. I began to wonder if the two of you were closer than brothers."

"Secrets. And, no, I'm not telling you squat about me and Scott. Or me and Jarrett. Deal with it."

"I only want to know about you. Whoever you are."

"Dani knows some. I told her to help her with her battle against the cancer. She asked. And I asked if knowing would help her, and she said it would. So I told her what I could. She says it helped. I'm glad I told her. But I never would have if it hadn't been important."

"Are you afraid I'll love you less if I know these secrets?"

"Yes."

"I won't. Look how many secrets I thought I knew, and I didn't love you less. I thought you were crazy."

"I have been. I am."

"And I'm still here.

"I've got my time line set. I'll do it all then. Locks of Love. I'll even write the secrets down to be sure I don't forget any."

# Chapter Twenty-two

It was Katie at the backdoor steps of the house on Olympia Avenue. She had found her confident in a reluctant Jarrett Daniels. Jarrett felt as though he were in a soap opera. He swung the screen door open and Katie stomped up the steps and into the kitchen. Jarrett closed the screen door behind her. Katie twisted nervous fingers.

"He is who he is no matter who he says he is."

"Missy, that was one train-wreck of a sentence. My youngest boy talks like that when he's all messed up in his head. You all messed up in your head?"

Katie burst into tears and flung herself on Jarrett's chest.

"I love him. What am I going to do?"

Jarrett nervously patted her back.

"Uh, marry him? Do you think you could do that? I'd appreciate a few more grandbabies, but that's not necessary. Tadpole'll do fine."

"I'll feel like some cheap floozy, marrying him for his money."

"Believe me, I've known cheap floozies and you're not one of them. Do you really love him? Do you love my baby boy?"

"Yes."

"Well, then, marry the poor son-of-a-bitch, will ya? He's suffered enough, doncha think?"

Katie stood away from Jarrett, snuffling. Her eyes were red and swollen and her face blotchy. She was wiping her eyes with the backs of her hands, but the tears kept coming.

"I don't have anybody to ask. I don't have anyone to advise me. I don't want to make a bad decision again. I can't. I just can't.

"I been there, little girl. Did it, done it, been there, got the T-shirt. Takes guts to commit. You got guts?"

"Yes, I do."

"Then go for it, girl. He'll never knowingly hurt you, or your little boy. My baby's a good man. I raised him up right."

Mary came into the kitchen and, quickly assessing the situation, slid her arm around Katie's waist.

"I know Trevor can be a little overwhelming at times. He never lost his unbridled enthusiasm for life. Or his headlong pursuit of sensation and experience. He was a joy to watch as a baby and a frightening charge to guide as a teenager. Establishing limits has always been the hardest task, both external and internal. He stayed wide-eyed and breathless well into his twenties, a true Peter Pan."

Mary smiled to herself.

"Jarrett and I took him to San Francisco and to New Orleans and to Paris and to a dozen other places around the world when he was a boy. As we walked the streets arm in arm, before or after one of my concerts, Trevor would race on ahead of us, hair flying, and come racing back to us, laughing and jabbering about what he'd seen and heard and smelled and felt and thought. He never grew weary of exploration, and Jarrett and I never grew weary of hearing him tell us all about it."

Jarrett led them into the living room and sat down in his recliner, leaning forward.

"We wanted him to have wings, Katie. Grammy and Mary and I. He'd been so repressed all his young life. Maybe we should have seen the signs, any or all of us. But what the heck difference would it have made? As it turns out, what we did for Trevor was the best thing we could have done anyway. We gave him love and understandin'. A good firm base he could depend on. A sense of responsibility for his actions and the knowledge of the consequences of those actions. We taught him how to live his own life and how to channel and control his really enormous talent."

Jarrett leaned back in his recliner and Katie perched on the couch beside Mary. Jarrett shook his head, remembering.

"When I first met Trevor, he was about five feet of boy with three foot of hair. It didn't take me more than a week, tops, to figure out he had about seven foot of talent jammed in there and that it was gettin' top-heavy and about to topple him. Mary and Grammy and I taught him how to get it out and down, and how to use it. We were intent, all four of us, Trevor included, on teachin' him to fly. We forgot to teach him how to land."

Katie's eyes widened.

"Good grief, Jarrett."

"Well, maybe not as bad as it sounds. We did teach how to take breaks. I thought. How to rest in a tree for a while. But he still takes off and flies better than he lands. He used to land, stagger, and bounce. The big tour before you met him? Richmond? He landed, staggered, and crashed. He didn't bounce. He stuck. We scooped him up in a spoon after Richmond and brought him home. We kept it quiet. Fans and the media didn't need to know. Nothin' that rest, relaxation, the proper medication, food and gettin' away from the business couldn't and didn't cure."

Jarrett shook his head.

"He's real susceptible to chest colds. Mary thinks it's from that year or so he lived on his own outdoors. You know, sleepin' outside in freezin' weather? That may be it."

"That's horrible. He's a singer. His lungs are his living."

"Well, yeah, I guess. He gets just about anythin' goin' around. Gets it and hides it. Tryin' to bogart his way through it. Never works. He crashes and burns. You'd think he'd have learned his lesson by now, but, no, gotta try to be a hero or somethin'. Can't fool the lungs, though. And here we are with him again. Tryin' to crash and burn over love. 'Goin' down in flames; burnin' up with love'. I swear."

Mary slid her hand into Katie's cold one as Jarrett shook his head again.

"And as soon as he can stagger up on those legs again, he's stretchin' up with his wings to go flyin' some more. When you first met Trevor, how'd he seem to you? Was he eatin' right? Actin' right?"

Katie thought about that.

She tried to see again–in her mind's eye–Ski the construction worker without the more recent overlay of Trevor Lane Daniels, superstar. She remembered the scruffy man who'd given her a lift. The shadow in the back at Big Dog's while she played and sang. The sleeping figure on her sofa. The kind-eyed man on the floor by Robbie, exchanging silent, secret knowledge with her baby.

"He seemed perfectly normal to me. Perfectly ordinary."

Then she remembered Trevor hiding in her closet and smiled.

"Well, maybe not perfectly normal. He was angry that I was hitchhiking."

"As well he might be."

Katie smiled more, remembering.

"Oh, yes. Definitely angry. But he was trying to figure out solutions for me. I was so wrapped up in my own problems. We ate at Big Dog's but I don't think he was hungry. I know I wasn't, but that's because of the stage fright. Before and after. He shared a bowl of cereal with Robbie the next morning. He was the one who got it for both of them. He was kind and considerate. He was concerned about my car, and about me, and about Robbie. He slept in his clothes. Well, he had no choice there. He didn't shave the next morning. Again, no choice. He watched cartoons with Robbie, then drove us to day care, and me to work. What he did for food between then and 5:30 p.m? I have no idea. I know now he was busy arranging the car for me. And the cell phone. Buying Keturah's and the day care."

Jarrett nodded.

"He was busy and active and distracted out of himself. Good. He handled his crazies. He called us that mornin' of the day you met. Did you know that? Before he met up with you on I-75, he was headin' home to be with us. He'd sounded tired, maybe a little depressed, on the phone.

498

He and Scott had worked that whole day movin' him from
The Ice Palace to Gill Street. Mary and I were worried. We
thought we'd have to step in and slow him down again."

"He's a big boy, Jarrett."

"He's a man, Kate. But the daddy in me is hard to
rein in sometimes. He'll always be my little boy. But when
he called to cancel with us, he sounded fine. Distracted, but
fine. I guess you were the distraction."

"I suppose so. The wonder is he didn't wash his
hands of me. I was very prickly. Very defensive. I got on his
nerves. But I only made him really angry when it came to
Robbie. And it wasn't really me he was angry with."

"Make's perfect sense, Kate. Robbie would be a
priority with him. But the whole incident of meetin' you and
helpin' you stopped any potential downward spiral he might
have been havin'. And he knew it. That's why he cancelled
with us. He'd found another solution."

"I'm the solution to Trevor Daniels' problems?
Great. No stress there."

"Trevor's like a force of nature, Katie. He needs to
go to ground. You ground him. It's that simple."

"It can't be."

"Why not? What is love but need and want gettin'
together on both sides?"

"I don't know."

"He's workin' hard, Katie. He wants this badly."

"He'll sweep me away. He's like a force of nature.
He's like a tidal wave. I'll be submerged and swept away."

"He's not that good, little girl. Time you separated
your Ski from your Trevor from your trained monkey up
there on stage. They're all Trevor, mind you. But you're
scared of the monkey, and the monkey's the least of it.
You're okay with Ski. You can handle him. But you need to
get to know Trevor. That's not easy. That takes time and
patience. But, by God, it's worth it. I've rarely met a better
man in my life, and never his equal. I'm partial to him. He's
my son. But he's also a helluva good man. You try to get to
know that Trevor, little girl."

499

\*    \*    \*    \*    \*

Katie called Jarrett from the noisy backstage area of the Cincinnati concert, her cell phone pressed close to her ear over the pandemonium.

"This is incredible. This is horrible! I can't live like this."

"Don't say that, little girl. You signed on for the whole Midwest tour. You're in."

"I didn't know it was going to be like this."

"Not somethin' you want to do for a livin', huh?"

"Absolutely not. I don't know how he does it. I don't know why he does it!"

"Can't stop himself. Driven, little girl. Your man is driven. Hard from within. It's your job to be there when he runs out of fuel. To catch him before he crashes and burns."

"That's a huge responsibility. I can't do that."

"Who else but you? You're the chosen one."

"Great. We're all in trouble now. Who did it before?"

"Mary and I did in the beginnin'. Scott's been doin' what he can. Trevor's been flyin' solo mostly."

"My God! The guys in the band?"

"Got their own worries, little girl. Real pressure-cooker, the road. Kills off the weak. Destroys marriages and relationships. Pulls a band together or blows it apart. The guy at the top's always alone. He's the boss, the decision-maker. The umpire for squabbles. The strong one to lean on. He can't falter or it all goes down."

"And I'm in charge of this?"

"Yep."

"There isn't enough money in the world for this!"

Silence on the other end of the phone. Then Jarrett rumbled his reply.

"Is there enough love, little girl?"

Katie drew in a breath, steadying herself. Trevor had taught her how to do that to calm herself and to focus. She

500

wanted to be honest with this honest man who was Trevor's father–as honest as she could be.

"I don't know. I hope so. I'm not giving up. It's just way more than I ever realized."

"Do what you can, little girl. Anythin' you can do'll be a help. It beats Trevor tryin' to fly solo."

*　　　*　　　*　　　*　　　*

Katie and Trevor were in the kitchenette of the tour bus as Jesse drove. Katie was standing, swaying gently to the movement of the bus. Trevor was seated, intent on a crossword puzzle. The door separating Jesse from them was closed.

Katie pointed her chin at Trevor.

"All right. You mentioned having trouble with establishing limits. I've been on this tour now three weeks. I've been talking to Carla and Manny. Carla and I agree that Manny's cooking is perfectly nutritional and none of the ingredients he uses seem to trigger your lung problems."

Trevor looked up from his crossword puzzle.

"Huh? What?"

"Carla has been functioning as your ad hoc medical advisor. She and I have been discussing what might be beneficial or harmful to your lungs. Food allergies came up as a possibility and we've been experimenting and observing, with Manny's help."

"I'm a lab rat now?"

"You don't seem to have any food allergies."

"I'm allergic to starving. You know, lack of food."

"No, you're not. You forget to eat. It lowers your resistance. And milk and other dairy products make you phlegmy. That effects your lungs. And your singing. That means no pizza while you're on tour."

"What! The heck it does."

"Carla and I set up a tentative schedule that has some form of decent food going into you every three hours. Have you ever been tested for hypoglycemia?"

501

"Hypo-what? Heck, no. I go to docs, reluctantly, when I'm sick."

"You are such a guy. That is such a guy thing. Never mind. We'll work around it. The next thing Carla and I discussed was possible air pollution concerns. Scott has the bus on a routine schedule to change out the diesel filters, but I, for one, can still smell fumes. He's going to work on that problem. Dani and I will be creating or buying seat covers–at least three sets–to put on the cushions up here in the kitchenette. Curtains, too. Every week, those will be taken down and replaced. The dirty ones will be washed, dried and stored. You already shower after every concert, but we need to put that shower and hair wash and change of clothes into practice before you come out to sign autographs, not after. In cold weather, Margaret will blow dry your hair to avoid a chill."

A stunned Trevor laid his crossword puzzle down.

"Not doable. It'll mess up the schedule."

"Doable. I checked with Scott and Jesse about that. It will rearrange the sequence of events from fans-shower-sleep to shower-fans-sleep, but no more than fifteen to twenty minutes will inconvenience the fans."

"I don't want to inconvenience the fans at all."

"They waited to get in. Some waited for tickets. They wait for you to come out. They can wait fifteen to twenty minutes more."

Trevor scowled at her.

"They waited to get in. Some waited for tickets. They wait for me to come out. I don't want to make them wait more than they have to."

Katie flung wide her arms in exasperation.

"Ten minutes then. Shower and change fast. It's your life and your health, God damn it! Don't you count for something? Don't you think your fans would be amenable to this change if they knew it was for your continued good health?"

Trevor blinked. He sensed some heat rising on his face and felt a smile creeping in. He reached out a finger to stroke Katie's arm.

"You're doing all this because you like me."

"Well, of course, I am. Yes, I like you. And I love you. But that's beside the point."

"Not to me it isn't. You love me."

"I'm stubborn. Are we going to try this?"

Trevor felt his smile growing.

"Yep. We'll try this. Got any other suggestions?"

"Sleep."

"Don't tempt me."

"Quit that. Rest. Naps."

"Naps? Do I look like Robbie to you? Or some geezer?"

"Sometimes. Sometimes both. Limits. You work to the point of exhaustion and then drop. Who benefits from that? You worry your loved ones. You leave your resistance weakened and the germs have an easy time pulling you down. Naps."

"When? How? Every three hours? After another snack? Do I get my own blankey?"

"Carla, Scott and I researched the schedules. Anywhere from 3:00 p.m. to 5:00 p.m. most days is available."

"3:00 p.m. to 5:00 p.m? What am I usually doing then? I have no idea."

"Nothing. Most recently, crayoning. Or watching Scott doodle. Carla's concerned about Scott's health."

"Scottie? What's wrong?"

"Nothing. Nothing at all. But the both of you treat your bodies as though you were sixteen year olds, and you're not. Scott has two years on you. It's past time for good nutrition and a sensible lifestyle."

"Sensible lifestyle? I'm on tour! What's sensible about that?"

"Not much. But Carla, Scott, Manny and I have hopes. You've made some major changes yourself. After the

Richmond incident, I think you sensed it was time to reassess and regroup. Manny's cooking. Basketball. Gold's Gym. Carla and I are just trying to formalize the timing more."

Katie sat down at the table next to Trevor and clasped his hands.

"You told me once that setting limits is hard for you. I'm trying to set some limits for you, but not so many that you'll feel caged and restricted."

"You love me."

"Did you hear anything I said?"

"Oh, yeah. But nothing nearly as important to me."

"All of this should be important to you. I'm trying to improve and prolong your life. And Scott's. Maybe even mine and Carla's and the whole traveling circus."

"You love me."

"Yes. Deal with it."

"Are you going to bat my hands away if I try to hug and kiss you?"

Katie narrowed her eyes at him.

"No. But we've been this far before."

Trevor shook his head slowly, smiling.

"Oh, no, we haven't."

Trevor slowly reached up his hands to Katie's face and then brushed a lazy kiss across her lips, his smiling eyes half-closed. He drew her closer and onto his lap, relaxing himself and remembering the feel of love he got from Jarrett. Remembering the feel of finally connecting with Mary. Opening up to love.

He closed his eyes to help him concentrate on the opening up. He closed his arms around Katie and began to smooth her back and shoulders, listening to the soft shush of material under his hands, feeling her warmth and the movement her heart made as it beat against his chest.

He snuggled his face into her neck, and let himself go.

In his mind, he soared into the sky with Katie in his arms, up into clouds and sunshine, way up into the beyond, far away from anything to bring him down. No dark pits. No snares. No closed dark rooms. No closets. Only light and air and sunshine. Warmth and well being. Love.

Trevor felt Katie's arms slide around him and her hands move into his hair. Her lips were on his face and neck. She kissed him and he kissed her back, losing track of actual body geography. Neck, face, breast, arms, legs, stomach. Hands, lips, mouth. Feeling. All feeling.

Katie whispered in his ear.

"Trevor?"

"Hmm?"

"You've let me in."

"Hmm."

Trevor snuggled into her like a puppy and she lay down with him on the seat, nuzzling him back and letting him do wonderful things to her with his hands and his mouth.

Moving her clothes out of his way with gentle hands, Trevor slid into Katie, hearing her gasp and stealing her breath away with a hungry kiss that devoured her mouth. He swirled her mindlessly into the sky with him again on a hedonistic updraft of sensation. Releasing inside her quickly, Trevor stayed inside Katie as long as he could afterwards, reveling in the shared closeness. He fell blissfully asleep with Katie's arms around him, safe and secure at last in his love for her and her love for him.

$$*\qquad*\qquad*\qquad*\qquad*$$

Life on the road changed subtly during the Midwest tour that encompassed Indiana, Illinois, Iowa, Nebraska, Ohio and Missouri.

The roadies grumbled about the changes in scheduling, but no one quit over it, and eventually they got used to it. Trevor forced Katie to turn a blind eye to the excesses of his troops and to leave their morals alone as well.

"You can't save 'em all, Hasselhoff. Concentrate on your willing victims. If you improve the quality of my life, and Scottie's, the good vibes will trickle down to the troops.

Pay no attention to anything you might hear about bimbos sleeping with the boss. They'll get over it. Or hit the road. Whatever. Leave their nookie and their liquor alone. And their gambling. Drugs I won't put up with."

Carla and Katie undertook a cleaning schedule for the bus. On off-hours, they took the Hyundai to local K-Marts and Walmarts, looking for cheap curtains and seat covers. They added to the collection of bedding for the built-in bunk beds. They got Jesse a cushion for his butt in the driver's seat.

The brothers worked out an unofficial schedule of when the tour bus would be available for intimacy without letting Carla or Katie know about it. Scott was better in the mornings. Trevor was ready all the time.

Margaret and Dani had stayed off the road for this tour, keeping to Dani's schedule of chemo. Carla and Katie took over wardrobe, the cleaning and laundry and the repairs of all the clothing for the entire group, on or off-stage. Since neither of them had Dani's flair for designing hair styles for Trevor nor Margaret's surprising cleverness at executing those styles, Trevor reverted to wearing his hair straight down, or pulled back with a band, or braided down his back. The absence of hair spray was voted a good thing.

Scott had had the diesel filters cleaned before the tour, but checked ahead on their schedule for down time and increased the frequency of changing them out on his maintenance schedule. He booked the bus into a fleet service three days hence, alerting the band and the roadies so they could plan ahead to meet anyone they knew in that area.

The girls did laundry, Trevor helping to fold, while Scott stayed with the bus at the fleet service and Jesse and Manny disappeared with the roadies. Other members of the band including the back up singers, Eloise and Linda, escaped to nearby friends, family or floozies as they chose.

For the four members of the tour at the top, life was as close to what it would have been in Punta Gorda, Florida, as they could make it. Katie kept Trevor to his nap schedule, sleeping with him sexlessly to lure him into bed, and his energy level improved overall. The fans didn't seem to mind the extra wait at the end of the concerts and Trevor's lungs stayed clearer. Carla checked his lungs and blood pressure and temperature daily, which amused Trevor but didn't bother him much.

"Hello, Des Moines! How's it goin'?"

"Hello, Valparaiso!"

"Hello, Omaha!"

"Hello, Chicago! How's it goin'?"

They played county fairs and municipal auditoriums. They played concert halls and chili cook-offs and colleges. They played to fourteen hundred and they played to forty thousand. Trevor varied the content, depending on the locale. In general, the Midwesterners were more conservative than the Texans had been. And the college students were definitely not the county fair crowd.

Most members of the band, and Jake especially, had been with Trevor so long that they picked up cues from his body language alone about changes in tempo or when he was about to spring a surprise 'Take it away, Wes' or 'Take it away, Sarah Jane' on them. Trevor was more than willing to try anything to keep the grind from becoming too boring or the band too stale. He promised them a surprise every night, and delivered it, keeping his band interested and on its toes.

"Hello, Kent State! How's it goin'?"

Trevor got a huge pop and roar from the crowd of collegiates. He loved playing colleges. He felt they were the most receptive audiences to changes of material, tempo and direction. He played the first set along traditional lines. 'Little Pussy,', 'Fun, Fun, Fun,' 'Free.' But after 'Free,' Trevor threw them all a curve.

"Ladies and gentlemen! Oh, yeah, you college guys, too."

A huge whoop and cat calls.

"I'm gonna step off stage here for a bit. But before I go, I want to introduce a member of this band you all know from his awards and his talent. Mr. Jake Benson, bass guitar, winner of five best in beer awards. Seriously, best bass player in the country and maybe the whole world. Take it away, Jake!"

And he casually un-slung Blondie, set her on a stand and walked off stage. Scott met him in the wings, hissing at him.

"Jesus Christ, moron. What the hell are you up to?"

"Watch. Listen."

After a momentary lull, Jake organized his rattled musicians and stepped to the mike.

"Thank you, Trevor Daniels. I'll get you for this."

Jake swung into his opening chords.

"Goin' down in flames,

Burnin' up with love…"

And the band followed him. Trevor grinned mischievously at Scott.

"I'm not an idiot. Well, not about the music. I knew Jake and the band had been rehearsing this. I wrote it, but it's not my style. I'm just taking the band in a different direction. Spicing it up. Great crowd, huh?"

"It's your crowd. Not Jake's."

"They'll tolerate this. Jake needs this. He really is good. He always has been. He needs his chance."

"What? To steal your audience? Your fans?"

"As if. No, to maybe steal some of the band. I don't know. He's a creative musician and writer. He needs to fly. I know I did. I do."

"An outlet for your weirder stuff?"

"Maybe. His way is best for 'Scream in Pain'."

Scott and Trevor listened to the driving beat of heavy metal flow from Jake's fingers on bass and his screaming delivery of 'Goin' Down in Flames'. The crowd stayed with him, stomping the beat and starting a crowd surf. The band stayed with him, grinning to one another.

Scott grabbed his walkie-talkie off his belt.

"Watch it out there. This crowd is changin' character."

He clicked off and watched his troops come more tightly up to the front of the stage.

508

"Jesus Christ, Trevor. You've started a riot."

Trevor grinned.

"Not me. I'm right here. Jake's starting the riot. If any. Woke 'em up, didn't I?"

"You're gonna give me a heart attack one of these days, or an ulcer."

"Geezer."

"Flake."

Back on the stage after Jake's applause died down, Trevor slowed the crowd back down a little with 'Surviving' and mellowed them out further with 'Every Love Song Always Sounds the Same.' He ended the concert as usual with 'Guitar-Man,' perched on his solitary stool, relaxed and mesmerizing as the roadies broke down the set behind and around him.

"Guitar-Man, tie some feathers in you hair.
Come tonight, you're gonna fly.
Wild and free
As you should be,
Fling your spirit to the sky.

Guitar-Man, burnin' up inside,
Let your music start to flow.
Pain or joy,
Little boy,
Let the magic in you show.

Guitar-Man, got a dream.
Hope to God it comes out right.
Time for fun.
Your past is done.
Know I'm there to hold you tight.

Guitar-Man, glory-bound,
Play your music soft and sweet.
You will learn
It's your turn.
Live your music in your sleep."

Trevor made a point of bringing Jake up to take what he thought of as a final curtain call with him, and listened to the added volume of applause when he did so, carefully laying the groundwork for Jake to strip him of key band members and drop into the groove of playing colleges himself, if he chose to do so. It was both a different audience and the same, Trevor felt. Colleges were different. Texas honky-tonks would never buy Jake's hard rock versions of his own music. Colleges would. Even Texas Aggies.

*   *   *   *   *

Everyone finished the Midwest tour healthier, happier and more relaxed than usual. Trevor was back in a better relationship with Jake than he'd had in several years. They would never share more than the music and longevity, but their professional roots went long and deep.

Jake had thrown a long arm around Trevor as they wobbled off stage together at Kent State, applause still rolling in swells behind them.

"Dude. I thought I was gonna have to kill you. 'Take it away, Jake'? Jesus."

"You did fine. That's payback for you and Dani conning me into singing 'Guitar-Man' at Big Dog's."

"Thirty years ago?"

"Watch it. We both were there. Wasn't more than twenty, tops."

"Still. That's some long range revenge there, dude."

"I knew you'd been rehearsing."

"It darned near blew me away!"

"Good for you. Crowd liked you. Want to pilfer the band and go off on your own? You could, you know. I'm agreeable."

"No, dude. I like a paycheck. You point and I'll play. I liked it, though. What a rush! Been a while since I got a rush on stage."

510

"We need to do that more. Bring in more of your stuff. It's got to be the right crowd, though. I can play your style, but I can't sing it. You do the vocals. We'll double our draw once the word gets out. Brings a whole new meaning to country-rock, doesn't it?"

"You devil, you. Had it all planned, didn't ya?"

"Not all. Been thinking. Time seemed right. 'Take it away, Jake'."

"You retirin'?"

"As if. But I got my interests elsewhere, so to speak."

"Nice lady."

"Yeah."

"Next time, why don't you surprise Mitch instead? Let him drum up some business, pardon the pun."

Trevor grinned.

"Might be Linda and Eloise next. I hear them doing rap when they think I'm not listening. This I gotta see. Ghetto-country-rap."

"You're scarin' me now."

"Me? I'm harmless."

"Huh."

*　　*　　*　　*　　*

The Midwest tour was over.

A California tour was on the horizon.

Trevor, Katie and Robbie had settled into the Gill Street house in an easy fashion. But Katie was on the phone now to Jarrett, her hands not quite steady.

"Jarrett, I'm really worried about Trevor."

"What's he done now?"

"Nothing. I mean, that's it. He's doing nothing. He sits and stares."

"Has he stopped talkin' and eatin'?"

"He's stopped talking. I haven't been able to get a word out of him all day. I don't know if he's eating or not. I didn't notice."

511

"Is he there now?"

"Yes. Right here with me in the kitchen. I'm on the cordless."

"Goddammit, he's gone Ferndale on us. Put him on the phone. Trevor!"

"Yes, sir?"

"Don't you go Ferndale. Katie says you're not talkin'. You eatin'? Trevor?"

"Sir?"

"Are you eatin'? Don't make me have to come over there and kick your butt.

When Trevor chuckled, Jarrett relaxed somewhat.

"That's more like it, Trevor. What's happenin', son?"

"Jake."

"What about Jake? Talk to me, Trevor."

"He's overdosed."

"Jesus, Mary and Joseph. Is he okay? Where is he?"

"Tampa General."

"Mary and I are comin' over. I want three scrambled eggs in you before I get there. And I'll check your breath to be sure. Put Katie back on."

"Jarrett? What in the world is going on?"

"Mary and I are comin' over. It's one of the boys in his band. Man from his band, I should say. One of his oldest friends in a lousy business. Jake's in the hospital with an overdose, Katie. I didn't even know he had a drug problem. This is devastatin' to Trevor. Not as bad as dead, but dead might be comin' next and soon. Like I said, we'll be over. Probably in about five minutes. Trevor has his orders to eat three scrambled eggs. Is he movin' yet?"

"Yes. He stood up. How did you do that?"

"He didn't come with no owner's manual, Katie. I found out that when I wanted most to cuddle and coddle him was when he needed me most to be strong and be stern with him. Not angry. Not hurtful. Just lay down the law and force him to do the most basic things. Eat. Talk. Breathe. I'm half of the opinion he might be what they call these days bi-polar. But mostly he can handle it himself. He's gotten real good

512

over the years at backin' off the manic, or channelin' it into his music, or work, or his rollerblades, or that fast little car of his and fast little boat. Runnin'. The depressive side is harder for him. He about doesn't see it comin'. Then he stops talkin' so he can't tell anybody about it. Hearin' this about Jake blindsided him. He must have gone down before he knew it. He up scramblin' eggs yet?"

"No."

"Put the phone to his ear. Trevor! Right now! Into the fridge! Out with the eggs! Got it?"

"Yes, Dad."

"Good. Shove the phone back to Katie."

Katie breathed into the phone that Trevor handed her.

"He's doing it! You got him out of his chair and heading for the refrigerator. Amazing. Jarrett, I know when that call came in. I wondered, because Trevor's eyes just went dead. But he didn't crash. He told me he had to go to Tampa. He took the truck, not the MG. And he didn't tear out of here. He wouldn't tell me where or what, but he said he might be back late and to not wait up."

"That's good. That's darned good, considerin'. Usin' some sense. He had it under control at that point. Call came in when?"

"Yesterday about noon. Trevor came back this morning. About five hours ago now. He hasn't shaved or showered or changed his clothes. He's finished scrambling his eggs, Jarrett. He has them out on a plate with the fork he cooked them with."

"That's Trevor. Is he eatin' them yet?"

"Yes. He's sitting at the table watching me watch him. And he's starting to smile at me."

"He knows what's goin' on. Good. Get him showered and shaved and changed. We'll be over."

Jarrett hung up and Katie hit the off button on the cordless phone.

Trevor, unshaven and hollow-eyed from lack of sleep, smiled at her, forking a piece of egg into his mouth.

Katie set down the cordless phone.

"Why didn't you tell me, Trevor?"

Trevor shrugged and Katie frowned at him through narrowed eyes.

"Oh, no, you don't, mister. I understand I have to insist on words."

Trevor grinned and chuckled, eating more eggs.

"Okay, okay. Hard to snap out of it. Sometimes I can't. Dad knows. Heck, you know now."

"That's it?"

Trevor sighed and shook his head. Katie scowled at him.

"Keep eating, mister. Jarrett and Mary are coming over. Jarrett's going to do a Breathalyzer test on you for eggs. Why do I think it'll be my fault if you haven't eaten?"

Trevor laughed out loud now and Katie was somewhat reassured by the sound and by the overall lightening she saw in Trevor's face as he stood up from the table.

"No, it won't be your fault. I expect I've got orders to clean up, too."

Trevor finished the eggs and turned to the sink, picking up the dish pad and beginning to wash off the plate, the fork and the frying pan. His back was to Katie, his long strong legs spread in a firm stance, his shoulders straight and broad. He looked stable and indestructible.

Katie knew better now.

"Trevor, please don't shut me out. You said you wanted me in your life. Well, I'm in it. Robbie and I live here now with you, again. But I want into your real life, too."

"I've been trying to wow you with my charm and good looks. Not too romantic to have a dirty lump sitting there."

Katie came up behind Trevor at the sink and put her arms around his middle from behind. She laid her head against his back in its day-old T-shirt and breathed in his scent.

"I like the whole package, Trevor. Not just the good stuff. You frightened me, because I knew something was wrong and I didn't know what to do to help. That wasn't fair, Trevor."

Trevor finished the dishes, set them in the drain, turned off the water, ripped off a sheet of paper towel from the roll under the counter and dried his hands, still with his back to Katie.

"I'm not proud of it, Katie."

"Trevor! There's nothing to be proud of or ashamed of. It just is. I'm not proud of my ears…"

"You should be."

"Just shut up!"

Trevor laughed, relaxing into the feel of Katie's arms around him, even when she momentarily tightened those arms in anger to give him a shake.

"My ears are my ears. God-given. Lucky for me I don't have to keep my eyes on them…"

"Very! That'd be a stretch."

"Stop it. Just stop it!"

Katie gave Trevor another angry squeeze, but held on to him.

"Quit trying to be flip and charming, will you? This is serious to me."

"To me, too. I live with it."

"I want to live with it, too, Trevor. God damn it, let me in!"

Trevor sighed and moved his hands up to cover Katie's around his middle.

"That's tough, Katie. I hate showing weakness. In my past…well, the heck with that. No guy alive wants to show weakness."

"So, it's okay for me to blubber and cringe. But not you?"

"Yeah. That's about it."

"Bull. Was what I saw today as bad as it gets? Tell me the truth. I've got to know."

"Uh, no. Not nearly as bad as it gets. It was heading there, though. Good call phoning up Dad."

"I can't be calling Jarrett every time for this. I need to know how to do CPR on your psyche myself. You need to tell me what triggers it, or what signs I should look for."

Trevor turned in her arms now and wrapped his own arms around her, resting his chin on her head. Katie continued to hold him close, listening to the steady beat of Trevor's heart and surrounded by the essence of him.

He smoothed his hands over her back.

"Anything not normal, Kate. Lot of possibilities there. In both directions. Too happy, too glad, too fast. Too anything. You've seen today the too quiet, the too sedentary, and the too numb. Hard to figure out where top dead center is on my engine. Hard for me to figure out. And not all warning signs are always warning signs. Sometimes if I'm quiet, I'm just quiet. Thinking, or hearing the music in my head. Half an hour to an hour's okay. Five hours is not acceptable."

Trevor rocked Katie gently back and forth.

"Sometimes I'm sleeping because I'm tired. Like when I crashed at your place out in Arcadia after that move from The Ice Palace. I was bushed. I needed to recharge my batteries. Ten, twelve, sixteen hours of sleep then is okay. But the same amount of sleep for no good reason isn't. Sometimes I don't eat because I'm into the music and I don't want to stop for a break. So that's okay. But today? This morning? Nope. I hadn't eaten since noon yesterday. You didn't know that. I wasn't likely to pass out or anything. And you heard Dad. He made me get up and fix it myself. Physical activity keeps me centered. It breaks the down cycle for me. It reins in the manic cycle, too, but speed works better there. Physical activity to jump-start the energy. Speed to drain off the excess energy. Always seeking the middle ground. Never sure, even in my own mind, when I've found it."

Katie, in turn, smoothed Trevor's back slowly, enjoying the feel of his solid muscle under her hands.

"You've got a lot of different Trevors in there, don't you?"

"Yep. Quite a crowd."

"I like them all, so far."

"I don't have a truly mean one, Katie. I've got one with a bad temper, and darned little self-control. But he's never yet started something. Well, not since I was about fifteen years old. Dad found him and busted him. I know his hot buttons. He's been under control for years now. He and Dad had a lot of fun through my teens! I don't have any strangers living in me, Katie. They're all me."

Katie stood back out of Trevor's arms enough to be able to look up into his face, but still keep her arms around him.

"Why is all this such a big secret, Trevor? I don't see any problem here."

Trevor laughed, tilting back his head, his long hair swinging free as he shook his head.

"God knows. It sure sounds simple when you say that. Most people don't like crazy. Most people are afraid of crazy. I'm an emotional cripple, Katie."

"You're not crazy. And you're not a cripple."

Katie gave Trevor another shake.

"I'll bet there's medication out there for this."

"There is. And I'm not taking any of it. I hate drugs. I've had my own demons to battle there. You can ask Dad. I hate all drugs. It's hard to get me to a doctor if I'm sick. I even hate taking aspirin. And I really hate hospitals. I got into drugs and then, with Dad's help, I got back out of them."

"You went to a hospital yesterday."

"Yep. For Jake. He's out of ICU now, by the way. But the problem? Oh, geez, why...?"

Katie watched as Trevor slumped back against the sink and closed his eyes. She reached up and tenderly touched her thumbs to the corners of his eyes, then smoothed the long hair behind his ears, tracing her fingers over the lines of misery she saw across his brow. Trevor's face relaxed somewhat. Katie drew her fingers down the sides of his face, then smoothed the stubble on his jaw with the backs of her hands. She ran her fingers up into the hair at the back of his neck and slowly massaged the tensed muscles she felt there. Finally she planted a kiss over his heart.

"Come on upstairs, baby. We'll take a shower together. I'll wash your hair. You better shave yourself. Then I'll brush your hair for you, if you want."

"I'd like that. That'd feel good."

Trevor opened his eyes and smiled wanly.

"Sorry I almost cried on you."

Katie kissed his chest again through the fabric of his shirt and put her arms back around him.

"That's not crazy, Trevor. That's normal. You're worried about your friend. You're concerned for his future. It's perfectly normal to be sad about that. It's a sad situation."

"You're good for me."

"I hope so. You're good for me. And for Robbie. We both love you very much. Should I phone Jarrett and Mary and tell them not to come over?"

Trevor stood away from the sink, breathing in through his nose.

"Nope. I like my parents. Both of them. I'm happy to see them anytime, anyplace, anywhere. They set out to help me through the down cycle. To help you help me through it. They might as well get the pleasure of seeing normal as long as they're coming anyway. You know, I'd still be living at home if Mary and Dad hadn't thrown me out and told me go set up a place of my own."

Katie took his hand and led him upstairs to the master bedroom and into the bathroom there. She started the shower going, blending the water. She smiled at Trevor standing passively beside her.

"You have choices. I could undress you. You could undress you. You could undress me…"

Trevor glimmered a smile.

"I get the picture. I like that you-could-undress–me idea. And I'll take a piece of that I-can-undress-you."

"We can't take too long. Jarrett and Mary are coming over, remember."

Trevor slowly hooked his finger into the front of Katie's jeans.

"I think they'll figure it out if we're late coming downstairs."

"My orders are clean, not sexually satisfied."

"Maybe we can do both. Surely sex is healthy for me."

"Much you'd care. But at least you're talking and moving."

"I'm living. I'm alive. Do you want to see how well I can move? Loofah my back?"

"I'll loofah you all over."

\*     \*     \*     \*     \*

Trevor shook off his depression.

Jake went into a twelve-step program.

Back on the road—or more accurately in the Lear jet—Katie faced Trevor and a grinning Carla in the whispering hum of the small aircraft as Scott flew them to the first of the California tour dates where they would meet up with the tour bus that Jesse had driven out in advance. She'd just thrown Trevor another curve ball and his jaw was dropping.

"Dance lessons?"

"Yes. I've been thinking. You love to move. I've watched you on stage. Running around with that tail velcroed on your jeans for 'Little Pussy'. On fast numbers, you're out to the far sides of the stage both right and left. Performing gives you a jolt of energy. I would imagine it would be difficult at times for you to stand still."

"Dance lessons?"

"Eloise and Linda are moving almost all the time. Jake wanders around. So does Sarah Jane on violin."

"Fiddle. Sarah Jane plays fiddle. Dance lessons?"

"What harm could there be? You have a natural sense of rhythm, I'd think. You wouldn't dance to the slow ones. Well, maybe to the waltzes."

519

"Waltzes? What waltzes? Dance lessons? When? How?"

"Maybe Eloise and Linda could teach you some simple steps. I couldn't. I can't dance. But I love to see you move. I can't be in the minority there. You're very graceful."

"That's embarrassing."

"You'd sell more CDs. Get more fans. Women love to watch beautiful men move. Women love good-looking butts dancing."

"My wife-to-be is suggesting I wriggle my worm?"

"That, too. But I was suggesting dancing. A few simple steps you could do while you play guitar. Nothing fancy. Just a teaser."

Scott, from the open door of the cockpit, chuckled.

"Best give it a shot, Trev. We'll watch the ratin's on it. See if we can pick up a vote. Maybe even get DJs to ask folks to phone in to their radio stations to vote. You best be dancin' your fine Daniels butt off up on stage while anyone wants to see it. They ain't gonna want to see it move much once it's all tired and saggy."

"My butt's not going to get tired and saggy."

"Sure it is. Everyone's does. Best use it while you can. If you can."

"I can. I'm not sure I want to."

"Give it a try, rat boy. Can't hurt."


Eloise and Linda taught him some boot scootin' and after Trevor stopped falling over his own feet, they tried it in rehearsal. They kept trying it until Trevor stopped either missing chords or watching his feet. They simplified the moves.

Finally, Trevor was allowed to try out the merest hint of a routine live for 'Fun, Fun, Fun'. When he got applause and shrieks, Trevor smiled and got into it more. By the time he'd finished the simple song, he was practically dancing a cha cha with Blondie. There was no doubt which way the audiences in California voted. They didn't need the open phone lines to radio stations later to figure that out.

When Trevor played Candlestick Park, he played it like he'd never played it before. The open-air theatre reverberated with stomping feet and chants of 'Tre! Vor! Tre! Vor!'

Trevor grinned.

Dancing was in.

# Chapter Twenty-three

It was December and finally they were up in New York City for the Locks of Love concert. Trevor was already on stage, dancing little steps with Blondie in his arms and laughingly working the huge crowd. Katie, backstage, was as used to the darkness and wires and flashes of stage light and overpowering noise level as it was possible to be. She caught Scott grinning at her and was puzzled for a moment.

She didn't stay puzzled for long.

Trevor broke into a warbling boogie-woogie ballad that left her mouth dropping open.

"Boys, let me tell ya.
Got your lady tonight?
Grab ahold and kiss her
And hold her real tight.
I lost my lady.

I don't give a damn
About the car I drive.
I don't really care
If I'm dead or alive.
I lost my lady.

Everybody says
I'll be all right
But I'm the one who's sleepin'
Single tonight.
I lost my lady.

She don't give a damn
About the lies I've told.
But I lost her real fast.
I couldn't give her my soul.
I lost my lady.

Katydid, listen up.
I'm still your man.

522

Come back to me.
Got my soul in my hand
For my lady."
Trevor boot-scooted off stage to a huge pop from the stirred-up crowd.

Katie punched him in the arm and he grinned at her, unrepentant and uncaring that their conversation would be heard by every last soul in the packed concert because of the headset he wore.

"Ow!"

"You're courting me on stage," Katie hissed, "I can't believe you're doing this."

"Whatever it takes. I'm goal-oriented."

"You are so full of shit."

"Kate, I'm serious."

"Then propose like a serious man."

Trevor dropped to his knees.

"Marry me."

"Get up. You're still screwing around."

"I am not!"

"Up."

Trevor got back up again. He dusted off his jeans, ignoring a swell of laughter from the crowd, Blondie slung over his back temporarily, the electric cord of a pick-up trailing behind him.

"What the heck's it going to take?"

"Maybe just one night of total and complete emotional honesty from you."

"You had that with Ski."

"Before he fell in love with me? Yes. Not a moment since unless I back you into a corner."

Trevor ripped open his Dani-shirt, buttons flying in all directions, and began to unzip his jeans.

Katie waved panic-stricken hands at him as another roar of support came from the crowd.

"Jesus Christ, Trevor! What the hell are you doing?"

"Getting naked. Getting honest."

"Not here, you moron. Jesus! There's a crowd of people out front. Roadies all over the back here. You have a show to finish. Switch off that headset. Good. Tonight. Somewhere away from everybody. Away from the tour. Away from The Life. Away. Got it? Jesus. Put your shirt back on. I swear to God."

"Tonight. Right? We're taking the Hyundai. Best Western. Day's Inn. Whatever. We're getting naked and we're getting honest here. I'm way past nuts now. I purely don't have a thing to lose. That always makes it easier for me to let go. Got no other choice."

"Yes. Tonight. After the concert. After the haircut. No shower. No fans. Fuck 'em."

"No fans?"

"Send your regrets. And a stack of CDs. Pre-signed. T-Shirts. Whatever."

"No fans. Got it."

"Hyundai. Be there. I'll drive."

"Oh, no, you won't. Your feet don't reach the pedals."

"Fine. You drive. No speeding."

"Darn straight."

"I'll make the reservations. In my name. I will not have a crowd of people waiting there for us."

"Done."

"Good."

"I love you."

"Shut up and play."

Katie flung herself into Trevor's arms as the crowd howled, stared up at him briefly, and smacked a kiss onto his lips.

"Knock 'em dead, Ski."

Trevor kissed her hard on the mouth, applause behind him, and stepped back onto the stage, feeling wobbly and light-headed.

He threw his heart and every spare ounce of energy he had into the concert. Security had to tighten up considerably.

He finished with 'Guitar-Man', as always, and handed Blondie off to Jesse Tweak who took her to safety in the tour bus.

Stagehands rolled a platform with a barber chair out. Margaret, in tears, brought out a pair of gold-plated shears tied with a big red bow and, while the crowd grew silent and expectant and the TV cameras rolled, sliced, in four neat passes, Trevor's long, dark hair off to the base of his skull.

Women fainted.

Grown men cried.

An hysterical Margaret had to be helped off stage by two of Scott's security team. A volunteer from the audience—planted by Trevor himself in the form of Rick Bissonette from Bisous–at-the-Spa in Punta Gorda—came up to shave the rest of his hair off as if he were going into the Marine Corps.

Cameras clicked and rolled.

More women fainted.

Trevor sucked it in. After all, it was his plan, he thought.

The deed done, Scott thoughtfully handed him a ski jacket and a knit ski cap as he came off stage. He grinned at his brother and hugged him. The ski cap was in his favorite shade of bright blue and had Ski Colorado embroidered on the front in yellow.

Trevor pulled the cap on over his ears and stumbled his way to the side exit to meet Katie in the Hyundai, pulling on the ski jacket as he went. He was soaking wet from sweat, wired, tired, and desperate.

Katie was waiting for him in the passenger seat, the engine running and the heater on. He opened the driver's side door and fell into the car, closing the door behind him.

Katie looked over at him.

"Nice hat. New?"

"Gift from Scott. Cold night air."

"Very thoughtful."

"Yep. Which way do I go?"

Katie grinned at him.

525

"'Second star to the right and on to morning'."

"Wiseguy."

"I get that from my boyfriend. Actually, we aren't driving that far."

Trevor pulled out of the parking lot, following the one-way signs. Katie pointed into the darkness.

"Go straight here. Turn left. Okay. Right over there."

"We're still in the parking garage, Kate."

"You bet. I'm taking no chances on stray fans. A cab's meeting us out front in fifteen minutes."

"We'll never find a slot."

"Oh, yes, we will. I planned ahead. See, there's Carla, holding down the fort."

Carla's laughing face was caught in the headlights, her body standing in an open slot for compact cars and waving them in like the ground crew at an airport. As Trevor pulled into the slot, Carla thumped the body of the car gleefully before running out of sight.

Katie turned smugly to Trevor.

"See? I have my minions, too"

"Am I on my honeymoon?"

"Maybe. Depends. Let's see what you've got when we get there."

Katie got out of the car and reached into the back seat to haul out a diaper bag. Trevor gave her a puzzled look.

"A diaper bag? My God, woman."

"They're very handy for carrying things."

"Things?"

"Supplies. Accoutrements. Whatever."

"You're scaring me."

"As if."

Trevor crawled out of the tiny car, grabbing his sunglasses out of the glove box and sliding them on from force of habit.

The Hyundai had plenty of leg and headroom in it for his and Scott's length and bulk. Katie had looked like a child on the passenger seat, Trevor thought.

A disturbing image for him.

"Let me take the bag."

"You're on, big boy. Follow me."

Katie was wearing a tank top and jeans and a denim jacket against the chill of New York City. As he watched her tiny figure in the darkness ahead of him, Trevor thought to himself how poetic it was that he had come back to New York City for this, the most important night of his life. Full-circle, he mused. What a world.

"God has a sense of humor."

"Did you ever doubt it? Look at penguins."

"He's having fun with a two-legged man-child tonight."

Katie grinned back at him.

"Nope. That's my job. I hope."

"Lead on, McDuff."

Trevor shouldered the diaper bag and stuck his hands in his pockets. He followed Katie down some concrete stairs to another level. The sounds around him reminded him very much of the New York City of his youth. He caught the smell of diesel fumes and fried food and felt the wet chill of New York City air feather around the back of his naked neck.

"This cab better have a heater."

"Wuss-boy. You won't need it for long."

Katie considered the man beside her, standing with his ski cap on, his sunglasses worn after dark, his baggy jacket zipped to his chin and the bag over his shoulder.

"It's a good thing you're not black."

"It is? Why?"

"I think it's the ski cap. You never looked like this in baseball caps. You look like a desperate criminal."

"I am desperate. And this could get criminal."

Katie shook her head at him.

A yellow cab pulled up to them and Trevor opened the back door for Katie, who slid over to let him in, giving her destination to the cabbie.

And they were off.

Trevor hunched down in the seat.

"You got funds for this operation? You know I don't even have my wallet with me."

"I've got funds. My picnic, my ticket."

Trevor glanced up to the reflection of their cabdriver he saw in the rearview mirror and his comic devil nudged him.

"Good. Don't leave me stranded. If you don't like my work tonight, at least slide me twenty bucks for the effort."

The cabbie glanced back at them in his rearview mirror, and Katie punched Trevor in the arm, making him laugh.

"Ow! Just no violence. Okay? I'm not into violence."

"Shut up."

"I'm shutting."

Katie sat stiffly beside him now. Trevor began to hum a tune that had been rattling around in his head. Katie looked over at him, barely able to see him in the darkened cab.

"Did you bring the ring?"

"What ring?"

"The engagement ring."

"What engagement ring?"

"You proposed to me and you don't even have an engagement ring?"

"I thought you weren't in it for the money."

"I'm not."

"Well, then?"

"Ape."

Trevor grinned at her in the dark. Katie could see his bright white teeth reflecting his fun.

"We'll go shopping together for it later, darlin'. History, by way of Dad, has taught me not to get the ring before I get the answer. And never get the ring without the lady."

Their cabbie chimed in on that one.

"Amen to that, buddy. Waste of good money."

Trevor threw his head back in laughter.

"God, I love New York."

Up in the hotel room with the door locked, they faced one another.

Katie took the diaper bag from Trevor and put it on the floor. She took off her jacket and hung it over the back of a chair.

Trevor hadn't said anything since they'd gotten to the hotel room. He stood now silent and motionless.

Katie glanced at him worriedly.

"Are you all right?"

Trevor licked his lips.

"Flashbacks for me. We'll see if I'm all right. I'm coming clean."

Trevor removed his sunglasses and laid them on the table. He removed the ski cap and waited for Katie's reaction to his bald head. She hadn't witnessed what he thought of biblically as the shearing of Samson.

Getting no reaction from Katie, Trevor placed his ski cap on the table as well.

Watching Katie solemnly the whole time, Trevor slowly began to undress.

He took off his jacket and dropped it over a chair. He took off his shirt and dropped it to the floor. He took off his worn sneakers. He unbuttoned his jeans, unzipped them and took them down the long length of his legs, taking his socks off with each pant leg and letting the bundle join his shirt and shoes on the floor.

He removed his boxers.

Totally naked, Trevor got down on his knees and sat back on his heels.

Finally, he took off the necklace Dani had given him for his sixteenth birthday and that he had never taken off since she had clasped it around his neck.

He placed the necklace with his clothing.

He was hugely conscious of his nakedness from his head to his heels.

He knew every scar he'd ever had was showing. His leg. The base of his skull. Others near his hairline, just above

529

his forehead. Scars that no one had ever seen. His long hair was finally gone. He had no protection at all.

Trevor licked dry lips and swallowed.

"My name is Trevor Lane Daniels. I love you. I want to marry you."

Katie dropped to the floor in front of Trevor.

She was speechless and stunned. She reached her hands out to slowly touch his knees, where even more scars showed, the kinds of scars any little boy might get playing on his knees or slipping and falling. She doubted somehow that Trevor had gotten these scars that way.

She reached for Dani's necklace and held it out to Trevor, then finally coaxed him to bend forward with her fingertips. Trevor did so and Katie clasped the necklace around his neck again, fingering the scars at the base of his skull. She sat up further and leaned close to him, brushing her lips over scars as she found them and making him shiver. She traced her fingers over his shoulders, kissing behind her touch. She placed her fingers and her hands and her lips slowly everywhere over his body, kissing and caressing, smoothing and soothing. Trevor never moved.

"You're a beautiful person, Ski," she breathed.

"I'm Trevor."

"You're a beautiful person, Trevor."

"Marry me."

"I will. I shouldn't. I have scars, too. Mental ones. Lots of them."

"You never asked about the scar on the back of my leg."

"I wouldn't, Ski. I saw it. I thought it was a birth defect."

An odd smile tugged at Trevor's lips.

"Yeah. A birth defect. I like that."

"You never asked me about the scars from my caesarian. Or my stretch marks."

"I love your stretch marks. You got them carrying a baby. They're beautiful."

"Oh, Ski. That's so sweet."

530

"No crying. Stop that right now. Be my bride, Katie. Please?"

Katie nuzzled her face into his shoulder and inhaled his scent. Soap and water and sweat and male.

"I love you so much. Whoever you are. I'll never leave you. I'll never cheat on you. I'll never be intentionally cruel to you. I don't believe in divorce, even though I've had one."

"I don't cheat. I do lie, but I don't do it well, and never for evil. I'm moody and self-absorbed and arrogant and stupid. I'll never leave you. I'll never break our wedding vows. I love you. Be my wife. Please?"

Katie kissed his neck in the hollow above his collarbone.

"Yes."

Katie sat back from him then and fixed her eyes firmly on Trevor's eyes.

"You're an asthmatic manic-depressive."

Trevor grimaced and planted a weak version of the idiot-grin on his face.

"Yeah."

"You're a childish, selfish brat who uses his family to gain his ends."

"I'm working on the selfish thing. And I prefer the term 'child-like'."

"You are a ruthless sociopathic liar."

"Okay."

"Is it possible to insult you?"

"Not when you're telling the truth."

"Have I missed anything?"

"I'm extremely goal-oriented. I can focus. I can dig in. I'm hardworking."

"I'm not trying to list your merits. I'm trying to list all your flaws."

"Oh. Sorry. Lots of people consider those to be flaws in me."

"I don't. I might consider your charm to be a flaw. I'm not sure about that."

531

Trevor sobered again.

"Do you want me to list what I consider to be my flaws? See if they match your list?"

"You're a very strange man."

"Is that a flaw?"

"No. Oddly enough, I like that. I like your originality. Very well then. List your flaws."

Trevor chewed on his bottom lip.

"I'll start with the one I have the hardest struggle with."

Katie tilted her head, trying to assess his sincerity. Trevor swallowed.

"I have trouble with drawing a line in the sand I won't cross."

"What?"

"I have trouble setting limits or parameters for myself. I lack good judgment at times. Lots of times. I scare myself with the depths to which I won't go. I truly scare myself then, because I haven't found the bottom of my morality yet."

"This from the man who gives blankets and cracker packs to the homeless? Bull."

"It's true, Kate. There's probably nothing I wouldn't stoop to doing. And a lot I've done."

"You're clever. Very clever. Are you forcing me to list your merits to counteract what you claim are your flaws?"

"No."

"Well, I can't seem to help myself. Cruelty. You are never cruel. I can't imagine you being cruel."

"I've been cruel."

"Regretted it?"

"Yes."

"It doesn't count then. Repentance is everything. Next?"

Trevor chuckled.

532

"How did you do that? I was dead serious. I am dead serious. I'm trying to list my worst flaws and you're making me laugh. This is serious."

"You say you have no sense of boundaries or limitations. Of course, you don't. You're an artist."

"Well, I should at least have some sort of internal barrier system. Something that gives me a jolt when I hit it as a reminder to myself that I don't want to cross it."

"You've got your boundaries. You didn't force sex on me. You never made me feel dependent on you."

"That's easy. I'll never do anything that's been done to me that I didn't like. But look how I lie. I think nothing of lying to achieve a goal."

"You think plenty about it."

"Afterward. When it's too late."

"It's never too late."

"I want to stop it before it starts. I want barriers."

"Here's some more flaws. You brood. You're moody. You're absent-minded. You're thoughtless."

"Thoughtless?"

He was plainly puzzled, Katie thought, frowning at her, but with a look of introspection on his face. He repeated the accusation.

"Thoughtless?"

"Yes. You have a wonderful family that loves you and you think nothing of worrying them."

"I do. I regret it. Everytime."

"Then stop worrying them."

"How?"

"What worries them? Your health worries them. Your judgment."

"You see? My judgment. My judgment is tied up with my health."

"Then learn better. Stop worrying your family. They love you. God knows why."

"I'm manipulative."

533

"That may be part of it. But they always seem to see you coming with that. They just go along with it because they love you."

Trevor took a deep breath.

"Are you ready for my monolog? I think I've got it all together in one place."

Katie nodded briefly.

"Yes, I'm ready."

"I'm the legitimate son of Lisa Buck Lane, now Lisa Sabatino."

Trevor considered his statement.

"Well, she was Lisa Lane Buck Sabatino when I last saw her. That was when I was fifteen years old. My first father was Shawn Lane, composer, musician, and homosexual. My parents divorced when I was about two years old, my father having come out of the closet."

Trevor paused briefly to organize his thoughts.

"Custody was awarded to my mother, who moved me out-of-state and away from my father, against whom she had a restraining order, and away from her sister, my Aunt Mary. I never saw my birth father from age two onwards."

Trevor frowned.

"Because of the flaws inherent in the legal system, I remained in my mother's sole custody, except for short spans of time spent in hospitals and foster care, until she married Nick Sabatino when I was about ten."

Trevor shivered slightly and then carefully relaxed his hands.

"My mother beat me, and starved me, tied me up in closets, and left me for days on end in the dark. She tricked me out to some of her johns. She's the one who gave me that long cut on the back of my right leg. She came after me with a knife. I was six years old."

Trevor looked up, then down again. Katie remained silent.

"I lived on the streets. I lived in fear. When she married Nick, he beat me up and tossed me officially out of the house. You've heard my song about Darryl's grandfather?"

Katie nodded.

"He was real, Katie. He found me a home. Such as it was. With a sado-masochistic pedophile who kept me locked in a house for three months, a dog collar around my neck, naked and squatting in my own filth. One Christopher de Nunzio."

Trevor huffed out a breath.

"I agreed to that arrangement in order to earn the guitar you and the whole world know I call Blondie. Three months. He had porno pictures taken of me. Of us. There's at least another video still out there someplace. Dad, Scott and I found one of them. Parts of that video will be coming out as film background for Jake Benson's cover of my 'Scream in Pain.' People will probably think it's fake. It's not."

Trevor drew a breath in through his nose and held it a moment before releasing it.

"After three months, this person Chris gave me Blondie, twenty bucks, some condoms and a backpack with some pitiful, little, childlike belongings in it. He told me to go to Key West, Florida, to play guitar. I was ten years old. I played guitar. I started heading for Key West. On foot."

Katie was sitting with her hand over her mouth now. Trevor glanced up at her again and then down.

"It's a long walk to Key West, Florida, from New York City. I slept outside in the cold. In the rain. In the heat. In the snow."

"Your lungs. Jarrett mentioned your sleeping outside. Mary thinks it caused your asthma."

"Could be. Doesn't matter now. My asthma's a fact of life. Like my scars. And my fears."

Trevor shifted his weight slightly.

"I headed south. I played guitar for tips. I hitchhiked. I was free."

He looked up at Katie again and smiled ironically.

"I was free to do absolutely anything I wanted to do. No limits. No barriers. No protection. No advice. But I'm tough and I learn quickly. I sold my body for food, or money, whatever I needed. I stole. I lied. I survived. My songs are my life, Katie. My music was my friend and my salvation."

Katie shifted closer to him, laying her hands on his knees and smoothing his thighs with her hands. Trevor looked up and didn't break eye contact with her again.

"I was still heading for Key West."

He chuckled.

"Side trips to New Orleans. California. Texas. Truckers, God bless them. I love truckers. I never had to sell my body to a trucker. Just play my music and chatter to keep them awake. There's not a state in the union I hadn't been in before I got to Charlotte County, barring Alaska and Hawaii. I'm real well-traveled. But I kept heading for the Keys."

Trevor drew in another breath and let it out, finding it easier to relate his history to Katie than he had thought it would be.

"I got mugged in Charlotte County at old Exit 31 up on the interstate. And raped in the boonies. Three local boys, the youngest being nineteen. The Spath boys. I wasn't quite fifteen. They stole Blondie and hocked her. Stole my backpack with my measly possessions in it. And my music. Left me for dead behind a strip mall."

He smiled.

"That's when things actually started looking up for me, only I didn't know it then. I was out cold. Dad worked for the Charlotte County Sheriff's Department back then. He scooped me up in his cruiser and got me to a hospital. The rest is history."

"Your birth mother?"

"Oh, my, yes. Re-entered my life when Dad wanted to adopt me. Dad and I together found Mary. Lisa–the woman I refer to as my former-mom–you already know I don't like the name Lisa–found us through Mary. That wasn't Mary's fault. It worked out for the best. Mary is Mary Buck, now Daniels. She was a concert violinist."

"You told me that."

536

"I wanted to be sure I didn't miss anything. Lisa came, but Mary faced her down. Quite the lady, my aunt. I got adopted. Everything from then on you can read in any biography on me. You probably have."

"Your birth father? Shawn Lane?"

"Oh. Yeah. Forgot. Mary brought me my father. She'd always loved him, but, well, it didn't work out. I've met Shawn's life partner, Doug Henshaw. Nice guy. Real loyal. Good man. My father died of AIDS contracted before he met Doug. I never knew my father. I told you that much. Mary gave me my father. Mary and Dad together. And then they gave me my life. Dad was married before Mary. Another witch. Scott's mom. Mary and I found a way to get Scott reconnected with Dad. Scott was sixteen when we met. Can't keep us apart now."

"You're a beautiful person, Trevor."

Trevor shook his head.

"I've known dirt, Kate. I've wallowed in dirt. I was smoking and dealing and doing drugs before I was even out of elementary school. I don't think there's a thing about sex I don't know and darned little I haven't done. I have no morals. Dad loaned me his. I have no self-respect. Grammy gave me what I have. I have no pride in self. Mary's sharing hers with me. I have no center, no core. I'm empty. Hollow. All I have is the music machine inside me, sucking up experience and turning it into music and words. I create beauty. Don't confuse the creation with the creator, Kate."

"You're a beautiful person, Trevor. You are very much a self-made man. You're like a phoenix rising from its own ashes."

Trevor shook his head.

"You're romanticizing me."

"Who quit smoking? Who quit drugs? Who quit selling his body? Who quit drinking?"

"I still drink."

"You know what I mean. And I haven't seen you drink so much as a beer since we met. It's always Dr. Pepper."

537

"Mary and Dad and Grammy made me what I am today. I'm the hollow-man."

"They loved you. They guided you. They didn't create you. You did. You are a beautiful person, Trevor. I love you. Will you marry me?"

Trevor bit his lip, his eyes worried.

"Are you sure?"

"Yes."

"I may backslide. I'll probably always need help."

"Trevor. We help one another. No debts of gratitude. No pity fucks. You make me feel pretty and desirable. I love the way you look at me. I love the way you love Robbie. I love the way you love life. I love your extremes, even when they frighten me or exasperate me."

Trevor gritted his teeth and spewed out another piece of his darkness.

"I come from an abusive mother. Can you trust me not to be an abusive parent? Can I trust myself? Child abuse. It's the gift that keeps on giving. Not AIDS."

Katie leaned forward to smooth her hands slowly up Trevor's arms.

"Is this your worst fear?"

Trevor nodded.

"I love babies. I love children. I would take my own life if I ever found myself hurting one."

"Ssh. I think that you are so mindful of what has been done to you in the past that that will never be an issue. You never do to others what you don't wish done to you. Ever. This will not be a problem. You'll probably be a lousy father because you'll spoil our children with too little discipline."

"Our children?"

"I hope so. Marry me?"

"I'd like to marry you. I didn't buy a ring. Remember?"

Katie sat back on her heels and drew a breath.

"I remember. So. That's it? You have no more secrets?"

Trevor chewed on his bottom lip.

"I've got more secrets, but they're not mine. They're other peoples' secrets, and I'm not giving them up. But secrets of my own? I may find others later, but I'm pretty sure you've got them all."

"Well. If that was all you've been worried about all these years, what's the big deal?"

Silence.

Trevor felt a huge weight lifting off his shoulders. It was the same sensation he'd felt as the weight of his long hair fell away under Margaret's scissors. He felt his face crinkling into a grin and then a chuckle beginning deep in his chest. He closed his eyes, threw his head back and let the first of the laughter roll up from his toes and out his mouth. He fell right flat back on his back with it and spread his arms wide, laughing and rolling his head from side to side.

Katie scrambled to his side.

"Trevor! Sweetheart, please watch the back of your head. You have nothing there to protect you now. Be careful."

Katie's tiny hands reached out to him.

Trevor's eyes flashed open. He grabbed Katie fast and rolled with her, landing on top and grinning down at her.

"I feel so light and airy! This is great! Marry me. Love me. Be my bride forever. Make babies with me. Katie, Katie, Katie. Beautiful Katie."

"You're nuts."

"Oh, my, yes. Ask anyone. Hey. Watcha got in the diaper bag, little girl?"

"Goodies."

"Goodies? I love goodies. Can I see? Can I play with your goodies, little girl? 'Can I give you a lick; will you flick my Bic, Little Pussy?' Oh. I forgot. I have a degree in marine biology. Just in case."

Katie laughed up at him.

"You can't even swim!"

"But I love water."

"So. Not just another pretty face. Brains, too."

"I guess. Got no common sense, though."

539

"You've got enough."

"Street smarts."

"Translate: common sense."

Trevor toned his grin down to a warm, intimate smile.

"Thanks. So. Whatcha really got in the diaper bag?"

"Baby oil."

Trevor brightened considerably.

"Got plans?"

"I believe I do."

"No rapes."

"I don't believe it's possible to rape the willing on either side."

"Protection?"

"Against what? Disease? We neither of us have been with anyone else for several, several months. Years in my case. Correct?"

"Correct."

"Pregnancy? I believe you mentioned twenty-five children. Time's a-wastin'."

Trevor sucked in a breath and grinned again.

"Yes, it is. Screw the protection."

### BLESSING

Never look behind you.
Never look ahead.
Look right there beside you
Lying in your bed.

What's done is gone. It can't be changed.
What's coming up,
Who knows?
The sweetest time is right here now,
So stop and smell a rose.

I've looked behind me almost all my life.
Running scared and frightened of the strife.

I've planned ahead.
God's laughed and let me bleed.
But what I'll wed
Is really all I need.

Love and trust and sanity
Take the place of vanity.
The past is done and gone.
The future is unknown.
Right now is all the blessing that I need.
Right now is all the blessing that I need.

\*     \*     \*     \*     \*

Trevor flew home from New York City with Katie on a regular commercial airline, wearing neither a baseball cap nor sunglasses. Then they picked up a rental car in Ft. Myers and drove home to Punta Gorda. While Katie went to check on Robbie, Trevor went over to his old home on Olympia Avenue.

Jarrett was now running his hands over Trevor's naked skull, his face intent, while Trevor blushed.

"Darn, Trevor. You sure do go to extremes. I ain't never broke you of that habit. How's it feel?"

Trevor grinned at him and Jarrett watched the play of muscle under the pale skin of Trevor's scalp.

"Weird. I feel naked. People warned me about that, but I really wasn't prepared for the shock. My head feels so light it might drift off my shoulders. Like it had helium in it. I feel like I've got no clothes on. I keep reaching for it, the hair, and it's not there. I go to fling it over my shoulder, and it's not there. It's just not there."

"You better start wearin' a hat for real now. You'll get sunburned. They didn't leave you much past some peach fuzz. Why? You didn't have to do that. Got all them scars showin' in the back now. And a couple up front here I didn't know about."

541

Jarrett reached his concerned hands to touch those areas of his son's head and Trevor ducked his head in embarrassment.

"Those scars were before your time, Dad. The hair? It'll grow back. I figured, get it cut, get it cut. I kind of wish I hadn't. But I'll look like Dani for sure now."

"I don't hardly recognize you without that hair."

"I hardly recognize myself. It was like a whole separate person, Dad. Like Siamese twins being separated. I thought I was going to bawl right there on national TV. I saw the tapes later. I saw my face. And the faces of a lot of fans. Men, too. Not just chicks. It was still a good thing to do. Dani'll get honest-to-God Trevor-hair wigs. We'll auction 'em off after Dani doesn't need them anymore. We got the medical expenses covered. And the event drew a lot of attention to the cause."

"But you still feel naked."

"Yeah. But I feel better than Dani and the other folks on chemo do. I've got short hair, not cancer. Mine'll grow back."

"So will theirs, Trev. Ya done good. Ya make me proud, son. Ya gonna get a nice tattoo up there? Maybe have some lightnin' bolts carved into your hair or wear it buzzed like mine?"

"No. I'm going to wear a hat and grow this stuff back out fast. Maybe keep it shorter. Maybe to my ears. Or my neck. It's a helluva lot cooler in the Florida heat."

"Makes ya look like you done joined the Marine Corps right now. Just wait till Mary sees it."

"I can hardly wait."

Jarrett kept looking at Trevor's head and running his hands over it.

"Darn, boy. You look like Mr. Clean. No earring, though. Yet. You ever had your hair this short in your whole life? I sure didn't hardly recognize you. It's you, though. I can see you peepin' out them eyes of yours at me. God Almighty."

Trevor laughed, blushing and bashful.

Jarrett watched again in fascination as muscles and veins moved under the taunt skin covering Trevor's skull. There were his former-mom's ears, Jarrett thought, revealed at last. There were the scars from his attack by the Spath boys, a distorted crisscross at the nape of his neck as he turned his head. And there were other marks, near the temples, above his forehead at the hairline and behind one ear that Jarrett hadn't known about.

Jarrett put a hand up to the one at Trevor's temple now, sobering Trevor.

"It was a long time ago, Dad. Before you."

"I hardly know you."

Trevor put up a hand to cover Jarrett's, now cupped behind his ear.

"I hardly know myself, Dad. Got nowhere to hide now. And nothing to hide with. All my scars are showing. At least, all the scars in places that won't get me arrested for having them show. But it's me, Dad. It's really me."

Trevor smiled lovingly at the man still running concerned hands over his shaved scalp.

"Daddy, please. I'm all right. Really."

"I've seen more hair on a cue ball."

"I know. It'll grow."

"It better. You're gonna look right silly about five o'clock tonight when your face is darker than your head."

"Maybe I'll grow a goatee. Or a Fu Manchu."

Jarrett playfully slammed Trevor's shoulder with the palm of one hand.

"Don't mess with me, boy. Just wait till your aunt sees this. They didn't show this on the station Mary and I were watching."

"She's probably seen this hairstyle on me before. Like when I was born maybe. I don't think they showed this part on TV. Probably saving it for special release. Margaret was having a fit. I thought she was going to have a heart attack on stage, her hands were shaking so much. She did the deed and then broke down crying. I didn't know she could cry at all, least of all over me. That shook me up, I can tell you. I had this shorter haircut done by Rick Bissonette. You know. The guy who owns Bisous-at-the-Spa. I don't think Margaret knows about this yet."

Trevor grinned at his father and then shrugged.

"I figured, get it cut. Get it really cut."

He sobered for a moment.

"That hair is absolutely and positively the last thing that was left over from the olden days, Dad. It was always what was always mine. What I couldn't loose. And it couldn't be stolen from me or thrown out. I think I know why, as an adult, Lisa let my hair grow long. It really did make me look more like Shawn."

Trevor eyes saddened.

"I idolized her. You know? Back when? She was my mom. I remember sitting on the bed, watching her get dressed up, making herself pretty. She'd smile. She'd smooth my hair. She'd laugh and flirt. I was Shawn to her. I didn't know that then. I didn't understand. I adored her. That all stopped for both of us after the knife attack. But now the long hair finally makes sense."

Trevor quirked a smile again at his still-stunned father.

"And I finally found a good enough reason to get it all cut off."

"Makes more sense than what you've done now with this skinhead look. Gonna have to wear a hat all the time or put some sunscreen on there. Be gettin' a real nasty burn."

Trevor chuckled.

"I wanted to start fresh, Dad. I wanted to start all over again for Katie's sake. I'll grow the hair, but probably not as long as before. I like the freedom this gives me. I don't look like Trevor Daniels. Flying down here with Katie, not one person came up for my autograph. Katie's shown me her scars, too, Dad. Fair was fair."

"Swappin' scars, huh? Helluva lady."

"She is. She's a keeper."

"Be yourself, boy. Anythin' else is a fraud. Not good for either of you."

544

"I'm trying. It's sometimes hard for me to remember just who I am. I've been covering it up for years."

"Give it your best shot, boy. You always do."

Jarrett smoothed his hands over Trevor's skull again.

"Makin' peace with your past. That's a good thing, Trevor. Makin' peace and movin' on. Good for you, son."

"Yeah. It is. Hey. Want to come to a wedding?"

"Anyone I know?"

"I think so. Scruffy kid you picked up next to a dumpster a couple of years back. He's bald now. But I hear he's gorgeous."

"It'd be my pleasure, son. No tie, though. I ain't wearin' no tie."

"Absolutely not. Neither am I."

"Good for you, son."

"Yeah. It is."

# Chapter Twenty-four

Attorney-at-law Stephan B. Widmeyer was enjoying the easy task of handling Katie's child support, visitation, and dissolution of marriage agreement enforcement business. At his offices in Port Charlotte, he leaned back now in his chair, stroking his handlebar mustache, a twinkle in his blue eyes as he glanced from Trevor to Katie Mercer seated across the desk from him.

"For me, it's like playing tennis. I'm not even breaking a sweat. Your ex's attorney asks for visitation, Mrs. Mercer, and I counter with the threat of molestation charges. I ask for the transfer of the deed to the house, they panic but counter with a demand for your address. I counter with the threat of abuse charges and ask for increased child support. You lose nothing. He gains nothing. But it keeps him very high profile. Hard to get away with things like throwing you out of your own home, or attempting to sell it, when another attorney's involved. I'm sure his attorney had no idea Mr. Smallwood did that. What was the point? Spite and malice. That'll make a judge real sympathetic."

Katie chewed on her bottom lip.

"I don't understand why Charlie suddenly decided to do that."

"Does he know about Trevor?"

"I didn't think he did. How could he? I didn't know."

"Well, not Trevor *per se* then. Did he have a way to find out if you were seeing another man? Having a man over to the house, perhaps?"

"I don't think so. But who knows? If he'd been spying on me, he could have found out where I worked. He could have seen Trevor meeting me there those few times. But there were no letters. No phone calls. Just, 'For Sale'. All of a sudden."

"How did you meet Trevor? If you don't mind my asking?"

"Oh, I don't mind."

Trevor sat forward.

"Well, I mind. The hell with Charlie Smallwood. I know you're having a good time, Steve, but I don't think Katie's getting as much of a charge out of this little war as you are. I want a way to get this guy geographically out of Katie's and my way. Buy him off. Find out what it'll take to make him disappear forever out of her and Robbie's lives. Money? Career? Whatever."

Katie laid a hand on Trevor's arm.

"It doesn't seem right to me to reward him for what he's done to Robbie and to me."

Trevor gave her a steely look.

"Yes, ma'am, it does. Keep your friends close and your enemies even closer. I want him sucked in so tight it'd kill him to mess with you. And I want to know exactly where he is. What's he always dreamed about doing or having?"

Katie gnawed on her bottom lip, trying to remember what she would have preferred to forget.

"Charlie always talked about owning a night club on the south side of Chicago where he could play guitar and sell watered-down drinks to customers."

Trevor snorted.

"That's it? That was his dream? A captive audience and a two-bit hustle? Steve? Make it happen. Stipulation of giving up Robbie for adoption and no further contact with either him or Katie, ever. Don't be cheap. Keep me posted."

Steve Widmeyer nodded.

Trevor slid back his chair and stood up, stretching his arms over his head.

"Are we through here? We've wasted enough of this beautiful day the Good Lord gave us on this worthless sack of shit. Katie? You coming?"

Katie stood and slid her hand into Trevor's.

They exited Steve Widmeyer's office and crossed US 41 on foot, heading for the parking lot of Julien French Bakery.

Katie squeezed Trevor's hand.

"I don't feel right about this, Ski. It still feels as though we're rewarding Charlie for all the horrible things he's done."

"We're buying him off, plain and simple."

"It still feels like a reward to me. Fulfilling his life's dream. It just seems wrong."

"What it is, Katydid, is Machiavellian. I got a fair notion of this guy's character from what he's done to you and all you haven't said. I'm guessing he's going to choke to death on his own dream and save us all a lot of trouble in the long run. I give him five years, tops, before he fucks up badly enough to cause his own death, one way or another."

Katie shook her head.

"I don't get it."

"I'm running with my mean streak here and it feels pretty darned good. Charlie's earned this."

Trevor opened the door to Julien French Bakery and allowed Katie to precede him.

"Come have a pastry with me here. Always celebrate your victories. We just had one, babe."

Trevor waited until William had brought a slice of tiramisu for him and a berry tartlet for Katie and departed.

He leaned across the small bistro table, grinning at Katie.

With his hair just long enough now to brush his collar and fall over his brow, he looked just like any other guy, Katie thought. Any other gorgeous guy, she amended mentally.

Without its own weight to drag it down, Trevor's hair, when it began to grow back in, had shown a tendency to wave gently. Now it flopped around his face, but Trevor no longer used it for a shield of any kind. He only used his sunglasses out in the bright Florida sun, and only used a baseball cap to keep his nose from burning in that same sun.

He was eager and relaxed as he gazed into Katie's eyes.

"Revenge, as Worf on 'Star Trek: Next Generation' would say, is a dish best served cold. Imagine the

548

possibilities, Kate. Roll in the possibilities like a kid in fall leaves up north. Enjoy it. One of the first things I learned about having a lot of money is what it couldn't buy. It's also something I have to keep relearning all the time. I've watched you doing Stephie's parties, going around in the limo. You really don't care about the money. Not about the really gross magnitude of what the family has. It's kind of like never-never land. Totally unbelievable. But if a person has the mentality that money is their life goal—your mom's money or maybe gypping customers out of drinks—well, then money will bring them crashing down when they get it. They spend it. They blow it. They waste it."

Trevor forked a bite of his tiramisu into his mouth and savored the moment before speaking again.

"I'm hoping he wastes it on drugs myself. Or running with the wrong crowd. I'm guessing he'll flaunt the money. Someone's always out there to take it away. Women. Con artists. Does he gamble? There you go. He might blow it gambling. Fast cars. I've been there myself. I love fast cars. But I've learned to pace myself with big-ticket items. And I've got deeper pockets than Charlie Smallwood will ever think to have. I'm not saying that in a conceited way. He'll get his Southside bar, because Steve will buy it for him, fully stocked, good clientele established, total turnkey operation. He'll play his guitar, screw up the management of the bar, spend what he doesn't have, probably get in with your basic bent-nosed bad guys of Chicago and, like I said, probably disappear in five years, tops. Another real moron gone down the tubes, greased by his dream-come-true. I love it."

Katie nibbled at her berry tartlet while Trevor luxuriated in the flavor of his tiramisu, smiling at her all the while. She shook her head at him, returning his smile.

"That is Machiavellian. How do you know Charlie won't make a success of this bar?"

Trevor snorted.

"Please. Tell me you saw the seeds of success in the man and I'll be happy for him. What was he like as a provider while you were married?"

549

"He worked. Not often. Not long. His bosses were always giving him problems, he said. Or his co-workers. He made good money when he worked, though."

"Did you support the three of you?"

"No. Charlie didn't like me working. He moved in and out of the house. In and out of our lives. When he was out, I collected welfare and took in sewing. I was very young–in my head–when we met and married. My mother never liked him. After she died, he talked me into marrying him, hoping, I suppose, to get the nest egg she left me. Before we married, I'd never seen the cruelty. Nor understood the periods of unemployment. Naïve. Stupid."

"Quit with the twenty-twenty hindsight."

Katie smiled.

"Okay. Fair enough. And you're right. He blew our nest egg, what there was of it, on buying the orange grove."

Trevor frowned.

"What orange grove?"

"Oh. The house outside Arcadia. You might not have noticed. There's an orange grove behind it. There's an orange grove behind every house up in that area. Acres of them sometimes. It's like wheat fields in Kansas or rocks in Colorado. It just is."

"My Uncle Richard has orange groves. Successful ones. I wonder if there's any potential there with that one."

"Well, Charlie didn't know anything about orange groves. Or trees or fruit or anything. Neither do I, actually. But I'd never get into anything I didn't understand."

"I can testify to that."

"I understand you now."

"And, God knows you're into me."

Katie grinned.

"Yes, I am."

"See? Charlie'll choke on the money and screw up the bar."

"Then he'll come back."

"Oh, no, he won't. This is a one-time offer. The offer of a lifetime. Trust me, he'll be getting so much money he won't be able to know it's not there till he's shaking sand out of a can and wondering why. We're not talking a couple of thousand here. We're not even talking a couple of hundred thousand. When Charlie Smallwood chokes on dick, I want to be sure he's got a big, fat one to choke on."

Trevor leaned across the table, whispered a number into Katie's ear and had the pleasure of seeing her eyes grow wide and her face lose all color.

"Ski!"

"Don't sweat it. Sell some more CDs. You're good at that. We'll make it up in less than a month. Just a speed bump in the game of life for us, darlin'."

"I don't think the Devil went down to Georgia, Trevor. I think he's sitting in Julien French Bakery eating pastry."

Trevor grinned at her.

"Fallen angel. I prefer the term 'fallen angel'."

"Jesse and Becky got married last weekend."

"Jesus Christ."

"Who couldn't see that coming?"

"Me. I couldn't see it coming. I'm supposed to be the leader of the band. Not the follower. Is Becky coming on the road with Jess? Where was our invitation to this wedding?"

"She is. She figured if Carla and I could take it, so could she. Their wedding was small. It was just both sets of their parents, back up in Tidewater, Virginia."

"One big happy family. We better start thinking seriously about a traveling nanny and a day care bus. When are we getting married? Does anybody know? Do I know?"

Katie laughed at him.

"How about Father's Day?"

"I had plans for Father's Day. Tentative plans. Not a problem. Plans can be changed. A June wedding? In Florida? Best not be outdoors. We'll all sweat to death. And I'm not wearing a tie. Neither is Dad."

"Good. Neither am I."

"You get it all lined up. You and Stephie or you and Carla and Mary. Scott and Dad. Make them my best men.

551

They are anyway. Just point me in the right direction on the day in question."

Katie giggled and curled her toes in delight.

"Silly."

\*     \*     \*     \*     \*

Trevor finished his CD of songs for Jarrett.

Margaret's book came out.

It was time to celebrate more victories.

Trevor scratched his head.

"Kate, I don't want to upstage the wedding, but we'll have everybody here for it anyway. Can I tag this gift to Dad on somewhere? And Margaret's book? She worked darned hard on that. Uphill most of the way, 'cause she doesn't like me much."

"Stephie's doing the job of a wedding planner. Let her know what you have in mind. Carla and Mary and I are just doing the fun stuff."

"I think my bachelor party might be milkshakes at Mickey D's."

"Right."

"Well, maybe burgers at Big Dog's."

Trevor and Katie set their wedding date for June and Stephie blocked off a wing of the Best Western Water Front to house out-of-town guests.

Trevor snagged the early part of his bachelor party at Big Dog's for his gift to Jarrett.

Jarrett held the boxed CD in his hands, grinning from ear to ear.

"You little weasel. Come here and give me sugar."

Jarrett folded a willing and grinning Trevor into his arms.

"Happy Father's Day, Dad."

"It ain't Father's Day yet. That's later in June sometime."

"Any day is Father's Day as far as I'm concerned. I'm about to be a father myself to Robbie. I just couldn't wait for an official date, Dad. It was Scottie's idea to do the CD. We figured out which songs to go on it between us. They're all new. I've never even done any of them live in concert. It's all just for you."

"'Daddy Let Me'. I declare. You ought not to just let them stay on this one CD, son."

"I might not now. But they were written for you. You get them first."

"Thank you, son. Who did the artwork on the label?"

"Well, Robbie and I did. We're both into coloring. He's better than I am. Scott scanned our artwork into his computer and he's got some sort of CD label making program. I don't understand all that stuff. Just give me a box, six strings, a pencil and piece of paper. I'm happy. Simplest is best for me."

\*　　　\*　　　\*　　　\*　　　\*

A week after the wedding, Trevor was holding Katie's hand in the kitchen on Gill Street over their usual shared breakfast of scrambled eggs. He was happily rubbing his finger over her small diamond engagement ring.

"You never got the romantic dinners."

"What could be more romantic than dining tête-à-tête with Trevor Lane Daniels, Sarasota's fifth most eligible bachelor?"

"Not any more, he's not. We never flew to Vegas in the Lear jet."

"I don't gamble. Why bother?"

"We could have spent our honeymoon anywhere we wanted to."

"We really are married? I'm so glad."

"Of course we are."

Katie sighed in bliss.

"I just wondered if that was true. I was having Trevor Daniels' love child, you know."

"You been reading the tabloids again?"

"No."

Trevor blinked.

The information took a moment to sink in.

He jumped straight out of his chair.

"You're pregnant!?"

\* \* \* \* \*

Mary looked up from her needlepoint and over to Jarrett in his recliner.

"There goes that whooping sound again."

"Trevor."

"I suppose. Do you think it's a birth announcement this time?"

"Could be."

\* \* \* \* \*

"Pregnant? You're pregnant?"

Katie nodded.

Awed, Trevor gasped and shivered in delight and sudden fear.

"I'm pregnant?"

Katie broke into a laugh.

"No, silly. I'm pregnant."

"Trust me. I'm pregnant, too. I'll be weepy and bloated."

"That's PMS, Trevor."

"I'll get fat and throw up."

"My turn first in the bathroom."

"Fair. That's fair. Pregnant. Wow. We're pregnant. I'm going to be a father. How far along? When are you due? When are we due? Oh, my, God."

"Trevor?"

"Yeah?"

" Calm down."

"Oh. Okay. You, too."

They sat at the breakfast table clutching one another's hands. Katie drew one hand away to cover her

554

narrow middle and Trevor sat with the stunned look of a man hit in the head with a two by four.

"Pregnant. Oh, my, yes. Pregnant. Baby. Let me listen to the baby."

"The baby's not moving yet, Trevor."

"Can I put my head on your stomach? Will it hurt you? Will it hurt the baby?"

"Tranquilizers for you, Daddy."

"Daddy. Oh, my God."

\*      \*      \*      \*      \*

Katie stood on the steps of the house on Olympia Avenue. Jarrett stood on the threshold, squinting into the distance.

"Where's Trevor?"

"Running all over town screaming at the top of his lungs, 'I'm a Daddy,' 'We're pregnant,' and variations of that same theme. He was doing cartwheels down the sidewalk fronting Gilchrist Park. I lost track of him when he ran down Shreve Street."

Mary slid from behind Jarrett and put her arm around Katie's waist, drawing her up the steps.

"So like his father. That seems to be the traditional reaction of the Lane male to news of pregnancy."

Jarrett loomed over them from behind.

"He's a Daniels."

Mary smiled up at him.

"He's both today, Jarrett. You taught him parenting skills. He'll need that more than joy, Grandpa."

"Grandpa. Sounds old. Sounds good, though."

Jarrett fixed his eyes on Mary's face.

"Shawn Lane had two years of in-house fatherhood before the shit hit his fan. While Trevor's still out there whoopin' it up, I want some basic information from Katie."

Mary put a hand on his arm.

"It's not our place, Jarrett."

"If not us, then who? I can't be sure what that boy might be tryin' to hide. This is important for all our futures. I'm gonna ask you somethin', Katie. And I want a straight answer."

Katie raised her chin.

Jarrett considered his words.

"Would you ever deny my boy his child?"

"No! Never. The child will be as much Trevor's as mine."

"You're denyin' Robbie to his father."

"That's different. You know it is. And Charlie hasn't expressed any interest in visitation with Robbie now that he's gotten the offer of his bar. If he had wanted visitation, I would have permitted it. But it would have had to have been supervised visitation. I would never permit Charlie to be alone with Robbie ever again."

"Good. Good answer. Stick with those answers, little girl."

"I love your son, Jarrett. I have one failed marriage behind me. I don't want another. I've tried to get to know Trevor as well as anyone can get to know another before I even committed to a kiss, let alone a relationship. I can't predict the future. Who can? If he cheats on me, I will divorce him. We've discussed that. If he ever abuses me or Robbie, I will divorce him."

"I'll kill him. It'll never happen, Katie."

"Those are my ground rules as of now."

Jarrett chuckled.

"Got some fire in there, do you? Good. You'll need it."

His face sobered.

"Trevor tell you about his past?"

Katie licked her lips.

"Lisa. Shawn. Chris. Spath boys."

"All right. I guess I'm mostly concerned with your opinion of the Shawn-thing, or the Chris-thing maybe."

556

Katie gnawed on her bottom lip. She could hear the echo of Trevor's shouts across the sleepy streets of Punta Gorda.

"Your son is a wonderful man. He loves me and he loves Robbie. I love him. I wouldn't want to share him in our marriage. I've already had a marriage to an abusive cheater. I will not tolerate another. If Trevor wants to fall in love or sleep with someone else, he'll have to divorce me. That's my stand right now. I can't see the future. I've seen the past. So has Trevor. I don't think any of that is going to be a problem."

"Fair enough, little girl. Fairer than most. Them secrets you've got now are lock-box-bank-box secrets. Go-to-your-grave-with-them secrets. Ain't no one ever tried to cash in on them secrets and lived. Welcome to the family."

\*　　\*　　\*　　\*　　\*

## TREVOR'S WEDDING SONG

"With this ring, I thee wed."
Better words I've never said
To any woman in my life.
You are my wife.

Hand in hand
And heart to heart
From this moment now
We start
To build a life together for all time.

Love. Come to me, love.
God above
I love you so.
Even more today than yesterday,
But not as much
As tomorrow.

"With this ring, I thee wed."
Lay down with me in my bed.
Stay beside me till we're dead
And evermore.

Love. Come to me, love.
God above
I love you so.
Even more today than yesterday,
But not as much as tomorrow.

\*       \*       \*       \*       \*

Katie watched Trevor on stage as she fingered her wedding band. The sweeping moves. The personality projecting to the farthest dark corner of the vast hall, all the way up to the highest tier. Trevor was playing the St. Pete Times Forum, nicknamed The Ice Palace.

His stage presence was magnetic; larger than life, she thought. He was a brilliant, hard-working, focused man, driven by his talent to produce and perform. He survived in a business that often brought other performers to their knees. A fast-paced pressure cooker, her beloved had called it. A runaway train. And Trevor was doing it all while he fought his own personal demons.

She loved him with every fiber of her being. But Katie also felt proud, and honored, to have her role as the one who helped him keep himself sane. She was a member of the team, along with his parents, his brother, his friends and his extended family. His music, his personality, the good he brought to others would outlive his actual life span.

Parts of Trevor Lane Daniels were for the ages.

But she kept him happy and grounded in the here and now of Trevor Lane Daniels, the man, the husband, the father, the father-to-be and the son. She helped him fulfill Trevor's own personal dream of safe contentment.

\*       \*       \*       \*       \*

Trevor looked over to his brother as they carried boxes into the garage of Scott's newly-acquired house at the corner of Retta Esplanade and Chasteen Street.

"Kate's pregnant. It's a girl."

"Carla's pregnant, too. It's a girl."

"Gonna be a race then."

"Yeah."

"Sweet."

Trevor shoved the carton he was carrying onto one of his brother's newly-installed work benches.

"Katie doesn't like her name. Keturah. I think it's sweet."

"I think you're soft in the head. Maybe we should name on of the girls Ski. Somebody should be Ski."

"Ski Daniels. Not bad. Go out to Glenwood Springs, Colorado, and buy up the old Sunlight Ski Area. Rename it Ski Daniels. Then everybody can Ski Daniels."

"Well, at least the family could ski free."

"Free. That's it! I like it!"

"Free? Are you nuts? No man in his right mind wants his daughter named Free."

"Oh. Yeah. Forgot."

"Darned straight. Ain't never gonna be nothin' free about no Daniels women."

Trevor inhaled the scent of oil and particle board from the warm closeness of his brother's garage as Scott slid the carton he was carrying onto one of the many built-in shelves that he had installed. In his mind, he could hear strains of new music building and evolving and growing.

"Shawn called me his pride and joy. Dad called me his country pride and joy. I've got the perfect name for my daughter–pending Katie's approval, of course. Joy Daniels. She'll be my very own pride and joy. I like that."

# EPILOGUE

On a brisk Punta Gorda evening some eighteen months after his wedding, Trevor gathered his family into the big, warm hall of his house on Gill Street.

"I got another brain storm. Comes of looking at all these pictures of me as a baby that Mary has with me in a knit hat when I had no hair. Mary said babies—well, people—lose their body heat through their heads. That problem I never had before. Thick hair. Lots of it. I'd just hunch down in my coat or shirt or blanket and blow on my fingers. No sweat. Cold, but doable. Well, now that I've got no hair to speak of–like a baby–I can feel the difference. My head is cold in the winter! And having babies in the family has made me very aware of the importance of protecting heads. So, I thought, here we go. I've got it!"

Trevor looked expectantly at his gathered family. He caught Mary smiling at him and Katie looking puzzled. Carla with her baby daughter in her arms and Robbie at her feet with Junior, looked resigned. Scott was shaking his head.

"What have you got now, moron?"

Mary folded her hands in her lap.

"Trevor, darling, I'd like a few more details."

Katie tilted her head, still puzzled.

"Ski?"

"Yes. That's it. Ski caps. From Ski. Perfect!"

Scott gave a reluctant chuckle.

"Priceless. Gonna be givin' out ski caps this time. Now every bum in the woods of Charlotte County is gonna be called Ski."

"Ironic, isn't it?"

Mary smiled softly.

"I think that's a wonderful idea, Trevor. Distribution similar to blankets and cracker packets?"

"Yep. Seems to work. Corporate is always coming up with ways we can donate to charity on a really huge scale. They won't miss this money. Grammy would say it was the purest level of giving–where neither the giver nor the recipient ever knows to whom or from whom the gift comes or goes. Messy sentence, but you all catch my drift?"

Katie smiled at him while Jarrett eased their baby Joy out of her arms.

"Ski, I think it's perfect."

If you enjoyed this book, then read below an excerpt from Punta Gorda Storms , due to be released in 2006.

Matt Fisher gave Joy Daniels one of the mystified looks that intrigued her so much.

"You're tall?"

"Yes, I am. I'm five foot seven."

"No, you're not."

"Am, too."

Matt shook his head ruefully. Joy scowled at him.

"In my mind, I am five foot seven inches tall, I weigh a hundred and ten pounds, tops, have long, flowing straight blonde hair and am really rather flat-chested. Maybe my hips are a little too broad."

"You're right about the hips."

Joy punched him sharply in the upper arm, causing him to give a mock yelp.

"Ow!"

Matt's eyes laughed at her as he rubbed his stinging upper arm. He stepped back from her in case she didn't like his laughter, but she followed him anyway.

"I said I wanted honesty, not scathing honesty. Your nose is too long."

"I don't care. It works. That's all I care about. Why is it so important to you to be five foot seven?"

"Because I hate being short."

"You're not short. You're not tall. You're sure not flat chested. Get real Get out a measuring tape. Your body goes out, in, and then out again. I was only messing with you about the hips. You look fine."

"Is that a compliment?"

"Were you fishing for one?"

"No."

"Good. Don't. A compliment? No. Just a statement of fact. I've read enough poetry to be able to give you a really good snow job, but you're the one who wanted this honesty thing. You don't float when you walk. You sort of tromp. You're not willowy. You're no slender reed. You're rounded. How's that? You're rounded."

"Is that a good thing or a bad thing?"

"I don't know. It just is. Like my nose. It works. Okay?"

"Okay. And your nose is cute."

"Geez."

Joy drew herself up to her fullest height and narrowed her eyes at the enigma before her.

"Daddy says everything is illusion."

Joy hummed with taut energy as she laid the statement between them. Matt, sensing deeper issues, rubbed his chin, buying time to consider her words. It was no part of his plan to cross swords with the powerful and possessive Trevor Daniels in any way whatsoever, but Joy Daniels had asked him for honesty. Matt was finding honesty to be increasingly difficult to find lately, both within himself and in the world that had recently crumbled around him.

"I draw. I can create illusion. I could draw you taller. Maybe you are taller. Maybe the Joy Daniels you see inside your head is more real than the one going toe-to-toe with me right now over silly stuff."

Joy growled and Matt held up both hands defensively.

"Bad choice of words. No diplomacy. Honest, though. You said you wanted honesty. I'm trying to give it my best shot. 'Everything is illusion'? How everything is everything? Your face? No two artists would ever draw it the same way. No two people would ever see it the same way. You don't see it the way I see it, or the way your dad sees it. Scientifically speaking, light hits a surface and in a combination of bounce-off and absorb, sends messages into our eyes that are registered and interpreted in our brains. That's surface. That's art. That's what I do. I can easily draw you to be a five foot seven Joy Daniels with long blonde hair. That's imagination. Illusion has to do with what you are able to make other people see or think they see. It's got nothing to do with who you are inside, unless you're fooling yourself as well. Your dad's made a fortune out of illusion built on solid talent and hard work, but is the illusion who he is?"

"No."

Joy threw her arms wide and wailed.

"I don't know who I am!"

Matt, by now used to her frequent impassioned outbursts and seemingly random jumps from topic to topic, lifted an eyebrow at her.

"Oh, come on. My best guess here is that you're Trevor Daniel's daughter. Am I getting close?"

"You asshole! You know that's not what I meant."

"Stipulate, then."

"Daddy plays guitar. And sings. And writes. He has musical talent. He has, I don't know, charisma. Uncle Scott says Daddy could sell ice cubes to Eskimos. Aunt Mary plays violin. Robbie plays guitar. Junior cracks jokes. Erin is all drama. I can barely remember the Pledge of Allegiance."

"Your mom?"

"She knows how to play guitar and sing. Daddy won't let her. It's some sort of private joke between the two of them. Daddy was the one to sing us lullabies and tuck us into bed. Well, Mom did the tucking."

"So grab a guitar and teach yourself the notes. That's how I found out I could draw. I grabbed a pencil and a piece of paper and had at it."

Joy frowned.

"I did. I can play and sing. I suck."

"Oh. Well, best give it up then."

"I don't know who I am! I'm surrounded by massive talent. If I weren't my father's daughter, I'd starve in the streets."

Matt cracked up, laughing even harder as Joy's scowl deepened.

"The heck you would. Maybe you can't remember the words to Shakespeare's plays but you've more than got Erin's knack for drama. Maybe you've got your mom's musical genes. None. Junior does comedy. Right now, you're funny to me. I'm laughing. See? Ow! Quit punching me."

Matt danced out of the range of her tiny fists.

"Take up boxing, why don't you? You got a good right jab there."

"I took karate. I couldn't remember my left from my right. I couldn't remember the katas. Daddy made sure I had 'every opportunity'. I don't do anything really, really well. I want to do something really, really well."

Matt sobered. He owed Joy Daniels for the good that she had brought into his life. She was asking for help. She was asking for honesty. He was drawn to her. She wanted to know what her talent was.

What could he tell her?

If you haven't read the first book in this series, <u>Country Pride and Joy,</u> indulge yourself with a great Southern read!

*March 18, 2004*

*Dear Ms. Simon:*

*I just finished your first book and am overjoyed to finally come across an author that can write a novel that people can relate to. I thoroughly enjoyed this book and look forward to the others. Keep writing, you are a rare gem!*

*Sincerely,*
*Michele Jasinski*

To purchase these fine books, check our website for locations nearest you. www.sallysimonbooks.com
Or phone 941-391-2331